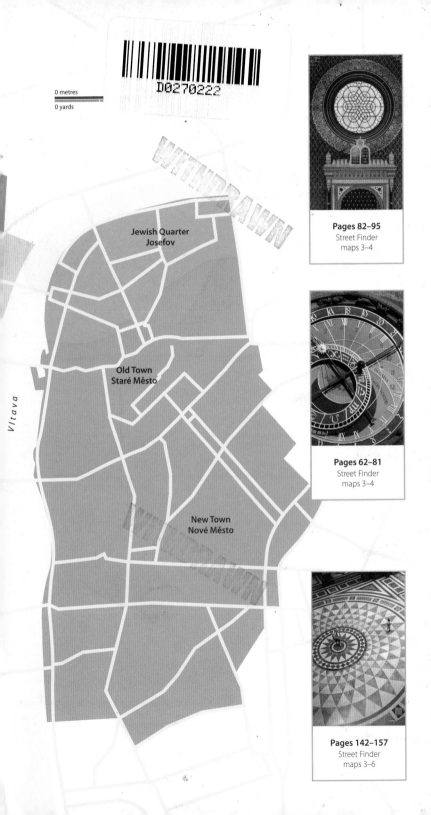

0 metres

0 yards

D0270222

Jewish Quarter
Josefov

Old Town
Staré Město

V l t a v a

New Town
Nové Město

**Pages 82–95**
Street Finder
maps 3–4

**Pages 62–81**
Street Finder
maps 3–4

**Pages 142–157**
Street Finder
maps 3–6

# PRAGUE

EYEWITNESS TRAVEL

# PRAGUE

Main Contributor **Vladimír Soukup**

LONDON, NEW YORK,
MELBOURNE, MUNICH AND DELHI
www.dk.com

**Project Editor** Heather Jones
**Art Editor** Lisa Kosky
**Editors** Ferdie McDonald, Carey Combe
**Designers** Louise Parsons, Nicki Rawson

**Contributors**
Petr David, Vladimír Dobrovodský, Nicholas Lowry,
Polly Phillimore, Joy Turner-Kadečková, Craig Turp

**Photographers**
Jiří Doležal, Jiří Kopřiva, Vladimír Kozlík, František Přeučil,
Milan Posselt, Stanislav Tereba, Peter Wilson

**Illustrators**
Gillie Newman, Chris Orr, Otakar Pok, Jaroslav Staně

This book was produced with the assistance of
Olympia Publishing House, Prague.

Printed and bound in China by
L. Rex Printing Co. Ltd.

First published in the UK in 1994 by
Dorling Kindersley Limited
80 Strand, London,
WC2R 0RL, UK

13 14 15 16 10 9 8 7 6 5 4 3 2

**Reprinted with revisions**
1994, 1995, 1996, 1997, 1998, 1999, 2000,
2001, 2002, 2003, 2004, 2005, 2006, 2008, 2009, 2010, 2011, 2012, 2013

1994, 2013 © Dorling Kindersley Limited, London
A Penguin Company

A CIP catalogue record is available from the British Library.

ISBN 978-1-40938-000-9

Floors are referred to throughout in accordance with
European usage; ie the "first floor" is the floor above ground level.

MIX
Paper from
responsible sources
FSC™ C018179
www.fsc.org

**The information in this
DK Eyewitness Travel Guide is checked annually.**
Every effort has been made to ensure that this book is as up-to-date as possible
at the time of going to press. Some details, however, such as telephone numbers,
opening hours, prices, gallery hanging arrangements and travel information are
liable to change. The publishers cannot accept responsibility for any consequences
arising from the use of this book, nor for any material on third party websites, and
cannot guarantee that any website address in this book will be a suitable source of
travel information. We value the views and suggestions of our readers very highly.
Please write to: Publisher, DK Eyewitness Travel Guides, Dorling Kindersley,
80 Strand, London, WC2R 0RL, UK, or email travelguides@dk.com.

Front cover main image: View over the rooftops of Old Town, Prague

◀ The majestic Prague Castle and the Vltava River on a clear night

# Contents

How to Use this Guide **6**

Rudolph II (ruled 1576–1612)

# Introducing
# Prague

Great Days in Prague **10**

Putting Prague on
the Map **14**

The History of Prague **18**

Prague at a Glance **38**

Prague Through
the Year **52**

A River View of Prague **56**

Outdoor café tables

## Prague Area by Area

Old Town **62**

Jewish Quarter **82**

Prague Castle and Hradčany **96**

Wallenstein Palace and Garden in the Little Quarter

Church of Our Lady before Týn

Little Quarter **122**

New Town **142**

Further Afield **158**

Day Trips **168**

Four Guided Walks **172**

## Travellers' Needs

Where to Stay **184**

Where to Eat and Drink **192**

Shopping in Prague **210**

Entertainment in Prague **216**

## Survival Guide

Practical Information **224**

Getting to Prague **234**

Getting around Prague **238**

Street Finder **244**

General Index **256**

Acknowledgments **268**

Phrase Book **271**

Transport Map
*Inside back cover*

Fiacre, Old Town Square

Baroque façades of houses at the southern end of Old Town Square

# HOW TO USE THIS GUIDE

This Eyewitness Travel Guide helps you get the most from your stay in Prague with the minimum of difficulty. The opening section, *Introducing Prague*, locates the city geographically, sets modern Prague in its historical context and describes events through the entire year. *Prague at a Glance* is an overview of the city's main attractions, including a feature on the River Vltava. Section two, *Prague Area by Area*, starts on page 60. This is the main sightseeing section, which covers all the important sights, with photographs, maps and drawings. It also includes day trips from Prague and four guided walks around the city. Carefully researched tips for hotels, restaurants, shops and markets, cafés and bars, entertainment and sports are found in *Travellers' Needs*. The last section, the *Survival Guide*, contains useful practical advice on all you need to know, from making a telephone call to using the public transport system.

## Finding Your Way Around the Sightseeing Section

Each of the five sightseeing areas in the city is colour-coded for easy reference. Every chapter opens with an introduction to the part of Prague it covers, describing its history and character, followed by a Street-by-Street map illustrating the heart of the area. Finding your way around each chapter is made simple by the numbering system used throughout. The most important sights are covered in detail in two or more full pages.

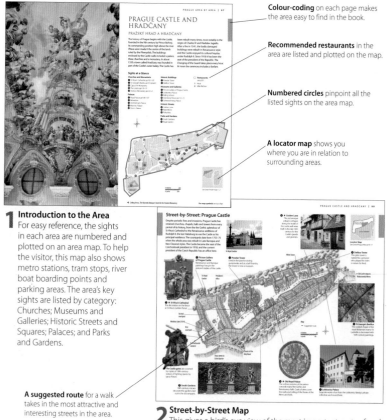

**Colour-coding** on each page makes the area easy to find in the book.

**Recommended restaurants** in the area are listed and plotted on the map.

**Numbered circles** pinpoint all the listed sights on the area map.

**A locator map** shows you where you are in relation to surrounding areas.

**1 Introduction to the Area**
For easy reference, the sights in each area are numbered and plotted on an area map. To help the visitor, this map also shows metro stations, tram stops, river boat boarding points and parking areas. The area's key sights are listed by category: Churches; Museums and Galleries; Historic Streets and Squares; Palaces; and Parks and Gardens.

**A suggested route** for a walk takes in the most attractive and interesting streets in the area.

**2 Street-by-Street Map**
This gives a bird's eye view of the most important parts of each sightseeing area. The numbering of the sights ties in with the area map and the fuller descriptions on the pages that follow.

## Prague Area Map

The coloured areas shown on this map *(see inside front cover)* are the five main sightseeing areas of Prague – each covered in a full chapter in Prague Area by Area *(pp60–157)*. They are highlighted on other maps throughout the book. In Prague at a Glance *(pp38–51)*, for example, they help locate the top sights. They are also used to plot the routes of the river trip *(pp57–9)* and the four guided walks *(p173)*.

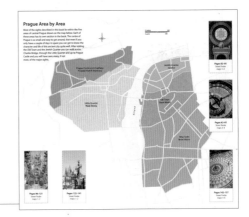

**Practical Information**
lists all the information you need to visit every sight, including a map reference to the Street Finder *(pp250–55)*.

**Numbers** refer to each sight's position on the area map and its place in the chapter.

**3** **Detailed Information on each Sight**
All the important sights in Prague are described individually. They are listed in order, following the numbering on the area map. Practical information on opening hours, telephone numbers, admission charges and facilities available is given for each sight. The key to the symbols used can be found on the back flap.

**The Visitors' Checklist**
provides the practical information you will need to plan your visit.

**The façade** of each major sight is shown to help you spot it quickly.

**Stars** indicate the most interesting architectural details of the building, and the most important works of art or exhibits on view inside.

**Numbered circles** point out key features of the sight listed in a key.

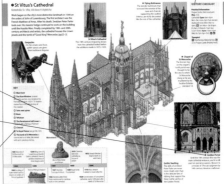

**4** **Prague's Major Sights**
Historic buildings are dissected to reveal their interiors; and museums and galleries have colour-coded floorplans to help you find important exhibits.

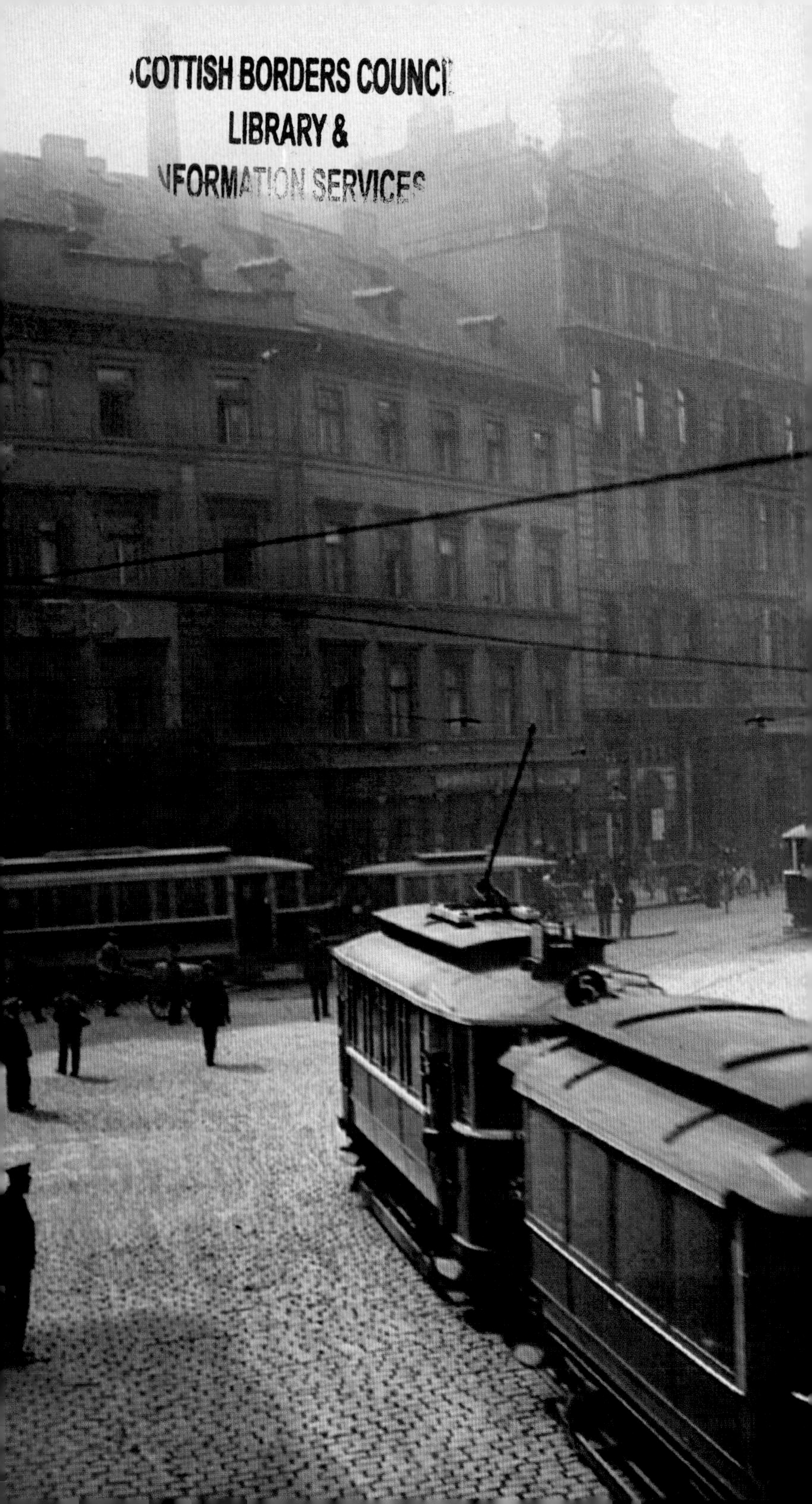
COTTISH BORDERS COUNCI
LIBRARY &
NFORMATION SERVICES

# INTRODUCING PRAGUE

Great Days in Prague          10–13

Putting Prague on the Map     14-15

The History of Prague         18–37

Prague at a Glance            38–51

Prague Through the Year       52–55

A River View of Prague        56–59

# GREAT DAYS IN PRAGUE

Few cities have as much to offer as Prague, so it can be difficult to decide how best to spend your time. The Old Town is a joy in itself, and you could amble around here admiring its old houses for days. Yet, with some planning you can see much more of what makes this historic city special. Here are itineraries for some of the best of the attractions, arranged first by theme and then by length of stay. Price guides on pages 10–11 include travel, food and admission for two adults, while family prices are for two adults and two children.

## National Treasures

**Two adults**
allow at least Kč2,800

- Hradčany Square guards
- Lunch in the Little Quarter
- Cross the Charles Bridge
- Watch the Town Hall clock
- Majestic art or church

### Morning

Starting at **Hradčany Square**, admire the Prague Castle guards in their elaborate costumes then walk through První nádvoří to **St Vitus's Cathedral** (see pp102–105), the soul of the Castle. Take a short tour around here before moving on to the "Story of Prague Castle" permanent exhibition in **Royal Palace** (see pp106–107). For souvenir shopping, go for the artisans' cottages on **Golden Lane** (see p99). Alternatively, head to **Lobkowicz Palace**, and tour the exhibition inside (see p101). Walk down U Zlaté

The sumptuous interior of the Spanish synagogue

studně and Sněmovní to **Little Quarter Square** (see p129), where you can enjoy a late lunch and admire the architectural gems of the **Little Quarter** (see pp122–41).

### Afternoon

It is a short walk from here to **Charles Bridge** (see pp136–9), and on to Old Town Square. Time your arrival on the hour to see the **Old Town Square's Astronomical Clock** (see p76) in action. The **Old Town Hall Tower** (see p75) is well worth a visit for amazing views of Prague Castle and the Little Quarter. Next, choose between seeing the art in the Rococo **Kinský Palace** (see p72) or the bare majesty of **Church of St Nicholas** (see p72–3). The narrow streets and shops of the Týn courtyard now await exploration. Enjoy dinner in the elegant surroundings of the **La Truffe** restaurant (see p199), or for a lighter meal try **Maitrea** (see p198).

## Literary, Art and Religious Landmarks

**Two adults**
allow at least Kč4,900

- "Kafka's café"
- The Jewish Quarter
- Decorative and Medieval Art collections
- Quality Shopping

### Morning

Jewish Prague and Franz Kafka are inseparable, so you may want to start the day with a coffee at **Grand Café Praha** (see p207) in Old Town Square. Kafka lived above here and the café was once named after his journalist girlfriend, Milena. Refreshed, head along Pařížská into the **Jewish Quarter** (see pp82–95). Stop at the **Maisel Synagogue** (see p92), then cross the road to the historic **Old Jewish Cemetery** (see pp88–9). A good walk around here, as well as a look inside the **Klausen Synagogue** (see p87) sets you up for lunch. Try one of the local Jewish restaurants or **Barock** (see p200).

A little respite for visitors at an outdoor café in Old Town Square

◀ A tram carrying passengers past the entrance to Municipal House (c. 1912–1922)

### Afternoon

Admire the Gobelin tapestries at the **Museum of Decorative Arts** *(see p86)*. Stroll along to the **Jewish Town Hall** *(see p87)*, and the **Old-New Synagogue** *(see pp90–91)*. The eastern side of the Jewish Quarter is home to two must-see sights: the glorious **Spanish Synagogue** *(see pp92–3)* and the medieval art in **St Agnes of Bohemia Convent** *(see pp94–5)*. After a day of high cultural input, it's time for a little quality shopping on Pařížská – a large thoroughfare in the Jewish Quarter. Eat at **King Solomon**, one of Prague's best Jewish restaurants *(see p200)*.

## Family Day

**Family of four**
allow at least Kč2,600

- **Funicular ride and tower**
- **Mirror Maze**
- **Peacocks and caves**
- **Church of St James**

### Morning

Take the funicular railway up **Petřín Hill** *(see p141)*, to see Prague's mini-Eiffel Tower – the Observation Tower *(see p140)* which has a spiral stair- case to the top. The **Mirror Maze** *(see p140)*, a short walk away, will keep youngsters happy, as will the nearby **Štefánik's Observatory** *(see p140)*. Take the funicular halfway back down the hill for lunch at the **Nebozízek**, *(see p201)* with its outdoor patio and panoramic views.

### Afternoon

Take a stroll on **Střelecký Ostrov**, where the swans await the remnants of your lunchtime bread. There's more wildlife to be seen at the **Wallenstein Palace** *(see p126)*, home to peacocks and a bizarre replica of a limestone cave. Walk or take the metro over the river to catch the **Old Town Square's Astronomical Clock** *(see p76)* in action. Eat at one of the cafés

Wenceslas Square and monument in front of the National Museum

on the square. Then on to the **Church of St James** *(see p67)*. Children will be intrigued by the mummified arm, which has been hanging above the church entrance for several centuries.

## History and Heroes

**Two adults**
allow at least Kč1,000

- **Wenceslas Square – the rise and fall of Communism**
- **Lunch in splendid style**
- **Wartime history**
- **Shopping for antiques**

### Morning

Start the day with a walk along **Wenceslas Square** *(see pp144–6)*

The Mirror Maze, great fun for young and old alike

to see where the communist regime was toppled. Walk the length of the square and imagine it lined with people as it was for weeks in 1989. Pay your respects at the **Monument to the Victims of Communism** *(see p145)*, and to anti-communist martyr Jan Palach, who set him self alight here in 1969 in protest at the Soviet invasion. Just off the Square is the former **Gestapo HQ** on Politických vězňů (now the national trade office) where thousands of Czechs were imprisoned during WWII. Stop for lunch at the Art Nouveau **Hotel Europa** *(see p147)* on Wenceslas Square.

### Afternoon

Walk to the Baroque **Church of St Cyril and St Methodius** *(see p152)*, where Czech resistance fighters took their own lives in 1942. Bullet holes can still be seen on the wall of the crypt, where a museum chronicles the events. End the day antique-browsing. **Military Antiques** in Charvátova *(see p212)*, is a treasure-trove of relics from the Nazi and Soviet occupations, and military bric-a-brac from all periods.

## 2 days in Prague

- Tour Prague Castle, a Gothic gem
- Watch the Town Hall Clock strike the hour in Old Town Square
- Visit the poignant sights of the Jewish Quarter

Aerial view of Old Town Square, with the Jan Hus Monument in its centre

### Day 1
**Morning** Catch scenic tram route 22 up Hradčany hill to **Prague Castle** (*pp98–9*). Take a tour of the Gothic architectural wonder **St Vitus's Cathedral** (*pp102–105*) and the **Royal Palace** (*pp106–107*).

**Afternoon** Wander through the stately **Royal Garden** (*p111*), then make your way down picturesque **Nerudova Street** (*p130*) to cross **Charles Bridge** (*pp136–9*), lined with statues of saints. Head to **Old Town Square** (*pp68–71*) to watch the **Town Hall Clock** (*p76*) on the **Old Town Hall** (*pp74–5*) chime the hour. The pretty **Kinský Palace** (*p72*) features ancient art in the shadow of the spire-topped **Church of Our Lady Before Týn** (*p72*). End the day by shopping for crafts at the market on Havelská Street.

### Day 2
**Morning** Begin by exploring the **Jewish Quarter** (*pp82–95*). Visit the **Old Jewish Cemetery** (*pp88–9*), with its tilting tombstones marked by symbols for family names, the **Pinkas Synagogue** (*pp86–7*) memorial to Holocaust victims and the 13th-century **Old-New Synagogue** (*pp90–91*).

**Afternoon** Cross the Vltava to the **Little Quarter** (*pp122–41*), where characterful shops stand alongside cafés and beer gardens. On **Little Quarter Square** (*p127*) the **Church of St Nicholas** (*pp128–9*) is the height of High Baroque and worthy of a peek inside. Go for a leisurely stroll in **Wallenstein Palace and Garden** (*p126*) amid bronze statues and wandering peacocks, then see celebrated sculptures and paintings in the **Kampa Museum of Modern Art** (*p135*).

## 3 days in Prague

- Cross fortified Charles Bridge, looking at its statues
- Explore the narrow streets and Baroque palaces of the romantic Little Quarter

### Day 1
**Morning** Marvel at Prague's most venerated Gothic survivor, **St Agnes of Bohemia Convent** (*pp94–5*), and its medieval art collection. Then walk to **Old Town Square** (*pp68–71*) to take in the Baroque **Kinský Palace** (*p72*) and the imposing **Church of Our Lady before Týn** (*p72*). Don't miss the **Old Town Hall** (*pp74–5*) and its crowd-pleasing astronomical clock, which strikes the hour.

**Afternoon** Admire the Cubist House of the Black Madonna on **Celetná Street** (*p67*) en route to the **Powder Gate** (*p66*), a former

St Vitus's Cathedral, a medieval Gothic masterpiece completed in the 20th century

city fortification. Afterwards, visit the **Estates Theatre** (*p67*), where Mozart conducted operas, the **Church of St Gall** (*p73*) and Havelská Street market for knick-knacks. It's a short walk from here to the magnificent **Charles Bridge** (*pp136–9*).

### Day 2
**Morning** Devote your morning to **Prague Castle** (*pp98–9*). Survey the city from Hradčanské náměstí before venturing into **St Vitus's Cathedral** (*pp102–105*) and **St George's Basilica** (*pp100–101*). Take a tour of the **Royal Palace** (*pp106–107*) and the **Royal Garden** (*p111*), and if there's time walk along **Golden Lane** (*p101*) with its brightly painted cottages.

**Afternoon** Head down **Nerudova Street** (*p130*) to meander the narrow streets of the **Little Quarter** (*pp122–41*) and pop into the **Church of St Nicholas** (*pp128–9*). The monumental **Wallenstein Palace and Garden** (*p126*), peaceful **Kampa Island** (*p131*) and the **Kampa Museum of Modern Art** (*p135*) are all nearby.

### Day 3
**Morning** Visit the **Jewish Quarter** (*pp82–95*), where the **Old Jewish Cemetery** (*pp88–9*), **Old-New Synagogue** (*pp90–91*) and **Pinkas Synagogue** (*pp86–7*) honour life in the former ghetto.

**Afternoon** Take a half-hour train ride to Charles IV's striking summer retreat, **Karlstein Castle** (*p169*), which stands in isolation above a wooded valley.

## 5 days in Prague

- Admire St Agnes of Bohemia Convent
- Listen to a Mozart opera at the Estates Theatre
- Take a trip to Charles IV's breathtaking country retreat, Karlstein Castle

### Day 1
**Morning** Tour **Old Town Square** (pp68–71), taking in the Gothic steeples of the **Church of Our Lady Before Týn** (p72), **Kinský Palace** (p72) and the **Old Town Hall** (pp74–5), where the astronomical **Town Hall Clock** (p76) delights crowds on the hour with its procession of the 12 Apostles. Ride the metro to the **Little Quarter** (pp122–41) and ascend the Old Castle Steps to **Prague Castle** (pp98–9), the historic heart of Bohemia. Explore the **Royal Palace** (pp106–107) and the **Royal Garden** (p111), then visit Romanesque **St George's Basilica** (pp100–101) and the gravity-defying **St Vitus's Cathedral** (pp102–105), where St Wenceslas is interred in a chapel.

**Afternoon** Set opposite the castle complex, the Baroque **Sternberg Palace** (p112–15) houses the National Gallery's Old Masters. Walk up to the opulent 17th-century shrine of **The Loreto** (pp118–19), then make your way to **New World** (p116), a charming street of cottages where royal astronomers and goldsmiths once lived. Take tram 22 to the **Strahov Monastery** (pp120–21), whose ornate library holds thousands of obscure tomes.

### Day 2
**Morning** Spend your morning exploring the **New Town** (pp142–57). **Wenceslas Square** (pp144–6) showcases early 20th-century architecture and highlights include the Art Nouveau **Hotel Europa** (p147). The **National Museum** (p147) here is still marked by the scars of the 1968 Warsaw Pact invasion, while the **Mucha Museum** (p147) features the early work of Art Nouveau avatar Alphonse Mucha.

**Afternoon** Head to the Gothic **New Town Hall** (p155), where Hussites defenestrated their Catholic overlords in 1419. Off **Charles Square** (pp150–51 & 152), a former medieval cattle market, is the **Church of St Cyril and St Methodius** (p152), where Czech partisans slugged it out with German troops in 1942. The grand **National Theatre** (pp156–7) is a cultural treasure where historic operas by Smetana are put on.

Neo-Classical elegance of the Estates Theatre, where *Don Giovanni* had its debut

### Day 3
**Morning** Immerse yourself in the spirit of medieval Bohemia at **St Agnes of Bohemia Convent** (pp94–5), which is packed with 13th–16th-century paintings and sculptures. Next, marvel at the simplicity of the **Old-New Synagogue** (pp90–91) and the pseudo-Moorish style of the **Spanish Synagogue** (pp92–3) in the **Jewish Quarter** (pp82–95). Nearby, the **Old Jewish Cemetery** (pp88–9) and **Pinkas Synagogue** (pp86–7) contain memorials to Prague's Holocaust victims.

**Afternoon** Explore the back streets of the **Old Town** (pp62–81). Start at the **Powder Gate** (p66) and walk down **Celetná Street** (p67). Turn off for the **Church of St Gall** (p73) and **Bethlehem Chapel** (p77), where martyr Jan Hus preached austerity. **Charles Street** (p80), lined with Baroque and Renaissance façades, leads to the **Charles Bridge** (pp136–9).

### Day 4
**Morning** Journey by train to Charles IV's imposing **Karlstein Castle** (p169). Don't miss the Chapel of St Catherine, the walls of which are decorated with gems.

**Afternoon** Back in the city, browse the designer shops on Národní Street, and then enjoy an evening at the **Estates Theatre** (p67) or **Rudolfinum** (p86).

### Day 5
**Morning** Wander the **Little Quarter** (pp122–41) and the **Wallenstein Palace and Garden** (p126). On **Little Quarter Square** (p127) is the stunning Baroque **Church of St Nicholas** (pp128–9), and close by, pretty **Nerudova Street** (p130) is lined with intriguing house signs.

**Afternoon** For inspiring art, visit the **Kampa Museum of Modern Art** (p135). Then wind down with a stroll around **Kampa Island** (p131) and the **Little Quarter Riverside** (pp132–3).

The Little Quarter, its buildings largely unchanged since the 18th century

# Putting Prague on the Map

Prague has a population of just over 1 million and covers 500 sq km (200 sq miles) at its outer limits. It is the capital of the Czech Republic and head of the region of Bohemia. Prague's geographical position at the centre of Europe makes it a convenient base from which to visit both the Bohemian countryside and many other major cities, such as Nuremberg, Vienna, Bratislava and Budapest.

## Prague and Environs

| 0 km | 10 |
| 0 miles | 5 |

Slaný
Kralupy n. Vltavou
Neratovice
Brandýs n. Labem-Stará Boleslav
Vltava
Elbe
D8
Roztoky
Čakovice
Čelákovice
D11
Kladno
Prague
Václav Havel
10
See next page
Úvaly
Český Brod
12
Unhošť
Rudná
Říčany
2
D5
Beroun
Zbraslav
Jílové u Prahy
D1
Karlštejn
Berounka
Řevnice
4
Vltava
Sázava
3

POLAND
Oder
3
Legnica
A4
Wrocław
3
8
Elbe
33
Hradec Králové
35
35
Olomouc
35
D1
Leoš Janáček
Ostrava
48
Ostrava
Kraków-Balice
Kraków
Bielsko-Biała
7
REPUBLIC
11
hlava
Brno
D1
Zlín
35
Žilina
Brno-Tuřany
Morava
D2
Trenčín
Banská Bystrica
Zvolen
303
D1
SLOVAKIA
Vienna
Bratislava
Nitra
D2
Polten
Bratislava
Váh
Vienna International
A4
2
Eisenstadt
Gyor
M3
A2
Tatabánya
M1
Budapest
Budapest Ferenc Liszt
HUNGARY
M7
Szekesfehérvár
Szolnok
Rába
Lake Balaton
aribor
M7
Zagreb

| 0 kilometres | 50 |
| 0 miles | 30 |

### Key

Greater Prague

Motorway

Major road

Railway line

Country boundary

**For additional map symbols** *see back flap*

# Central Prague

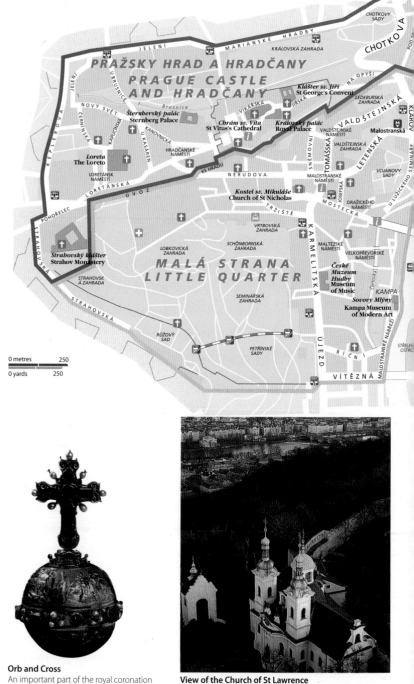

0 metres 250
0 yards 250

**Orb and Cross**
An important part of the royal coronation
regalia, this orb is now kept at St Vitus's
Cathedral *(see pp102–105).*

**For key to symbols** *see back flap*

**View of the Church of St Lawrence**
Petřín Park offers outstanding views of Prague *(see p141
and Four Guided Walks, pp176–7).*

**Painted House Façade**
The Old Town has many Renaissance and Baroque houses. Some have colourful mural paintings like this one in Old Town Square (*see pp68–71*).

**Art Nouveau Statue**
The New Town has many examples of Art Nouveau architecture (*see pp148–9*).

Map labels:

FRANTIŠKU

*Klášter sv. Anežký*
**St Agnes's Convent**

NA
**JOSEFOV
JEWISH QUARTER**

*Staronová synagóga*
**Old-New Synagogue**

*Starý židovský hřbitov*
**Old Jewish Cemetery**

REVOLUČNÍ

NÁBŘEŽÍ
NÁMĚSTÍ
CURIEOVÝCH

DVOŘÁKOVO
PAŘÍŽSKÁ

U MILOSRDNÝCH
U OBECNÍHO DVORA

HRADEBNÍ

HAŠTALSKÁ

VĚZEŇSKÁ

KOZÍ

DLOUHÁ

MASNÁ

RYBNÁ

KRÁLODVORSKÁ

NÁMĚSTÍ JANA
PALACHA

V
i
t
a
v
a

Mánesův most

KŘIŽOVNICKÁ

Staroměstská

VALENTINSKÁ

MAISELOVA

ŠIROKÁ

ZÁTECKÁ

PAŘÍŽSKÁ

STAROMĚSTSKÉ
NÁMĚSTÍ

*Staroměstská radnice*
**Old Town Hall**

OVOCNÝ
TRH

PLATNÉŘSKÁ

MARIÁNSKÉ
NÁMĚSTÍ

U RADNICE

MALÉ
NÁMĚSTÍ

**STARÉ MĚSTO
OLD TOWN**

KARLOVA

ANENSKÉ
NÁMĚSTÍ

HUSOVA

RYTÍŘSKÁ

NA MŮSTKU

NEKÁZANKA

PANSKÁ

RŮZOVA

SMETANOVO NÁBŘEŽÍ

BETLÉMSKÉ
NÁMĚSTÍ

SKOŘEPKA

PERLOVA

28. ŘÍJNA

V CÍPU

JINDŘIŠSKÁ

POLITICKÝCH

NA PERŠTÝNĚ

UHELNÝ
TRH

**Můstek**

VÁCLAVSKÉ
NÁMĚSTÍ

**Můstek**

Karlův most

post Legií

NÁRODNÍ

NÁRODNÍ

SPÁLENÁ

**Národní třída**

JUNGMANNOVA

VLADISLAVOVA

ŠTĚPÁNSKÁ

VE SMEČKÁCH

KRAKOVSKÁ

OPLETALOVA

VÁCLAVSKÉ
NÁMĚSTÍ

WASHINGTONOVA

WILSONOVA

LEGEROVA

VĚZEŇSKÚ

*Národní divadlo*
**National Theatre**

OSTROVNÍ

V JIRCHÁŘÍCH

OPATOVICKÁ

ČERNÁ

LAZARSKÁ

VODIČKOVA

MEZIBRANSKÁ

SOKOLSKÁ

SLOVANSKÝ
OSTROV

NA STRUZE

MASARYKOVO NÁBŘEŽÍ

PŠTROSSOVA

KŘEMENCOVA

SPÁLENÁ

**Muzeum**

ČELAKOVSKÉHO
SADY

**NOVÉ MĚSTO
NEW TOWN**

MYSLÍKOVA

NÁPL. LÁVNÍ

ODBORŮ

ŽITNÁ

Jiráskův most

JIRÁSKOVO
NÁMĚSTÍ

NA ZDERAZE

DITTRICHOVA

KARLOVO
NÁMĚSTÍ

**Karlovo náměstí**

NA RYBNÍČKU

HÁLKOVA

LIPOVÁ

**RESSLOVA**

VÁCLAVSKÁ

KARLOVO
NÁMĚSTÍ

**JEČNÁ**

Palackého most

RAŠÍNOVO

GORAZDOVA

TROJANOVA

NA MORÁNI

U NEMOCNICE

KATEŘINSKÁ

KE KARLOVU

VINIČNÁ

PALACKÉHO
NÁMĚSTÍ

**Karlovo náměstí**

NÁMĚSTÍ POD
EMAUZY

NÁBŘEŽÍ

BENÁTSKÁ

BOTANICKÁ
ZAHRADA

APOLINÁŘSKÁ

NA SLUPI

KOSÁRKOVO
NÁBŘEŽÍ

Čechův most

ČECHŮV

LISTOPADU
17

552   16

# THE HISTORY OF PRAGUE

Prague's position at the crossroads of Europe has made it a magnet for foreign traders since prehistoric times. By the early 10th century Prague had become a thriving town with a large market place, the Old Town Square, and two citadels, Prague Castle and Vyšehrad, from where its first rulers, the Přemyslids, conducted their many family feuds. These were often bloody: in AD 935, Prince Wenceslas was murdered by his brother Boleslav. Wenceslas was later canonized and became the Czechs' best-known patron saint.

During the Middle Ages Prague prospered, especially during the reign of the Holy Roman Emperor, Charles IV. Under the government of this wise and cultured ruler, Prague grew into a magnificent city, larger than Paris or London. Charles instigated the founding and building of many institutions in Prague, including the first university in Central Europe, Charles University. One of the University's first Czech rectors was Jan Hus, the reforming preacher whose execution for alleged heresy in 1415 led to the Hussite wars. The radical wing of the Hussites, the Taborites, were finally defeated at the Battle

of Lipany in 1434. During the 16th century, after a succession of weak kings, the Habsburgs gained control, beginning a rule that would last for almost 400 years. One of the more enlightened of all the Habsburg Emperors was Rudolph II. He brought the spirit of the Renaissance to Prague through his love of the arts and sciences. Soon after his death, in 1618, Prague was the setting for the Protestant revolt which led to the Thirty Years' War. The war's aftermath caused a serious decline in the fortunes of the city that would revive only in the 18th century. Prague's many fine Baroque churches and palaces date from this time.

The 19th century saw a period of national revival and the burgeoning of civic pride. The great public monuments – the National Museum, the National Theatre and Rudolfinum – were built. But the Habsburgs still ruled the city, and it was not until 1918 that Prague became the capital of an independent Republic. World War II brought occupation by the German army, followed by four decades of Communism. After the "Velvet Revolution" of 1989, Prague has embraced a new era.

View of Prague Castle and Little Quarter, 1493

◄ *St Wenceslas and St Vitus*, by Bartholomaeus Spränger, c.1600

# Rulers of Prague

Three great dynasties have shaped the history of Prague: the Přemyslids, the Luxemburgs and the Habsburgs. According to Slavic legend, the Přemyslids were founded by Princess Libuše *(see p23)*. Her line included St Wenceslas and Přemysl Otakar II, whose death in battle at Marchfeld paved the way for the Luxemburgs. This family produced one of the city's greatest rulers, Charles IV, who was King of Bohemia and Holy Roman Emperor *(see pp26–7)*. In 1526, Prague came under the control of the Austrian House of Habsburg whose rule lasted 400 years, until after World War I, when the newly formed Czechoslovakia gained its independence and was governed by a succession of presidents. Following the dissolution of Czechoslovakia in 1993, the modern day Czech Republic continues to elect presidents.

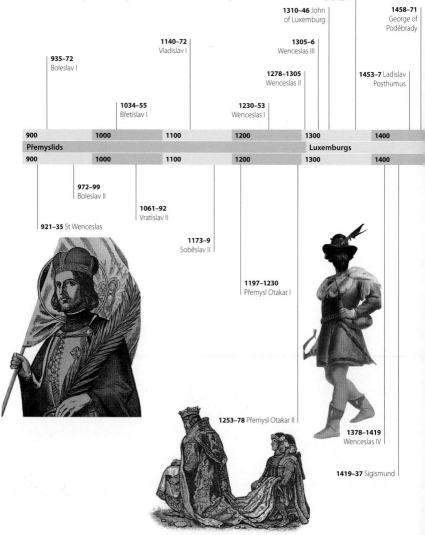

**1346–78**
Charles IV

**1310–46** John
of Luxemburg

**1458–71**
George of
Poděbrady

**1305–6**
Wenceslas III

**1140–72**
Vladislav I

**935–72**
Boleslav I

**1278–1305**
Wenceslas II

**1453–7** Ladislav
Posthumus

**1034–55**
Břetislav I

**1230–53**
Wenceslas I

| 900 | 1000 | 1100 | 1200 | 1300 | 1400 |

Přemyslids / Luxemburgs

| 900 | 1000 | 1100 | 1200 | 1300 | 1400 |

**972–99**
Boleslav II

**1061–92**
Vratislav II

**921–35** St Wenceslas

**1173–9**
Soběslav II

**1197–1230**
Přemysl Otakar I

**1253–78** Přemysl Otakar II

**1378–1419**
Wenceslas IV

**1419–37** Sigismund

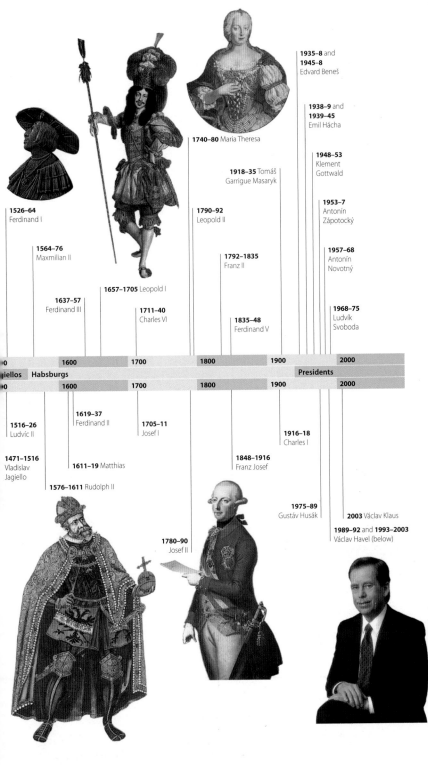

**1935–8** and **1945–8** Edvard Beneš

**1938–9** and **1939–45** Emil Hácha

**1948–53** Klement Gottwald

**1740–80** Maria Theresa

**1918–35** Tomáš Garrigue Masaryk

**1953–7** Antonín Zápotocký

**1526–64** Ferdinand I

**1790–92** Leopold II

**1957–68** Antonín Novotný

**1564–76** Maxmilian II

**1792–1835** Franz II

**1657–1705** Leopold I

**1968–75** Ludvík Svoboda

**1637–57** Ferdinand III

**1711–40** Charles VI

**1835–48** Ferdinand V

1600 | 1700 | 1800 | 1900 | 2000

giellos | Habsburgs | Presidents

1600 | 1700 | 1800 | 1900 | 2000

**1516–26** Ludvíc II

**1619–37** Ferdinand II

**1705–11** Josef I

**1916–18** Charles I

**1471–1516** Vladislav Jagiello

**1611–19** Matthias

**1848–1916** Franz Josef

**1576–1611** Rudolph II

**1975–89** Gustáv Husák

**2003** Václav Klaus

**1989–92** and **1993–2003** Václav Havel (below)

**1780–90** Josef II

# Prague Under the Přemyslids

Early Celtic tribes, from 500 BC, were the first inhabitants of the area around the Vltava valley. The Germanic Marcomans arrived in 9–6 BC, and gradually the Celts left. The first Slavic tribes came to Bohemia in about 500 AD. Struggles for supremacy led to the emergence of a ruling dynasty, the Přemyslids, around 800 AD. They built two fortified settlements: the first at Prague Castle *(see pp96–111)*, the second at Vyšehrad, a rocky headland on the right bank of the Vltava *(see pp180–81)*. These remained the seats of Czech princes for hundreds of years. One prince crucial to the emerging Czech State was the pious Wenceslas. He enjoyed only a brief reign but left an important legacy in the founding of St Vitus's rotunda *(see p104)*.

**Extent of the City**
▨ 1000 AD  ▨ Today

**Boleslav's henchman** raises his sword to strike the fatal blow.

**St Cyril and St Methodius**
Originally Greeks from Salonica, these two brothers brought Christianity to Great Moravia in about 863. They baptized early Přemyslid, Bořivoj, and his wife Ludmila, grandmother of St Wenceslas.

**Second assassin** grapples with the Prince's companion.

**Early Coin**
Silver coins like this denar were minted in the royal mint of Vyšehrad during Boleslav II's reign from 967–99.

**Wild Boar Figurine**
Celtic tribes made small talismans of the wild animals that they hunted for food in the forested areas around Prague.

**6th century** Slavs settle alongside Germanic tribes in Bohemia

**623–658** Bohemia is part of an empire formed by Frankish merchant, Samo

**600 AD**

**700**

**500 BC** Celts in Bohemia. Joined by Germanic Marcomans in 1st century AD

*Bronze head of a Celtic goddess*

**8th century** Tribe of Czechs settle in central Bohemia

*Vyšehrad acropolis – first Czech settlement on the right bank of the Vltava*

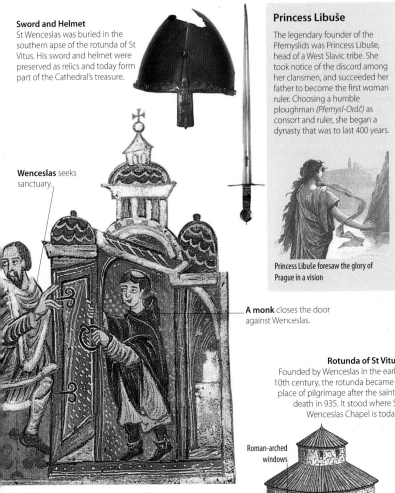

**Sword and Helmet**
St Wenceslas was buried in the southern apse of the rotunda of St Vitus. His sword and helmet were preserved as relics and today form part of the Cathedral's treasure.

**Princess Libuše**
The legendary founder of the Přemyslids was Princess Libuše, head of a West Slavic tribe. She took notice of the discord among her clansmen, and succeeded her father to become the first woman ruler. Choosing a humble ploughman (*Přemysl-Oráč*) as consort and ruler, she began a dynasty that was to last 400 years.

Princess Libuše foresaw the glory of Prague in a vision

**Wenceslas** seeks sanctuary.

**A monk** closes the door against Wenceslas.

**Rotunda of St Vitus**
Founded by Wenceslas in the early 10th century, the rotunda became a place of pilgrimage after the saint's death in 935. It stood where St Wenceslas Chapel is today.

Roman-arched windows

**Assassination of Prince Wenceslas**
*In 935, the young Wenceslas was murdered on the orders of his brother, Boleslav. This manuscript illustration of 1006 shows the moment when the assassins caught up with the prince as he was about to enter the church for the morning mass.*

Curving stone walls

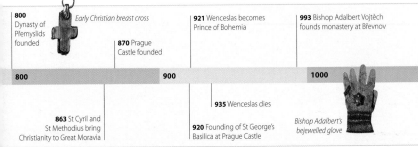

**800** Dynasty of Přemyslids founded

*Early Christian breast cross*

**870** Prague Castle founded

**921** Wenceslas becomes Prince of Bohemia

**993** Bishop Adalbert Vojtěch founds monastery at Břevnov

**800**　**900**　**1000**

**863** St Cyril and St Methodius bring Christianity to Great Moravia

**920** Founding of St George's Basilica at Prague Castle

**935** Wenceslas dies

*Bishop Adalbert's bejewelled glove*

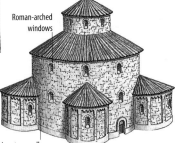

# Early Medieval Prague

Prague Castle steadily grew in importance from the beginning of the 9th century onwards. Prone to frequent fires, its wooden buildings were gradually replaced by stone and the area developed into a sturdy Romanesque fortress with a palace and religious buildings. Clustered around the original outer bailey was an area inhabited by skilled craftsmen and German merchants, encouraged to come and stay in Prague by Vladislav II and, later, Přemysl Otakar II. This came to be known as the "Little Quarter" and achieved town status in 1257. It was joined to the Old Town by a bridge, known as the Judith Bridge.

**Extent of the City**
◻ 1230      ◻ Today

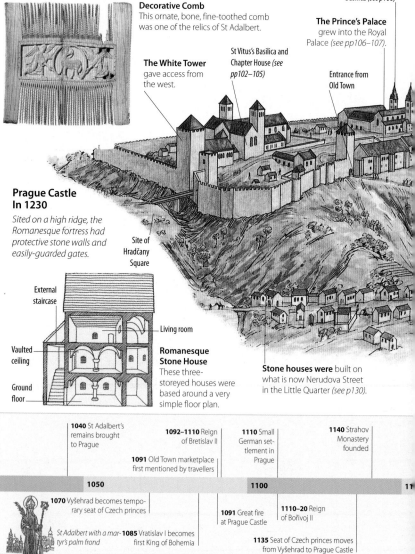

**St George's Convent and Basilica** *(see p100)*

**Decorative Comb**
This ornate, bone, fine-toothed comb was one of the relics of St Adalbert.

**The Prince's Palace**
grew into the Royal Palace *(see pp106–107)*.

**St Vitus's Basilica and Chapter House** *(see pp102–105)*

**The White Tower**
gave access from the west.

**Entrance from Old Town**

**Prague Castle In 1230**
*Sited on a high ridge, the Romanesque fortress had protective stone walls and easily-guarded gates.*

**Site of Hradčany Square**

External staircase

Vaulted ceiling

Ground floor

Living room

**Romanesque Stone House**
These three-storeyed houses were based around a very simple floor plan.

**Stone houses were** built on what is now Nerudova Street in the Little Quarter *(see p130)*.

---

**1040** St Adalbert's remains brought to Prague

**1091** Old Town marketplace first mentioned by travellers

**1092–1110** Reign of Bretislav II

**1110** Small German settlement in Prague

**1140** Strahov Monastery founded

**1050**

**1100**

**11**

**1070** Vyšehrad becomes temporary seat of Czech princes

*St Adalbert with a mar-**1085** Vratislav I becomes tyr's palm frond      first King of Bohemia*

**1091** Great fire at Prague Castle

**1110–20** Reign of Bořivoj II

**1135** Seat of Czech princes moves from Vyšehrad to Prague Castle

**St Agnes of Bohemia**
Sister of Wenceslas I, this devout woman built a convent for the order of the Poor Clares (the female counterparts of the Franciscans) (*see pp94–5*). She was not canonized until 1989.

## Where to see Romanesque Prague

Remains of Prague's fascinating history can be seen in the crypt of St Vitus's Cathedral (*pp102–105*), and the Royal Palace (*pp106–107*).

**St George's Basilica**
The vaulting in the crypt dates from the 12th century (*p100*).

**The Black Tower** was the exit to Bohemia's second town, Kutná Hora (*see p168*).

**Vratislav II**
The Vyšehrad Codex, an illuminated selection from the gospels, was made to mark Vratislav's coronation in 1061.

Little Quarter Square

**St Martin's Rotunda**
This well-preserved building is in Vyšehrad (*p180*).

**Přemysl Otakar II**
The last great Přemyslid king was killed in battle after trying to carve out a huge empire.

**Little Quarter Coat of Arms**
Vladislav II's portrait was incorporated into this 16th-century miniature painting.

Romanesque stone head from Judith Bridge Tower

**1182** Romanesque construction of Prague Castle completed

**1233** Founding of St Agnes's Convent

**1257** Little Quarter receives town status

**1258–68** Strahov Monastery rebuilt in Gothic style after fire

**1200**

**1250**

**1172** Judith Bridge built (*see pp136–9*)

**1212** Přemysl Otakar I receives the Sicilian Golden Bull, confirming the sovereignty of Bohemian kings

Sicilian Golden Bull

**1278** Přemysl Otakar II dies at Marchfeld

# Prague's Golden Age

In the late Middle Ages, Prague attained the height of its glory. The Holy Roman Emperor Charles IV chose Prague as his Imperial residence and set out to make the city the most magnificent in Europe. He founded a university (the Carolinum) and built many fine churches and monasteries in the Gothic style. Of major importance were his town-planning schemes, such as the reconstruction of Prague Castle, the building of a new stone bridge to replace the Judith Bridge, and the foundation of a new quarter, the New Town. A devout Catholic, he owned a large collection of relics which were kept, along with the Crown Jewels, at Karlstein Castle *(see pp168–9)*.

**Extent of the City**
🔲 1350    🔲 Today

**Charles IV**
wears the Imperial crown, set with sapphires, rubies and pearls.

**St Wenceslas Chapel**
Proud of his direct descent from the Přemyslids, Charles had this shrine to St Wenceslas built in St Vitus's Cathedral *(see pp102–105)*.

**The Emperor**
places the piece of the cross in its reliquary.

**St Wenceslas Crown**
Worn by Charles at his coronation in 1347, the Bohemian crown was based on early Přemyslid insignia.

**1280** Old-New Synagogue completed in Gothic style

*Town Hall, Old Town Square*

**1338** John of Luxemburg gives permission to Old Town to build a town hall

**1333** Charles IV makes Prague his home

**1348** Charles IV founds Charles University

| 1305 | 1320 | 1335 |
|---|---|---|

**1306** Přemyslid dynasty ends

*Portal of Old-New Synagogue*

**1310** John of Luxemburg occupies Prague

*Votive panel showing Charles, Archbishop Jan Očko and Bohemia's patron saints*

**1344** Elevation of Prague bishopric to archbishopric

**1348** Charles IV founds Prague New Town

**St Vitus by Master Theodoric**
This is one of a series of paintings of saints by the great Bohemian artist for the Holy Rood Chapel at Karlstein Castle (c1365).

**A jewelled reliquary cross** was made to house the new relic.

**University Seal, 1348**
The seal depicts the Emperor offering the foundation documents to St Wenceslas.

## Where to see Gothic Prague

Prague's rich Gothic legacy includes three of its best-known sights – St Vitus's Cathedral (pp102–105), Charles Bridge (pp136–9) and the Old-New Synagogue (pp90–91). Another very important building from Charles IV's reign is the Carolinum (p67). Churches that have retained most of their original Gothic features include the Church of Our Lady before Týn (p72).

**Building the New Town**
This manuscript records Charles IV supervising the building of the New Town during the 14th century.

**Carolinum** This fine oriel window was part of the university (p67).

## Charles IV and his Relics

*Charles collected holy relics from all over the Empire. In about 1357 he received a part of Christ's cross from the Dauphin. This mural in Karlstein Castle is thought to be the best likeness of the Emperor.*

**Old Town Bridge Tower**
The sculptural decoration is by Peter Parler (p139).

Sculpture of young Wenceslas IV by Peter Parler in St Vitus's Cathedral

**1357** Charles Bridge begun

**1378** Reign of Wenceslas IV begins

*Bethlehem Chapel*

| 350 | 1365 | 1380 | 1395 |
|---|---|---|---|

**1361** Wenceslas IV born, oldest son of Charles

**1378** Charles dies

**1391** Bethlehem Chapel founded

# Hussite Prague

In the early 15th century, Europe shook in fear of an incredible fighting force – the Hussites, followers of the reformist cleric, Jan Hus. Despite simple weapons, they achieved legendary military successes against the Emperor's Catholic crusades, due largely to their religious fervour and to the discipline of their brilliant leader, Jan Žižka, who invented mobile artillery. The Hussites split into two camps, the moderate "Utraquists" *(see p77)* and the radical "Taborites" who were finally defeated at the Battle of Lipany in 1434, paving the way for the moderate Hussite king, George of Poděbrady.

**Extent of the City**
☐ 1500    ☐ Today

**Nobles' Letter of Protest**
Several hundred seals of the Bohemian nobility were affixed to a letter protesting about the execution of Jan Hus.

**The priest** held a gilded monstrance.

Jan Žižka

## God's Warriors
*The early-16th-century Codex of Jena illustrated the Hussite successes. Here the Hussites, who included artisans and barons, are shown singing their hymn, with their blind leader, Jan Žižka.*

**War Machine**
For maximum effect, farm waggons were tied together to form a shield. A chilling array of weapons were unleashed including crossbows, flails and an early form of howitzer.

*Jan Hus preaching*

**1402–13** Jan Hus preaches at Bethlehem Chapel *(see p77)*

**1415** Jan Hus burned at the stake at Constance

**1419** Defenestration of councillors from New Town Hall

**1434** Battle of Lipany

*The Taborites made lethal weapons from simple farm tools*

**1400**

**1420**

**1440**

**1410** Jan Hus excommunicated. Building of Old Town Clock

*The chalice, symbol of the Utraquists*

**1424** Jan Žižka dies

**1448** Prague conquered by troops of George of Poděbrady

**1420** Hussites victorious under Jan Žižka at Vitkov and Vyšehrad

**Satan Dressed as the Pope**
Lurid images satirizing the corruption of the church were painted on placards and carried through the streets.

**The banner** was decorated with the Hussite chalice.

**A variety of farm implements** were used as makeshift weapons by the peasants.

**The peasant** army marched behind Jan Žižka.

**Hussite Shield**
Wooden shields like this one that bears the arms of the city of Prague, were used to fill any gaps in the waggon fortress's tight formation.

## Reformer, Jan Hus

Born to poor parents in a small Bohemian town, Jan Hus became one of the most important religious thinkers of his day. His objections to the Catholic Church's corrupt practices, opulent style and wealth were shared by many Czechs – nobles and peasants alike. His reformist preaching in Prague's Bethlehem Chapel earned him a huge following, noticed by the Roman Papacy, and Hus was excommunicated. In 1412 Wenceslas IV, brother of the Emperor Sigismund, asked him to leave Prague. In October 1414, Hus decided to defend his teaching at the Council of Constance. Even though he had the Emperor's safe conduct, he was put in prison. The following year he was declared a heretic and burned at the stake.

**Jan Hus at the Stake in 1415**
After suffering death at the hands of the Church on 6 July 1415, Jan Hus became a revered martyr of the Czech people.

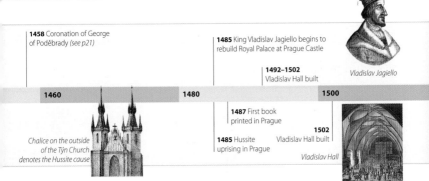

**1458** Coronation of George of Poděbrady *(see p21)*

**1485** King Vladislav Jagiello begins to rebuild Royal Palace at Prague Castle

**1492–1502** Vladislav Hall built

*Vladislav Jagiello*

1460 — 1480 — 1500

**1487** First book printed in Prague

**1485** Hussite uprising in Prague

**1502** Vladislav Hall built

*Chalice on the outside of the Týn Church denotes the Hussite cause*

*Vladislav Hall*

# The Renaissance and Rudolph II

With the accession of the Habsburgs, the Renaissance reached Prague. Art and architecture were dominated by the Italians who enjoyed the patronage of the Imperial court, especially that of Rudolph II. The eccentric Rudolph often neglected politics, preferring to indulge his passions for collecting and science. His court was a haven for artists, astrologers, astronomers and alchemists, but his erratic rule led to revolts and an attempt by his brother Matthias to usurp him. In the course of the Thirty Years' War *(see pp32–3)* many works of art from Rudolph's collection were looted.

**Extent of the City**
1550  Today

Dalibor Tower

Fish pond

Belvedere

Pergola

**Rudolph II**
A connoisseur of the bizarre, Rudolph was delighted by this vegetable portrait by Giuseppe Arcimboldo (1590).

Orchard

Formal flower beds

Lion House

**Mosaic Desk Top**
Renaissance table tops with Florentine themes of fountains and gardens were made at Rudolph's court in semi-precious stones.

**Rabbi Löw**
A revered Jewish sage, he was said to have invented a Golem *(see pp90–91)*.

**1526** Habsburg rule begins with Ferdinand I

*Ferdinand I*

**1541** Great fire in Little Quarter, the Castle and Hradčany

**1556** Ferdinand I invites Jesuits to Prague

**1520**　　**1540**　　**1560**

**1538–63** Belvedere built

**1547** Unsuccessful uprising of towns of Prague against Ferdinand I

*Charter for manglers and dyers*

**Sense of Sight**
Jan Brueghel's allegorical painting shows the extent of Rudolph II's huge collection – from globes to paintings, jewels and scientific instruments.

**Tycho Brahe**
The Danish astronomer spent his last years living in Prague.

Ball Game Hall

**A covered bridge** connected the Palace to the garden.

## Where to see Renaissance Prague

The Royal Garden (p111) preserves much of the spirit of Renaissance Prague. Paintings and objects from Rudolph's collections can be seen in the Sternberg Palace (pp112–15), the Picture Gallery of Prague Castle (p100) and the Museum of Decorative Arts (p86).

**At the Two Golden Bears** Built in 1590, the house is famous for its symmetrical, carved doorway, one of the most graceful in Prague (p73).

**Belvedere** The palace is decorated with stone reliefs by Italian architect, Paolo della Stella (p110).

**Ball Game Hall** Beautiful Renaissance sgraffito, heavily restored, covers the façade of this building in the Royal Garden (p111).

## Royal Palace Gardens
*No longer a medieval fortress, Prague Castle and its gardens were given over to the pleasure of the King. Here Rudolph enjoyed ball games, exotic plants and his menagerie.*

**1583** Prague becomes seat of Imperial court of Rudolph II; great art collection begun

**1609** Publication of Rudolph's Imperial Charter on religious freedom

**1620** Battle of the White Mountain

**1621** Execution in Old Town Square of 27 Protestant leaders

**1612** Rudolph II dies

**1580**

**1600**

**1620**

*A ten-ducat coin (1603)*

**1614** Matthias Gate at Prague Castle built

**1618** Defenestration of two royal governors from Royal Palace (see p107)

# Baroque Prague

In 1619 the Czech nobles deposed Habsburg Emperor Ferdinand II as King of Bohemia and elected instead the Protestant ruler Frederick of the Palatinate. The following year they paid for their defiance at the Battle of the White Mountain, the beginning of the Thirty Years' War. There followed a period of persecution of all non-Catholics, accompanied by the Germanization of the country's institutions. The leaders in the fight against Protestantism were the Jesuits and one of their most powerful weapons was the restoration of Prague's churches in Baroque style. Many new churches also adopted this style.

**Extent of the City**
🏛 1750    🏛 Today

Mirror Chapel

**Church of St Nicholas**
This outstanding High Baroque church in the Little Quarter was the work of the great Dientzenhofers *(see pp128–9)*.

Grape Courtyard

**Measuring the World**
Some monasteries were seats of learning. Strahov *(see pp120–21)* had two libraries built, decorated with Baroque painting. This fresco detail is in the Philosophical Hall.

Holy Saviour Church

---

**1627** Beginning of Counter-Reformation committee in Prague

*Old Town coat of arms – embellished with the Imperial eagle and 12 flags in recognition of the defence of the city against the Swedes*

**1706–14** Decoration of Charles Bridge with statues

**1625**    **1645**    **1665**    **1685**    **1705**

**1648** Swedes occupy Prague Castle. Treaty of Westphalia and end of Thirty Years' War

**1704–53** Building of Church of St Nicholas in the Little Quarter

**1631** Saxon occupation of Prague

**1634** Wallenstein killed by Irish mercenaries

**1676–8** New bastions built to fortify Vyšehrad

A sculpture of
**Atlas** (1722) adorns
the top of the tower.

Observatory Tower

**Battle of the White Mountain**
In 1620 the Czech army was defeated
by Habsburg troops at Bílá Hora (White
Mountain), a hill west of Prague
(see p163). After the battle, Bohemia
became a de facto province of Austria.

**St Clement's Church** gave its
name to the whole complex.

Italian Chapel

**Monstrance**
Baroque monstrances
– used to display the
communion host –
became increasingly
elaborate and ornate
(see pp118–19).

## Clementinum

*The Jesuits exercised enormous power over
education. Between 1653 and 1723 they built this
College. It was the largest complex of buildings after
Prague Castle and included three churches, smaller
chapels, libraries, lecture halls and an observatory.*

## Where to see
## Baroque Prague

The Baroque is everywhere in
Prague. Almost all the churches
were built or remodelled in
Baroque style, the finest being
St Nicholas (pp128–9). There are
also the grand palaces and
smaller houses of the Little
Quarter (pp122–41), the façades
in the Old Town (pp62–81), and
statues on churches, street
corners and along the parapets
of Charles Bridge.

**Nerudova Street** At the Golden Cup,
No. 16, has preserved its typical
Baroque house sign (p130).

**Charles Bridge** This statue of St
Francis Borgia by Ferdinand Brokof
was added in 1710 (pp136–9).

| | | | |
|---|---|---|---|
| **1748** Bohemian Chancellery loses last vestiges of power | **1757** Prague besieged by Prussians | **1773** Jesuit Order dissolved | **1782** Convents and monasteries closed<br>**1784** Four towns of Prague united to form a single city |
| **1725** | **1745** | **1765** | **1785** |
| | **1740** Accession of Empress Maria Theresa<br><br>*Maria Theresa* | *Mozart at Bertramka* (p160) | **1787** Mozart stays at Bertramka preparing for the premiere of *Don Giovanni* at the Estates Theatre (see p67) |

# The National Revival in Prague

The 19th century was one of the most glorious periods in the history of Prague. Austrian rule relaxed, allowing the Czech nation to rediscover its own history and culture. Silent for so long, Czech was re-established as an official language. Civic pride was rekindled with the building of the capital's great showpieces, such as the National Theatre, which utilized the talents of Czech architects and artists. The Jewish Quarter and New Town underwent extensive redevelopment and, with the introduction of public transport, Prague grew beyond its ancient limits.

**Extent of the City**
| 1890 | Today |

December

Days of the year

**Smetana's Libuše**
Written for the scheduled opening of the National Theatre in 1881, the opera drew on early Czech legend *(see pp22–3)*.

**Months** and zodiac signs revolve around the centre.

Old Town coat of arms

**Rudolfinum**
A major concert venue beside the Vltava, the building *(see p86)* is richly decorated with symbols of the art of music.

## Old Town Clock Tower Calendar

*In 1866, the revolving dial on Prague's most enduring landmark was replaced by a new one by celebrated artist, Josef Mánes. His studies of Bohemian peasant life are incorporated into pictures symbolizing the months of the year.*

**1805** Czechs, Austrians and Russians defeated by Napoleon at Battle of Slavkov (Austerlitz)

**1818** National Museum founded

*Restored clock from the east face of the Town Hall Tower*

**1848** Uprising of people of Prague against Austrian troops

| 1800 | 1820 | 1840 |
| --- | --- | --- |

**1815** First public demonstration of a vehicle driven by a steam engine

**1845** First train arrives in Prague

*The battle of Slavkov*

**1833** Englishman Edward Thomas begins production of steam engines

**1838–45** Old Town Hall undergoes reconstruction

**Expo 95 Poster**
Vojtěch Hynais designed this poster for the ethnographic exhibition of folk culture in 1895. In the Art Nouveau style, it reflected the new appreciation of regional traditions.

## Where to see the National Revival

Many of Prague's remarkable monuments, the National Museum for example, were built around this period. One fine example of Art Nouveau architecture is the Municipal House (p66), where the Mayor's Room has murals by Mucha. The Rudolfinum (p86) and the National Theatre (pp156–7) have gloriously-decorated interiors by great artists of the day. The Prague Museum has many objects from the late 19th and early 20th centuries as well as the original painting for Mánes' Old Town Clock.

Sagittarius

**Municipal House**
Allegories of civic virtues painted by Alfons Mucha adorn this Art Nouveau interior.

**Jewish Quarter**
From 1897 onwards, the slum housing of the ghetto was replaced with new apartment blocks.

**National Museum** The Neo-Renaissance façade dominates the skyline (p147).

**National Theatre** The decor has murals by Czech artists, including Aleš (pp156–7).

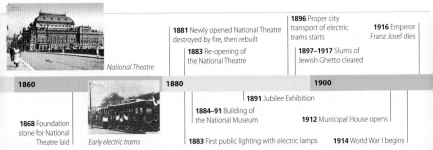

**1881** Newly opened National Theatre destroyed by fire, then rebuilt

**1883** Re-opening of the National Theatre

**1896** Proper city transport of electric trams starts

**1897–1917** Slums of Jewish Ghetto cleared

**1916** Emperor Franz Josef dies

National Theatre

**1860**

**1880**

**1900**

**1891** Jubilee Exhibition

**1884–91** Building of the National Museum

**1912** Municipal House opens

**1868** Foundation stone for National Theatre laid

Early electric trams

**1883** First public lighting with electric lamps

**1914** World War I begins

# Prague after Independence

Just 20 years after its foundation in 1918, the Czechoslovak Republic was helplessly caught up in the political manoeuvring that preceded Nazi domination of Europe. Prague emerged from World War II almost unscathed by bombings, no longer part of a Nazi protectorate but of a Socialist republic. Any resistance was brutally suppressed. Ultimately, the intellectuals spoke out, demanding observance of civil rights. Denial of such rights led these dissidents to unite and prepare for the "Velvet Revolution". In the end, it was a playwright, Václav Havel, who was swept into power at Prague Castle to lead the country at the start of a long and often difficult return to independence.

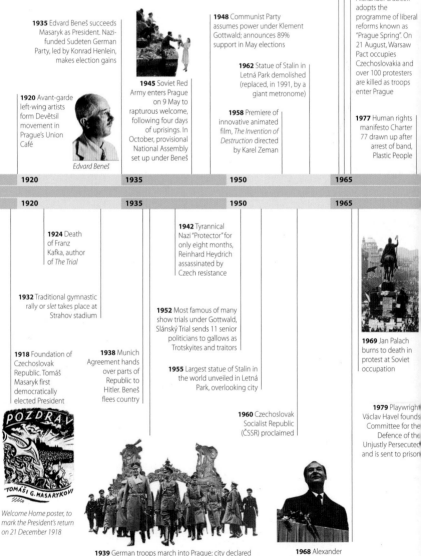

**1966** Jiří Menzel's *Closely Observed Trains* wins Oscar for Best Foreign Film, drawing the world's attention to Czech cinema

**1967** First Secretary and President, Antonín Novotný, imprisons dissident writers

**1968** Moderate Alexander Dubček adopts the programme of liberal reforms known as "Prague Spring". On 21 August, Warsaw Pact occupies Czechoslovakia and over 100 protesters are killed as troops enter Prague

**1977** Human rights manifesto Charter 77 drawn up after arrest of band, Plastic People

**1935** Edvard Beneš succeeds Masaryk as President. Nazi-funded Sudeten German Party, led by Konrad Henlein, makes election gains

**1948** Communist Party assumes power under Klement Gottwald; announces 89% support in May elections

**1962** Statue of Stalin in Letná Park demolished (replaced, in 1991, by a giant metronome)

**1945** Soviet Red Army enters Prague on 9 May to rapturous welcome, following four days of uprisings. In October, provisional National Assembly set up under Beneš

**1958** Premiere of innovative animated film, *The Invention of Destruction* directed by Karel Zeman

**1920** Avant-garde left-wing artists form Devětsil movement in Prague's Union Café

*Edvard Beneš*

**1920**          **1935**          **1950**          **1965**

---

**1920**          **1935**          **1950**          **1965**

**1924** Death of Franz Kafka, author of *The Trial*

**1942** Tyrannical Nazi "Protector" for only eight months, Reinhard Heydrich assassinated by Czech resistance

**1932** Traditional gymnastic rally or *slet* takes place at Strahov stadium

**1952** Most famous of many show trials under Gottwald, Slánský Trial sends 11 senior politicians to gallows as Trotskyites and traitors

**1969** Jan Palach burns to death in protest at Soviet occupation

**1918** Foundation of Czechoslovak Republic. Tomáš Masaryk first democratically elected President

**1938** Munich Agreement hands over parts of Republic to Hitler. Beneš flees country

**1955** Largest statue of Stalin in the world unveiled in Letná Park, overlooking city

**1960** Czechoslovak Socialist Republic (ČSSR) proclaimed

**1979** Playwright Václav Havel founds Committee for the Defence of the Unjustly Persecuted and is sent to prison

*Welcome Home poster, to mark the President's return on 21 December 1918*

**1939** German troops march into Prague; city declared capital of Nazi Protectorate of Bohemia and Moravia. Emil Hácha is President under the German protectorate

**1968** Alexander Dubček elected to post of First Secretary

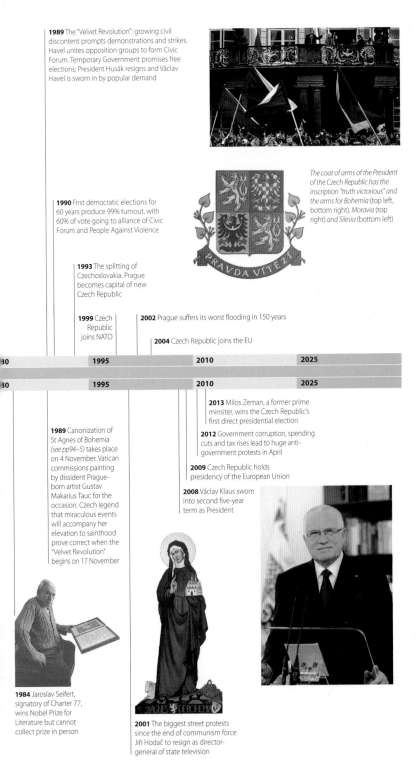

**1989** The "Velvet Revolution": growing civil discontent prompts demonstrations and strikes. Havel unites opposition groups to form Civic Forum. Temporary Government promises free elections; President Husák resigns and Václav Havel is sworn in by popular demand

*The coat of arms of the President of the Czech Republic has the inscription "truth victorious" and the arms for Bohemia (top left, bottom right), Moravia (top right) and Silesia (bottom left)*

**1990** First democratic elections for 60 years produce 99% turnout, with 60% of vote going to alliance of Civic Forum and People Against Violence

**1993** The splitting of Czechoslovakia. Prague becomes capital of new Czech Republic

**1999** Czech Republic joins NATO

**2002** Prague suffers its worst flooding in 150 years

**2004** Czech Republic joins the EU

**1995** | **2010** | **2025**

**1995** | **2010** | **2025**

**2013** Milos Zeman, a former prime minister, wins the Czech Republic's first direct presidential election

**2012** Government corruption, spending cuts and tax rises lead to huge anti-government protests in April

**2009** Czech Republic holds presidency of the European Union

**2008** Václav Klaus sworn into second five-year term as President

**1989** Canonization of St Agnes of Bohemia (see pp94–5) takes place on 4 November. Vatican commissions painting by dissident Prague-born artist Gustav Makarius Tauc for the occasion. Czech legend that miraculous events will accompany her elevation to sainthood prove correct when the "Velvet Revolution" begins on 17 November

**1984** Jaroslav Seifert, signatory of Charter 77, wins Nobel Prize for Literature but cannot collect prize in person

**2001** The biggest street protests since the end of communism force Jiří Hodač to resign as director-general of state television

# PRAGUE AT A GLANCE

There are almost 150 places of interest described in the *Area by Area* section of this book. A broad range of sights is covered: from the ancient Royal Palace, which was the site of the Defenestration of 1618 *(see p107)*, to cubist houses built in the Jewish Quarter in the 1920s *(see p93)*; from the peaceful oasis of Petřín Park *(see p141)*, to the bustle of Wenceslas Square *(see pp144–5)*. To help you make the most of your stay, the following 12 pages are a time-saving guide to the best Prague has to offer visitors. Museums and galleries, churches and synagogues, palaces and gardens all have their own sections. Each sight has a cross reference to its own full entry. Below are the attractions that no visitor should miss.

## Prague's Top Ten Sights

**Old Town Square**
See pp68–71.

**Old Town Hall**
See pp74–6.

**Old Jewish Cemetery**
See pp88–9.

**St Agnes's Convent**
See pp94–5.

**Prague Castle**
See pp98–9.

**St Vitus's Cathedral**
See pp102–105.

**Wallenstein Palace and Garden**
See p126.

**Church of St Nicholas**
See pp128–9.

**Charles Bridge**
See pp136–9.

**National Theatre**
See pp156–7.

◀ A view of the Old Town and Charles Bridge, bustling with people

# Prague's Best: Museums and Galleries

With more than 20 museums and almost 100 galleries and exhibition halls, Prague is a city of unexpected and rare delights. Religious masterpieces of the Middle Ages vie with the more recent opulence of Art Nouveau and the giants of modern art. Several galleries have opened since 1989 with many more temporary exhibitions. There are museums devoted to the history of the state, the city of Prague and its people, many of them housed in buildings that are historical landmarks and works of art in themselves. This map gives some of the highlights, with a detailed overview on pages 42–3.

**Picture Gallery of Prague Castle**
Among the art on display are paintings from the famous collection of Emperor Rudolph II, as well as over 100 works by Titian, Aachen and Rubens.

**Prague Castle and Hradčany**

**Little Quarter**

**Sternberg Palace**
The collection of European art here is outstanding, represented in works such as *The Feast of the Rosary* by Albrecht Dürer (1506).

**The Loreto**
The offerings of devout local aristocrats form the basis of this collection of religious decorative art. In 1721 this jewel-encrusted, tree-shaped monstrance was given to the treasury by Countess Wallenstein.

**Schwarzenberg Palace**
The ornate Renaissance palace, formerly the home of the Museum of Military History, is now a gallery exhibiting Baroque art.

**Smetana Museum**
The life and work of this 19th-century Czech composer are remembered beside the river that inspired one of his most famous pieces – the *Vltava*.

**Museum of Decorative Arts**
Five centuries of arts and crafts are
represented here, with particularly
impressive collections of Bohemian glass,
graphic art and furniture. This carved and
painted chest dates from 1612.

**St Agnes of Bohemia
Convent**
This collection includes
the 14th-century
*Resurrection of Christ* by
the Master of the
Třeboň Altar.

**Maisel Synagogue**
One of the most important collections of
Judaica in the world is housed in the Maisel
Synagogue and other buildings of the State
Jewish Museum. The displays include
religious artefacts, furnishings and books. This
illuminated page is from the manuscript of
the Pesach *Haggadah* of 1728.

Jewish
Quarter

Old Town

0 metres 500
0 yards 500

**National Museum**
The vast skeleton of a
whale dominates the
other exhibits in one of
seven grand halls
devoted to zoology.
The museum will be
closed until 2015
while it undergoes
extensive renovation.

New
Town

**Dvořák Museum**
This viola, which belonged to the influential 19th-century
Czech composer, is among the personal effects and musical
scores on display in the charming Michna Summer Palace.

# Exploring the Museums and Galleries

The city's museums give a fascinating insight into the history of the Czechs and of Prague's Jewish population. Also a revelation to visitors unfamiliar with the culture is the art of the Gothic and Baroque periods and of the 19th-century Czech National Revival. The National Gallery's plans to show more collections are underway, with Salmovský Palace the home of temporary exhibitions.

## Czech Painting and Sculpture

The most important and wide-ranging collection in Prague is that of the National Gallery. Its holdings of Czech art are shown at two venues: medieval art is housed at **St Agnes's Convent**, and 20th- to 21st-century art is on display at at the Trade Fair Palace.

The **Picture Gallery of Prague Castle** is a reminder of Emperor Rudolph II's once-great art collection. Alongside the paintings are documents and other evidence of just how splendid the original collection must have been.

14th-century *Madonna Aracoeli*, St Vitus Treasure, Prague Castle

For some of the best Bohemian art, you must visit the Baroque works at the **Schwarzenberg Palace**, just outside the main gate of the Castle. These include examples by Baroque masters Karel Škréta and Petr Brandl. On permanent display within the Castle is the St Vitus Treasure, a collection of religious pieces including a Madonna from the School of Master Theodoric.

Centuries of Czech sculpture are housed in the Lapidarium at the **Exhibition Ground**. Among its exhibits is statuary formerly found on the Charles Bridge, and the Marian pillar that used to stand in the Old Town Square.

The collection at the **St Agnes of Bohemia Convent** includes Bohemian and central European Gothic painting and sculpture, including panels painted for Charles IV by Master Theodoric. Works by 19th- and 20th-century Prague artists can be seen at the Prague Gallery. Its branches include the Baroque **Troja Palace**, where the architecture makes a great backdrop. Exhibitions are drawn from the gallery's 3,000 paintings, 1,000 statues and 4,000 prints. The superb museum of 20th- and 21st-century art at the **Trade Fair Palace** represents almost every 20th-century artistic movement. Cubism and Art Nouveau are both represented, as are the 1920s figures of Otto Gutfreund. The development of such ground breaking

*Commerce* by Otto Gutfreund (1923), Trade Fair Palace

groups as Osma, Devětsil, Skupina 42 and the 12.15 group is also well documented.

## European Painting and Sculpture

On view at **Sternberg Palace** is an exceptional range of masterpieces by Europe's finest artists from antiquity to the 18th century.

The most treasured work in the collection is the *Feast of the Rosary* by Albrecht Dürer. Works by 17th-century Dutch masters such as Rubens and Rembrandt also feature.

The museum of 20th- and 21st-century art at the **Trade Fair Palace** has a fine collection of Picassos and Rodin bronzes, as well as works from almost every Impressionist, Post-Impressionist and Fauvist. Three notable self-portraits are those of Paul Gauguin (*Bonjour Monsieur Gauguin*, 1889), Henri Rousseau (1890) and Pablo Picasso (1907). Modern German and Austrian painting is also on show, with works by Gustav Klimt and Egon Schiele. The *Dance of Life*, by Norwegian Edvard Munch, is considered greatly influential upon Czech avant-garde art.

The other main venue for European art is the **Picture Gallery of Prague Castle**, which focuses on European painters of the 16th to 18th centuries. As well as Titian's superb *The Toilet of a Young Lady*, there are also works in the collection by Rubens and Tintoretto. The exquisite building of **Schwarzenberg Palace** now houses a gallery of Baroque art.

## Music

Two Czech composers merit their own museums. The **Smetana Museum** is a memorial to the father of Czech music, Bedřich Smetana, whose musical style became closely linked to the national revival. The **Dvořák Museum**, housed in the Michna Summer Palace, explores the life and work of Antonín Dvořák. Both museums contain personal memorabilia, musical scores and correspondence.

The **Museum of Music** has many rare and historic instruments, and a number of scores by famous composers.

## History

The historical collections of the **National Museum** are held at the main Wenceslas Square building. The **Prague Museum** centres on the history of the city, with period rooms, historical prints and a model of Prague in the 19th century, made of paper and wood by the lithographer Antonín Langweil.

Bohemian Baroque glass goblet (1730), Museum of Decorative Arts

A branch of the museum at Výtoň, on the banks of the Vltava, depicts the way of life of a former settlement. Another at Vyšehrad records the history of this royal seat.

The Museum of Military History, housed in the Schwarzenberg Palace since 1945 but now on U Památníku 3, displays battle charts, weaponry, uniforms and other military regalia. The Lobkowicz Collection, housed in the 16th century **Lobkowicz Palace** at Prague Castle, includes rare books and manuscripts.

The Jewish Museum is made up of various sites in the Jewish Quarter, including the **Spanish Synagogue, Maisel Synagogue** and the **Old Jewish Cemetery**. Among its collections are holy artefacts taken from other Jewish communities and brought to Prague by the Nazis as part of a chilling plan for a museum of "an extinct race". Another moving display is of drawings made by children from the Terezín concentration camp.

## Decorative Arts

With glassware spanning centuries, from medieval to modern, porcelain and pewterware, furniture and textiles, books and posters, the **Museum of Decorative Arts** in the Jewish Quarter is one of Prague's best, but only a small selection of its holdings is on show. Look out for specialized temporary exhibitions mounted either at the museum itself or at other venues in Prague.

Many other museums have examples of the decorative arts, ranging from grandiose monstrances – including one with 6,222 diamonds – in the treasury of **The Loreto** to simple everyday furnishings in the **Prague Museum**. There is also a fascinating collection of pre-Columbian artefacts from Central America in the **Náprstek Museum**.

16th-century astrolabe from the National Technical Museum

## Science and Technology

A vast exhibition hall holds the transport section of the **National Technical Museum**. Ranks of vintage cars, motorcycles and steam engines fill the space, and over them hang examples of early flying machines. Other sections in the museum trace the progress of sciences such as electronics. The museum's many other fascinating exhibits include displays on architecture, astronomy and printing and communications.

### Finding the Museums and Galleries

Dvořák Museum *p154*
Exhibition Ground *p162*
Kampa Museum of Modern Art *p135*
Lobkowicz Palace *p101*
The Loreto *pp118–19*
Maisel Synagogue *p92*
Mozart Museum *p160*
Museum of Decorative Arts *p86*
Museum of Music *p141*
Náprstek Museum *p77*
National Museum *p147*
National Technical Museum *p162*
Old Jewish Cemetery *pp88–9*
Picture Gallery of Prague Castle *p100*
Prague Museum *p161*
St Agnes of Bohemia *pp94–5*
Schwarzenberg Palace *p116*
Smetana Museum *p81*
Spanish Synagogue *pp92–3*
Sternberg Palace *pp112–15*
Trade Fair Palace *pp164–5*
Troja Palace *pp166–7*

# Prague's Best: Churches and Synagogues

The religious buildings of Prague vividly record the city's changing architectural styles, and many are treasure houses of religious art. But they also reflect Prague's times of religious and political strife, the lives of its people, its setbacks and growth as a city. This map features highlights of their architecture and art, with a more detailed overview on pages 46–7.

**St George's Basilica**
St George, sword raised to slay the dragon, is portrayed in this late-Gothic relief, set above the doorway of the magnificent early Renaissance south portal.

**St Vitus's Cathedral**
The jewel of the cathedral is the Chapel of St Wenceslas. Its walls are decorated with semi-precious stones, gilding and frescoes. Elizabeth of Pomerania, the fourth and last wife of Charles IV, is shown at prayer in the fresco above the Gothic altar.

**Prague Castle and Hradčany**

**Little Quarter**

**The Loreto**
This shrine to the Virgin Mary has been a place of pilgrimage since 1626. Each hour, its Baroque clock tower chimes a hymn on the carillon of 27 bells.

**Church of St Thomas**
The skeleton of the martyr St Just rests in a glass coffin below a Crucifixion by Antonín Stevens, one of several superb works of religious art in this church.

**Church of St Nicholas**
In the heart of the Little Quarter, this is Prague's finest example of High Baroque. The dome over the high altar is so lofty that early worshippers feared it would collapse.

**Old-New Synagogue**
Prague's oldest synagogue dates from the 13th century. Its Gothic main portal is carved with a vine which bears twelve bunches of grapes symbolizing the tribes of Israel.

**Church of Our Lady before Týn**
Set back behind a row of arcaded buildings, the many-spired twin towers of the church dominate the eastern end of Old Town Square. The Gothic, Renaissance and Baroque features of the interior create striking contrasts.

**Church of St James**
Consecrated in 1374, this church was restored to new Baroque glory after a fire in 1689. Typical of its grandeur is this 18th-century monument to chancellor Jan Vratislav of Mitrovice. Fine acoustics and a superb organ make the church a popular venue for concerts.

Jewish Quarter

Old Town

**Slavonic Monastery Emauzy**
These cloisters hold a series of precious frescoes from three Gothic masters depicting scenes from the Old and New Testaments.

New Town

0 metres 500
0 yards 500

**Church of St Peter and St Paul**
Remodelled many times since the 11th century, the design of this church is now 1890s Neo-Gothic. This striking relief of the Last Judgment marks the main entrance.

# Exploring Churches and Synagogues

Religious building began in Prague in the 9th century, reaching its zenith during the reign of Charles IV *(see pp26–7)*. The remains of an 11th-century synagogue have been found, but during the 19th-century clearance of the overcrowded Jewish ghetto three synagogues were lost. Many churches were damaged during the Hussite rebellions *(see pp28–9)*. The political regime of the 20th century also took its toll, but now churches and synagogues have been reclaimed and restored, with many open to visitors.

## Romanesque

Three reasonably well-preserved Romanesque rotundas, dating from the 11th and 12th centuries, still exist in Prague. The oldest is the **St Martin's Rotunda**; the others are the rotundas of the Holy Rood and of St Longinus. All three are tiny, with naves only 6 m (20 ft) in diameter.

By far the best-preserved and most important Romanesque church is **St George's Basilica**, founded in 920 by Prince Vratislav I. Extensive

11th-century Romanesque Rotunda of St Martin in Vyšehrad

reconstruction was carried out after a fire in 1142, but its chancel, with some exquisite frescoes on its vaulting, is a Late-Romanesque gem.

The **Strahov Monastery**, founded in 1142 by Prince Vladislav II *(see pp24–5)*, has retained its Romanesque core in spite of fire, wars and extensive renovation.

## Gothic

Gothic architecture, with its ribbed vaulting, flying buttresses and pointed arches, reached Bohemia in about 1230 and was soon adopted into religious architecture.

The first religious building in Gothic style was the **St Agnes of Bohemia Convent**, founded in 1233 by Wenceslas I's sister, Agnes. Prague's oldest synagogue, the **Old-New Synagogue**, built in 1270, is rather different in style to the churches but is still a superb example of Early Gothic.

The best example of Prague Gothic is **St Vitus's Cathedral**. Its fine tracery and towering nave

High, Gothic windows at the east end of St Vitus's Cathedral

epitomize the style. Other notable Gothic churches are **Our Lady before Týn** and **Our Lady of the Snows**.

Important for its historical significance is the reconstructed Gothic **Bethlehem Chapel** where Jan Hus *(see p29)* preached for 10 years.

The superb Gothic frescoes found in abundance at the **Slavonic Monastery Emauzy**, were badly damaged in World War II, but have been restored.

## Renaissance

In the 1530s the influence of Italian artists living in Prague sparked the city's Renaissance movement. The style is more clearly seen in secular than religious building. The Late-Renaissance period, under Rudolph II (1576–1611), offers the best remaining examples.

## Domes and Spires

The domes and spires of Prague's churches are the city's main landmarks, as the view from the many vantage points will confirm. You will see a variety of spires, towers and domes: Gothic and Neo-Gothic soar skywards, while Baroque often have rounded cupolas and onion domes. The modern top of the 14th-century Slavonic Monastery, added after the church was struck in a World War II air raid, is a rare example of modernist religious architecture in Prague. Its sweeping, intersecting twin spires are a bold reinterpretation of Gothic themes, and a striking addition to the city's skyline.

*Gothic*

Church of Our Lady before Týn (1350–1511)

*Baroque*

Church of St Nicholas in the Little Quarter (1750)

The **High Synagogue** and the **Pinkas Synagogue** retain strong elements of the style: the former in its 1586 exterior, the latter in the reworking of an original Gothic building.

The Church of St Roch in the **Strahov Monastery** is probably the best example of Late-Renaissance "Mannerism".

Renaissance-influenced vaulting, Pinkas Synagogue (1535)

## Baroque

The Counter-Reformation *(see pp32–3)* inspired the building of new churches and the revamping of existing ones for a period of 150 years. Prague's first Baroque church was **Our Lady Victorious**, built in 1611–13.

**St Nicholas** in the Little Quarter took almost 60 years to build. Its lush interior and frescoed vault make it Prague's most important Baroque building, followed by **The Loreto** (1626–1750), adjoining the **Capuchin Monastery**. The father-and-son team, Christoph and Kilian Ignaz Dientzenhofer designed both buildings, and **St John on the Rock** and **St Nicholas** in the Old Town.

A special place in Prague's history was occupied by the Jesuit **Clementinum**. This influential university's church was the **Holy Saviour**. The Baroque style is closely linked with Jesuit teachings: Kilian Ignaz Dientzenhofer was educated here.

**Klausen Synagogue** (now the Jewish Museum) was built in 1689 with Baroque stuccoed barrel vaults.

Many early buildings were given Baroque facelifts. The Gothic nave of **St Thomas** has Baroque vaulting, and the once-Gothic **St James** went Baroque after a fire in 1689.

19th-century Neo-Gothic portal, Church of St Peter and St Paul

## Neo-Gothic

During the height of the 19th-century Gothic Revival *(see pp34–5)*, **St Vitus's Cathedral** was completed, in accordance with the original Gothic plan. Work by Josef Mocker, the movement's leader, aroused controversy but his **St Peter and St Paul** at Vyšehrad is a well-loved landmark. The triple-naved basilica of **St Ludmilla** in Náměstí Míru was also designed by Mocker.

### Finding the Churches and Synagogues

St Agnes of Bohemia *pp94–5*
Bethlehem Chapel *p77*
Capuchin Monastery *pp116–17*
Clementinum *p81 (see also History of Prague p33)*
St George's Basilica *p100*
High Synagogue *p87*
Holy Saviour *(see Knights of the Cross Square p81)*
St James *p67*
St John on the Rock *p153*
Klausen Synagogue *p87*
The Loreto *pp118–19*
St Ludmilla *(see Náměstí Míru p161)*
St Martin's Rotunda *(see Vyšehrad Walk p180)*
St Nicholas in the Little Quarter *pp128–9*
St Nicholas in the Old Town *p72*
Old-New Synagogue *pp90–91*
Our Lady before Týn *p72*
Our Lady of the Snows *p146*
Our Lady Victorious *p130*
St Peter and St Paul *(see Vyšehrad Walk p181)*
Pinkas Synagogue *p86*
Slavonic Monastery Emauzy *p150*
Strahov Monastery *pp120–21*
St Thomas *p127*
St Vitus's Cathedral *pp102–105*

Nave ceiling of the Church of St Nicholas in the Little Quarter

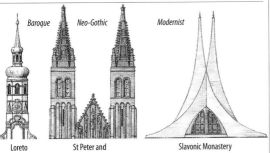

Baroque    Neo-Gothic    Modernist

Loreto (1725)    St Peter and St Paul (1903)    Slavonic Monastery Emauzy (1967)

# Prague's Best: Palaces and Gardens

Prague's palaces and gardens are among the most important historical and architectural monuments in the city. Many palaces house museums or galleries *(see pp40–43)*, and some are concert venues. The gardens range from formal, walled oases with fountains and grand statuary, to

open spaces beyond the city centre. This map features some of the best palaces and gardens, with a detailed overview on pages 50–51.

**Belvedere**
The Singing Fountain (1568) stands in front of the exquisite Renaissance summer palace.

**Royal Garden**
Though redesigned in the 19th century, the Renaissance garden preserves much of its original character. Historic statues still in place include a pair of Baroque lions (1730) guarding the entrance.

**Prague Castle and Hradčany**

**Little Quarter**

**South Gardens**
Starting life as the Castle's defensive bastions, these gardens afford a wonderful view of Prague. First laid out as a park in 1891, their present design was landscaped by Josip Plečnik 40 years later.

**Wallenstein Palace**
Built in 1624–30 for Duke Albrecht of Wallenstein, this vast Baroque palace was intended to outshine Prague Castle. Over 20 houses and a town gate were demolished to make room for the palace and garden. This Fountain of Venus (1599), stands in front of the arches of the *sala terrena.*

**Wallenstein Garden**
The garden statues are copies of 17th-century bronzes. The originals were plundered by the Swedes in 1648.

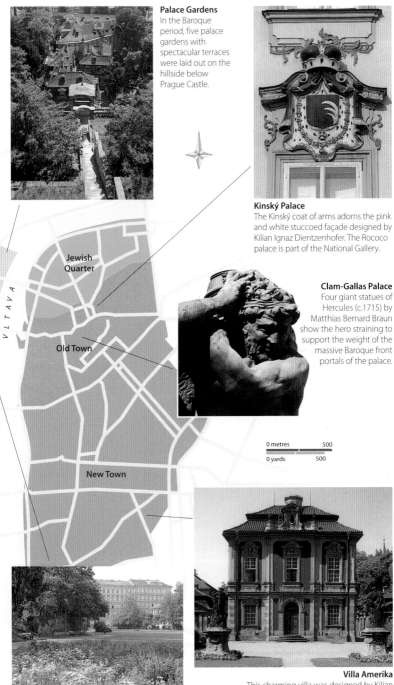

**Palace Gardens**
In the Baroque period, five palace gardens with spectacular terraces were laid out on the hillside below Prague Castle.

**Kinský Palace**
The Kinský coat of arms adorns the pink and white stuccoed façade designed by Kilian Ignaz Dientzenhofer. The Rococo palace is part of the National Gallery.

**Clam-Gallas Palace**
Four giant statues of Hercules (c.1715) by Matthias Bernard Braun show the hero straining to support the weight of the massive Baroque front portals of the palace.

Jewish Quarter

VLTAVA

Old Town

New Town

0 metres 500
0 yards 500

**Villa Amerika**
This charming villa was designed by Kilian Ignaz Dientzenhofer in 1712. It now houses the Dvořák Museum. The garden's sculptural decorations are from the workshop of Antonín Braun.

**Kampa Island**
A tranquil waterside park was created on the island after the destruction of its original gardens in World War II.

# Exploring the Palaces and Gardens

Prague boasts an amazing number of palaces and gardens, spanning centuries. Comparatively few palaces were lost to the ravages of war. Instead, they tended to evolve in style during restoration or enlargement. Palace gardens became fashionable in the 17th century, but could only be laid out where there was space, such as below Prague Castle. More vulnerable to change, most have been relandscaped several times. In the 19th century, and again after 1989, many of the larger parks and private gardens were opened up to the public.

Bronze Singing Fountain in the Royal Garden by the Belvedere

## Medieval Palaces

The oldest palace in Prague is the **Old Royal Palace** at Prague Castle. In the basement is the Romanesque ground floor, started in about 1135. It has been rebuilt many times, particularly between the 14th and 16th centuries. The heart of the Palace, Vladislav Hall, dates from the 1490s and is late Gothic in structure. Less well known is the early Baroque **Tuscany Palace**, which has a number of Baroque statues in its attic. Several 17th-century frescoes were unearthed during its reconstruction in the 1990s.

## Renaissance Palaces

One of the most beautiful Renaissance buildings in Prague is the 16th-century **Schwarzenberg Palace**. The work of Italian architects, its façade is entirely covered with geometric, two-tone sgraffito designs. Italians also worked on the **Belvedere**. Its graceful arcades and columns, all covered with rich reliefs, make this one of the finest Renaissance buildings north of the Alps. The **Martinic Palace**, built in 1563, was the first example of late-Renaissance building in Prague. Soon after came the **Lobkowicz Palace**. Its terracotta relief-decorated windows and plaster sgraffito have survived later Baroque modifications. The huge **Archbishop's Palace** was given a later Rococo façade over its Renaissance structure.

Southern façade of Troja Palace and its formal gardens

## Baroque Palaces

Many palaces were built in the Baroque style, and examples of all its phases still exist in Prague. A handsome, if ostentatious, early Baroque example is the

## Decorative Portals and Gates

The elaborate gates and portals of Prague's palaces are among the most beautiful and impressive architectural features in the city. Gothic and Renaissance portals have often survived, even where the buildings themselves have been destroyed or modified by renovations in a later architectural style. The period of most prolific building was the Baroque, and distinctive portals from this time can be seen framing many a grand entrance around the city. Statues of giants, heroes and mythological figures are often depicted holding up the doorways. These were not merely decorative but acted as an integral element of support.

Gateway to Court of Honour of Prague Castle (1768)

Wallenstein Palace. Similar ostentation is evident in the **Černín Palace**, one of Prague's most monumental buildings. The mid-Baroque had two strands, one opulent and Italianate, the other formal and French or Viennese in influence. **Troja Palace** and **Michna Summer Palace** are in Italian villa style while the **Sternberg Palace** on Hradčanské náměstí is more Viennese in style. Troja was designed in 1679 by Jean-Baptiste Mathey, who, like the Dientzenhofers (see p129), was a master of the Baroque. The pairs of giants on the portals of the **Clam-Gallas Palace**, and the **Morzin Palace** in Nerudova Street, are a popular Baroque motif. The **Kinský Palace** is a superb Rococo design by Kilian Ignaz Dientzenhofer.

## Gardens

The finest of Prague's palace gardens, such as the **Wallenstein Garden**, are in the Little Quarter. Though the style of Wallenstein Palace is Early Baroque, the garden still displays the geometric formality of the Renaissance, also preserved in the **Royal Garden** behind Prague Castle. The **South Gardens** on the Castle's old ramparts were redesigned in the 1920s.

Many more gardens were laid out in the 17th and 18th centuries, when noble families vied with each other to have fine winter residences in the Little Quarter below the Castle. Many are now the grounds of embassies, but others have been opened to the public. The Ledebour Garden has been combined with several neighbouring gardens. Laid out on a steep hillside, the **Palace Gardens**, in particular, make ingenious use of pavilions, stairs and terraces from which there are wonderful views of the city. The **Vrtba Garden**, landscaped on the site of former vineyards, is a similar Baroque creation with statues and splendid views. Former palace gardens were also used to create a park on **Kampa Island**.

Ancient trees in Stromovka

The many old gardens and orchards on Petřín Hill have been transformed into the large public area of **Petřín Park**. Another former orchard is **Vojan Park**, laid out by archbishops in the 13th century. The **Botanical Garden** are one of the few areas of green open to the public in the New Town.

Generally, the larger parks are situated further out of the city. **Stromovka** was a royal deer park, while **Letná Park** was developed in 1858 on the open space of Letná Plain.

The Royal Garden of Prague Castle, planted with spring flowers

### Where to Find the Palaces and Gardens

Archbishop's Palace p111
Belvedere pp110–11
Botanical Gardens p153
Černín Palace p117
Clam-Gallas Palace p80
Kampa Island p131
Kinský Palace p72
Letná Park p161
Lobkowicz Palace p101
Martinic Palace p116
Morzin Palace
    see Nerudova Street p130
Palace Gardens p135
Petřín Park p141
Royal Garden p111
Royal Palace pp106–107
Schwarzenberg Palace p116
South Gardens p110
Sternberg Palace pp112–13
Stromovka p162
Troja Palace pp166–7
Villa Amerika
    see Dvořák Museum p154
Vojan Park p135
Vrtba Garden p130
Wallenstein Palace and
    Garden p126

Troja Palace (c.1703)

Clam-Gallas Palace (c.1714)

# PRAGUE THROUGH THE YEAR

Springtime in Prague sees the city burst into colour as its gardens start to bloom. Celebrations begin with the Prague Spring Music Festival. In summer, visitors are entertained by street performers and the city's glorious gardens come into their own. When the weather begins to turn cooler, Prague hosts the Musica International Music Fair.

The year often draws to a close with snow on the streets. The ball season starts in December, and in the coldest months, most events are held indoors. At Prague Castle, an all-year-round attraction is the changing of the guard around midday. For details of activities, check the listings magazines (see p217) or the Prague Information Service (see p216).

Concert at Wallenstein Palace during the Prague Spring Music Festival

## Spring

As Prague sees its first rays of spring sunshine, the city comes alive. A mass of colours, blooms and cultural events makes this one of the most exciting times of the year to visit. The city's blossoming parks and gardens open their gates again, after the colder months of winter. During April the temperatures rise and an entertainment programme begins – dominated by the Prague International Spring Music Festival.

### Easter

**Easter Monday** (dates vary) is a public holiday. Easter is observed as a religious holiday but it is also associated with a bizarre pagan ritual in which Czech men beat their women with willow sticks in order to keep them fertile during the coming year. The women retaliate by throwing water over their male tormentors. Peace is finally restored when the women present the men with a painted egg. Church services are held during the entire Easter period (see p233).

### March

**Young Prague** (end of March). International festival which celebrates young musicians – choirs and orchestras perform and compete.

### April

**Boat trips** (1 April). A number of boats begin trips up and down the Vltava.

**Witch-burning** (30 April), at the Exhibition Ground (see p164). Concerts accompany this 500-year-old tradition where old brooms are burnt on bonfires, in a symbolic act to rid nature of evil spirits.

### May

**Labour Day** (1 May). Public holiday celebrated with numerous cultural events.

**Mozart's Prague** (early May). Celebration of Mozart. International orchestras perform in music halls and churches.

**Anniversary of Prague Uprising** (5 May). At noon sirens are sounded for one minute. Flowers are laid at the commemorative plaques of those who died (see p36).

**Day of Liberation from Fascism** (8 May). Public holiday for VE day. Wreaths are laid on the graves of soldiers at Olšany cemeteries.

**Prague International Book Fair** (third week in May), Industrial Palace (see p162). The best of Czech and international authors.

**Prague International Marathon** (dates vary).

### The Prague Spring International Music Festival

This international festival presents a busy programme of concerts, ballet and opera from 12 May to 3 June. Music lovers can hear a huge selection of music played by some of the best musicians in the world. The main venue is the Rudolfinum (see p86) but others include churches and palaces – some of which are only open to the public on these occasions. The festival begins on the anniversary of Bedřich Smetana's death (see p81). A service is held at his grave in Vyšehrad (see p180), and in the evening there is a concert at the Municipal House (see p66) where musicians perform his most famous work, Má Vlast (My Country). Municipal House is also where the festival ends.

Bedřich Smetana

## Average Daily Hours of Sunshine

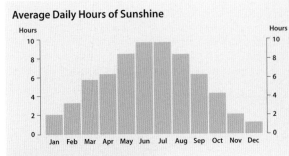

Hours

Jan Feb Mar Apr May Jun Jul Aug Sep Oct Nov Dec

**Sunshine Chart**
Prague's longest and
hottest days fall
between May and
August. At the height of
summer, daylight starts
at 5am. The snow-
covered city looks
stunning on a sunny
winter's day. But sunny
days can be spoiled by
thick smog (see p55).

Czechs and tourists enjoying the beauty of Vyšehrad Park on a sunny afternoon

## Summer

Summer arrives with high temperatures, frequent, sometimes heavy, showers and thousands of visitors. This is a beautiful, if busy, time to visit. Every weekend, Czechs set out for the country to go hiking in the surrounding hills or stay in country cottages. Those remaining in Prague visit the reservoirs and lakes (see p221), just outside the city to try and escape the heat. There is a wealth of entertainment on offer as culture moves into the open air taking over the squares, streets and gardens. Street performers, buskers and classical orchestras all help to keep visitors entertained. Many cafés have tables outside allowing you to quench your thirst while watching the fun.

### June

**Mayoral Boat Race** (first weekend in June), Primátorky. Rowing races are held on the river Vltava, just below Vyšehrad. **Summer**

**Concerts** (throughout the summer). Prague's gardens (see pp48–51) are the attractive and popular setting for a large number of free classical and brass-band concerts. One of the most famous, and spectacular, outdoor classical concerts is held by Křižík Fountain at the Exhibition Ground (see p162). Full orchestras play to the stunning backdrop of coloured lights and water, synchronized to the music by computer.

**Prague Museum Night** (second Saturday in June). From 7pm until midnight buses take visitors from Staroměstská metro station to various museums and galleries, with free entry.

**Anniversary of the Murder of Reinhard Heydrich's Assassins** (18 June). A mass is held in remembrance at the Church of St Cyril and St Methodius (see p152) for those who died there.

**Battle Re-enactments** (throughout summer), held in Prague's palaces and gardens.

**Dance Prague** (end of May to last week of June). An international festival of contemporary dance at the Ponec Theatre (see p219).

### July

**Remembrance of the Slavonic Missionaries** (5 July). Public holiday in honour of St Cyril and St Methodius (see p152).

**Anniversary of Jan Hus's Death** (6 July). A public holiday when flowers are laid at the the memorial of 15th-centruy religious reformer and martyr Jan Hus (see p28).

### August

**Fortuna Czech Open** (third week of August). International youth music festival.

Changing of the Guard at Prague Castle

## Average Monthly Rainfall

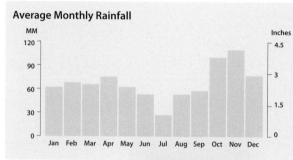

**Rainfall Chart**
Prague has plenty of rain throughout the year. The wettest months are October and November, but there are frequent light showers in the summer months as well. Winter snowfalls can be quite heavy, but they are rarely severe.

## Autumn

When the gardens below Prague Castle take on the shades of red and gold, and visitors start to leave, the city gets ready for the cold winter months. This is also the traditional mushroom-gathering season when you encounter people with baskets full of freshly picked mushrooms. Market places are flooded with fruit and vegetables. The tree-lined slopes above the Vltava take on the beautiful colours of autumn. September and October still have a fair number of warm and sunny days, although November often sees the first snowfalls. Football fans fill the stadiums and the popular steeplechase course at Pardubice reverberates to the cheers of fans.

Jazz musicians playing at the International Jazz Festival

### September

**Prague Grand Prix** *(second Saturday in September)*. Running competition in the centre of Prague.
**Dvořákova Praha** *(dates vary)*, International music festival in the Rudolfinum *(see p86)*.
**Kite competitions** *(third Sunday in September)*, on Letná Plain in front of Sparta Stadium. Very popular competition for children but open to anyone, with a kite, young or old.
**St Wenceslas** *(28 September)*. A sacred music festival is held for the feast of the patron saint.
**Běchovice-Praha** *(last Sunday in September)*. This 10-km (6-mile) road race has been run since 1897. The race starts from Běchovice, a suburb of Prague, and ends in Žižkov.

### October

**Golden Prague** *(time varies)*, Žofín Palace. International TV festival of prize-winning programmes.
**The Great Pardubice Steeplechase** *(second Sunday in October)*, held at Pardubice, east of Prague. This horse race has been run since 1874 and is considered to be the most difficult in Europe.
**Tina B** *(mid-October–mid-November)*. Contemporary themed art festival featuring international artists and introducing new techniques and the latest trends in new media.
**The Day of the Republic** *(28 October)*. Despite the splitting up of Czechoslovakia into two separate republics, the founding of the country in 1918 is still a public holiday.

### November

**Velká Kunratická** *(second Sunday in November)*. Popular, but gruelling, cross-country race in Kunratice forest. Anyone can enter.
**Celebration of the Velvet Revolution** *(17 November)*. Peaceful demonstrations take place around Wenceslas Square *(see pp144–5)*.

A view of St Vitus's Cathedral through autumn trees

## Average Monthly Temperature

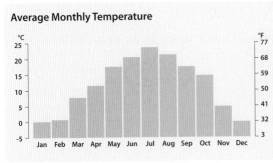

**Temperature Chart**
The chart shows the average minimum and maximum temperatures for each month in Prague. The summer usually remains comfortably warm, while the winter months can get bitterly cold and temperatures often drop below freezing.

## Winter

If you are lucky enough to catch Prague the morning after a snowfall with the sun shining, the effect is magical. The view over the Little Quarter rooftops with their pristine white covering is a memorable sight. Unfortunately Prague is rarely at its best during the winter months. The weather is changeable. Foggy days with temperatures just above freezing can quickly go down to -5° C (23° F). Pollution and Prague's geographical position in the Vltava basin, lead to smog being trapped just above the city.

As if to try and make up for the winter weather's shortcomings, the theatre season reaches its climax and there are a number of premieres. Balls and dances are held in these cold months. Just before Christmas Eve large barrels containing live carp – which is the traditional Czech Christmas delicacy – appear on the streets. Christmas trees adorn the city, and carol singers

View of the Little Quarter rooftops covered in snow

can be heard on street corners. Christmas mass is held in most churches and New Year's Eve is celebrated, in time-honoured style, throughout the entire city.

### December

**Christmas markets** *(throughout December)*, Můstek and Anděl metro stations, Náměstí Míru, Palackého náměstí, Old Town Square. Stalls sell Christmas decorations, gifts, hot wine, punch and the traditional Czech carp *(see p211)*.
**Christmas Eve, Christmas Day and Boxing Day** *(24, 25 and 26 December)*. Public holidays. Mass is held in churches throughout the city.
**Swimming competitions in the Vltava** *(26 December)*. Hundreds of hardened and determined swimmers gather at the Vltava to swim in temperatures of around 3° C (37° F).
**New Year celebrations** *(31 December)*. Crowds of people congregate around Wenceslas and Old Town Square.

### January

**New Year's Day** *(1 January)*. Public holiday.

### February

**Dances and Balls** *(early February)*.
**Bohemian Carnevale Praha** *(second and third weeks of February)*. Museums, schools and shops host performances of traditional Czech festivities.

### Public Holidays

New Year's Day *(1 Jan)*
Easter Monday
Labour Day *(1 May)*
Day of Liberation from Fascism *(8 May)*
Remembrance of the Slavonic Missionaries *(5 July)*
Anniversary of Jan Hus's death *(6 July)*
St Wenceslas *(28 Sep)*
Foundation of Czechoslovakia *(28 Oct)*
Fall of Communism *(17 Nov)*
Christmas Eve, Christmas Day, Boxing Day *(24–26 Dec)*.

Barrels of the traditional Christmas delicacy, carp, on sale in Prague

# A RIVER VIEW OF PRAGUE

The Vltava river has played a vital part in the city's history *(see pp22–3)* and has provided inspiration for artists, poets and musicians throughout the centuries.

Up until the 19th century, parts of the city were exposed to the danger of heavy flooding. To try and alleviate the problem, the river's embankments have been strengthened and raised many times, in order to try to prevent the water penetrating too far (the foundations of today's embankments are made of stone or concrete). During the Middle Ages, year after year of disastrous flooding led to the decision to bury the areas affected under 2 m (6 ft) of earth to try to minimize the damage. Although this strategy was only partially effective, it meant that the ground floors of many Romanesque and Gothic buildings were preserved and can still be seen today *(see pp80–81)*. In 2002 however, a state of emergency was declared as flooding devastated large parts of the city. Despite its destructive side, the Vltava has provided a vital method of transport for the city, as well as a source of income. As technology improved, the river became increasingly important; water mills, weirs and water towers were built. In 1912 a large hydroelectric power plant was built on Štvanice Island, supplying almost a third of Prague's electricity. To make the river navigable, eight dams, a large canal and weirs were constructed along the Slapy-Prague-Mělník stretch, where the Vltava flows into the river Elbe. For the visitor, an excursion on one of the many boats and paddle steamers that travel up and down the river is worthwhile. There are trips to Troja *(see pp166–7)* and as far as Slapy Lake. Catching a boat from one of the piers on the river is one of the best ways of seeing the city.

A view of the steamboat landing stage (přístaviště parníků) on Rašínovo nábřeží

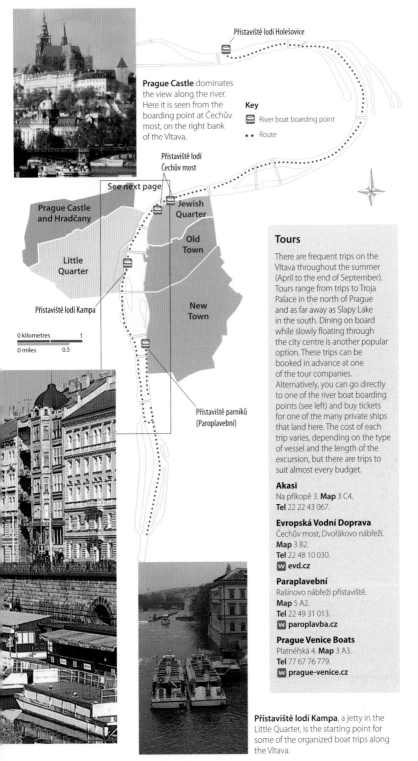

Přístaviště lodí Holešovice

**Prague Castle** dominates the view along the river. Here it is seen from the boarding point at Čechův most, on the right bank of the Vltava.

**Key**

🚢 River boat boarding point

•• Route

Přístaviště lodí Čechův most

See next page

Prague Castle and Hradčany

Jewish Quarter

Little Quarter

Old Town

Přístaviště lodí Kampa

New Town

0 kilometres 1

0 miles 0.5

Přístaviště parníků (Paroplavební)

## Tours

There are frequent trips on the Vltava throughout the summer (April to the end of September). Tours range from trips to Troja Palace in the north of Prague and as far away as Slapy Lake in the south. Dining on board while slowly floating through the city centre is another popular option. These trips can be booked in advance at one of the tour companies. Alternatively, you can go directly to one of the river boat boarding points (see left) and buy tickets for one of the many private ships that land here. The cost of each trip varies, depending on the type of vessel and the length of the excursion, but there are trips to suit almost every budget.

**Akasi**
Na příkopě 3. **Map** 3 C4.
**Tel** 22 22 43 067.

**Evropská Vodní Doprava**
Čechův most, Dvořákovo nábřeží.
**Map** 3 B2.
**Tel** 22 48 10 030.
🌐 evd.cz

**Paraplavební**
Rašínovo nábřeží přístaviště.
**Map** 5 A2.
**Tel** 22 49 31 013.
🌐 paroplavba.cz

**Prague Venice Boats**
Platnéřská 4. **Map** 3 A3.
**Tel** 77 67 76 779.
🌐 prague-venice.cz

**Přístaviště lodí Kampa**, a jetty in the Little Quarter, is the starting point for some of the organized boat trips along the Vltava.

# Prague River Trip

Taking a trip on the Vltava gives you a unique view of many of the city's historic monuments. Although the left bank was the site of the first Slavonic settlement in the 9th century, it was the right bank, heavily populated by merchants and traders, that developed into a thriving and bustling commercial centre, and the tradition continues today. The left bank was never developed as intensively and much of it is still an oasis of parks and gardens. The river's beauty is enhanced by the numbers of swans which have made it their home.

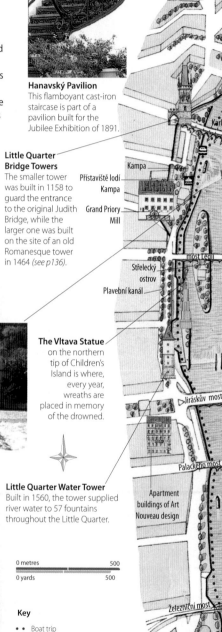

**Hanavský Pavilion**
This flamboyant cast-iron staircase is part of a pavilion built for the Jubilee Exhibition of 1891.

**Little Quarter Bridge Towers**
The smaller tower was built in 1158 to guard the entrance to the original Judith Bridge, while the larger one was built on the site of an old Romanesque tower in 1464 (see p136).

**Vltava Weir**
The thickly wooded slopes of Petřín Hill tower above one of several weirs on the Vltava. During the 19th century this weir, along with others on this stretch, were built to make the river navigable to ships.

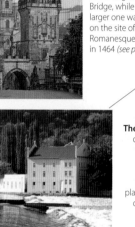

**The Vltava Statue**
on the northern tip of Children's Island is where, every year, wreaths are placed in memory of the drowned.

**Little Quarter Water Tower**
Built in 1560, the tower supplied river water to 57 fountains throughout the Little Quarter.

| 0 metres | | 500 |
|---|---|---|
| 0 yards | | 500 |

**Apartment buildings of Art Nouveau design**

**Key**

• • Boat trip

Map labels (right side):
- Karlův
- Kampa
- Přístaviště lodí Kampa
- Grand Priory Mill
- most Legií
- Střelecký ostrov
- Plavební kanál
- Jiráskův most
- Palackého most
- Železniční most

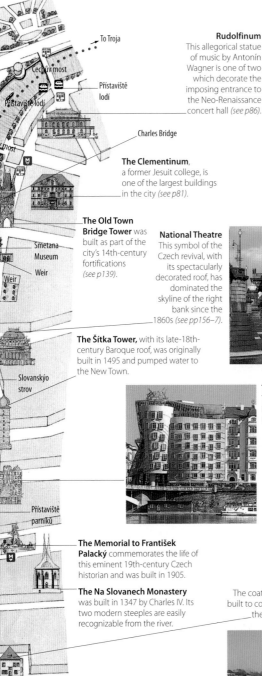

To Troja

Cechův most

Přístaviště
lodí

Přístaviště lodí

iv most

The Clementinum,
a former Jesuit college, is
one of the largest buildings
in the city (see p81).

Charles Bridge

Smetana
Museum

Weir

Slovanskýo
strov

Přístaviště
parníků

### Rudolfinum
This allegorical statue
of music by Antonín
Wagner is one of two
which decorate the
imposing entrance to
the Neo-Renaissance
concert hall (see p86).

### The Old Town
**Bridge Tower** was
built as part of the
city's 14th-century
fortifications
(see p139).

### National Theatre
This symbol of the
Czech revival, with
its spectacularly
decorated roof, has
dominated the
skyline of the right
bank since the
1860s (see pp156–7).

**The Šítka Tower,** with its late-18th-
century Baroque roof, was originally
built in 1495 and pumped water to
the New Town.

### The Dancing House
This charming, quirky office building
has become a symbol of post-Velvet
Revolution modern architecture.

### The Memorial to František
**Palacký** commemorates the life of
this eminent 19th-century Czech
historian and was built in 1905.

### The Na Slovanech Monastery
was built in 1347 by Charles IV. Its
two modern steeples are easily
recognizable from the river.

### Výtoň Excise House
The coat of arms on this 16th-century house –
built to collect duty on timber transpored along
the river – is of the New Town from 1671.

### Church of St Peter and St Paul
The Neo-Gothic steeples on this
much-rebuilt church were designed
by František Mikeš and erected in
1903. They are the dominant feature
of Vyšehrad rock (see pp180–81).

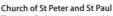

An aerial view of Prague's attractive Staromestska Square ▶

# PRAGUE AREA BY AREA

Old Town                          60–79
Jewish Quarter                    80–93
Prague Castle and Hradčany  94–119
Little Quarter                    120–139
New Town                          140–155
Further Afield                    156–165
Day Trips                         166–169
Four Guided Walks                 170–179

# OLD TOWN
## STARÉ MĚSTO

The heart of the city is the Old Town and its central square. In the 11th century the settlements around the Castle spread to the right bank of the Vltava. A market-place in what is now Old Town Square (Staroměstské náměstí) was mentioned for the first time in 1091. Houses and churches sprang up around the square, determining the random network of streets, many of which survive. The area gained the privileges of a town in the 13th century, and, in 1338, a Town Hall. This and other great buildings, such as Clam-Gallas Palace and the Municipal House, reflect the importance of the Old Town.

## Sights at a Glance

### Churches
- 4 Church of St James
- 8 Church of Our Lady before Týn
- 11 Church of St Nicholas
- 14 Church of St Gall
- 15 Church of St Martin in the Wall
- 17 Church of St Giles
- 18 Bethlehem Chapel
- 22 Church of St Francis

### Museums and Galleries
- 16 Náprstek Museum
- 24 Smetana Museum

### Historic Streets and Squares
- 3 Celetná Street
- 7 Old Town Square pp68–71
- 20 Mariánské Square
- 21 Charles Street
- 25 Knights of the Cross Square

### Historic Monuments and Buildings
- 1 Powder Gate
- 2 Municipal House
- 6 Carolinum
- 10 Jan Hus Monument

- 12 Old Town Hall pp74–6
- 13 House at the Two Golden Bears
- 23 Clementinum

### Theatres
- 5 Estates Theatre

### Palaces
- 9 Kinský Palace
- 19 Clam-Gallas Palace

☐ **Restaurants** see pp198–9
1 Las Adelitas
2 Ambiente Brasileiro
3 Bellevue
4 Bohemia Bagel
5 Buddha Bar
6 Caffrey's
7 Country Life
8 Divinis
9 Francouzská Restaurace
10 Kabul
11 Kogo
12 Lehká hlava
13 Maitrea
14 Mlýnec
15 Parnas
16 Phenix
17 Pizza Nuova
18 Platina
19 Plzeňská
20 Red Pif
21 Le Saint-Tropez
22 Sarah Bernhardt
23 Století
24 Le terroir
25 La Truffe
26 U Provaznice
27 U Tří růží
28 U Závoje
29 V Zátiší
30 VinodiVino
31 Zdenek's Oyster Bar

See Street Finder maps 3, 4

◀ A close up of the famous Astronomical Clock

For map symbols see back flap

# Street-by-Street: Old Town (East)

Free of traffic (except for a few horse-drawn carriages) and ringed with historic buildings, Prague's Old Town Square (Staroměstské náměstí) ranks among the finest public spaces in any city. Streets like Celetná and Ovocný trh are also pedestrianized. In summer, café tables spill out onto the cobbles, and though the area draws tourists by the thousands, the unique atmosphere has not yet been destroyed.

**❽ Church of Our Lady before Týn**
The church's Gothic steeples are the Old Town's most distinctive landmark.

**❾ Kinský Palace**
This stunning Rococo palace now serves as an art gallery.

**⓫ Church of St Nicholas**
This Baroque church's imposing façade dominates a corner of the square.

STAROMĚSTSKÉ NÁMĚSTÍ

MALÉ NÁMĚSTÍ

ŽELEZNÁ

**❼ ★ Old Town Square**
This late-19th-century watercolour by Václav Jansa shows how little the Square has changed in over a century.

**❿ Jan Hus Monument**
Religious reformer Hus is a symbol of integrity, and the monument brings together the highest and lowest points in Czech history.

**The Štorch house** has painted decoration based on designs by Mikuláš Aleš showing St Wenceslas on horseback.

**⓭ House at the Two Golden Bears**
The carved Renaissance portal is the finest of its kind in Prague.

**U Rotta** is a former ironmonger's shop, decorated with colourful paintings by the 19th-century artist Mikuláš Aleš.

**⓬ ★ Old Town Hall**
The famous astronomical clock draws a crowd of visitors every hour.

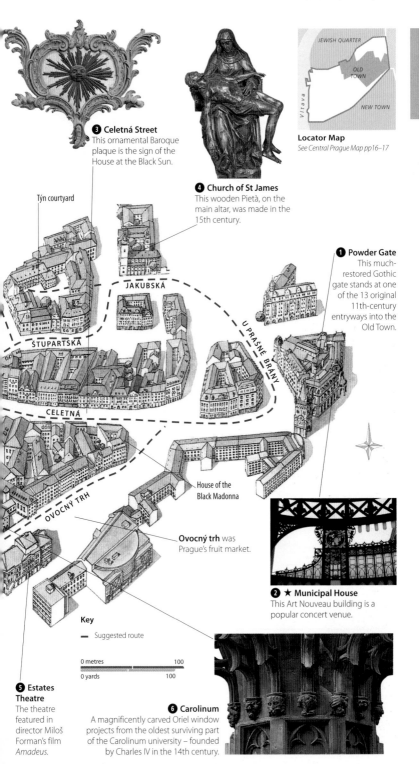

**3 Celetná Street**
This ornamental Baroque plaque is the sign of the House at the Black Sun.

Týn courtyard

**4 Church of St James**
This wooden Pietà, on the main altar, was made in the 15th century.

**Locator Map**
See Central Prague Map pp16–17

JEWISH QUARTER

OLD TOWN

NEW TOWN

Vltava

**1 Powder Gate**
This much-restored Gothic gate stands at one of the 13 original 11th-century entryways into the Old Town.

JAKUBSKÁ

ŠTUPARTSKÁ

U PRAŠNÉ BRÁNY

CELETNÁ

OVOCNÝ TRH

House of the Black Madonna

**Ovocný trh** was Prague's fruit market.

**2 ★ Municipal House**
This Art Nouveau building is a popular concert venue.

**Key**

— Suggested route

0 metres           100
0 yards            100

**5 Estates Theatre**
The theatre featured in director Miloš Forman's film *Amadeus*.

**6 Carolinum**
A magnificently carved Oriel window projects from the oldest surviving part of the Carolinum university – founded by Charles IV in the 14th century.

# ❶ Powder Gate
*Prašná Brána*

Náměstí Republiky. **Map** 4 D3. **Tel** 72 49 11 556. Ⓜ Náměstí Republiky. 🚋 5, 8, 24, 26. **Open** 10am–6pm daily (to 8pm Mar & Oct; to 10pm Apr–Sep). 🌐 **praguetowers.com**

There has been a gate here since the 11th century, when it formed one of the 13 entrances to the Old Town. In 1475, King Vladislav II laid the foundation stone of the New Tower, as it was to be known. A coronation gift from the city council, the gate was modelled on Peter Parler's Old Town bridge tower built a century earlier. The gate had little defensive value; its rich sculptural decoration was intended to add prestige to the adjacent palace of the Royal Court. Building was halted eight years later when the king had to flee because of riots. On his return in 1485 he opted for the safety of the Castle. Kings never again occupied the Royal Court.

The gate acquired its present name when it was used to store gunpowder in the 17th century. The sculptural decoration, badly damaged during the Prussian occupation in 1757, was replaced in 1876.

The Powder Gate viewed from outside the Old Town

Karel Špillar's mosaic *Homage to Prague* on Municipal House's façade

# ❷ Municipal House
*Obecní Dům*

Náměstí Republiky 5. **Map** 4 D3. **Tel** 22 20 02 101. Ⓜ Náměstí Republiky. 🚋 5, 8, 24, 26. Gallery **Open** for exhibitions only, 10am– 7pm daily. 🎧 by arrangement. ♿ 🌐 **obecnidum.cz**

Prague's most prominent Art Nouveau building stands on the site of the former Royal Court palace, the King's residence between 1383 and 1485. Abandoned for centuries, what remained was used as a seminary and later as a military college. It was demolished in the early 1900s to be replaced by the present cultural centre (1905–11) with its exhibition halls and auditorium, designed by Antonín Balšánek assisted by Osvald Polívka.

The exterior is embellished with stucco and allegorical statuary. Above the main entrance there is a huge semicircular mosaic entitled *Homage to Prague* by Karel Špillar. Inside, topped by an impressive glass dome, is Prague's principal concert venue and the core of the entire building, the Smetana Hall, sometimes also used as a ballroom. The interior of the building is decorated with works by leading Czech artists of the first decade of the century, including Alfons Mucha *(see p149)*.

There are numerous smaller halls, conference rooms and offices that are normally closed but for which you can arrange a guided tour, or you can simply relax in one of the cafés or restaurants. On 28 October, 1918, Prague's Municipal House was the scene of the momentous proclamation of the new independent state of Czechoslovakia.

Decorative detail by Alfons Mucha

Hollar Hall

Foyer

Mayor's Salon with paintings by Alfons Mucha

Entrance hall

Entrance to Art Nouveau café

Restaurants

### ❸ Celetná Street
*Celetná Ulice*

**Map** 3 C3. ⓂNáměstí Republiky, Můstek.

One of the oldest streets in Prague, Celetná follows an old trading route from eastern Bohemia. Its name comes from the plaited bread rolls that were first baked here in the Middle Ages. It gained prestige in the 14th century as a section of the Royal Route *(see p172)* used for coronation processions. Foundations of Romanesque and Gothic buildings can be seen in some of the cellars, but most of the houses with their picturesque signs are Baroque remodellings.

At No. 34, the House of the Black Madonna is a fine example of Cubist architecture. The building was designed by Josef Gočár in 1911 and is home to the historic Grand Café Orient, the only surviving Cubist café in the world. The building also hosts temporary exhibitions.

### ❹ Church of St James
*Kostel Sv. Jakuba*

Malá Štupartská 6. **Map** 3 C3. Ⓜ Můstek, Náměstí Republiky. **Tel** 22 48 28 816. **Open** 9:30am–noon, 2–4pm Mon–Sat (to 3:30pm Fri), 2–4pm Sun.. 🕆 6:45am Mon–Fri, 5pm Thu–Fri, 8am Sat, 8:30am & 10:30am Sun.

This church was originally the Gothic presbytery of a Minorite monastery. The order (a branch of the Franciscans) was invited

Baroque organ loft in the Church of St James

to Prague by King Wenceslas I in 1232. The church was rebuilt in the Baroque style after a fire in 1689, allegedly started by agents of Louis XIV. Over 20 side altars were added, decorated with works by painters such as Jan Jiří Heinsch, Petr Brandl and Václav Vavřinec Reiner. The tomb of Count Vratislav of Mitrovice (1714–16), designed by Johann Bernhard Fischer von Erlach and executed by sculptor Ferdinand Brokof, is the most beautiful Baroque tomb in Bohemia. The count is said to have been accidentally buried alive – his corpse was later found sitting up in the tomb. Hanging on the right of the entrance is a mummified forearm. It has been there for several centuries, ever since a thief tried to steal the jewels from the Madonna on the high altar. The Virgin grabbed his arm and held on so tightly it had to be cut off.

Because of its long nave, the church has excellent acoustics,

and many concerts and recitals are given here. There is also a magnificent organ built in 1702.

### ❺ Estates Theatre
*Stavovské Divadlo*

Ovocný trh 1. **Map** 3 C4. **Tel** 22 49 01 448 (tickets), 22 49 02 231 (guided tours; call between 9am–5pm Mon–Fri). Ⓜ Můstek. **Open** for guided tours and performances only. ♿ 🌐 **narodni-divadlo.cz**

Built by Count Nostitz in 1783, this opera theatre is one of Prague's finest examples of Neo-Classical elegance. It is a mecca for Mozart fans *(see p218)*. On 29 October 1787, Mozart's opera, *Don Giovanni* had its debut here with Mozart conducting. In 1834 the musical *Fidlovačka* premiered here; one of the songs, "Where is my Home?", became the Czech national anthem.

### ❻ Carolinum
*Karolinum*

Ovocný trh 3. **Map** 3 C4. **Tel** 22 44 91 251. Ⓜ Můstek. **Closed** to the public. **Open** for special exhibitions.

At the core of the university founded by Charles IV in 1348 is the Carolinum. The chapel, arcade and walls still survive, together with a fine oriel window, but in 1945 the court-yard was reconstructed in Gothic style. In the 15th and 16th centuries the university played a leading role in the movement to reform the church. After the Battle of the White Mountain *(see pp32–3)*, the university was taken over by the Jesuits.

Smetana Hall
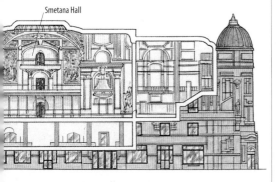

# ❼ Old Town Square: East and North Sides

*Staroměstské náměstí*

Some of Prague's colourful history is preserved around the Old Town Square in the form of its buildings. On the north side of the Square, the Pauline Monastery is the only surviving piece of original architecture. The east side boasts two superb examples of the architecture of their times: the House at the Stone Bell, restored to its former appearance as a Gothic town palace, and the Rococo Kinský Palace. An array of pastel-coloured buildings completes the Square.

★ **House at the Stone Bell**
At the corner of the building, the bell is the sign of this medieval town palace.

**Kinský Palace**
C G Bossi created the elaborate stucco decoration on the façade of this Rococo palace *(see p72)*.

**East Side**

**North Side**

## KEY

① Statues by Ignaz Platzer from 1760–65

② Rococo stucco work

③ Entrance to Týn Church

④ A solid gold effigy of the Virgin Mary

⑤ Romanesque arcaded house with 18th-century façade

⑥ Restaurant U Sv. Salvatora façade dates from 1696

★ **Church of St Nicholas**
Besides its original purpose as a parish church and, later, a Benedictine monastery church, this has served as a garrison church and a concert hall *(see p72)*.

East and north side

Jan Hus Monument

★ **Church of Our Lady before Týn**
Astronomer and astrologer Tycho Brahe is buried in Týn Church *(see p72)*.

**Týn School**
Gothic rib vaulting is a primary feature of this building, which was a school from the 14th to the mid-19th century.

**Ministerstvo pro místní rozvoj**
Architect Osvald Polívka designed this Art Nouveau building in 1898, with figures of firefighters on the upper façade. It houses the Ministry of Local Development.

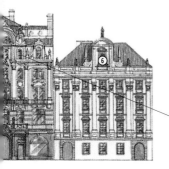

**Staroměstské náměstí, 1793**
The engraving by Filip and František Heger shows the Old Town Square teeming with people and carriages. The Old Town Hall is on the left.

# ❼ Old Town Square: South Side

*Staroměstské náměstí*

A colourful array of houses of Romanesque or Gothic origin, with fascinating house signs, graces the south side of the Old Town Square. The block between Celetná Street and Železná Street is especially attractive. The Square has always been a busy focal point, and today offers visitors a tourist information centre, as well as a number of restaurants, cafés, shops, and galleries.

### Franz Kafka (1883–1924)

The author of two of the most influential novels of the 20th century, *The Trial* and *The Castle*, Kafka spent most of his short life in the Old Town. From 1893 to 1901 he studied in the Golz-Kinský Palace (see p72), where his father later had a shop. He worked as an insurance clerk, but frequented Berta Fanta's literary salon at the Stone Ram, Old Town Square, along with others who wrote in German. Hardly any of his work was published in his lifetime.

**U Lazara (At Lazarus's)**
Romanesque barrel vaulting testifies to the house's early origins, though it was rebuilt during the Renaissance. The ground floor houses the Staroměstská restaurace.

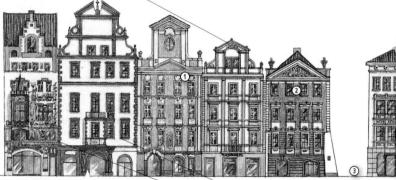

## South Side

### ★ Štorch House
The late-19th-century painting of St Wenceslas on horseback by Mikuláš Aleš appears on this ornate Neo-Renaissance building, also known as At the Stone Madonna.

### KEY

① At the Stone Table
② At the Golden Unicorn
③ Železná Street
④ At the Storks
⑤ **The arcade** houses the Grand Café Praha.
⑥ At the Blue Star
⑦ U Orloje restaurant
⑧ Melantrichova Passage

### ★ At the Stone Ram
The early 16th-century house sign shows a young maiden with a ram. The house has been referred to as At the Unicorn due to the similarity between the one-horned ram and a unicorn.

**Melantrichova Passage**
Václav Jansa's painting (1898) shows the narrow passageway leading to the Old Town Square.

 South side

 Jan Hus Monument

**At the Red Fox**
A golden Madonna and Child look down from the Baroque façade of an originally Romanesque building.

**At the Ox**
Named after its 15th-century owner, the burgher Ochs, this house features an early 18th-century stone statue of St Anthony of Padua.

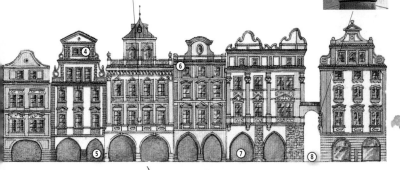

**1338** Old Town becomes municipality

*Leopold II's Royal Procession through the Old Town Square in 1791*

**1735** Church of St Nicholas completed

**1948** Klement Gottwald proclaims Communist state from balcony of Golz-Kinský Palace

| 1150 | 1300 | 1450 | 1600 | 1750 | 1900 | 2050 |
|---|---|---|---|---|---|---|

**1200** Square is meeting point of trade routes and important market

**1365** Building of present Týn Church

**1621** Execution of 27 anti-Habsburg leaders in square *(see p33)*

**1689** Fire destroys large part of Old Town

**1784** Unification of Prague towns

**1915** Unveiling of Jan Hus Monument

*Hus Monument (detail)*

Statue of the Madonna on Our Lady before Týn

## ➑ Church of Our Lady before Týn
*Kostel Matky Boží Před Týnem*

Týnská, Štupartská. **Map** 3 C3.
**Tel** 60 24 57 200. Ⓜ Staroměstská,
Můstek. **Open** 10am–1pm, 3–5pm
Tue–Sat, 10:30am–noon Sun. ⊞
6pm Tue–Thu, 8am Sat, 9:30am &
9pm Sun. ✉ Ⓦ tyn.cz

Dominating the Old Town
Square are the magnificent
multiple steeples of this historic
church. The present Gothic
church was started in
1365 and soon became
associated with the
reform movement in
Bohemia. From the
early 15th century
until 1620 Týn was
the main Hussite
church in Prague.
The Hussite king,
George of Poděbrady,
took Utraquist
communion *(see
Church of St Martin in the Wall
p75)* here and had a gold
chalice – the Utraquist symbol –
mounted on the façade. After
1621 the chalice was melted
down to become part of the
statue of the Madonna that
replaced it.

Kinský arms on
Golz-Kinský Palace

On the northern side of the
church is a beautiful entrance
portal (1390) decorated with
scenes of Christ's passion. The
dark interior has some notable
features, including Gothic
sculptures of *Calvary*, a pewter
font (1414) and a 15th-century
Gothic pulpit. Behind the church
is the Týn Courtyard, with its
numerous architectural styles.

## ➒ Kinský Palace
*Palác Kinských*

Staroměstské náměstí 12. **Map** 3 C3.
**Tel** 22 48 10 758. Ⓜ Staroměstská.
**Open** 10am–6pm Tue–Sun. ⊞ ✉
✉ ♿ Ⓦ ngprague.cz

This lovely Rococo palace,
designed by Kilian Ignaz
Dientzenhofer, has a pretty pink
and white stucco façade
crowned with statues of the
four elements by Ignaz Franz
Platzer. It was bought from the
Golz family in 1768 by
Štěpán Kinský, an Imperial
diplomat. In 1948
Communist leader,
Klement Gottwald,
used the balcony
to address a huge
crowd of party
members – a key
event in the crisis
that led up to his
*coup d'état*. The
National Gallery
now uses the Kinský Palace
for art exhibitions.

## ➓ Jan Hus Monument
*Pomník Jana Husa*

Staroměstské náměstí. **Map** 3 B3.
Ⓜ Staroměstská.

At one end of the Old Town
Square stands the massive
monument to the religious
reformer and Czech hero, Jan
Hus *(see pp28–9)*. Hus was burnt
at the stake after being
pronounced a heretic by the
Council of Constance in 1415.
The monument by Ladislav
Šaloun was unveiled in 1915 on
the 500th anniversary of his
death. It shows two groups of
people, one of victorious Hussite
warriors, the other of Protestants
forced into exile 200 years later,
and a young mother symbolizing
national rebirth. The dominant
figure of Hus emphasizes the
moral authority of the man who
gave up life rather than his beliefs.

## ⓫ Church of St Nicholas
*Kostel Sv. Mikuláše*

Staroměstské náměstí. **Map** 3 B3.
**Tel** 60 29 58 927. Ⓜ Staroměstská.
**Open** 10am–5pm Mon (to 4pm Tue–
Sat, from 11:30am Sun). ⊞ 10am Sun.
Ⓦ svmikulas.cz

There has been a church here
since the 12th century. It was the
Old Town's parish church and
meeting place until Týn Church
was completed in the 14th
century. After the Battle of the
White Mountain in 1620 *(see
pp32–3)* the church became
part of a Benedictine
monastery. The present
church by Kilian Ignaz
Dientzenhofer, was
completed in 1735. Its
dramatic white façade
is studded with
statues by Antonín
Braun. When in 1781
Emperor Joseph II

Defiant Hussites on the Jan Hus Monument in Old Town Square

Church of St Nicholas in the Old Town

closed all monasteries not engaged in socially useful activities, the church was stripped bare. In World War I the church was used by the troops of Prague's garrison. The colonel in charge took the opportunity to restore the church with the help of artists who might otherwise have been sent to the front. The dome has frescoes of the lives of St Nicholas and St Benedict by Kosmas Damian Asam. In the nave is a huge crown-shaped chandelier. At the end of the war, the church of St Nicholas was given to the Czechoslovak Hussite Church. The church is now a popular concert venue.

## ⓬ Old Town Hall
*Staroměstská Radnice*

See pp74–5.

## ⓭ House at the Two Golden Bears
*Dům U Dvou Zlatých Medvědů*

Kožná 1. **Map** 3 B4. Ⓜ Můstek.
**Closed** to the public.

If you leave the Old Town Square by the narrow Melantrichova Street, make a point of turning into the first alleyway on the left to see the portal of the house called "At the Two Golden Bears". The present Renaissance building was constructed from two earlier houses in 1567. The portal was added in 1590, when a wealthy merchant, Lorenc Štork, secured the services of court architect Bonifaz Wohlmut, who had designed the spire on the tower of St Vitus's Cathedral *(see pp102–105)*. His ornate portal with reliefs of two bears is one of the most beautiful Renaissance portals in Prague. Magnificent arcades, also dating from the 16th century, have been preserved in the inner courtyard. In 1885 Egon Erwin Kisch, known as the "Furious Reporter", was born here. He was a German-speaking Jewish writer and journalist, feared for the force of his left-wing rhetoric.

## ⓮ Church of St Gall
*Kostel Sv. Havla*

Havelská. **Map** 3 C4. Ⓜ Můstek.
**Tel** 60 24 57 200. **Open** 11:30am–1pm daily. ✝ 12:15pm Mon–Fri, 8am Sun. ♿ ⬡ ⬡ **tyn.cz**

Dating from around 1280, this church was built to serve an autonomous German community in the area known as Gall's Town (Havelské Město). In the 14th century this was merged with the Old Town. In the 18th century the church was given a Baroque facelift by Giovanni Santini-Aichel, who created a bold façade decorated with statues of saints by Ferdinand Brokof. Rich interior furnishings include paintings by the leading Baroque artist Karel Škréta, who is buried here. Prague's best-known market has been held in Havelská Street since the middle ages, selling flowers, vegetables, toys, and clothes.

One of nine statues on façade of St Gall's

Carved Renaissance portal of the House at the Two Golden Bears

# ⑫ Old Town Hall

*Staroměstská Radnice*

One of the most striking buildings in Prague is the Old Town Hall, established in 1338 after King John of Luxembourg agreed to set up a town council. Over the centuries a number of old houses were knocked together as the Old Town Hall expanded, and it now consists of a row of colourful Gothic and Renaissance buildings, most of which have been carefully restored after heavy damage inflicted by the Nazis in the 1945 Prague Uprising. The tower is 69.5 m (228 ft) high and offers a spectacular view of the city.

**Old Town Coat of Arms**
Above the inscription, "Prague, Head of the Kingdom", is the coat of arms of the Old Town, which was adopted in 1784 for the whole city.

**Gothic Door**
This late Gothic main entrance to the Town Hall and Tower was carved by Matthias Rejsek. The entrance hall is filled with wall mosaics after designs by the Czech painter Mikuláš Aleš.

## KEY

① Temporary art exhibitions

② Tourist information and entrance to Tower

③ Former house of Volflin of Kamen

④ Entrance hall decorated with mosaics

⑤ Viewing gallery

⑥ Steps to gallery

⑦ Calendar *(see pp34–5)*.

**Old Council Hall**
This 19th-century engraving features the well-preserved 15th-century ceiling.

**★ Old Town Hall Tower**
In 1364 the tower was added
to what was the private house
of Volflin of Kamen. Its gallery
provides a fine city view.

**Oriel Chapel**
The original stained-glass
windows on the five-sided
chapel were destroyed in the
last days of World War II, but
were replaced in 1987.

**Oriel Chapel Ceiling**
The chapel, which was built on the first floor of
the tower in 1381, has an ornate ceiling.

**★ Astronomical
Clock**
Mechanical figures
perform above the
zodiac signs in
the upper section
*(see p76)*; the lower
section is a calendar.

## Executions in the Old Town Square

A bronze tablet below the Old Town Hall chapel records
the names of the 27 Protestant leaders executed here by
order of the Catholic Emperor Ferdinand on 21 June 1621.
This was the humiliating aftermath of the Battle of the
White Mountain *(see pp32–3)*. This defeat led to the
emigration of Protestants unwilling to give up their faith,
a Counter-Reformation drive and Germanization.

# Town Hall Clock

*Orloj*

The Town Hall acquired its first clock at the beginning of the 15th century. According to legend, in 1490, when it was rebuilt by a master clockmaker called Hanuš (real name Jan Z Růže), the councillors were so anxious to prevent him from recreating his masterpiece elsewhere, that they blinded the poor man. Though the clock has been repaired many times since, the mechanism was perfected by Jan Táborský between 1552 and 1572.

The Apostles

Vanity and Greed

Arabic numerals 1–24

Astronomical Clock with the sun in Aries

Blue, representing the daylight hours

Calendar by Josef Mánes *(see pp32–3)*

Death

The Turk, a symbol of lust

Vojtěch Sucharda's Apostles, sculpted after the last set was burnt in 1945

## Apostles

The centrepiece of the show that draws a crowd of spectators every time the clock strikes the hour is the procession of the 12 Apostles. First the figure of Death, the skeleton on the right of the clock, gives a pull on the rope that he holds in his right hand. In his left hand is an hourglass, which he raises and inverts. Two windows then open and the clockwork Apostles (or to be precise 11 of the Apostles plus St Paul) move slowly round, led by St Peter.

At the end of this part of the display, a cock crows and the clock chimes the hour. The other moving figures are a Turk, who shakes his head from side to side, Vanity, who looks at himself in a mirror and Greed, adapted from the original medieval stereotype of a Jewish moneylender.

## Astronomical Clock

The clockmaker's view of the universe had the Earth fixed firmly at the centre. The purpose of the clock was not to tell you the exact time but to imitate the supposed orbits of the sun and moon about the Earth. The hand with the sun, which points to the hour, in fact records three different kinds of time. The outer ring of medieval Arabic numerals measures Old Bohemian time, in which a day of 24 hours was reckoned from the setting of the sun. The ring of Roman numerals indicates time as we know it. The blue part of the dial represents the visible part of the sky. This is

divided into 12 parts. In so-called Babylonian time, the period of daylight was divided into 12 hours, which would vary in length from summer to winter.

The clock also shows the movement of the sun and moon through the 12 signs of the zodiac, which were of great importance in 16th-century Prague.

The figures of Death and the Turk

## ⑮ Church of St Martin in the Wall
*Kostel Sv. Martina Ve Zdi*

Martinská 8. **Map** 3 B5. **Tel** 602 766 643. Národní třída, Můstek. 6, 9, 17, 18, 21, 22. **Open** 2–4pm daily (except Sun). 7:30pm Sun.
**w martinvezdi.eu**

This 12th-century church became part of the city wall during the fortification of the Old Town in the 13th century, hence its name. It was the first church where blessed wine, usually reserved for the clergy, was offered to the congregation as well as bread. This was a basic tenet of belief of the moderate Hussites *(see pp28–9)*, the Utraquists, who took their name from the Latin *sub utraque specie*, "in both kinds". In 1787 the church was converted into workshops, but rebuilt in its original form in the early years of this century.

## ⑯ Náprstek Museum
*Náprstkovo Muzeum*

Betlémské náměstí 1. **Map** 3 B4. **Tel** 22 44 97 511. Národní třída, Staroměstská. 6, 9, 17, 18, 22. **Open** 10am–6pm Tue–Sun.
**w nm.cz**

Vojta Náprstek, art patron and philanthropist, created this museum as a tribute to modern industry following a decade of exile in America after the 1848 revolution *(see pp34–5)*. On his return in 1862, inspired by London's Victorian museums, he began his collection. He created the Czech Industrial Museum by joining five older buildings together, and in the process virtually destroyed the family brewery and home – an 18th-century house called At the Haláneks (U Halánků). He later turned to ethnography and the collection now consists of artefacts from Asian, African and Native American cultures, including weapons and ritual objects from the Aztecs, Toltecs and Mayas. The museum is part of the National Museum. Regular temporary exhibitions on a range of subjects are also staged here.

Ceiling fresco by Václav Vavřinec Reiner in Church of St Giles

## ⑰ Church of St Giles
*Kostel Sv. Jiljí*

Husova 8. **Map** 3 B4. **Tel** 22 42 20 235. Národní třída. 6, 9, 18, 22. **Open** 4–6pm Mon, Wed, Fri. 7am & 6:30pm Mon–Fri, 6:30pm Sat, 9:30am, noon & 6:30pm Sun.
**w kostel-praha.cz**

Despite the Gothic portal on the southern side, this church is essentially Baroque. Founded in 1371 on the site of a Romanesque church, it became a Hussite parish church in 1420. Following the Protestant defeat in 1620 *(see pp32–3)*, Ferdinand II presented the church to the Dominicans, who built a huge friary on its southern side. It has now been returned to the Dominicans, religious orders having been abolished under the Communists.

The vaults of the church are decorated with frescoes by the painter Václav Vavřinec Reiner, who is buried in the nave before the altar of St Vincent. The main fresco, a glorification of the Dominicans, shows St Dominic and his friars helping the pope defend the Catholic Church from non-believers.

## ⑱ Bethlehem Chapel
*Betlémská Kaple*

Betlémské náměstí 4. **Map** 3 B4. **Tel** 22 42 48 595. Národní třída, Staroměstská. 6, 9, 17, 18, 22. **Open** Apr–mid-Oct 10am–6pm daily; mid-Oct–Mar 10am–5pm daily. **Closed** 24, 31 Dec.

The present "chapel" is a reconstruction of a hall built by the followers of the radical preacher Jan Milíč z Kroměříže in 1391–4. The hall was used for preaching in Czech. Between 1402 and 1413 Jan Hus *(see pp28–9)* preached in the Chapel. Influenced by the teachings of the English religious reformer John Wycliffe, Hus condemned the corrupt practices of the Church, arguing that the Scriptures should be the sole source of doctrine. After the Battle of the White Mountain in 1620 *(see pp32–3)*, when Protestant worship was outlawed, the building was handed over to the Jesuits, who rebuilt it with six naves. In 1786 it was almost demolished. After World War II the Chapel was reconstructed following the design shown in old illustrations.

16th-century illustration showing Jan Hus preaching in Bethlehem Chapel

# Street-by-Street: Old Town (West)

The narrow streets near Charles Bridge follow Prague's medieval street plan. For centuries Charles Street (Karlova) was the main route across the Old Town. The picturesque, twisting street is lined with shops and houses displaying Renaissance and Baroque façades. In the 17th century the Jesuits bought up a vast area of land to the north of the street to house the complex of the Clementinum university.

**The Old Town Bridge Tower** dates from 1380. The Gothic sculptural decoration on the eastern façade was from Peter Parler's workshop. The kingfisher was the favourite personal symbol of Wenceslas IV (son of Charles IV) in whose reign the tower was completed *(see p139)*.

**㉒ Church of St Francis**
This Baroque church is noteworthy for its huge cupola and its underground corridors, which are all that remains of the original Church of St Francis.

**㉓ ★ Clementinum**
This plaque records the founding in 1783 of a state-supervised seminary in place of the old Jesuit university.

**㉔ ★ Smetana Museum**
A museum devoted to the life and work of composer Bedřich Smetana is housed in this Neo-Renaissance building set on the riverfront, which was once an old waterworks.

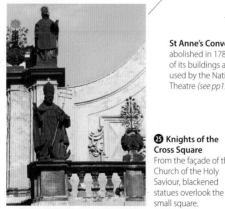

**St Anne's Convent** was abolished in 1782. Some of its buildings are now used by the National Theatre *(see pp156–7)*.

**㉕ Knights of the Cross Square**
From the façade of the Church of the Holy Saviour, blackened statues overlook the small square.

ANANSKA

0 metres 100
0 yards 100

**Key**
— Suggested route

For key to symbols *see back flap*

**20 Mariánské Square**
The square used to be flooded so often, it was called "the puddle". The Art Nouveau sculptures on the balcony of the New Town Hall, built here in 1911, are by Stanislav Sucharda.

**Locator Map**
*See Central Prague Map pp16–17*

Observatory tower

MARIÁNSKÉ NÁMĚSTÍ

**19 Clam-Gallas Palace**
One of Prague's grandest Baroque palaces and full of wonderful statuary, the restored Clam-Gallas is open for concerts.

KARLOVA

LILIOVÁ

HUSOVA

To Old Town Square

ŘETĚZOVÁ

**21 Charles Street**
Among the many decorated houses along the ancient street, be sure to look out for this Art Nouveau statue of the legendary Princess Libuše *(see p23)* surrounded by roses at No. 22/24.

**17 Church of St Giles**
Much of the Baroque sculpture, like this angel on the altar (1738), is by František Weiss.

**18 Bethlehem Chapel**
In this spacious chapel, rebuilt in the 1950s, Hus and other reformers preached to huge congregations.

### ⓲ Clam-Gallas Palace
*Clam-Gallasův Palác*

Husova 20. **Map** 3 B4.
🚇 Staroměstská. **Open** for concerts and temporary exhibitions only; usually 10am–6pm Tue–Sun.

The interior of this magnificent Baroque palace suffered during its use as a store for the city archives, but it has been restored to its former glory. The palace, designed by Viennese court architect Johann Bernhard Fischer von Erlach, was built in 1713–30 for the Supreme Marshal of Bohemia, Jan Gallas de Campo. Its grand portals, each flanked by two pairs of Hercules sculpted by Matthias Braun, give a taste of what lies within. The main staircase is also decorated with Braun statues, set off by a ceiling fresco, *The Triumph of Apollo* by Carlo Carlone. Clam-Gallas Palace also has a theatre, where Beethoven is known to have performed.

### ⓴ Mariánské Square
*Mariánské Náměstí*

**Map** 3 B3. 🚇 Staroměstská, Můstek.

Two statues dominate the square from the corners of the forbidding Town Hall, built in 1912. One illustrates the story of the long-lived Rabbi Löw *(see p90)* finally being caught by the Angel of Death. The other is the Iron Man, a local ghost condemned to roam the Old Town after murdering his mistress. A niche in the garden wall of the Clam-Gallas Palace houses a statue of the River Vltava, depicted as a nymph pouring water from a jug. There is a story that an old soldier once made the nymph sole beneficiary of his will.

A 19th-century sign on the House at the Golden Snake

### ⓴ Charles Street
*Karlova Ulice*

**Map** 3 A4. 🚇 Staroměstská.

Dating back to the 12th century, this narrow, winding street was part of the Royal Route *(see pp174–5)*, along which coronation processions passed on the way to Prague Castle. Many original Gothic and Renaissance houses remain, most converted into shops to attract tourists.

A café at the House at the Golden Snake (No. 18) was established in 1714 by an Armenian, Deodatus Damajan, who handed out slanderous pamphlets from here. It is now a restaurant. Look out for At the Golden Well (No. 3), which has a magnificent Baroque façade and stucco reliefs of saints including St Roch and St Sebastian, who are believed to offer protection against plagues.

### ⓴ Church of St Francis
*Kostel Sv. Františka*

Křižovnické náměstí 3.
**Map** 3 A4. **Tel** 22 11 08 289.
🚇 Staroměstská. 🚋 17, 18. 🚌 207.
**Open** 10am–7pm daily.

The Baroque Church of St Francis was constructed between 1679 and 1685 by architects Gaudenzio Casanova and Domenico Canevalle, and was built on the remains of the original church of St Francis of Assisi of 1270. The church has a striking 40m- (130ft-) high cupola. Statues of Bohemian patrons stand in alcoves in the façade. The interior is richly appointed with frescoes and important artwork.

Matthias Braun's statues on a portal of the Clam-Gallas Palace (c.1714)

Former Jesuit Church of the Holy Saviour in the Clementinum

Underground corridors contain tombstones and fragments of the former church.

# ㉓ Clementinum

*Klementinum*

Křižovnická 190, Karlova 1, Mariánské náměstí 5. **Map** 3 A4. **Tel** 22 22 20 879 (tours). Ⓜ Staroměstská. 🚊 17, 18. Library **Open** 9am–10pm Mon–Sat (to 7pm Sat). Church of the Holy Saviour **Open** for services and events. ✝ 7pm Tue, 2pm & 8pm Sun. 🎒 ✉ ♿ 📷 every half hour from 10am–5pm daily. 🌐 **klementinum.com**

In 1556 Emperor Ferdinand I invited the Jesuits to Prague to help bring the Czechs back into the Catholic fold. They established their headquarters in the former Dominican monastery of St Clement, hence the name Clementinum. This soon became an effective rival to the Carolinum (*see p67*), the Utraquist university. Prague's first Jesuit church, the Church of the Holy Saviour (Kostel sv. Salvátora) was built here in 1601. Its façade, with seven large statues of saints by Jan Bendl (1659), is dramatically lit up at night. Expelled in 1618, the Jesuits were back two years later more determined than ever to stamp out heresy. In 1622 the two universities were merged, resulting in the Jesuits gaining a virtual monopoly on higher education in Prague. They searched for books in Czech and then burnt them by the thousand. Between 1653 and 1723 the Clementinum expanded eastwards. Over 30 houses and three churches were pulled down to make way for the new complex. When in 1773 the pope dissolved their order, the Jesuits had to leave Prague and education was secularized. The Clementinum became the Prague University library, today the National Library. Look out for classical concerts performed in the beautiful Mirror Chapel (Zrcadlová kaple). You can also take a tour of the library and Mirror Chapel.

# ㉔ Smetana Museum

*Muzeum Bedřicha Smetany*

Novotného lávka 1. **Map** 3 A4. **Tel** 22 22 20 082. Ⓜ Staroměstská. 🚊 17, 18. **Open** 10am–5pm Wed–Mon. 📷 for a fee. 🌐 **nm.cz**

A former Neo-Renaissance waterworks beside the Vltava has been turned into a memorial to Bedřich Smetana (1824–1884), the father of Czech music. The museum contains documents, letters, scores and instruments detailing the composer's life and work. Smetana was a fervent patriot, and his music helped inspire the Czech national revival. Deaf towards the end of his life, he never heard his cycle of symphonic poems *Má Vlast* (My Country), being performed.

Statue of Charles IV (1848) in Knights of the Cross Square

# ㉕ Knights of the Cross Square

*Křižovnické Náměstí*

**Map** 3 A4. **Tel** 22 11 08 259. Ⓜ Staroměstská. 🚊 17, 18. 🚌 207. Church of St Francis: **Open** 10am–7pm for services and concerts. ✝ 7am Mon–Fri, 9am Sun. 📷 ♿

This small square in front of the Old Town Bridge Tower offers fine views across the Vltava. On the north side is the Church of St Francis (kostel sv. Františka, *see p80*), once part of the monastery of the crusading Knights of the Cross with the Red Star. In summer, concerts of popular Classical and Baroque music take place in this beautiful Baroque church most evenings at 8pm. To the east is the Church of the Holy Saviour, part of the huge Clementinum complex. In the square stands a large bronze Neo-Gothic statue of Charles IV.

Sgraffito façade of the Smetana Museum

# JEWISH QUARTER
## JOSEFOV

In the Middle Ages there were two distinct Jewish communities in Prague's Old Town: Jews from the west had settled around the Old-New Synagogue, Jews from the Byzantine Empire around the Old Shul (on the site of today's Spanish Synagogue). The two settlements gradually merged and were confined in an enclosed ghetto. For centuries Prague's Jews suffered from oppressive laws – in the 16th century they had to wear a yellow circle as a mark of shame. Rudolph II's more enlightened reign saw the Jewish Mayor Mordechai Maisel *(see p92)* appointed chief financial advisor. Discrimination was further relaxed by Joseph II, and the Jewish Quarter was named Josefov after him. In 1850 the area was officially incorporated as part of Prague. In the 1890s the city authorities decided to raze the ghetto slum because the lack of sanitation made it a health hazard. However, the Town Hall, a number of synagogues and the Old Jewish Cemetery were saved.

## Sights at a Glance

### Synagogues and Churches
4 Pinkas Synagogue
5 Klausen Synagogue
6 Old-New Synagogue pp90–91
7 High Synagogue
9 Maisel Synagogue
10 Church of the Holy Ghost
11 Spanish Synagogue
13 Church of St Simon and St Jude
14 Church of St Castullus

### Concert Hall
1 Rudolfinum

### Museums and Galleries
2 Museum of Decorative Arts
15 St Agnes of Bohemia Convent pp94–5

### Historic Buildings
8 Jewish Town Hall
12 Cubist Houses

### Cemeteries
3 Old Jewish Cemetery pp88–9

### Restaurants
See pp200–201
1 Aldente Trattoria Vineria
2 Barock
3 La Belle Epoque
4 Bílkova 13
5 Cartouche
6 La Casa Argentina
7 Chagall's
8 CottoCrudo
9 La Degustation
10 La Finestra in Cucina
11 Grosseto Marina
12 King Solomon
13 Lokál
14 Mistral Café
15 La Veranda
16 La Vita e Bella
17 Zlatá Praha

See Street Finder maps 3, 4

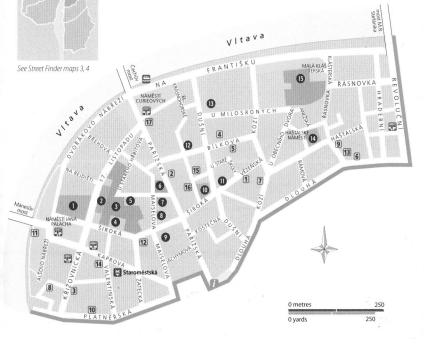

◀ The ornate interior of the Spanish Synagogue

For map symbols see back flap

# Street-by-Street: Jewish Quarter

Though the old ghetto has disappeared, much of the area's fascinating history is preserved in the synagogues around the Old Jewish Cemetery, while the newer streets are lined with many delightful Art Nouveau buildings. The old lanes to the east of the former ghetto lead to the quiet haven of St Agnes's Convent, beautifully restored as a branch of the National Gallery.

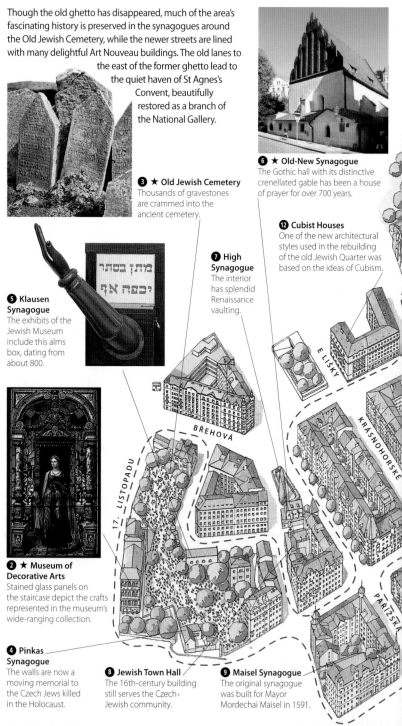

❻ ★ **Old-New Synagogue**
The Gothic hall with its distinctive crenellated gable has been a house of prayer for over 700 years.

❸ ★ **Old Jewish Cemetery**
Thousands of gravestones are crammed into the ancient cemetery.

⓬ **Cubist Houses**
One of the new architectural styles used in the rebuilding of the old Jewish Quarter was based on the ideas of Cubism.

❼ **High Synagogue**
The interior has splendid Renaissance vaulting.

❺ **Klausen Synagogue**
The exhibits of the Jewish Museum include this alms box, dating from about 800.

❷ ★ **Museum of Decorative Arts**
Stained glass panels on the staircase depict the crafts represented in the museum's wide-ranging collection.

❹ **Pinkas Synagogue**
The walls are now a moving memorial to the Czech Jews killed in the Holocaust.

❽ **Jewish Town Hall**
The 16th-century building still serves the Czech Jewish community.

❾ **Maisel Synagogue**
The original synagogue was built for Mayor Mordechai Maisel in 1591.

**⓯ ★ St Agnes of Bohemia Convent**
Christ on Clouds, by the Czech Master, is one of the Medieval and Gothic works on show in the converted convent.

Na Františku Hospital

**Locator Map**
*See Central Prague Map pp16–17*

Former Charnel House

**⓮ Church of St Castullus**
Some fine mid-14th-century Gothic vaulting has been preserved in this restored parish church.

U MILOSRDNÝCH

U OBECNIHO DVORA

BÍLKOVA

KOZÍ

Parsonage of St Castullus

**⓭ Church of St Simon and St Jude**
Part of the Na Františku Hospital since the 17th century, the church is now a popular venue for concerts.

ŠIROKÁ

**⑪ Spanish Synagogue**
The newest of the synagogues in this part of Prague, it was built in flamboyant imitation Moorish style in 1868.

| 0 metres | 50 |
| 0 yards | 50 |

**⑩ Church of the Holy Ghost**
This Baroque statue of St John Nepomuk by Ferdinand Brokof (1727) stands in front of the church.

**Key**

— Suggested route

**For key to symbols** *see back flap*

Stage of the Dvořák Hall in the Rudolfinum

## ❶ Rudolfinum

Alšovo nábřeží 12. **Map** 3 A3.
🚇 Staroměstská. 🚊 17, 18. 🚌 207.
Philharmonic: **Tel** 22 70 59 227. Galerie
Rudolphinum: **Tel** 22 70 59 309. **Open**
10am–6pm Tue–Sun (to 8pm Thu).
🚫 ♿ 🖥 **w** ceskafilharmonie.cz

Now the home of the Czech
Philharmonic Orchestra, the
Rudolfinum is one of the most
impressive landmarks on the
Old Town bank of the Vltava.
Many of the major concerts of
the Prague Spring music
festival (see p52) are held here.
There are several concert halls,
and the sumptuous Dvořák
Hall is one of the finest
creations of 19th-century
Czech architecture.

The Rudolfinum was built
between 1876 and 1884 to a
design by Josef Zítek and Josef
Schulz and named in honour of
Crown Prince Rudolph of
Habsburg. Like the National
Theatre (see pp156–7), it is an
outstanding example of Czech
Neo-Renaissance style. The
curving balustrade is decorated
with statues of distinguished
Czech, Austrian and German
composers and artists.

Also known as the House of
Artists (Dům umělců), the
building houses the Galerie
Rudolphinum, a collection of
modern art. Between 1918 and
1939, and for a brief period after
World War II, the Rudolfinum
was the seat of the
Czechoslovak parliament.

## ❷ Museum of Decorative Arts

*Uměleckoprůmyslové Muzeum*

17. listopadu 2. **Map** 3 B3. **Tel** 25 10 93
111. 🚇 Staroměstská. 🚊 17, 18.
🚌 207. **Open** 10am–6pm Tue–Sun
(to 7pm Tue). 🚫 🚫 ♿ 🖥
**w** upm.cz

For some years after its
foundation in 1885, the museum's
collections were housed in the
Rudolfinum. The present building,
designed by Josef Schulz in
French Neo-Renaissance style,
was completed in 1901. The
museum's glass collection is one
of the largest in the world, but
only a fraction of it is ever on
display. Pride of place goes to
the Bohemian glass, of which
there are many fine Baroque
and 19th- and 20th-century
pieces. Medieval and Venetian
Renaissance glass are also
well represented.

Among the permanent
exhibitions of other crafts are
Meissen porcelain, the Gobelin
tapestries and displays covering
fashion, textiles, photography
and printing. The furniture
collection has exquisitely carved
escritoires and bureaux from the
Renaissance. On the mezzanine
floor are halls for temporary
exhibitions and an extensive art
library housing more than
100,000 publications.

## ❸ Old Jewish Cemetery

*Starý Židovský Hřbitov*

See pp88–9.

## ❹ Pinkas Synagogue

*Pinkasova Synagóga*

Široká 3. **Map** 3 B3. **Tel** 22 23 17 191.
🚇 Staroměstská. 🚊 17, 18.
🚌 207. **Open** 9am–6pm Sun–Fri
(Nov–Mar: to 4:30pm). 🚫 🚫 ♿
**w** jewishmuseum.cz

The synagogue was founded
in 1479 by Rabbi Pinkas and
enlarged in 1535 by his great-
nephew Aaron Meshulam
Horowitz. It has been rebuilt
many times over the centuries.
Excavations have turned up
fascinating relics of life in the
medieval ghetto, including a

Names of Holocaust victims on Pinkas Synagogue wall

*mikva* or ritual bath. The core of the present building is a hall with Gothic vaulting. The gallery for women was added in the early 17th century.

The synagogue now serves as a memorial to all the Jewish Czechoslovak citizens who were imprisoned in Terezín concentration camp and later deported to various Nazi extermination camps. The names of the 77,297 who did not return are inscribed on the synagogue walls. The building now houses an exhibition of children's drawings from the Terezín concentration camp.

## ❺ Klausen Synagogue

*Klausová Synagóga*

U starého hřbitova 3a. **Map** 3 B3. **Tel** 22 23 17 191. Staroměstská. 17, 18. 207. **Open** 9am–6pm Sun–Fri (Nov–Mar: to 4:30pm). **jewishmuseum.cz**

19th-century Torah pointer in Klausen Synagogue

Before the fire of 1689, this site was occupied by a number of small Jewish schools and prayer houses known as *klausen*. The name was preserved in the Klausen Synagogue, built on the ruins and completed in 1694. The High Baroque structure has a fine barrel-vaulted interior with rich stucco decorations. It now houses Hebrew prints and manuscripts and an exhibition of Jewish traditions and customs, tracing the history of the Jews in Central Europe back to the early Middle Ages. Many exhibits relate to famous figures in the city's Jewish community including the 16th-century Rabbi Löw *(see p90)*, who, according to legend, created an artificial man out of clay.

Adjoining the synagogue is a building that looks like a tiny medieval castle. It was built in 1906 as the ceremonial hall

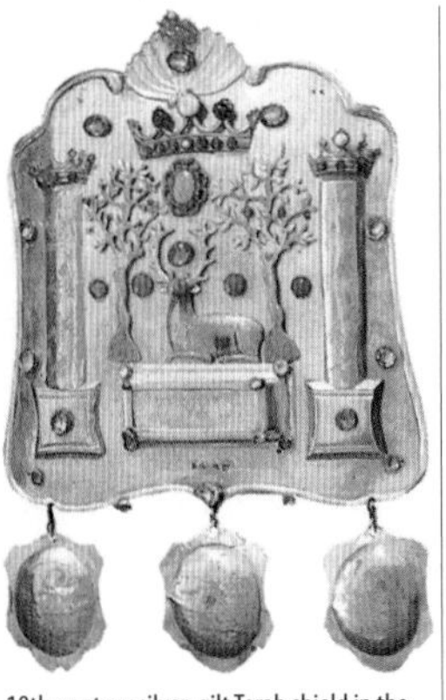

18th-century silver-gilt Torah shield in the High Synagogue

of the Jewish Burial Society. In 1944 an exhibition was put on here detailing the history of the Prague ghetto.

## ❻ Old-New Synagogue

*Staronová Synagóga*

*See pp90–91.*

## ❼ High Synagogue

*Vysoká Synagóga*

Červená 2. **Map** 3 B3. **Tel** 22 48 00 849. Staroměstská. 17, 18. 207. **Open** for services only: 8:30am–2pm Mon–Fri. **kehilaprag.cz**

Like the Jewish Town Hall, the building of the High Synagogue was financed by Mordechai Maisel, mayor of the Jewish Town, in the 1570s. Originally the two buildings formed a single complex and to facilitate communication with the Town Hall, the main hall of the synagogue was on the first floor.

It was not until the 19th century that the two buildings were separated and the synagogue was given a staircase and street entrance. You can still see the original Renaissance vaulting and stucco decoration.

## ❽ Jewish Town Hall

*Židovská Radnice*

Maiselova 18. **Map** 3 B3. **Tel** 22 48 00 849. Staroměstská. 17, 18. 207. **Closed** to the public.

The core of this attractive blue and white building is the original Jewish Town Hall, built in 1570–77 by architect Panacius Roder at the expense of the immensely rich mayor, Mordechai Maisel. In 1763 it acquired a new appearance in the flowery style of the Late Baroque. The last alterations date from 1908, when the southern wing was enlarged.

The building is one of the few monuments that survived far-reaching sanitation of this medieval part of Prague at the beginning of the 20th century. On the roof stands a small wooden clock tower with a distinctive green steeple. The right to build the tower was originally granted to the Jewish community after their part in the defence of Charles Bridge against the Swedes in 1648 *(see pp32–5)*. On one of the gables there is another clock. This one has Hebrew figures and, because Hebrew reads from right to left, hands that turn in an anti-clockwise direction. The Town Hall is now the seat of the Council of Jewish Religious Communities in the Czech Republic.

Façade and clock tower of the Jewish Town Hall

# ❸ Old Jewish Cemetery

*Starý Židovský Hřbitov*

This remarkable site was, for over 300 years, the only burial ground permitted to Jews. Founded in 1478, it was slightly enlarged over the years but still basically corresponds to its medieval size. Because of the lack of space people had to be buried on top of each other, up to 12 layers deep. Today you can see over 12,000 gravestones crammed into the tiny space, but several times that number are thought to have been buried here. The last burial was of Moses Beck in 1787.

View across the cemetery towards the western wall of the Klausen Synagogue

**David Gans' Tombstone**
The tomb of the writer and astronomer (1541–1613) is decorated with the symbols of his name – a star of David and a goose (*Gans* in German).

## KEY

① **The oldest tomb** is that of the writer Rabbi Avigdor Kara (1439).

② **The Pinkas Synagogue** is the second-oldest in Prague (*see p86*).

③ **Jewish printers**, Mordechai Zemach (d 1592) and his son Bezalel (d 1589), are buried under this square gravestone.

④ **Rabbi David Oppenheim (1664–1736)** was the chief rabbi of Prague. He owned the largest collection of old Hebrew manuscripts and prints in the city.

⑤ **Mordechai Maisel** (1528–1601) was Mayor of Prague's Jewish Town and a philanthropist.

⑥ **The Museum of Decorative Arts** (*see p86*).

⑦ **The Neo-Romanesque Ceremonial Hall**

⑧ **Klausen Synagogue** (*see p87*).

⑨ **The Nephele Mound** was where infants who died under a year old were buried.

⑩ **The gravestone of Moses Beck**

★ **14th-Century Tombstones**
Embedded in the wall are fragments of Gothic tombstones brought here from an older Jewish cemetery discovered in 1866 in Vladislavova Street in the New Town.

**Prague Burial Society**
Founded in 1564, the group carried out ritual burials and performed charitable work in the community. Members of the society wash their hands after leaving the cemetery.

★ **Tombstone of
Rabbi Löw**
The most visited grave in
the cemetery is that of
Rabbi Löw (1520–1609).
Visitors place hundreds of
pebbles and wishes on his
grave as a mark of respect.

Entrance

★ **Tombstone of Hendela Bassevi**
The highly decorated tomb (1628)
was built for the beautiful wife of
Prague's first Jewish nobleman.

## Understanding the Gravestones

From the late 16th century onwards, tombstones in the Jewish cemetery were decorated with symbols denoting the background, family name or profession of the deceased person.

**Blessing hands:**
Cohen family

**A pair of
scissors:** tailor

**A stag:** Hirsch or
Zvi family

**Grapes:** blessing
or abundance

# ❻ Old-New Synagogue

*Staronová Synagoga*

Built around 1270, this is the oldest synagogue in Europe and one of the earliest Gothic buildings in Prague. The synagogue has survived fires, the slum clearances of the 19th century and many Jewish pogroms. Residents of the Jewish Quarter have often had to seek refuge within its walls and today it is still the religious centre for Prague's Jews. It was originally called the New Synagogue until another synagogue was built nearby – this was later destroyed.

★ **Jewish Standard**
The historic banner of Prague's Jews is decorated with a Star of David and within it the hat that had to be worn by Jews in the 14th century.

## Rabbi Löw and the Golem

The scholar and philosophical writer Rabbi Löw, director of the Talmudic school (which studied the Torah) in the late 16th century, was also thought to possess magical powers. He was supposed to have created a figure, the Golem, from clay and then brought it to life by placing a magic stone tablet in its mouth.

The Golem went berserk and the Rabbi had to remove the tablet. He hid the creature among the Old-New Synagogue's rafters.

Rabbi Löw and the Golem

## KEY

① **Candlestick holder**.

② **14th-century stepped brick gable**.

③ **These windows** formed part of the 18th-century extensions built to allow women a view of the service.

④ **The tympanum** above the Ark is decorated with 13th-century leaf carvings.

⑤ **The cantor's platform** and its lectern is surrounded by a wrought-iron Gothic grille.

★ **Five-rib Vaulting**
Two massive octagonal pillars inside the hall support the five-rib vaults.

**Right-hand Nave**
The glow from the bronze chandeliers provides light for worshippers using the seats lining the walls.

## VISITORS' CHECKLIST

**Practical Information**
Červená.
**Map** 3 B2.
**Tel** 22 23 17 191.
**synagogue.cz**
**Open** 9:30am–6pm Sun–Fri (Nov–Mar: to 5pm).
**Closed** Jewish holidays.
9am & 7pm Sat.

**Transport**
Staroměstská. 17, 18 to Staroměstská, 17 to Law Faculty (Právnická fakulta). 207.

**★ Rabbi Löw's Chair**
A star of David marks the chair of the Chief Rabbi, placed where the distinguished 16th-century scholar used to sit.

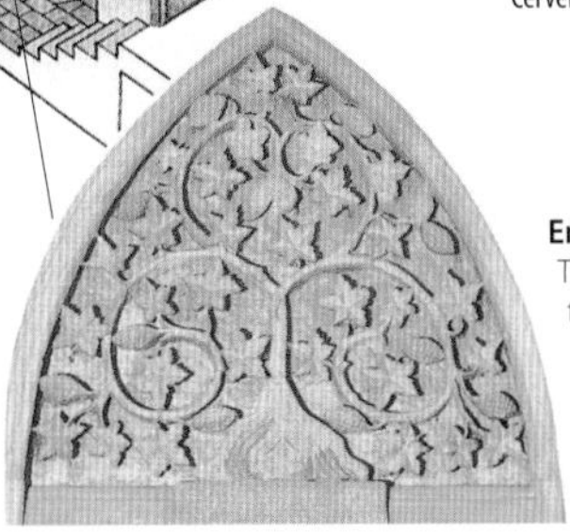

**Entrance Portal**
The tympanum above the door in the south vestibule is decorated with clusters of grapes and vine leaves growing on twisted branches.

**The Ark**
This shrine is the holiest place in the synagogue and holds the sacred scrolls of the Torah.

18th-century silver Torah crown in the Maisel Synagogue

## 9 Maisel Synagogue
*Maiselova Synagóga*

Maiselova 10. **Map** 3 B3. **Tel** 22 23 17 191. Ⓜ Staroměstská. 🚋 17, 18. 🚌 207. **Open** Apr–Oct: 9am–6pm Sun–Fri; Nov–Mar: 9am–4:30pm Sun–Fri. 🅿 ♿ 🎫 **W** jewishmuseum.cz

When it was first built, at the end of the 16th century, this was a private house of prayer for the use of mayor Mordechai Maisel and his family. Maisel had made a fortune lending money to Emperor Rudolph II to finance wars against the Turks, and his synagogue was the most richly decorated in the city. The original building was a victim of the fire that devastated the Jewish Town in 1689 and a new synagogue was built in its place. Its present crennelled, Gothic appearance dates from the start of the 20th century. Since the 1960s the Maisel Synagogue has housed a fascinating collection of Jewish silver and other metalwork dating from Renaissance times to the 20th century. It includes many Torah crowns, shields and finials. Crowns and finials were used to decorate the rollers on which the text of the Torah (the five books of Moses) was kept. The shields were hung over the mantle that was draped over the Torah and the

pointers were used to follow the text so that it was not touched by readers' hands. There are also objects such as wedding plates, lamps and candlesticks. By a tragic irony, nearly all these Jewish treasures were brought to Prague by the Nazis from synagogues throughout Bohemia and Moravia with the intention of founding a museum of a vanished people.

## 10 Church of the Holy Ghost
*Kostel Sv. Ducha*

Elišky Krásnohorské. **Map** 3 B3. **Tel** 602 301 639. Ⓜ Staroměstská. 🚋 17, 18. 🚌 207. **Open** only for services. 🕐 8am Mon–Sat, 9:30am Sun. 🎫 ♿

This church stands on the narrow strip of Christian soil that once separated the two Jewish communities of the Middle Ages – the Jews of the eastern and western rites. Built in the mid-14th century, the single-naved Gothic church was originally part of a convent of Benedictine nuns. The convent was destroyed in 1420 during the Hussite Wars (*see pp28–9*) and not rebuilt.

The church was badly damaged in the Old Town fire of 1689. The exterior preserves the original Gothic buttresses and high windows, but the vault of the nave was rebuilt in Baroque style after the fire. The furnishings

too are mainly Baroque. The high altar dates from 1760, and there is an altar painting of *St Joseph* by Jan Jiří Heintsch (c1647–1712). In front of the church stands a stone statue of St John Nepomuk (*see p85*) distributing alms (1727) by the Baroque sculptor Ferdinand Maximilian Brokof. Inside the church there are a few earlier statues, including a 14th-century *Pietà* (the heads of the figures are later, dating from 1628), a Late Gothic statue of St Ann and busts of St Wenceslas and St Adalbert from the early 16th century.

Church of the Holy Ghost

## 11 Spanish Synagogue
*Španělská Synagóga*

Vězeňská 1, Dušní 12. **Map** 3 B2. **Tel** 22 23 17 191. Ⓜ Staroměstská. 🚋 17, 18. 🚌 207. **Open** Apr–Oct: 9am–6pm Sun–Fri; Nov–Mar: 9am–4:30pm Sun–Fri. 🅿 ♿ **W** jewishmuseum.cz

Prague's first synagogue, known as the Old School (Stará škola), once stood on this site. In the 11th century the Old School was the centre of the community of Jews of the eastern rite, who lived strictly apart from Jews of the western rite, who were concentrated round the Old-New Synagogue. The present building dates from the second half of the 19th century. The exterior and

Motif of the Ten Commandments on the Spanish Synagogue's façade interior are both pseudo-Moorish in appearance. The rich stucco decorations on the walls and vaults are reminiscent of the Alhambra in Spain, hence the name. Once closed to the public, the Spanish Synagogue now houses a permanent exhibition dedicated to the history of the Jews of Bohemia.

# ⓬ Cubist Houses
*Kubistické Domy*

Elišky Krásnohorské, 10–14. **Map** 3 B2.
🚇 Staroměstská. 🚋 17, 18. 🚌 207.
**Closed** to the public.

The rebuilding of the old Jewish Quarter at the turn of the 20th century gave Prague's architects scope to experiment with many new styles. Most of the blocks in this area are covered with flowing Art Nouveau decoration, but on the corner of Bílkova and Elišky Krásnohorské there is a plain façade with a few simple repeated geometrical shapes. This is an example of Cubist architecture, a fashion that did not really catch on in the rest of Europe, but was very popular with the avant-garde in Bohemia and Austria before and after World War I. This block was built for a cooperative of teachers in 1919–21.

At No. 7 Elišky Krásnohorské you can see the influence of Cubism in the curiously geometric figures supporting the windows. Another interesting Cubist building is the House of the Black Madonna in Celetná *(see pp174–5)*.

Cubist-style figures framing a window in Elišky Krásnohorské Street

# ⓭ Church of St Simon and St Jude
*Kostel Sv. Šimona A Judy*

Dušní/U milosrdných. **Map** 3 B2.
**Tel** 22 23 21 068. 🚇 Staroměstská.
🚋 17, 18. 🚌 207. **Open** for concerts.
♿ 🅦 fok.cz

Members of the Bohemia Brethren built this church with high Late Gothic windows in 1615–20. Founded in the mid-15th century, the Brethren agreed with the Utraquists *(see p77)* in directing the congregation to receive both bread and wine at Holy Communion. In other respects they were more conservative than other Protestant sects, continuing to practise celibacy and Catholic sacraments such as confession. After the Battle of the White Mountain *(see pp32–3)*, the Brethren were expelled from the Empire.

The church was then given to a Catholic order, the Brothers of Mercy, becoming part of a monastery and hospital. Tradition has it that the monastery's wooden steps were built from the scaffold on which 27 Czechs were executed in 1621 *(see p74)*. In the 18th century the city's first anatomy lecture hall was

Detail of Baroque façade of Church of St Simon and St Jude

established here and the complex continues to serve as a hospital – the Na Františku. The church is now used as a venue for concerts.

# ⓮ Church of St Castullus
*Kostel Sv. Haštala*

Haštalské náměstí. **Map** 3 C2.
🚋 5, 8, 14, 26. 🚌 207. **Open** times vary. 🕯 11am 1st Sun of month; other times vary. 🚫 ♿

This peaceful little corner of Prague takes its name – Haštal – from the parish church of St Castullus. One of the finest Gothic buildings in Prague, the church was erected on the site of an older Romanesque structure in the second quarter of the 14th century. Much of the church had to be rebuilt after the fire of 1689, but the double nave on the north side survived. It has slender pillars supporting a delicate ribbed vault.

The interior furnishings are mainly Baroque, though there are remains of wall paintings of about 1375 in the sacristy and a metal font decorated with figures dating from about 1550. Standing in the Gothic nave is an impressive sculptural group depicting *Calvary* (1716) from the workshop of Ferdinand Maximilian Brokof.

# ⓲ St Agnes of Bohemia Convent

*Klášter Sv. Anežky České*

In 1234 a convent of the Poor Clares was founded here by Agnes, sister of King Wenceslas I. She was not canonized until 1989. The convent, one of the very first Gothic buildings in Bohemia, was abolished in 1782 and used to house the poor and as storage space, later falling into disrepair. Following painstaking restoration in the 1960s, it has recovered much of its original appearance and is now used by the National Gallery to display a large collection of medieval painting and sculpture from Bohemia and Central Europe, dating from 13th–16th centuries.

First floor

### Gallery Guide

*The permanent exhibition is housed on the first floor of the old convent in a long gallery and smaller rooms around the cloister. The works are arranged chronologically.*

Ground floor

★ **Votive panel of Archbishop Jan Očko of Vlašim**
This detailed panel, painted around 1370 by an anonymous artist, shows Charles IV kneeling before the Virgin in Heaven.

★ **The Annunciation of Our Lady**
Painted around 1350 by the renowned Master of the Vyšší Brod Altar, this panel is one of the oldest and finest works in the museum.

Steps to first-floor gallery

★ **Strakonice Madonna**
This 700-year-old statue evokes the Classical French sculpture found in such places as Reims Cathedral.

Terrace café

Upper part of Church of the Holy Saviour

Steps down to cloister

Upper part of concert hall

Chapel of St Mary Magdalene

## VISITORS' CHECKLIST

**Practical Information**
U Milosrdných 17.
**Map** 3 C2.
**Tel** 22 48 10 628.
🌐 **ngprague.cz**
**Open** 10am–6pm Tue–Sun (last guided tour: 5pm). 🚫 🚭 ♿
📷 🖥

**Transport**
Ⓜ Náměstí Republiky, Staroměstská. 🚊 17 to Law faculty, 5, 8, 14, 26 to Dlouhá třída. 🚌 207 to Řásnovka.

### Variant of the Krumlov Madonna
Dating from around 1400, this touching image of mother and child was crafted by an unknown sculptor, a follower of the Master of the Krumlov Madonna.

### Church of the Holy Saviour
This capital decorated with heads of five Bohemian queens is matched by one with five Přemyslid kings.

Church of St Francis and concert hall

Entrance to Convent

### Cloister
The Gothic vaulting around the cloister of the convent dates from the 14th century.

### Key

▨ Medieval and early Renaissance Art
☐ Cloister
☐ Churches
▨ Concert hall
▨ Special exhibitions
▨ Non-exhibition space

# PRAGUE CASTLE AND HRADČANY

## PRAŽSKÝ HRAD A HRADČANY

The history of Prague begins with the Castle, founded in the 9th century by Prince Bořivoj. Its commanding position high above the river Vltava soon made it the centre of the lands ruled by the Přemyslids. The buildings enclosed by the Castle walls included a palace, three churches and a monastery. In about 1320 a town called Hradčany was founded in part of the Castle's outer bailey. The Castle has been rebuilt many times, most notably in the reigns of Charles IV and Vladislav Jagiello. After a fire in 1541, the badly damaged buildings were rebuilt in Renaissance style and the Castle enjoyed its cultural heyday under Rudolph II. Since 1918 it has been the seat of the president of the Republic. The Changing of the Guard takes place every hour. At noon the ceremony includes a fanfare.

## Sights at a Glance

### Churches and Monasterie
2 St Vitus's Cathedral *pp102–105*
5 St George's Basilica and Convent
18 Capuchin Monastery
19 The Loreto *pp118–19*
22 Strahov Monastery *pp122–4*

### Palaces
4 Royal Palace *pp106–107*
10 Belvedere
13 Archbishop's Palace
15 Martinic Palace
20 Černín Palace

### Historic Buildings
3 Powder Tower
8 Dalibor Tower

### Museums and Galleries
1 Picture Gallery of Prague Castle
7 Lobkowicz Palace
12 Riding School
14 Sternberg Palace *pp112–15*
16 Schwarzenberg Palace

### Historic Streets
6 Golden Lane
17 New World
21 Pohořelec

### Parks and Gardens
9 South Gardens
11 Royal Garden

### Restaurants
*see p201*
1 Host
2 Villa Richter

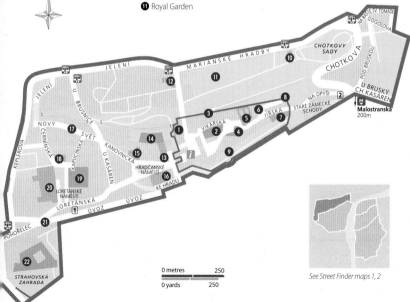

0 metres 250
0 yards 250

*See Street Finder maps 1, 2*

◀ Ceiling fresco, *The Heavenly Banquet*, found in the Strahov Monastery

**For map symbols** *see back flap*

# Street-by-Street: Prague Castle

Despite periodic fires and invasions, Prague Castle has retained churches, chapels, halls and towers from every period of its history, from the the Gothic splendour of St Vitus's Cathedral to the Renaissance additions of Rudolph II, the last Habsburg to use the Castle as his principal residence. The courtyards date from 1753–75 when the whole area was rebuilt in Late Baroque and Neo-Classical styles. The Castle became the seat of the Czechoslovak president in 1918, and the current president of the Czech Republic has an office here.

To Royal Garden

**❶ Picture Gallery of Prague Castle**
Renaissance and Baroque paintings hang in the restored stables of the castle.

**❸ Powder Tower**
Used in the past for storing gunpowder and as a bell foundry, the tower is now a museum.

To Royal Garden

President's office

**❷ ★ St Vitus's Cathedral**
The decoration on the fence at St Vitus's Golden Portal.

Second courtyard

Matthias Gate (1614)

First courtyard

To Hradčanské náměstí

Church of the Holy Rood

Steps down to Little Quarter

**The Castle gates** are crowned by copies of 18th-century statues of Fighting Giants by Ignaz Platzer.

**❾ South Gardens**
18th-century statues decorate the gardens laid out in the old ramparts.

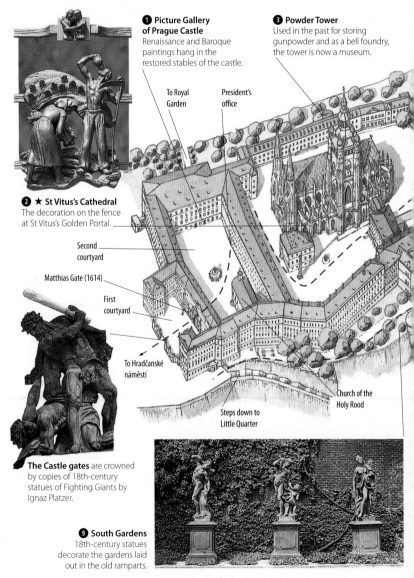

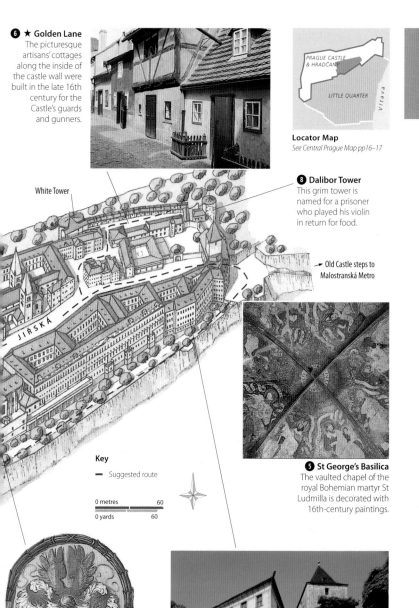

**❻ ★ Golden Lane**
The picturesque artisans' cottages along the inside of the castle wall were built in the late 16th century for the Castle's guards and gunners.

**Locator Map**
See Central Prague Map pp16–17

White Tower

**❽ Dalibor Tower**
This grim tower is named for a prisoner who played his violin in return for food.

→ Old Castle steps to Malostranská Metro

JIŘSKÁ

**Key**

— Suggested route

| 0 metres | 60 |
| 0 yards | 60 |

**❺ St George's Basilica**
The vaulted chapel of the royal Bohemian martyr St Ludmilla is decorated with 16th-century paintings.

**❹ ★ Old Royal Palace**
The uniform exterior of the palace conceals many fine Gothic and Renaissance halls. Coats of arms cover the walls and ceiling of the Room of the New Land Rolls.

**❼ Lobkowicz Palace**
Exquisite works of art from the Lobkowicz family's private collection are housed here.

### ❶ Picture Gallery of Prague Castle
*Obrazárna Pražského Hradu*

Prague Castle, the second courtyard.
**Map** 2 D2. **Tel** 22 43 73 531.
🚇 Malostranská, Hradčanská. 🚊 22.
**Open** 9am–4pm daily in winter,
9am–6pm daily in summer. 🅿️ ♿
**W** hrad.cz

The gallery was created in 1965 to hold works of art collected since the reign of Rudolph II *(see pp30–31)*. Though most of the collection was looted by the Swedes in 1648, many interesting paintings remain. Paintings from the 16th–18th centuries form the bulk of the collection, but there are also sculptures, among them a copy of a bust of Rudolph by Adriaen de Vries. Highlights include Titian's *The Toilet of a Young Lady*, Rubens' *The Assembly of the Olympic Gods* and Guido Reni's *The Centaur Nessus Abducting Deianeira*. Master Theodoric, Paolo Veronese, Tintoretto and the Czech Baroque artists Jan Kupecký and Petr Brandl are among other artists represented. The Picture Gallery houses many of Rudolph's best paintings.

You can also see the remains of the Castle's first church, the 9th-century Church of our Lady, thought to have been built by Prince Bořivoj, the first Přemyslid prince to be baptized a Christian *(see pp22–3)*. The site was discovered during reconstruction.

### ❷ St Vitus's Cathedral
*Chrám Sv. Víta*

*See pp102–105.*

### ❸ Powder Tower
*Prašná Věž*

Prague Castle, Vikářská. **Map** 2 D2.
**Tel** 22 43 71 111. 🚇 Malostranská,
Hradčanská. 🚊 22. **Open** Apr–Oct:
9am–6pm daily; Nov–Mar: 9am–4pm
daily. 🅿️ 🚫 ♿

A tower was built here in about 1496 by the King Vladislav II's architect Benedikt Ried as a cannon bastion overlooking the Stag Moat. The original was destroyed in the fire of 1541, but it was rebuilt as the home and workshop of gunsmith and bell founder Tomáš Jaroš. In 1549 he made Prague's largest bell, the 18-tonne Sigismund, for the bell tower of St Vitus's Cathedral.

During Rudolph II's reign (1576–1612), the tower became a laboratory for alchemists. It was here that adventurers such as Edward Kelley performed

**View of the Powder Tower from across the Stag Moat**

experiments that convinced the emperor they could turn lead into gold.

In 1649, when the Swedish army was occupying the Castle, gunpowder exploded in the tower, causing serious damage. Nevertheless it was used as a gunpowder store until 1754, when it was converted into flats for the sacristans of St Vitus's Cathedral. Today, the tower houses a perma-nent exhibition of Czech military history.

### ❹ Old Royal Palace
*Královský Palác*

*See pp106–107.*

### ❺ St George's Basilica and Convent
*Bazilika Sv. Jiří*

Jiřské náměstí. **Map** 2 E2. **Tel** 22 43 71
111. 🚇 Malostranská, Hradčanská.
🚊 22. **Open** Apr–Oct: 9am–6pm
daily; Nov–Mar: 9am–4pm daily.
🅿️ 🚫 ♿ **W** hrad.cz

Founded by Prince Vratislav (915–21), the basilica pre-dates St Vitus's Cathedral and is the best-preserved Romanesque

**Titian's *The Toilet of a Young Lady* in the Castle Picture Gallery**

church in Prague. It was enlarged in 973 when the adjoining St George's Convent was established here, and rebuilt following a fire in 1142. The massive twin towers and austere interior have been scrupulously restored to give a good idea of the church's original appearance. However, the rusty red façade was a 17th-century Baroque addition.

Buried in the church is St Ludmila, widow of the 9th-century ruler Prince Bořivoj (see pp22–3). She became Bohemia's first female Christian martyr when she was strangled as she knelt at prayer. Other members of the Přemyslid dynasty buried here include Vratislav. His austere tomb stands on the right-hand side of the nave at the foot of the curving steps that lead up to the choir. The impressive Baroque grille opposite en-closes the tomb of Boleslav II (973–99). The adjacent former Benedictine nunnery is the oldest convent building in Bohemia. It was founded in 973 by Princess Mlada, sister of Boleslav II. Throughout the Middle Ages the convent, together with the basilica, formed the heart of the castle complex.

Façade and towers of St George's Basilica

## ❻ Golden Lane
Zlatá Ulička

**Map** 2 E2. 🚇 Malostranská, Hradčanská. 🚃 22. 🅿

Named after the goldsmiths who lived here in the 17th century, this short, narrow street is one of the most picturesque in Prague. One side of the lane is lined with tiny, brightly

painted houses which were built right into the arches of the Castle walls. They were constructed in the late 1500s for Rudolph II's 24 Castle guards. A century later the goldsmiths moved in and modified the buildings. But by the 19th century the area had degenerated into a slum and was populated by Prague's poor and the criminal community. In the 1950s all the remaining tenants were moved out and the area restored to something like its original state. The house at number 20 is the oldest and the least altered in appearance. Most of the houses were converted into shops selling books, Bohemian glass and other souvenirs for tourists, who flock to the narrow lane.

Golden Lane has been home to some well-known writers, including the Nobel prize-winning poet Jaroslav Seifert, and Franz Kafka (see p70) who stayed at No. 22 with his sister for a few months in 1916–17. Because of its name, legends have spread about the street being filled with alchemists huddled over their bubbling alembics trying to produce gold for Rudolph II. In fact the alchemists had laboratories in Vikářská, the lane between St Vitus's Cathedral and the Powder Tower.

## ❼ Lobkowicz Palace
Lobkovický Palác

Jiřská 3. **Map** 2 E2. **Tel** 23 33 12 925 (to book a guided tour). 🚇 Malostranská. 🚃 12, 18, 20, 22. **Open** 10am–6pm daily. 🅿 ♿ 📷 💻 🌐 lobkowicz.cz Toy Museum: **Tel** 22 43 72 294. **Open** 9:30am–5:30pm daily. 🌐 ivan-steiger.de

Dating from 1570, this is one of the palaces that sprang up after the fire of 1541, when Hradčany was largely destroyed. Some original sgraffito on the façade has been preserved, but most of the present palace is Carlo Lurago's 17th-century reconstruction for the Lobkowicz family, who had inherited it in 1627. The most splendid room is the 17th-century banqueting hall with mythological frescoes by Fabian Harovník.

The palace once formed part of Prague's National Museum but has since been returned to the Lobkowicz family. It now houses the valuable Princely Collections, an exhibition of paintings, decorative arts, original music scores annotated by Beethoven and Haydn, and musical instruments.

Opposite the palace, at No. 6, is a delightful toy museum claiming to be the world's second largest, with toys from ancient Greece to the present. The collection includes toys made from wood and tin, dolls and teddy bears.

One of the tiny houses in Golden Lane

# ❷ St Vitus's Cathedral

*Katedrála Sv. Víta, Václava A Vojtécha*

Work began on the city's most distinctive landmark in 1344 on the orders of John of Luxembourg. The first architect was the French Matthew of Arras. After his death, Swabian Peter Parler took over. His masons' lodge continued to work on the building until the Hussite Wars. Finally completed by 19th- and 20th-century architects and artists, the cathedral houses the crown jewels and the tomb of "Good King" Wenceslas *(pp22–3)*.

**St Vitus's Cathedral**
This 19th-century engraving shows how the cathedral looked before the additions made in 1872–1929.

**Gargoyles**
On the ornate west front, gutter spouts are given their traditional disguise.

## KEY

① **West front**

② **The Rose Window**, located above the portals, was designed by František Kysela in 1925–7. It depicts scenes from the biblical story of the creation.

③ **Twin west spires**

④ **Nave**

⑤ **Triforium**

⑥ **The Renaissance bell tower** is capped with a Baroque "helmet".

⑦ **Chancel**

⑧ **To Royal Palace** *(see pp106–107).*

⑨ **The tomb of St Wenceslas** is connected to an altar, decorated with semi-precious stones.

Main entrance

| 926 Rotunda of St Vitus built by St Wenceslas | 1344 King John of Luxembourg founds Gothic cathedral. French architect Matthew of Arras begins work | *Bust of Peter Parler on triforium* | 1619 Calvinists take over cathedral as house of prayer | 1872 Joseph Mocker begins work on west nave |
|---|---|---|---|---|
| **1000** | **1200** | **1400** | **1600** | **1800** |
| 1060 Building of triple-naved basilica begins on orders of Prince Spytihněv | *Tomb of Přemysl Otakar II* | 1421 Hussites occupy St Vitus's    1356 Masterbuilder Peter Parler summoned to continue work on the cathedral | 1589 Royal tomb completed | 1770 New steeple added to tower after fire    1929 Consecration of completed cathedral, nearly 1,000 years after death of St Wenceslas |

**★ Flying Buttresses**
The slender buttresses that surround the exterior of the nave and chancel, supporting the vaulted interior, are richly decorated like the rest of the cathedral.

**★ Chapel of St Wenceslas**
The bronze ring on the chapel's north portal was thought to be the one to which St Wenceslas clung as he was murdered by his brother Boleslav *(see pp22–3)*.

**★ Golden Portal**
Until the 19th century this was the main cathedral entrance, and it is still used on special occasions. Above it is a mosaic of *The Last Judgment* by 14th-century Venetian craftsmen.

**Gothic Vaulting**
The skills of architect Peter Parler are never more clearly seen than in the delicate fans of ribbing that support the three Gothic arches of the Golden Portal.

# A Guided Tour of St Vitus's Cathedral

A walk around St Vitus's takes you back through a thousand years of history. Go in through the west portal to see some of the best elements of the modern, Neo-Gothic style and continue past a succession of side chapels to catch glimpses of religious artifacts, saintly relics and works of art from Renaissance paintings to modern statuary. Allow plenty of time to visit the richly decorated, jewel-encrusted St Wenceslas Chapel before you leave.

**② Chancel**
The chancel was built by Peter Parler from 1372. It is remarkable for the soaring height of its vault, counter-pointed by the intricacy of the webbed Gothic tracery.

Cathedral organ (1757)

New sacristy

**① Alfons Mucha Window**
The cathedral contains many superb examples of 20th-century Czech stained glass, notably *St Cyril and St Methodius.*

Main entrance (West Portal)

Thun Chapel

## The Four Eras of St Vitus's

Excavations have revealed sections of the northern apse of St Wenceslas's original rotunda, and architectural and sculptural remains of the later basilica, beneath the existing cathedral. The western, Neo-Gothic end is a faithful completion of the 14th-century plan.

Chapel of St Ludmilla

**Key**

☐ Rotunda, 10th century
▨ Basilica, 11th century
☐ Gothic cathedral, 14th century
☐ 19th- and 20th-century additions to cathedral

**Leopold II** is shown in a contemporary engraving being crowned King of Bohemia at the cathedral in September 1791. Mozart composed an opera, *La Clemenza di Tito*, in honour of the occasion.

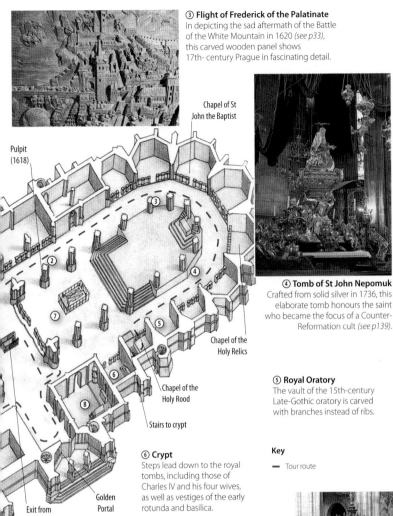

③ **Flight of Frederick of the Palatinate**
In depicting the sad aftermath of the Battle of the White Mountain in 1620 *(see p33)*, this carved wooden panel shows 17th-century Prague in fascinating detail.

Chapel of St John the Baptist

Pulpit (1618)

④ **Tomb of St John Nepomuk**
Crafted from solid silver in 1736, this elaborate tomb honours the saint who became the focus of a Counter-Reformation cult *(see p139)*.

Chapel of the Holy Relics

⑤ **Royal Oratory**
The vault of the 15th-century Late-Gothic oratory is carved with branches instead of ribs.

Chapel of the Holy Rood

Stairs to crypt

⑥ **Crypt**
Steps lead down to the royal tombs, including those of Charles IV and his four wives, as well as vestiges of the early rotunda and basilica.

Golden Portal

Exit from crypt

**Key**

— Tour route

⑧ **St Wenceslas Chapel**
Gothic frescoes with scenes from the Bible and the life of the saint cover the walls, interspersed with a patchwork of polished gemstones and fine gilding. Every object is a work of art – this golden steeple held the wafers and wine for Holy Communion.

⑦ **Royal Mausoleum**
Ferdinand I died in 1564. His beloved wife and son, Maximilian II, are buried alongside him in the mausoleum.

# ❹ Old Royal Palace

*Královský Palác*

From the time Prague Castle was first fortified in stone in the 11th century *(see pp24–5)*, the palace was the seat of Bohemian princes. The building consists of three different architectural layers. A Romanesque palace built by Soběslav I around 1135 forms the cellars of the present building. Přemysl Otakar II and Charles IV then added their own palaces above this, while the top floor, built for Vladislav Jagiello, contains the massive Gothic Vladislav Hall. During the period of Habsburg rule the palace housed government offices, courts and the old Bohemian Diet (parliament). In 1924 it was extensively restored.

**Riders' Staircase**
These wide and gently sloping steps, with their Gothic rib vault, were used by knights on horseback to get to Vladislav Hall for indoor jousting competitions.

**The Diet**, the medieval parliament, was also the throne room. Destroyed by fire in 1541, it was rebuilt by Bonifaz Wohlmut in 1563.

**An overhead passage** from the palace leads to the Royal Oratory in St Vitus's Cathedral *(see p105)*.

**Vladislav Hall**
The 17th-century painting by Aegidius Sadeler shows that the Royal Court was very like a public market. The hall's magnificent rib vaulting was designed by Benedikt Ried in the 1490s.

Entrance

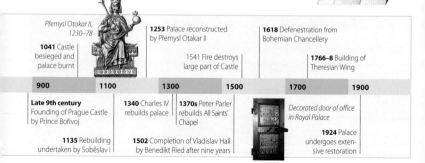

| | | | |
|---|---|---|---|
| *Přemysl Otakar II, 1230–78* | **1253** Palace reconstructed by Přemysl Otakar II | **1618** Defenestration from Bohemian Chancellery | |
| **1041** Castle besieged and palace burnt | **1541** Fire destroys large part of Castle | **1766–8** Building of Theresian Wing | |

| **900** | **1100** | **1300** | **1500** | **1700** | **1900** |
|---|---|---|---|---|---|

**Late 9th century** Founding of Prague Castle by Prince Bořivoj

**1340** Charles IV rebuilds palace

**1370s** Peter Parler rebuilds All Saints' Chapel

*Decorated door of office in Royal Palace*

**1135** Rebuilding undertaken by Soběslav I

**1502** Completion of Vladislav Hall by Benedikt Ried after nine years

**1924** Palace undergoes extensive restoration

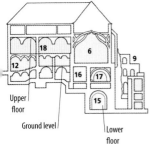

Upper floor

Ground level

Lower floor

**All Saints' Chapel** was built by Peter Parler for Charles IV. After the 1541 fire, its vault had to be rebuilt and it was redecorated in the Baroque style.

## Plan and Cross Section of Royal Palace

*The cross section of the palace shows the three distinct levels of the building, all constructed at different times. The plan shows how Vladislav Hall dominates the entire palace structure.*

### Key to Old Royal Palace

- ☐ Romanesque and Early Gothic
- ☐ Late Gothic
- ☐ Rebuilt after 1541 fire
- ☐ Baroque and later

| | |
|---|---|
| **1** Eagle Fountain | **10** All Saint's Chapel |
| **2** Vestibule | **11** Diet Hall |
| **3** Green Chamber | **12** Rider's staircase |
| **4** King's Bedchamber | **13** Court of Appeal |
| **5** Romanesque tower | **14** Palace courtyard |
| **6** Vladislav Hall | **15** Hall of the Romanesque palace |
| **7** Bohemian Chancellery | **16** Old Land Rolls |
| **8** Imperial Council Room steps | **17** Palace of Charles IV |
| **9** Terrace | **18** New Land Rolls |

**The Theresian Way** was built to house the office registers.

**Bohemian Chancellery**
This 17th-century Dutch-style stove decorates the former royal offices of the Habsburgs. The chancellery is the site of the 1618 defenestration.

## Defenestration of 1618

Painting by Václav Brožík, 1889

On 23 May, 1618, more than 100 Protestant nobles, led by Count Thurn, marched into the palace to protest against the succession to the throne of the intolerant Habsburg Archduke Ferdinand. The two Catholic Governors appointed by Ferdinand, Jaroslav Martinic and Vilém Slavata, were confronted and, after a row, the Protestants threw both the Governors and their secretary, Philipp Fabricius, out of the eastern window. Falling some 15 m (50 ft), they survived by landing in a dung heap. This event signalled the beginning of the Thirty Years' War. The Catholics attributed the survival of the Governors to the intervention of angels.

**The New Land Rolls**
These rooms are decorated with the crests of clerks who worked here from 1561 to 1774.

Old prison in the Dalibor Tower

## ❽ Dalibor Tower

*Daliborka*

Prague Castle, Zlatá ulička. **Map** 2 E2.
🚇 Malostranská. 🚊 12, 18, 20, 22.
**Open** 9am–6pm daily (Nov–Mar: to 4pm). 🚻 ♿

This 15th-century tower with a conical roof was part of the fortifications built by King Vladislav Jagiello *(see pp28–9)*. His coat of arms can be seen on the outer wall. The tower also served as a prison and is named after its first inmate, Dalibor of Kozojedy, a young knight sentenced to death for harbouring some outlawed serfs. While awaiting execution, he was kept in an underground dungeon, into which he had to be lowered through a hole in the floor.

According to legend, while in prison he learnt to play the violin. People sympathetic to his plight came to listen to his playing and provided him with food and drink, which they lowered on a rope from a window – prisoners were often left to starve to death. The story was used by Bedřich Smetana in his opera *Dalibor*. The tower ceased to serve as a prison in 1781. Visitors can see part of the old prison.

## ❾ South Gardens

*Jižní Zahrady*

Prague Castle (access from Hradčanské náměstí). **Map** 2 D3.
🚇 Malostranská. 🚊 12, 18, 20, 22.
**Open** Apr–Oct: 10am–6pm daily (May & Sep: to 7pm; Jun & Jul: to 9pm; Aug: to 8pm). 🌐 **hrad.cz**

The gardens occupy the long narrow band of land below the Castle overlooking the Little Quarter. Several small gardens have been linked to form what is now known as the South Gardens. The oldest, the Paradise Garden (Rajská zahrada), laid out in 1562, contains a circular pavilion built for Emperor Matthias in 1617. Its carved wooden ceiling shows the coloured emblems of the 39 countries of the Habsburg Empire. The Garden on the Ramparts (Zahrada Na valech) dates from the 19th century. It occupies a former vegetable patch and is famous as the site of the defenestration of 1618 *(see p107)*, when two Imperial governors were thrown from a first-floor window. Two obelisks were subsequently erected by Ferdinand II to mark the spots where they landed. Modifications were carried out in the 1920s by Josip Plečnik, who built the Bull Staircase leading to the Paradise Garden and the observation terrace. Below the terrace, in the former Hartig Garden, is a Baroque music pavilion designed by Giovanni Battista Alliprandi. Beside it stand four statues of Classical gods by Antonín Braun.

Alliprandi's music pavilion in the South Gardens

## ❿ Belvedere

*Belvedér*

Prague Castle, Royal Garden.
**Map** 2 E1. 🚇 Malostranská, Hradčanská. 🚊 22 to Královský Letohrádek. **Open** 10am–6pm Tue–Sun during exhibitions only. 🚻 ♿

Built by Ferdinand I for his beloved wife Anne, the Belvedere is one of the finest Italian Renaissance buildings north of the Alps. Also known as

The Belvedere, Emperor Ferdinand I's summer palace in the Royal Garden beside Prague Castle

◀ View of Prague Castle and the spires of St Vitus's Cathedral, Prague

Antonín Braun's statue of *The Allegory of Night* in front of the *sgraffito* decoration of the Ball Game Hall in the Royal Garden

Queen Anne's Summerhouse (Letohrádek Královny Anny), it is an arcaded building with slender Ionic columns topped by a roof shaped like an inverted ship's hull clad in blue-green copper. The main architect was Paolo della Stella, who was also responsible for the ornate reliefs inside the arcade. Work began in 1538 but was interrupted by the great Castle fire of 1541 and not completed until 1564.

In the middle of the small geometrical garden in front of the palace stands the Singing Fountain. Dating from 1568, it owes its name to the musical sound the water makes as it hits the bronze bowl, though you have to listen closely to appreciate the effect. The fountain was cast by Tomáš Jaroš, the famous bell founder, who lived and worked in the Powder Tower *(see p100)*.

Many of the Belvedere's works of art were plundered by the Swedish army in 1648. The statues stolen included Adriaen de Vries's 16th-century bronze of

*Mercury and Psyche*, now in the Louvre in Paris. Today, the Belvedere is used as an art gallery.

## ⓫ Royal Garden
*Královská Zahrada*

Prague Castle, U Prašného mostu. **Map** 2 D2. Ⓜ Malostranská, Hradčanská. 🚋 22. **Open** May–Oct: 10am–6pm daily (May & Sep: to 7pm; Jun & Jul: to 9pm; Aug: to 8pm). ♿ 🌐 **hrad.cz**

The garden was created in 1535 for Ferdinand I. Its appearance has been altered over time, but some examples of 16th-century garden architecture have survived, notably the Belvedere and the Ball Game Hall (Míčovna), built by Bonifaz Wohlmut in 1569. The building is covered in beautiful, though much restored, Renaissance *sgraffito*, a form of decoration created by cutting a

design through the wet top layer of plaster on to a contrasting undercoat. The garden is beautiful in spring when thousands of tulips bloom. This is where tulips were first acclimatized to Europe.

## ⓬ Riding School
*Jízdárna*

Prague Castle. **Map** 2 D2. **Tel** 22 43 73 232. Ⓜ Malostranská, Hradčanská. 🚋 22. **Open** 10am–6pm during exhibitions.

The 17th-century Riding School forms one side of U Prašného mostu, a road which runs to the northern side of Prague Castle via Deer Moat. In the 1920s it was converted into an exhibition hall, which now holds important exhibitions of painting and sculpture. A garden provides excellent views of St. Vitus's Cathedral and the northern fortifications of the castle.

## ⓭ Archbishop's Palace
*Arcibiskupský Palác*

Hradčanské náměstí 16. **Map** 2 D3. Ⓜ Malostranská, Hradčanská. 🚋 22. **Closed** to the public.

Ferdinand I bought this sumptuous palace in 1562 for the first Catholic Archbishop since the Hussite Wars *(see pp28–9)*. An imposing building, it has four wings and four courtyards. It replaced the old Archbishop's Palace in the Little Quarter, which had been destroyed during the wars, and has remained the Archbishop's seat in Prague ever since. In the period after the Battle of the White Mountain *(see pp32–3)*, it was a powerful symbol of Catholic domination of the city and the Czech lands. Its spectacular cream-coloured Rococo façade was designed by Johann Joseph Wirch in the 1760s for Archbishop Antonín Příchovský, whose coat of arms sits proudly above the portal.

Příchovský coat of arms

# ⓮ Sternberg Palace

*Šternberský Palác*

Franz Josef Sternberg founded the Society of Patriotic Friends of the Arts in Bohemia in 1796. Fellow noblemen would lend their finest pictures and sculpture to the society, which had its headquarters in the early 18th-century Sternberg Palace. Since 1949, the fine Baroque building has been used to house the National Gallery's collection of European art, with its superb range of Old Masters.

**The Lamentation of Christ**
The frozen, sculptural figures make this one of the finest paintings by Lorenzo Monaco (1408).

**Cardinal Cesi's Garden in Rome**
Henrick van Cleve's painting (1548) provides a valuable image of a Renaissance collections of antiquities. The garden was later destroyed.

First floor

Garden Room

Stairs to second floor

Ground floor

Stairs to first floor

Passageway to Hradčanské náměstí

Ticket office

## Gallery Guide

*The gallery is arranged on three floors around the central courtyard of the palace. The ground floor, reached from the courtyard, houses German and Austrian art from the 15th to 19th centuries. The stairs to the collections on the upper floors are just beyond the ticket office at the main entrance.*

★ **Scholar in his Study**
In this painting from 1634
Rembrandt used keenly
observed detail to
convey wisdom in the
face of the old scholar.

Chinese
Cabinet

Second
floor

**Paradise** (1618)
Roelandt Savery studied models of exotic
animals, brought to Prague by Persian nobles,
at the court of Emperor Rudolf II. He was then
able to paint real animals.

Stairs down to
other floors
and exit

★ **Head of Christ**
Painted by El Greco in
the 1590s, this portrait
emphasizes the
humanity of Christ. At
the same time the
curious square halo
framing the head gives
the painting the qualities
of an ancient icon.

★ **The Martyrdom of
St Thomas**
This magnificent work is by
Peter Paul Rubens, the
foremost Flemish painter of
the 17th century.

**Key**

▨ German and Austrian Art
   1400–1800

☐ Flemish and Dutch Art 1400–1600

▨ Italian Art 1400–1500

▨ Flemish and Dutch Art 1600–1800

☐ French Art 1400–1800

▨ Icons, Classical and Ancient Art

▨ Venice 1700–1800 and Goya

▨ Spanish Art 1400–1800

☐ Naples and Venice 1600–1700

☐ Italian Art 1500–1600

▨ Non-exhibition space

# Exploring the Sternberg Collections

The National Gallery's collection of European art at the Sternberg Palace ranks among the country's best collections. The museum is divided into three separate viewing areas. Its extensive holdings of German and Austrian art of the 15th–19th centuries are exhibited just off the courtyard on the ground floor. A small collection of art from antiquity and religious icons, as well as a larger display of early Italian and Dutch art, occupy the first floor. Most of the real treasures are on the second floor, where the museum displays works of Italian, Spanish, French and Dutch masters from the 16th–18th centuries.

## Icons, Classical and Ancient Art

Two small rooms on the first floor are occupied by an odd assortment of paintings that do not quite fit in with the rest of the collection. These include a *Portrait of a Young Woman* dating from the 2nd century AD, which was discovered during excavations at Fayoum in Egypt in the 19th century.

The second room, on the left as you enter the main viewing area, holds icons of the Orthodox church – some are Byzantine, some Italo-Greek and some Russian. A fine example on show here is a later 16th-century work, *Christ's Entry Into Jerusalem* from Russia. The collection of icons on display offers examples from a variety of the most important Mediterranean and Eastern European centres.

*Christ's Entry into Jerusalem*, a 16th-century Russian icon

## German and Austrian Art (1400–1800)

This collection is massive and it could take half a day to see everything. One of the most celebrated paintings in the Sternberg's collection is Albrecht Dürer's *The Feast of the Rosary*, painted during the artist's stay in Venice in 1506. The work has a particular

significance for Prague since it was bought by Emperor Rudolph II. The two figures in front of the Virgin and Child are Maximilian I (Rudolph's great-great-grandfather) and Pope Julius II.

The collection also includes works by several other important German painters of the Renaissance, including Hans Holbein the Elder and the Younger and Lucas Cranach the Elder. Cranach is represented by a striking *Adam and Eve* whose nudes show the spirit of the Renaissance, tempered by Lutheran Reform.

## Italian Art (1400–1700)

When you enter the gallery of early Italian art on the first floor, you are greeted by a splendid array of richly gilded early diptychs and triptychs from the churches of Tuscany and northern Italy. Most came originally from the d'Este collection at Konopiště Castle (*see p169*). Of particularly high quality are the two triangular panels of saints by the 14th-century Sienese painter Pietro Lorenzetti and a moving *Lamentation of Christ* by Lorenzo Monaco.

A fascinating element of the collection is the display of Renaissance bronze statuettes. Fashionable amongst Italian nobility of the 15th century, these little bronzes were at first cast from famous or newly discovered works of antiquity. Later, sculptors began to use the medium more freely – Padua, for example, specialized in the depiction of small animals – and producers also adapted items for use as decorative household goods such as oil lamps, ink pots and door knockers. This small collection has representative works from all the major Italian producers except Mantua and, while many variations can be found in other museums throughout the world, there are some pieces here that are both unique and outstanding examples of the craft. On the second floor, among the

*The Feast of the Rosary* by Dürer (1506)

*Don Miguel de Lardízábal* (1815) by Francisco Goya

16th-century Italian works on display, are some delightful surprises. These include *St Jerome* by the Venetian painter, Tintoretto, and *The Annunciation to the Shepherds* and *Portrait of an Elderly Man* by another Venetian, Jacopo Bassano. There is also an expressive portrait by the Florentine mannerist, Bronzino, of *Eleanor of Toledo*, the wife of Cosimo de' Medici.

## Flemish and Dutch Art (1400–1800)

The collections of Flemish and Dutch art on the first and second floors are rich and varied, ranging from rural scenes by Pieter Brueghel the Elder to portraits by Rubens and Rembrandt. Highlights of the former include an altarpiece showing the *Adoration of the Magi* by Geertgen tot Sint Jans. Other early works of great interest include *St Luke Drawing the Virgin* by Jan Gossaert (c1515), one of the first works of art from the Netherlands to show the clear influence of the Italian Renaissance. The

collection from the 17th century on the second floor includes several major works, notably by Peter Paul Rubens who, in 1639, sent two paintings to the Augustinians of the Church of St Thomas *(see p127)* in the Little Quarter. The originals were lent to the gallery in 1896 and replaced by copies. The violence and drama of *The Martyrdom of St Thomas* is in complete contrast

to the spiritual calm of *St Augustine*. Two other fine portraits are those of Rembrandt's *Scholar in His Study* and Frans Hals' *Portrait of Jasper Schade.*

Also on display is a wide assortment of paintings by other, less-prominent artists who nonetheless represent the enormous range and quality of this period.

## Spanish and French Art (1400–1800)

French art on the second floor is represented chiefly by the 17th-century painters Simon Vouet *(The Suicide of Lucretia)*, Sébastien Bourdon and Charles Le Brun. Spanish painting is even less well represented, but two of the collection's finest works are a haunting *Head of Christ* by El Greco, which is the only work by this important artist on display in the Czech Republic, and a noble half-length portrait of the politician *Don Miguel de Lardízábal* by Goya.

## The Chinese Cabinet

After several years of difficult restoration work, this curiosity on the second floor is once again open to the public. The richly decorated little chamber was part of the original furnishings of the Sternberg Palace, and was designed as an intimate withdrawing room away from the bustle of the grand state rooms. In its plethora of decorative styles, Baroque mingles with Far Eastern motifs and techniques, which were fashionable at the turn of the 18th century. The vaulted ceiling features the Star of the Sternbergs among its geometric decorations. Black lacquered walls are embellished with cobalt blue and white medallions in golden frames, while gilded shelves once held rare Oriental porcelain.

*Eleanor of Toledo* (1540s) by the Florentine Mannerist painter Agnolo Bronzino

## ⓯ Martinic Palace
*Martinický Palác*

Hradčanské náměstí 8. **Map** 1 C2.
**Tel** 77 77 98 040. Ⓜ Malostranská,
Hradčanská. 🚋 22. 🏛 only (call
ahead to arrange). 🅿
🅦 **martinickypalac.cz**

In the course of the palace's
restoration in the early 1970s,
workmen uncovered the
original 16th-century façade
decorated with ornate cream
and brown *sgraffito (see p111)*. It
depicts Old Testament scenes,
including the story of Joseph
and Potiphar's wife. More
*sgraffito* in the courtyard shows
the story of Samson and the
Labours of Hercules.

Martinic Palace was enlarged
by Jaroslav Bořita of Martinice,
who was one of the imperial
governors thrown from a
window of the Royal Palace in
1618 *(see p107)*.

According to an old legend,
between 11pm and midnight
the ghost of a fiery black dog
appears at the palace and acc-
ompanies walkers as far as the
Loreto *(see pp118–19)*. You can
tour the palace or visit a small
museum of musical machines,
such as gramophones.

## ⓰ Schwarzenberg Palace
*Schwarzenberský Palác*

Hradčanské náměstí 2. **Map** 2 D3.
**Tel** 23 30 81 730. Ⓜ Malostranská,
Hradčanská. 🚋 22. **Open** 10am–6pm
Tue–Sun. 🅿 ✉ 🅦 **ngprague.cz**

From a distance, the façade of
this grand Renaissance palace
appears to be clad in projecting
pyramid-shaped stonework. On
closer inspection, this turns out
to be an illusion created by
*sgraffito* patterns
incised on a flat
wall. Built originally

for the Lobkowicz
family by the Italian
architect Agostino Galli
in 1545–76, the gabled
palace is Florentine
rather than Bohemian
in style. It passed
through several
hands before the
Schwarzenbergs, a
leading family in the
Habsburg Empire,
bought it in 1719.
Much of the interior
decoration has survived,
including four painted
ceilings on the second
floor dating from 1580.
The palace once
housed the Museum of
Military History, now at
U Památníku 3. Following
renovation, the palace became
home to the National Gallery's
collection of Baroque art.

In the square outside is the
statue of Tomáš G Masaryk,
Czechoslovakia's first president.

## ⓱ New World
*Nový Svět*

**Map** 1 B2. 🚋 22, 25 to Brusnice.

Now a charming street of small
cottages, Nový Svět (New
World) used to be the name of
this area of Hradčany.
Developed in the mid-14th
century to provide houses for
the castle workers, the area was
twice destroyed by fire, the last
time being in 1541. Most of the
cottages date from the 17th
century. They have been
spruced up, but are otherwise
unspoilt and very different in
character from the rest of

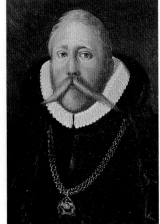
Tycho Brahe, Rudolph II's astronomer

Hradčany. In defiance of their
poverty, the inhabitants chose
golden house signs to identify
their modest houses – you
will see a Golden Pear, a
Grape, a Foot, a Bush and an
Acorn. Plaques identify No. 1
as the former home of
Rudolph II's brilliant court
astronomer, Tycho Brahe, and
No. 25 as the 1857 birthplace
of the great Czech violinist
František Ondříček.

## ⓲ Capuchin Monastery
*Kapucínský Klášter*

Loretánské náměstí 6. **Map** 1 B3.
🚋 22, 25. **Closed** to the public
except the church. 🕕 6pm Mon–Sat,
8:30am Sun.

Bohemia's first Capuchin
monastery was founded here in
1600. It is connected to the
neighbouring Loreto *(see
pp118–19)* by an overhead
roofed passage. Attached to the
monastery is the Church of Our
Lady Queen of Angels, a single-
naved building with plain
furnishings, typical of the
ascetic Capuchin order.

The church is famous for its
miraculous statue of the
Madonna and Child. Emperor
Rudolph II liked the statue so
much he asked the Capuchins
to give it to him to place in his
private chapel. The monks
agreed, but then the statue

The Carmelite monastery next to the Schwarzenberg Palace

The ornate altar, Church of the
Capuchin Monastery

somehow found its way back to
the church. Three times Rudolph
had the Madonna brought
back, but each time she
returned to her original position.
The Emperor eventually gave
up, left her where she was and
presented her with a gold
crown and a robe.

Each year, at Christmas, crowds
of visitors come to see the
church's Baroque nativity scene
of life-sized figures dressed in
period costumes.

# ⓲ The Loreto
*Loreta*

See pp118–19.

# ⓴ Černín Palace
*Černínský Palác*

Loretánské náměstí 5. **Map** 1 B3.
🚋 22, 25. **Closed** to the public.
🌐 **mzv.cz**

Built in 1668 for Count Černín
of Chudenice, the Imperial
Ambassador to Venice, the
Černín Palace is 150 m (500 ft)
long with a row of 30 massive
Corinthian half-columns
running the length of its upper
storeys. The palace towers over
the attractive, small, grassy
square that lies between it
and the Loreto.

The huge building suffered as
a result of its prominent position
on one of Prague's highest
hills. It was looted by the French
in 1742 and badly damaged in
the Prussian bombardment of
the city in 1757. In
1851 the impov-
erished Černín family
sold the palace to
the state and it
became a barracks.
After the creation
of Czechoslovakia in
1918 the palace was
restored to its original
design and became the
Ministry of Foreign Affairs.
A few days after the Communist
Coup in 1948 the Foreign
Minister, Jan Masaryk, the
popular son of Czechoslovakia's
first President, Tomáš Masaryk,
died as the result of a fall from a

Capital on Černín
Palace

top-floor window of the
Palace. He was the only non-
Communist in the government
that had just been formed.
No-one really knows whether he
was pushed or jumped, but he is
still widely mourned.

# ㉑ Pohořelec

**Map** 1 B3. 🚋 22, 25.

First settled in 1375, this is one
of the oldest parts of Prague.
The name is of more recent
origin: Pohořelec means "place
destroyed by fire", a fate the
area has suffered three times in
the course of its history – the
last time being in 1741. It is now
a large open square on a hill
high over the city and part of
the main access route to Prague
Castle. In the
centre stands a
large monument
to St John
Nepomuk (1752)
*(see p137),* thought
to be by Johann
Anton Quitainer.
The houses around the
square are mainly
Baroque and Rococo.

In front of the Jan Kepler
grammar school stands a
monument to Kepler and his
predecessor as astronomer at
the court of Rudolph II, Tycho
Brahe, who died in a house on
the school site in 1601.

Černín Palace, with its Corinthian half-columns

# ⑲ The Loreto

*Loreta*

Ever since its construction in 1626, the Loreto has been an important place of pilgrimage. It was commissioned by Kateřina of Lobkowicz, a Czech aristocrat who was very keen to promote the legend of the Santa Casa of Loreto *(see opposite)*. The heart of the complex is a copy of the house believed to be the Virgin Mary's. The Santa Casa was enclosed by cloisters in 1661, and a Baroque façade 60 years later by Christoph and Kilian Ignaz Dientzenhofer. The grandiose design and miraculous stories about the Loreto were part of Ferdinand II's campaign to recatholicize the Czechs *(see pp32–3)*.

**Bell Tower**
Enclosed in this large Baroque tower is a set of 30 bells cast 1683–91 in Amsterdam by Claudy Fremy.

**★ Loreto Treasury**
This gold-plated, diamond-encrusted monstrance, for displaying the host, is one of the valuable liturgical items in the Loreto treasury, most of which originated in the 16th–18th centuries.

Entrance from Loretánské náměstí

## KEY

① Chapel of St Ann

② Chapel of St Francis Seraphim

③ Fountain decorated with a sculpture of the Resurrection

④ Chapel of St Joseph

⑤ Chapel of the Holy Rood

⑥ Chapel of St Anthony of Padua

⑦ Chapel of Our Lady of Sorrows

⑧ **This fountain sculpture** is a copy of *The Ascension of the Virgin Mary*, taken from Jan Brüderle's 1739 sandstone statue, now in the Lapidarium *(see p162)*.

**Baroque Entrance**
The balustrade above the Loreto's front entrance is decorated with statues of St Joseph and St John the Baptist by Ondřej Quitainer.

**★ Santa Casa**
Stucco figures of many of the Old Testament prophets and reliefs from the life of the Virgin Mary by Italian artists decorate the chapel.

## VISITORS' CHECKLIST

**Practical Information**
Loretánské náměstí 7, Hradčany.
**Map** 1 C3.
**Tel** 22 05 16 740.
🌐 **loreta.cz**
**Open** 9am–12:15pm, 1–5pm daily (to 4pm winter). 📷
✝ 7:30am Sat, 10am & 6pm Sun.

**Transport**
🚋 22, 25 to Pohořelec.

**★ Church of the Nativity**
Gruesome relics, including fully clothed skeletons with death masks made of wax, line the walls of this 18th-century church. The frescoes are by Václav Vavřinec Reiner.

## Legend of the Santa Casa

The original house, said to be where the Archangel Gabriel told Mary about the future birth of Jesus, is in the small Italian town of Loreto. It was believed that angels transported the house from Nazareth to Loreto in 1278 following threats by infidels. After the Protestants' defeat in 1620 *(see pp32–3)*, Catholics promoted the legend, and 50 replicas of the Loreto were built in Bohemia and Moravia. This, the grandest, became the most important in Bohemia, and received many visitors.

The stuccoed Santa Casa

**17th-Century Cloister**
Built originally as a shelter for the many pilgrims who visited the shrine, the cloister is covered with frescoes.

# ㉒ Strahov Monastery

*Strahovský Klášter*

When it was founded in 1140 by an austere religious order, the Pre- monstratensians, Strahov rivalled the seat of the Czech sovereign in size. Destroyed by fire in 1258, it was rebuilt in the Gothic style, with later Baroque additions. Its famous library, in the theological and philosophical halls, is over 800 years old and despite being ransacked by many invading armies, is one of the finest in Bohemia. Strahov also escaped Joseph II's 1783 dissolution of the monasteries by changing its library into a research institute. It is now a working monastery and museum.

**Statue of St John**
A Late-Gothic, painted statue of St John the Evangelist situated in the Theological Hall, has the saint's prayer book held in a small pouch.

Entrance to main courtyard of the monastery

**★ Church of Our Lady**
The interior of this Baroque church is highly decorated. Above the arcades of the side naves, there are 12 paintings with scenes from the life of St Norbert, founder of the Premonstratensian order, by Jiří Neunhertz.

Entrance to Church of Our Lady

## KEY

① **Baroque organ on which Mozart played**

② **The Museum** of National Literature is devoted to Czech literature.

③ **Refectory**

④ **Baroque tower**

⑤ **The façade** of the Philosophical Hall is decorated with vases and a gilded medallion of Joseph II by Ignaz Platzer.

**Church Façade**
The elaborate statues, by Johann Anton Quitainer, were added to the western façade of the church when it was remodelled by the architect Anselmo Lurago in the 1750s.

**View from Petřín Hill**
A gate at the eastern end of the first courtyard leads to Petřín Hill, part of which was once the monastery's orchards.

**VISITORS' CHECKLIST**

**Practical Information**
Královská Kanonie Premonstrátů na Strahově. Strahovské nádvoří 1.
**Map** 1 B4.
**Tel** 23 31 07 711.
[W] strahovskyklaster.cz
**Open** 9am–noon, 12:30–5pm daily. Philosophical Hall, Theological Hall, Church of Our Lady, Picture Gallery: **Open** 9am–noon, 1–5pm daily, **Closed** Easter Sun, 24 & 25 Dec.

**Transport**
22, 25.

★ **Theological Hall**
One of the 17th-century astronomical globes by William Blaeu that line the hall. The stucco and wall paintings relate to librarianship.

★ **Philosophical Hall**
The ceiling fresco depicts the *Struggle of Mankind to Know Real History* by Franz Maulbertsch. It was built in 1782 to hold the Baroque bookcases and their valuable books from a dissolved monastery near Louka, in Moravia.

ance to
ries

**Strahov Gospel Book**
A facsimile of this superb and precious 9th-century volume, is now on display in the Theological Hall.

# LITTLE QUARTER
## MALÁ STRANA

The Little Quarter is the part of Prague least affected by recent history. Hardly any new building has taken place here since the late 18th century and the quarter is rich in splendid Baroque palaces and old houses with attractive signs. Founded in 1257, it is built on the slopes below the Castle hill with magnificent views across the river to the Old Town.

The centre of the Little Quarter has always been Little Quarter Square (Malostranské náměstí), dominated by the Church of St Nicholas. The Grand Prior's millwheel at Kampa Island still turns, pilgrims still kneel before the Holy Infant of Prague in the Church of Our Lady Victorious, and music rings out from churches and palaces as it did when Mozart stayed here.

## Sights at a Glance

### Churches
2 Church of St Thomas
4 Church of St Nicholas pp128–9
9 Church of Our Lady Victorious
13 Church of Our Lady beneath the Chain
23 Church of St Lawrence

### Parks and Gardens
8 Vrtba Garden
18 Vojan Park
20 Palace Garden
21 Observation Tower
22 Mirror Maze
24 Štefánik's Observatory
26 Petřín Park
27 Funicular Railway

### Museums
5 Museum Montanelli
17 Kafka Museum
19 Kampa Museum of Modern Art
28 Museum of Music

### Historic Monuments
25 Hunger Wall

### Historic Restaurants and Beer Halls
15 At the Three Ostriches

### Historic Streets and Squares
3 Little Quarter Square
6 Nerudova Street
7 Italian Street
10 Maltese Square
12 Grand Priory Square
16 Bridge Street

### Bridges and Islands
11 Kampa Island
14 Charles Bridge pp136–9

### Palaces
1 Wallenstein Palace and Garden
29 Michna Palace

### Restaurants
see pp201–202
1 Alchymist
2 Bar Bar

3 Café Lounge
4 Café de Paris
5 Café Savoy
6 Coda
7 Cowboys
8 Essensia
9 Gitanes
10 Kočár z Vídně
11 Konírna
12 Luka Lu
13 U Malého Glena
14 U Malířů
15 Malostranská beseda
16 Nebozízek
17 The Sushi Bar
18 Terasa U Zlaté Studně

◄ Statues and sculptures on Charles Bridge

For map symbols *see back flap*

# Street-by-Street: Around Little Quarter Square

The Little Quarter, most of whose grand Baroque palaces now house embassies, has preserved much of its traditional character. The steep, narrow streets and steps have an air of romantic mystery, and you will find fascinating buildings adorned with statues and house signs at every turn. Some of the old buildings now house smart restaurants.

**5 Museum Montanelli**
This contemporary museum hosts international exhibitions of modern art.

**At the Three Little Fiddles**, now a restaurant, acquired its house sign when it was the home of a family of violin makers around 1700.

**Thun-Hohenstein Palace** (1721–6) has a doorway crowned with two sculpted eagles by Matthias Braun. The palace is now the seat of the Italian embassy.

NERUDOVA

ANSKY VRŠEK

BŘETISLAVOVA

VLAŠSKÁ

TRŽI

**6 ★ Nerudova Street**
This historic street leading up to Prague Castle is named after the 19th-century writer Jan Neruda.

**Morzin Palace** has a striking Baroque façade with a pair of sculpted moors.

**7 Italian Street**
From the 16th to the 18th century, houses in the street, like the House at the Golden Scales, were occupied by Italian craftsmen.

**Key**

— Suggested route

| 0 metres | 100 |
| 0 yards | 100 |

**For key to symbols** *see back flap*

**8 Vrtba Garden**
Laid out in about 1725 by František Maximilián Kaňka, these fine Baroque terraces provide good views over the rooftops of the Little Quarter.

**Locator Map**
*See Central Prague Map pp16–17*

❶ ★ **Wallenstein Palace**
On the main hall ceiling, Albrecht von Wallenstein, the great general of the 30 Years' War, appears as the god Mars.

To Malostranská Metro

Czech National Assembly

Plague Column

TOMÁŠSKÁ

Wallenstein Gardens

Little Quarter Town Hall

MALOSTRANSKÉ NÁMĚSTÍ

❷ **Church of St Thomas**
A statue of St Augustine by Hieronymus Kohl (1684) decorates the church's dramatic Baroque façade.

❸ **Little Quarter Square**
This 18th-century view shows the lower half of the square between the church of St Nicholas and the Town Hall.

**Schönborn Palace**, now the American Embassy, is decorated with caryatids from the 17th century.

❹ ★ **Church of St Nicholas**
The cupola and bell tower of this Baroque church are the best-known landmarks of the Little Quarter.

# ❶ Wallenstein Palace and Garden

*Valdštejnský Palác*

Valdštejnské náměstí 4. **Map** 2 E3. 🚇 Malostranská. **Tel** 25 70 75 707. 🚊 12, 18, 20, 22. Palace: **Open** 10am–5pm Sat & Sun. 📞 call in advance to arrange. 🚻 ♿ from Valdštejnská. Garden: **Open** Apr–Oct: 10am–6pm daily (Jun–Sep: 10am–7pm). Riding school: **Open** for exhibitions 10am–6pm Tue–Sun ♿ from Valdštejnské náměstí. 🖥 🌐 senat.cz

The main hall of Wallenstein Palace

The first large secular building of the Baroque era in Prague, the palace stands as a monument to the fatal ambition of military commander Albrecht von Wallenstein (1581–1634). His string of victories over the Protestants in the 30 Years' War (*see pp32–3*) made him vital to Emperor Ferdinand II. Already showered with titles, Wallenstein started to covet the crown of Bohemia. When he dared to negotiate independently with the enemy, he was killed on the emperor's orders by mercenaries in 1634.

Wallenstein's intention was to overshadow even Prague Castle with his palace, built between 1624 and 1630. To obtain a suitable site, he had to purchase 23 houses, three gardens and the municipal brick kiln. The magnificent main hall rises to a height of two storeys with a ceiling fresco of Wallenstein himself portrayed as Mars, the god of war, riding in a triumphal chariot. The architect, Andrea Spezza, and nearly all the artists employed in the decoration of the palace were Italians.

Today the palace is used as the home of the Czech Senate, and following a central restoration is now open to the public. The gardens are laid out as they were when Wallenstein dined in the huge *sala terrena* (garden pavilion) that looks out over a fountain and rows of bronze statues. These are copies of works by Adriaen de Vries that were stolen by the Swedes in 1648 (*see pp32–3*). There is also a pavilion with fine frescoes showing scenes from the legend of the Argonauts and the Golden Fleece. Wallenstein was a holder of the Order of the Golden Fleece, the highest order of chivalry of the Holy Roman Empire. At the far end of the garden is a large ornamental pond with a central statue. Behind this stands the old Riding School, now used to house special exhibitions by the National Gallery. Both gardens and riding school have undergone substantial restoration.

Copy of a bronze statue of Eros by Adriaen de Vries

Palace

Sala terrena

Avenue of sculptures

Riding School

Valdštejnská Street entrance

**The grotesquery** is a curious imitation of the walls of a limestone cave, covered in stalactites.

Letenská Street entrance

Statue of Hercules

Klárov entrance

## ❷ Church of St Thomas
*Kostel sv. Tomáše*

Josefská 8. **Map** 2 E3. **Tel** 25 75 30 556. 🅼 Malostranská. 🚊 12, 20, 22. **Open** 9am–4pm daily. 🕆 12:15pm Mon–Sat (and 6pm Sat in English); 7pm Mon–Wed; 9:30am (Czech), 11am (English), 12:30pm (Spanish), 6pm (Czech) in summer and 5pm (Czech) in winter Sun. 🈂️ ♿

Founded by Wenceslas II in 1285 as the monastery church of the Augustinians, the original Gothic church was completed in 1379. In the Hussite period *(see pp28–9)* this was one of the few churches to remain Catholic. As a result, it suffered serious fire damage. During the reign of Rudolph II *(see pp30–31)*, St Thomas's developed strong links with the Imperial court. Several members of Rudolph's entourage were buried here, such as court architect Ottavio Aostalli and the sculptor Adriaen de Vries.

In 1723 the church was struck by lightning and Kilian Ignaz Dientzenhofer was called in to rebuild it. The shape of the original church was preserved in the Baroque reconstruction but, apart from the spire, the church today betrays little of its Gothic origins. The interior of the dome and the curving ceiling frescoes in the nave were painted by Václav Vavřinec Reiner. Above the altar are copies of paintings by Rubens – *The Martyrdom of St Thomas* and a picture of St Augustine. The originals are in

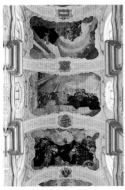

Baroque ceiling in the nave of the Church of St Thomas

Arcade in front of buildings on the north side of Little Quarter Square

the Sternberg Palace *(see pp112–15)*. The English-speaking Catholic community of Prague meets in this church.

## ❸ Little Quarter Square
*Malostranské Náměstí*

**Map** 2 E3. 🅼 Malostranská. 🚊 12, 20, 22.

The square has been the centre of life in the Little Quarter since its foundation in 1257. It had started life as a large marketplace in the outer bailey of Prague Castle. Buildings sprang up in the middle of the square dividing it in half – a gallows and pillory stood in its lower part.

Most of the houses around the square have a medieval core, but all were rebuilt in the Renaissance and Baroque periods. The centre of the square is dominated by the splendid Baroque church of St Nicholas. The large building beside it was a Jesuit college. Along the upper side of the square, facing the church, runs the vast Neo-Classical façade of Lichtenstein Palace. In front of it stands a column raised in honour of the Holy Trinity to mark the end of a plague epidemic in 1713.

Other important buildings include the Little Quarter Town Hall with its splendid Renaissance façade and the Sternberg Palace, built on the site of the outbreak of the fire of

1541, which destroyed most of the Little Quarter. Beside it stands the Smiřický; Palace. Its turrets and hexagonal towers make it an unmistakable landmark on the northern side of the lower square. The Baroque Kaiserstein Palace is situated at the eastern side. On the façade is a bust of the great Czech soprano Emmy Destinn, who lived there between 1908 and 1914. She often sang with the famous Italian tenor Enrico Caruso.

## ❹ Church of St Nicholas
*Kostel sv. Mikuláše*

See pp128–9.

## ❺ Montanelli Museum
*Muzeum Montanelli*

Nerudova 13. **Map** 2 D3. **Tel** 72 42 11 584. 🅼 Malostranská. 🚊 12, 20, 22. **Open** noon–6pm Tue–Sat, noon–4pm Sun. 🈂️ 📷 ♿ 🏠 💻 🆆 **muzeummontanelli.com**

The Montanelli Museum (MuMo) is one of a handful of small private museums in the Czech Republic. MuMo's aim is to present imaginative, modern art in a historical setting, while maintaining the DrAK Foundation's collection. There is an impressive selection of educational programmes for children, including weekend workshops.

# ❹ Church of St Nicholas

*Kostel sv. Mikuláše*

The Church of St Nicholas divides and dominates the two sections of Little Quarter Square. Building began in 1703, and the last touches were put to the glorious frescoed nave in 1761. It is the acknowledged masterpiece of father-and-son architects Christoph and Kilian Ignaz Dientzenhofer, Prague's greatest exponents of High Baroque *(see opposite)*, although neither lived to see the completion of the church. The statues, frescoes and paintings inside the church are by leading artists of the day, and include a fine *Crucifixion* of 1646 by Karel Škréta. Extensive renovation in the 1950s reversed the damage caused by 200 years of leaky cladding and condensation.

**Altar Paintings**
The side chapels hold many works of art. This painting of St Michael is by Francesco Solimena.

**★ Pulpit**
Dating from 1765, the ornate pulpit is by Richard and Peter Prachner. It is lavishly adorned with golden cherubs.

## KEY

① **Chapel of St Ann**

② **The curving façade** has a number of statues, one of which is St Paul, by John Frederick Kohl. The façade was completed in 1710 by Christoph Dientzenhofer, who was influenced by Italian architects Borromini and Guarini.

③ **The dome** was completed by Kilian Ignaz Dientzenhofer in 1751, shortly before his death.

④ **The belfry**, added in 1751–6, was the last part to be built. It houses a museum of musical instruments.

⑤ **Chapel of St Francis Xavier**

⑥ **Chapel of St Catherine**

Entrance from west side of Little Quarter Square

**Baroque Organ**
A fresco of St Cecilia, patron saint of music, watches over the superb organ. Built in 1746, the instrument was played by Mozart in 1787.

## VISITORS' CHECKLIST

**Practical Information**
Malostranské náměstí.
**Map** 2 E3.
**Tel** 25 75 34 215.
**Open** 9am–5pm daily
(Nov–Mar: to 4pm; last tour:
15 mins before closing).

**Transport**
Malostranská. 12, 20, 22.

**★ Dome Fresco**
František Palko's fresco, *The Celebration
of the Holy Trinity* (1753–4), fills the 70 m
(230 ft) high dome.

**High Altar**
A copper statue of St Nicholas by
Ignaz Platzer surmounts the high
altar. Below it, the painting of St
Joseph is by Johann Lukas Kracker,
who also painted the nave fresco.

Entrance to Belfry

**★ Statues of the Church Fathers**
The great teachers by Ignaz Platzer stand
at the four corners of the transept. St Cyril
dispatches a pagan with his crozier.

## The Dientzenhofer Family

Christoph Dientzenhofer (1655–1722)
came from a family of Bavarian
master builders. His son Kilian Ignaz
(1689–1751) was born in Prague and
educated at the Jesuit Clementinum
*(see p81)*. They were responsible for
the greatest treasures of Jesuit-influ-
enced Prague Baroque architecture.
The Church of St Nicholas, their last
work, was completed by Kilian's son-
in-law, Anselmo Lurago.

Kilian Ignaz Dientzenhofer

## ❻ Nerudova Street

*Nerudova Ulice*

**Map** 2 D3. 🚇 Malostranská. 🚊 12, 20, 22. 🚌 292.

A picturesque narrow street leading up to Prague Castle, Nerudova is named after the poet and journalist Jan Neruda, who wrote many short stories set in this part of Prague. He lived in the house called At the Two Suns (No. 47) between 1845 and 1857.

Up until the introduction of house numbers in 1770, Prague's houses were distinguished by signs. Nerudova's houses have a splendid selection of heraldic beasts and emblems. As you make your way up Nerudova's steep slope, look out in particular for the Red Eagle (No. 6), the Three Fiddles (No. 12), the Golden Horseshoe (No. 34), the Green Lobster (No. 43) and the White Swan (No. 49) as well as the Old Pharmacy museum (No. 32).

There are also a number of grand Baroque buildings in the street, including the Thun-Hohenstein Palace (No. 20, now the Italian embassy) and the Morzin Palace (No. 5, the Rumanian embassy). The latter has a façade with two massive statues of moors (a pun on the name Morzin) supporting the semicircular balcony on the first floor. Another impressive façade is that of the Church of Our Lady of Unceasing Succour, the church of the Theatines, an order founded during the Counter-Reformation.

Italian Street, heart of the former colony of Italian craftsmen

## ❼ Italian Street

*Vlašská Ulice*

**Map** 1 C4. 🚇 Malostranská. 🚊 12, 20, 22. 🚌 292.

Italian immigrants started to settle here in the 16th century. Many were artists or craftsmen employed to rebuild and redecorate the Castle. If you approach the street from Petřín, on the left you will see the former Italian Hospital, a Baroque building with an arcaded courtyard. Today it maintains its traditional allegiance as the cultural section of the Italian embassy.

The grandest building in the street is the former Lobkowicz Palace, now the German embassy. One of the finest Baroque palaces in Prague, it has a large oval hall on the ground floor leading out onto a magnificent garden. Look out too for the pretty stucco sign on the house called At the Three Red Roses, dating from the early 18th century.

## ❽ Vrtba Garden

*Vrtbovská Zahrada*

Karmelitská 25. **Map** 2 D4. **Tel** 27 20 88 350. 🚇 Malostranská. 🚊 12, 20, 22. **Open** Apr–Oct: 10am–6pm daily. 🅿 🚹 **vrtbovska.cz**

Behind Vrtba Palace lies a beautiful Baroque garden with balustraded terraces. From the highest part of the garden there are magnificent views of Prague Castle and the Little Quarter. The Vrtba Garden was designed by František Maximilián Kaňka in about 1720. The statues of Classical gods and stone vases are the work of Matthias Braun and the paintings in the *sala terrena* (garden pavilion) in the lower part of the garden are by Václav Vavřinec Reiner.

View of the Little Quarter from the terrace of the Vrtba Garden

## ❾ Church of Our Lady Victorious

*Kostel Panny Marie Vítězné*

Karmelitská 9. **Map** 2 E4. **Tel** 25 75 33 646. 🚊 12, 20, 22. **Open** 8:30am–7pm Mon–Sat, 8:30am–8pm Sun. 🚹 9am & 6pm (Czech) Mon–Fri, 5pm (English) Thu, 9am & 6pm (Czech), 5pm (Spanish) Sat, 10am & 7pm (Czech), noon (English), 5pm (French), 6pm (Italian) Sun. 🚹 **pragjesu.info**

The first Baroque building in Prague was the Church of the Holy Trinity, built for the German Lutherans by Giovanni Maria Filippi. It was finished in 1613 but after the Battle of the White Mountain *(see p33)* the Catholic authorities gave the church to the Carmelites, who rebuilt it

Sign at Jan Neruda's house, At the Two Suns, 47 Nerudova Street

and renamed it in honour of the victory. The fabric has survived including the portal. Enshrined on a marble altar in the right aisle is a glass case containing the Holy Infant Jesus of Prague (better known by its Italian name – *il Bambino di Praga*). This wax effigy has a record of miracle cures and is one of the most revered images in the Catholic world. It was brought from Spain and presented to the Carmelites in 1628 by Polyxena of Lobkowicz. A small museum adjacent to the church traces its history.

## ❿ Maltese Square

*Maltézské Náměstí*

**Map** 2 E4. 🚊 12, 20, 22.

The square takes its name from the Priory of the Knights of Malta, which used to occupy this part of the Little Quarter. At the northern end stands a group of sculptures featuring St John the Baptist by Ferdinand Brokof – part of a fountain erected in 1715 to mark the end of a plague epidemic.

Most of the buildings were originally Renaissance houses belonging to prosperous townspeople, but in the 17th and 18th centuries the Little Quarter was taken over by the Catholic nobility and many were converted to flamboyant Baroque palaces. The largest, Nostitz Palace, stands on the southern side. It was built in the mid-17th century, then in about 1720 a balustrade was added with Classical vases and statues of emperors. The palace now houses the Ministry of Culture and in summer, concerts are held here. The Japanese embassy is housed in the Turba Palace (1767), an attractive pink Rococo building designed by Joseph Jäger.

Čertovka (the Devil's Stream) with Kampa Island on the right

## ⓫ Kampa Island

*Kampa*

**Map** 2 F4. 🚊 6, 9, 12, 20, 22.

Kampa, an island formed by a branch of the Vltava known as the Devil's Stream (Čertovka), is a delightfully peaceful corner of the Little Quarter. The stream got its name in the 19th century, allegedly after the diabolical temper of a lady who owned a house nearby in Maltese Square. For centuries the stream was used as a millrace and from Kampa you can see the remains of three old mills. Beyond the Grand Prior's Mill the stream disappears under a small bridge below the piers of Charles Bridge. From here it flows between rows of houses. Predictably, the area has become known as "the Venice of Prague", but instead of gondolas you will see canoes.

For most of the Middle Ages there were only gardens on Kampa, though the island was also used for washing clothes and bleaching linen. In the 17th century the island became well-known for its pottery markets. There are some enchanting houses from this period around

Ferdinand Brokof's statue of John the Baptist in Maltese Square

Na Kampě Square. Most of the land from here to the southern tip of the island is a park, created from several old palace gardens.

The island all but vanished beneath the Vltava during the floods of 2002, which caused widespread devastation to homes, businesses and historic buildings, many of which needed to be restored.

## ⓬ Grand Priory Square

*Velkopřevorské Náměstí*

**Map** 2 F4. Ⓜ Malostranská. 🚊 12, 20, 22.

On the northern side of this small leafy square stands the former seat of the Grand Prior of the Knights of Malta. In its present form the palace dates from the 1720s. The doorways, windows and decorative vases were made at the workshop of Matthias Braun. On the opposite side of the square is the Buquoy Palace, now the French embassy, a delightful Baroque building roughly contemporary with the Grand Prior's Palace.

The only incongruous feature is a painting of John Lennon with "give peace a chance" graffitied alongside. The "Lennon Peace Wall" has graced the Grand Prior's garden since Lennon's death.

# Street-by-Street: Little Quarter Riverside

On either side of Bridge Street lies a delightful half-hidden world of gently decaying squares, picturesque palaces, churches and gardens. When you have run the gauntlet of the trinket-sellers on Charles Bridge, escape to Kampa Island to enjoy a stroll in its informal park, the views across the Vltava weir to the Old Town and the flocks of swans gliding along the river.

**The Church of St Joseph** dates from the late 17th century. The painting of *The Holy Family* (1702) on the gilded high altar is by the leading Baroque artist Petr Brandl.

**The House at the Golden Unicorn** in Lázeňská Street has a plaque commemorating the fact that Beethoven stayed here in 1796.

**16 Bridge Street**
A major thoroughfare for 750 years, the narrow street leads to Little Quarter Square.

To Little Quarter Square

**12 Grand Priory Square**
The Grand Prior's Palace is the former seat of the Knights of Malta and dates from the 1720s. Its street wall features colourful murals and graffiti.

**13 Church of Our Lady beneath the Chain**
Two massive towers survive from when this was a fortified priory.

**28 Museum of Music**
This museum houses a vast collection of beautifully hand-crafted musical instruments.

**9 Church of Our Lady Victorious**
This Baroque church houses the famous effigy, the Holy Infant of Prague.

MOSTECKÁ

LÁZEŇSKÁ

KARMELITSKÁ

NEBOVIDSKÁ

**10 Maltese Square**
Grand palaces surround the oddly shaped square. This coat of arms decorates the 17th-century Nostitz Palace, a popular venue for concerts.

| 0 metres | 100 |
| 0 yards | 100 |

**Key**

 — Suggested route

**For key to symbols** *see back flap*

**⑱ Vojan Park**
Quiet shady paths have been laid out under the apple trees of this former monastery garden.

U LUŽICKÉHO SEMINÁŘE

**⑮ At the Three Ostriches**
A restaurant and hotel have kept the sign of a seller of ostrich plumes.

**Locator Map**
*See Central Prague Map pp16–17*

**⑭ ★ Charles Bridge**
The approach to this magnificent 14th-century bridge, with its Baroque statues, passes under an arch below a Gothic tower.

Čertovka (the Devil's Stream)

NA KAMPĚ

Lichtenstein Palace

**The Grand Priory Mill**
has had its wheel meticulously restored, though it now turns very slowly in the sluggish water of the Čertovka, the former millrace.

**⑪ ★ Kampa Island**
This 19th-century painting by Soběslav Pinkas shows boys playing on Kampa. The island's park is still a popular place for children.

## ⓭ Church of Our Lady beneath the Chain
*Kostel Panny Marie Pod Řetězem*

Lázeňská/Velkopřevorské náměstí 4.
**Map** 2 E4. **Tel** 25 75 30 876.
Ⓜ Malostranská. 🚋 12, 20, 22.
**Open** for concerts and services.
✝ 5:30pm Wed, 10am Sun. ♿

This church, the oldest in the Little Quarter, was founded in the 12th century. King Vladislav II presented it to the Knights of St John, the order which later became known as the Knights of Malta. It stood in the centre of the Knights' heavily fortified monastery that guarded the approach to the old Judith Bridge. The church's name refers to the chain used in the Middle Ages to close the monastery gatehouse.

A Gothic presbytery was added in the 13th century, but a century later the original Romanesque church was demolished. Although a new portico was built with a pair of massive square towers, work was then abandoned, and the old nave became a courtyard between the towers and the church. This was given a Baroque facelift in 1640 by Carlo Lurago. The painting by Karel Škréta on the high altar shows the Virgin Mary and John the Baptist coming to the aid of the Knights of Malta in the naval victory over the Turks at Lepanto in 1571.

## ⓮ Charles Bridge
*Karlův Most*

See pp136–9.

Fresco that gave At the Three Ostriches its name

View along Bridge Street through the tower on Charles Bridge

## ⓯ At the Three Ostriches
*U Tří Pštrosů*

Dražického náměstí 12.
**Map** 2 F3. **Tel** 25 72 88 888.
Ⓜ Malostranská. 🚋 12, 20, 22.

Many of Prague's colourful house signs indicated the trade carried on in the premises. In 1597 Jan Fux, an ostrich-feather merchant, bought this house by Charles Bridge. At the time ostrich plumes were very fashionable as decoration for hats among courtiers and officers at Prague Castle. Fux even supplied feathers to foreign armies. So successful was his business that in 1606 he had the house rebuilt and decorated with a large fresco of ostriches. The building is now an expensive hotel and restaurant.

## ⓰ Bridge Street
*Mostecká Ulice*

**Map** 2 E3. Ⓜ Malostranská.
🚋 12, 20, 22.

Since the Middle Ages this street has linked Charles Bridge with the Little Quarter Square. Crossing the bridge from the Old Town you can see the doorway of the old customs house built in 1591 in front of the Judith Tower. On the first floor of the tower there is a 12th-century relief of a king and a kneeling man.

Throughout the 13th and 14th centuries the area to the north of the street was the Court of the Bishop of Prague. This was destroyed during the Hussite Wars (see pp28–9), but one of its Gothic towers is preserved in the courtyard of the house called At the Three Golden Bells. It can be seen from the higher of the two bridge towers. The street is lined with a mixture of Renaissance and Baroque houses. As you walk up to Little Quarter Square, look out for the house called At the Black Eagle on the left. It has rich sculptural decoration and a splendid Baroque wrought-iron grille. Kaunic Palace, also on the left, was built in the 1770s. Its Rococo façade has striking stucco decoration and sculptures by Ignaz Platzer.

## ⓱ Kafka Museum
*Kafkovo Muzeum*

Cihelná 2b. **Map** 2 F3. Ⓜ Malostranská.
**Tel** 25 75 35 373. 🚋 12, 18, 20, 22.
**Open** 10am–6pm daily. ♿
Ⓦ **kafkamuseum.cz**

This museum houses the long-term exhibition "The City of Franz Kafka and Prague". The author Franz Kafka was born in Prague in 1883. He wrote visionary works that are considered some of the most important of the 20th century, including *The Trial*, *The Metamorphosis* and *The Castle*.

The exhibition has two sections. Existential Space imagines Prague as a mystical space and explores how the city shaped Kafka's life, while Imaginary Topography examines how Kafka turned Prague into a fantastical place in his works, transcending reality.

## ⓲ Vojan Park
*Vojanovy Sady*

U lužického semináře 17. **Map** 2 F3.
**Tel** 25 75 31 839. Ⓜ Malostranská.
🚋 12, 18, 20, 22. **Open** 8am–5pm
daily (to 7pm in summer).

A tranquil spot hidden behind high white walls, the park dates back to the 17th century, when it was the garden of the Convent of Barefooted Carmelites. Two chapels erected by the Order have survived among the park's lawns and fruit trees. One is the Chapel of Elijah, who, because of his Old Testament associations with Mount Carmel, is regarded as the founder of the Order. His chapel takes the form of a stalagmite and stalactite cave. The other chapel, dedicated to St Theresa, was built in the 18th century as an expression of gratitude for the convent's preservation during the Prussian siege of Prague in 1757.

## ⓳ Kampa Museum of Modern Art
*Muzeum Kampa*

U Sovových mlýnů2. **Map** 2 F4.
**Tel** 25 72 86 147. 🚋 6, 9, 12, 20, 22.
**Open** 10am–6pm daily. ♿ 📷 📷
Ⓦ **museumkampa.cz**

Housed in the historic Sova mill, the Kampa Museum of Modern Art has an impressive collection of Central European art. The museum was founded by the Czech-American couple Jan and Meda Mládek to house their private collection of drawings, paintings and sculptures. Among the artists on display are abstract painter Frantisek Kupka and Czech cubist sculptor Otto Gutfreund.

18th-century statue of Hercules located in the Palace Gardens

## ⓴ Palace Gardens
*Palácové Zahrady*

Valdštejnské 14. **Map** 2 F3.
**Tel** 25 72 14 817. Ⓜ Malostranská.
🚋 12, 18, 20, 22. **Open** Apr & Oct:
9am–6pm; May & Sep: 9am–7pm; Jun
& Jul: 9am– 9pm; Aug: 9am–8pm daily.
♿ Ⓦ **palacove-zahrady.cz**

The steep southern slope below Prague Castle was covered with vineyards and gardens during the Middle Ages. But in the 16th century, nobles laid out formal terraced gardens based on Italian Renaissance models. Most of these gardens were rebuilt during the 18th century and decorated with Baroque statuary and fountains. Five of the gardens – including those belonging to the former Ledebour, Černín and Pálffy Palaces – have been linked together.

From their terraces, the gardens boast magnificent views of Prague. The Ledebour Garden, designed in the early 18th century, has a fine *sala terrena* (garden pavilion) by Giovanni Battista Alliprandi. The Pálffy Garden was laid out in the mid-18th century with terraces and loggias. The most beautiful of the five, and architecturally the richest, is the Kolowrat-Černín Garden, created in 1784 by Ignaz Palliardi. The highest terrace has a *sala terrena* with statues and Classical urns. Below this is an assortment of staircases and archways, and the remains of Classical statuary.

The foot of the Palace Gardens

# ⑭ Charles Bridge (Little Quarter Side)

*Karlův Most*

Prague's most familiar monument, Charles Bridge, was founded by Charles IV in 1357, and connects the Old Town with the Little Quarter. It is now pedestrianized but at one time could take four carriages abreast. Many of the statues on the bridge are copies; the originals are kept in the Lapidarium of the National Museum *(see p162)* and at Vyšehrad *(see p181)*. The Gothic Old Town Bridge Tower *(see p139)* is one of the finest buildings of its kind.

**★ View from Little Quarter Bridge Tower**
The tall pinnacled wedge tower, gives a superb view of the city of 100 spires. The shorter tower is the remains of Judith Bridge.

**St Adalbert, 1709**
Adalbert, Bishop of Prague, founded the Church of St Lawrence *(see p140)* on Petřín Hill in 991. He is known to the Czechs as Vojtěch.

Tower entrance

## KEY

① Little Quarter Bridge Tower

② Judith Bridge Tower, 1158

③ Steps to Saská Street

④ St Wenceslas, 1859

⑤ Christ between St Cosmas and St Damian, 1709

⑥ St Philip Benizi, 1714

⑦ St Cajetan, 1709

⑧ Steps to Kampa Island

⑨ St Nicholas Tolentino, 1708

⑩ St Augustine, 1708

⑪ St Jude Thaddaeus, 1708

⑫ St Francis of Assisi, with two angels, 1855

⑬ St Anthony of Padua, 1707

⑭ St Ludmilla with Little Václav, 1720

**St John de Matha, St Felix de Valois and the Blessed Ivan, 1714**
These saints, sculpted by Ferdinand Brokof, founded the Trinitarian Order of mendicants to collect money to buy the freedom of Christians enslaved by the infidels (represented at the foot of the sculpture).

**St Vitus, 1714**
This engraving of the statue shows the 3rd-century martyr with the lions which were supposed to maul him, but licked him instead. St Vitus is the patron saint of dancers and often invoked against convulsive disorders.

### ★ St Luitgard, 1710

This statue, regarded as the most artistically remarkable on the bridge, was sculpted by Matthias Braun when he was only 26. It is based on the blind Cistercian nun's celebrated vision when Christ appeared and she kissed his wounds.

### ★ St John Nepomuk, 1683

Reliefs on the bridge depict the martyrdom of St John Nepomuk. Here the saint is polished bright from people touching it for good luck.

**St Vincent Ferrer and St Procopius, 1712**
This detail shows a rabbi saddened by St Vincent's success in converting many Jews to Christianity. St Procopius is one of Bohemia's patron saints.

## St John Nepomuk

The cult of St John Nepomuk, canonized in 1729, was promoted by the Jesuits to rival the revered Jan Hus (see p29). Jan Nepomucký, vicar-general of the Archdiocese of Prague, was arrested in 1393 by Wenceslas IV along with the archbishop and others who had displeased him. The king had St John thrown off Charles Bridge, where he drowned. Statues modelled on the one placed here in 1683 are seen throughout central Europe, especially on bridges. Catholics would later argue that St John was killed for failing to reveal the confessions of the queen.

# ⓮ Charles Bridge (Old Town Side)

*Karlův most*

Until 1741, Charles Bridge was the only crossing over the Vltava. It is 520 m (1,706 ft) long and is built of sandstone blocks, rumoured to be strengthened by mixing mortar with eggs. The bridge was commissioned by Charles IV in 1357 to replace the Judith Bridge and built by Peter Parler. The bridge's original decoration was a simple cross. The first statue – of St John Nepomuk – was added in 1683, inspired by Bernini's sculptures on Rome's Ponte Sant'Angelo.

**St Francis Xavier, 1711**
The Jesuit missionary is supported by one Moorish, one Tartar and two Oriental converts, plus a pagan prince awaiting baptism.

**★ 17th-Century Crucifixion**
For 200 years, the wooden crucifix stood alone on the bridge. The gilded Christ dates from 1629 and the Hebrew words "Holy, Holy, Holy Lord", were paid for by a Jew as punishment for blasphemy.

## KEY

① **St Norbert, St Wenceslas and St Sigismund**, 1853

② **St Francis Borgia**, 1710

③ **St John the Baptist**, 1855

④ **St Christopher**, 1857

⑤ **St Cyril and St Methodius**, 1938

⑥ **St Ann**, 1707

⑦ **St Joseph with Jesus**, 1854

⑧ **Pietà**, 1859

⑨ **St Barbara, St Margaret and St Elizabeth**, 1707

⑩ **St Ivo**, 1711

⑪ **Old Town Bridge Tower**

**Thirty Years' War**
In the last hours of this war, the Old Town was saved from the Swedish army. The truce was signed in the middle of the bridge in 1648.

| | | | | | |
|---|---|---|---|---|---|
| | **1357** Charles IV commissions new bridge | **1621** Heads of ten Protestant nobles exhibited on the Old Town Bridge Tower | **1648** Swedes damage part of the bridge and Old Town Bridge Tower | | |
| | **1342** Judith Bridge destroyed by floods | | | *1890 flood damage* | |
| **1100** | **1300** | **1500** | **1700** | | **1900** |
| | **1158** Europe's second medieval stone bridge, Judith Bridge, is built | **1393** St John Nepomuk thrown off Bridge on the orders of Wenceslas IV | | **1890** Three arches destroyed by flood | **1938** Karel Dvořák's sculpture of St Cyril and St Methodius |
| | | *Sculptor Matthias Braun (1684–1738)* | | **1713** Bridge decorated with 21 statues by Braun, Brokof and others | |

**The Madonna, St Dominic and St Thomas, 1708**
The Dominicans, (known in a Latin pun as *Domini canes*, the dogs of God), are shown with the Madonna and their emblem, a dog.

**Madonna and St Bernard, 1709**
Cherubs and symbols of the Passion, including the dice, the cock and the centurion's gauntlet, form part of the statue.

Tower entrance

---

**★ Old Town Bridge Tower**

This magnificent Gothic tower, designed by Peter Parler, was built at the end of the 14th century. An integral part of the Old Town's fortifications, it was badly damaged in 1648 and the west side still bears the scars.

**Bridge Tower sculptures** by Peter Parler include St Vitus, the bridge's patron saint, Charles IV (*left*) and Wenceslas IV.

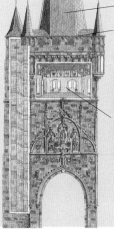

Pinnacled wedge spire

Roof viewing point

**The viewing gallery** is a rib-vaulted room, on the tower's first floor. It provides a wonderful view of Prague Castle and the Little Quarter.

# ㉑ Observation Tower

*Petřínská Rozhledna*

Petřín. **Map** 1 C4. **Tel** 72 49 11 497.
🚋 6, 9, 12, 20, 22, then take funicular railway. 🚌 143, 176. **Open** 10am–10pm daily (Mar, Oct: to 8pm; Nov–Feb: to 6pm). 🅿️ 🔊 ♿ 🖥️
**W** prazskeveze.cz

The most conspicuous landmark in Petřín Park is an imitation of the Eiffel Tower, built for the Jubilee Exhibition of 1891. The octagonally shaped tower is only 60 m (200 ft), a quarter the height of the Eiffel Tower. A spiral staircase of 299 steps leads up to the viewing platform. A lift is also available. On a clear day, you can see as far as Bohemia's highest peak, Sněžka in the Krkonoše (Giant Mountains), 150 km (100 miles) to the northeast.

# ㉒ Mirror Maze

*Zrcadlové Bludiště*

Petřín. **Map** 1 C4. **Tel** 72 49 11 497.
🚋 6, 9, 12, 20, 22, then take funicular railway. 🚌 143, 149, 176, 217. **Open** 10am–10pm daily (Mar, Oct: to 8pm; Nov–Feb: to 6pm). 🅿️ 🔊 ♿
**W** prazskeveze.cz

With its distorting mirrors, the maze (also known as The Labyrinth) is a relic of the Exhibition of 1891, like the Observation Tower. It is in a wooden pavilion in the shape of the old Špička Gate, part of the Gothic fortifications of Vyšehrad *(see pp180–81)*. This amusement house moved to Petřín at the end of the exhibition.

The 100-year-old Observation Tower overlooking the city

When you have navigated your way through the maze, your reward is to view the vivid diorama of *The Defence of Prague against the Swedes,* which took place on Charles Bridge *(see p138)* in 1648, badly damaging the tower.

# ㉓ Church of St Lawrence

*Kostel Sv. Vavřince*

Petřín. **Map** 1 C5. 🚋 12, 20, 22, 69 then take funicular railway. 🚌 176. ✝️ Easter–Oct: 5pm Fri. ♿

According to legend, the church was founded in the 10th century by the pious Prince Boleslav II and St Adalbert on the site of a pagan shrine. The ceiling of the sacristy is decorated with a painting illustrating this legend. The painting dates from the 18th century, when the Romanesque church was swallowed up by a large new Baroque structure, featuring a cupola flanked by two onion-domed towers. The small Calvary Chapel, dating from 1735, is situated to the left of the church.

# ㉔ Štefánik's Observatory

*Štefánikova Hvězdárna*

Petřín 205. **Map** 2 D5. **Tel** 25 73 20 540. 🚋 6, 9, 12, 20, 22, then funicular railway. **Open** Tue–Sun; opening hours vary monthly, so phone ahead or check the website. **Closed** Mon and Oct–Dec. 🅿️ 🔊 ♿
**W** observatory.cz

Since 1930, Prague's amateur astronomers have been able to enjoy the facilities of this observatory on Petřín Hill. You can use its telescopes to view the craters of the moon or unfamiliar distant galaxies. There is an exhibition of old astronomical instruments, and various special events for kids are held on Saturdays and Sundays.

# ㉕ Hunger Wall

*Hladová Zeď*

Újezd, Petřín, Strahovská.
**Map** 2 D5. 🚋 6, 9, 12, 20, 22, then funicular railway. 🚌 143, 176, 217.

The fortifications built around the southern edge of the Little Quarter on the orders of Charles IV in 1360–62 have been known for centuries as the Hunger Wall. Nearly 1,200 m (1,300 yards) of the wall survive, complete with crenellated battlements and a platform for marksmen on its inner side. It runs from Újezd across Petřín Park to Strahov. The story behind the name is that Charles commissioned its construction with the aim of providing employment to the poor during a period of famine. It is true that a great famine did break out in Bohemia in the 1360s, and the two events, the famine and the building of the wall, became permanently associated.

Diorama of *The Defence of Prague against the Swedes* in the Mirror Maze

Nebozízek, the station halfway up Petřín's funicular railway

## ㉖ Petřín Park
*Petřínské Sady*

**Map** 2 D5. 🚋 6, 9, 12, 20, 22, then take funicular railway. *See Four Guided Walks pp176–7.*

To the west of the Little Quarter, Petřín hill rises above the city to a height of 318 m (960 ft). The name derives either from the Slavonic god Perun, to whom sacrifices were made on the hill or from the Latin name Mons Petrinus, meaning "rocky hill". A forest used to stretch from here as far as the White Mountain *(see p33)*. In the 12th century the southern side of the hill was planted with vineyards, but by the 18th century most of these had been transformed into gardens and orchards.

Today a path winds up the slopes of Petřín, offering fine views of Prague. In the park is the *Monument to the Victims of Communism* (2002) by the sculptor Olbram Zoubek and a monument to Romantic poet Karel Hynek Mácha.

## ㉗ Funicular Railway
*Lanová Dráha*

Újezd. **Map** 2 D5. 🚋 6, 9, 12, 20, 22. In operation 9am–11:30pm daily (winter: to 11:20pm). 🎫 (also valid for public transport). ♿ 🌐 **dpp.cz**

Built to carry visitors to the 1891 Jubilee Exhibition up to the Observation Tower at the top of Petřín hill, the funicular was

Statue of Karel Hynek Mácha in Petřín Park

originally powered by water. In this form, it remained in operation until 1914, then between the wars was converted to electricity. In 1965 it had to be shut down because part of the hillside collapsed – coal had been mined here during the 19th century. Shoring up the slope and rebuilding the railway took 20 years, but since its reopening in 1985 it has proved a reliable way of getting up Petřín Hill. At the halfway station, Nebozízek, there is a restaurant *(see p201)* with fine views of the Castle and the city.

## ㉘ Museum of Music
*České Muzeum Hudby*

Karmelitská 2, Praha 1, Malá Strana. **Map** 2 E4. **Tel** 25 72 57 777. Ⓜ Malostranská. 🚋 12, 20, 22. **Open** 10am–6pm Mon, Wed–Sun. 🎫 ♿ 🌐 **nm.cz**

Housed in the former 17th-century Baroque Church of St Magdalene, the Museum of Music seeks to present musical instruments not only as fine specimens of craftsmanship and artistry but also as mediators between man and music.

The museum is run by the National Museum *(see p147)*. Exhibits include a look at the diversity of popular 20th-century music as preserved in film, television, photographs and sound recordings. Also examined is the production of handcrafted instruments, the

history of musical notation and the social occasions linked to certain instruments. Earphones offer high-quality sound reproduction of original recordings made on the instruments displayed. The museum's collections can be accessed via the study room, and there is a listening studio for the library of recordings.

## ㉙ Michna Palace
*Michnův Palác*

Újezd 40. **Map** 2 E4. **Tel** 25 70 07 111. 🚋 12, 20, 22.

In about 1580 Ottavio Aostalli built a summer palace here for the Kinský family on the site of an old Dominican convent. In 1623 the building was bought by Pavel Michna of Vacínov, a supply officer in the Imperial Army, who had grown rich after the Battle of the White Mountain. He commissioned a new Baroque building that he hoped would rival the palace of his late commander, Wallenstein *(see p126)*.

In 1767 the Michna Palace was sold to the army and over the years it became a crumbling ruin. After 1918 it was bought by Sokol (a physical culture association) and converted into a gym and sports centre with a training ground in the old palace garden. The restored palace was renamed Tyrš House in honour of Sokol's founder.

Restored Baroque façade of the Michna Palace (Tyrš House)

# NEW TOWN
## NOVÉ MĚSTO

The New Town, founded in 1348 by Charles IV, was carefully planned and laid out around three large central marketplaces: the Hay Market (Senovážné Square), the Cattle Market (Charles Square) and the Horse Market (Wenceslas Square). Twice as large as the Old Town, the area was mainly inhabited by tradesmen and craftsmen such as blacksmiths, wheelwrights and brewers. During the late 19th century, much of the New Town was demolished and completely redeveloped, giving it the appearance it has today.

## Sights at a Glance

### Churches and Monasteries
2 Church of Our Lady of the Snows
9 Church of St Ignatius
12 Church of St Cyril and
   St Methodius
14 Church of St John
   on the Rock
15 Slavonic Monastery Emauzy
17 Church of St Catherine
20 Church of St Stephen
23 Church of St Ursula

### Historic Buildings
5 Hotel Europa
10 Jesuit College
13 Faust House
21 New Town Hall

### Theatres and Opera Houses
7 State Opera
24 National Theatre pp156–7

### Historic Squares
1 Wenceslas Square
11 Charles Square

### Museums and Galleries
4 Museum of Communism

6 National Museum
8 Mucha Museum
19 Dvořák Museum

### Historic Restaurants and Beer Halls
18 Chalice Restaurant
22 U Fleků

### Parks and Gardens
3 Franciscan Garden
16 Botanical Gardens

☐ **Restaurants** see pp202–204
1 Alcron
2 Bresto
3 Café Louvre
4 Cafe Slavia
5 Celeste
6 Čestr
7 Cicala

8 Como
9 Dynamo
10 El Emir
11 Fama
12 Home Kitchen
13 Klub cestovatelů
14 Miss Saigon
15 Miyabi
16 Nota Bene
17 Novoměstský pivovar
18 Pagana
19 Le Patio
20 Renommé
21 Rotisserie
22 Solidní nejistota
23 Suterén
24 U Emy Destinnové
25 U Pinkasů
26 Ultramarin
27 Universal
28 Žofín
29 Zvonice

See Street Finder maps
3, 4, 5, 6

◄ The marble floor of the Pantheon at the National Museum

For map symbols see back flap

# Street-by-Street: Wenceslas Square

Hotels and restaurants occupy many of the buildings around
Wenceslas Square, though it remains an important commercial centre
– the square began life as a medieval horse market. As you walk along,
look up at the buildings, most of which date from the turn of last
century, when the square was redeveloped. There are fine
examples of the decorative styles used by Czech architects
of the period. Many blocks have dark covered arcades
leading to shops, clubs, theatres and cinemas.

**Koruna Palace** (1914) is
an ornate block of shops
and offices. Its corner
turret is topped with a
crown (*koruna*).

To Powder
Gate

**U Pinkasů** *(see p203)* became
one of Prague's most popular
beer halls when it started
serving Pilsner Urquell
*(see pp196–7)* in 1843.

NA PŘÍKOPĚ

Můstek Ⓜ

❷ **Church of Our Lady
of the Snows**
The towering Gothic building is only part of a vast
church planned during the
14th century.

Můstek Ⓜ

Můs

VODIČKOVA

❸ **Franciscan Garden**
An old monastery garden has
been laid out as a small park
with this fountain, rosebeds,
trellises and a children's
playground.

Lucerna
Palace

**Jungmann Square** is named after Josef
Jungmann (1773–1847), an influential scholar of
language and lexicographer, and there is a
statue of him in the middle. The Adria Palace
(1925) used to be the Laterna Magika Theatre
*(see p218)*, which was where Václav Havel's Civic
Forum worked in the early days of the 1989
Velvet Revolution.

**Wiehl House**, named after its architect Antonín
Wiehl, was completed in 1896. The five-storey
building is in striking Neo-Renaissance style, with
aloggia and colourful *sgraffito*. Mikuláš Aleš
designed some of the Art Nouveau figures.

**❶ ★ Wenceslas Square**
The dominant features of the square are the bronze, equestrian statue of St Wenceslas (1912) and the National Museum behind it. St Wenceslas, a former prince who was murdered by his brother Boleslav, is the patron saint of Bohemia.

**Locator Map**
*See Central Prague Map pp16–17*

**The Assicurazioni Generali Building** was where Franz Kafka *(see p70)* worked as an insurance clerk for 10 months in 1906–7.

**❺ ★ Hotel Europa**
Both the façade and the interior of the hotel (1906) preserve most of their original Art Nouveau features.

Café Tramvaj 11

DRTISSKÁ

**The Monument to the Victims of Communism** is close to the spot where Jan Palach immolated himself in 1969 in protest at the Warsaw Pact invasion. An unofficial shrine has been maintained here since 1989.

**❻ ★ National Museum**
The grand building with its monumental staircase was completed in 1890 as a symbol of national prestige.

St Wenceslas Monument

VÁCLAVSKÉ NÁMĚSTÍ

OPLETALOVA

WILSONOVA

SMEČKÁCH

KRAKOVSKÁ

Muzeum Ⓜ

Fénix Palace

Muzeum Ⓜ

0 metres 100
0 yards 100

**❼ State Opera**
Meticulously refurbished in the 1980s, the interior retains the luxurious red plush, crystal chandeliers and gilded stucco of the original late-19th-century theatre.

Memorial to Jan Palach, who died in protest against communism.

**Key**

— Suggested route

**For key to symbols** *see back flap*

Wenceslas Monument in Wenceslas Square

# ❶ Wenceslas Square

*Václavské Náměstí*

**Map** 3 C5. Ⓜ Můstek, Muzeum.
🚋 3, 9, 14, 24.

The square has witnessed many key events in Czech history. It was here that the student Jan Palach burnt himself to death in 1969, and in November 1989 a protest rally in the square against police brutality led to the Velvet Revolution and the overthrow of Communism.

Wenceslas "Square" is something of a misnomer, for it is some 750 m (825 yd) long and only 60 m (65 yd) wide. Originally a horse market, today it is lined with hotels, restaurants, clubs and shops, reflecting the seamier side of global consumerism. The huge equestrian statue of St Wenceslas that looks the length of the square from in front of the National Museum was erected in 1912. Cast in bronze, it is the work of Josef Myslbek, the leading Czech sculptor of the late 19th century. At the foot of the pedestal there are several other statues of Czech patron saints. A memorial near the statue commemorates the victims of the former regime.

# ❷ Church of Our Lady of the Snows

*Kostel Panny Marie Sněžné*

Jungmannovo náměstí 18. **Map** 3 C5.
**Tel** 22 22 46 243. Ⓜ Můstek. **Open** 7am–8pm Mon–Fri, 8am–8pm Sat & Sun. ✝ 7am, 8am, 6pm Mon–Fri, 8am, 6pm Sat, 9am, 10:15am, 11:30am, 6pm Sun. ♿ 🌐 **pms.ofm.cz**

Charles IV founded this church to mark his coronation in 1347. The name refers to a 4th-century miracle in Rome, when the Virgin Mary appeared to the pope in a dream telling him to build a church to her on the spot where snow fell in August. Charles's church was never completed, and the building we see today was just the presbytery of the projected church. Over 33 m (110 ft) high, it was finished in 1397, and was originally part of a Carmelite monastery. On the northern side there is a gateway with a 14th-century pediment that marked the entrance to the church graveyard.

A steeple was added in the early 1400s, but further building was halted by the Hussite Wars (*see pp28–9*). The Hussite firebrand Jan Želivský preached at the church and was buried here after his execution in 1422. The church suffered damage in the wars, and in 1434 the steeple was destroyed. For a long time the church was left to decay. In 1603 Franciscans restored the building. The intricate net vaulting of the ceiling dates from this period, the original roof having collapsed. Most of the interior decoration, apart from the 1450s pewter font,

is Baroque. The monumental three-tiered altar is crowded with statues of saints, and is crowned with a crucifix.

# ❸ Franciscan Garden

*Františkánská Zahrada*

Jungmannovo náměstí 18. **Map** 3 C5.
Ⓜ Můstek. **Open** Apr–Sep: 7am–10pm (Oct: to 8pm; Nov–Mar: 8am–7pm). ♿

Originally the garden of a Franciscan monastery, the area was opened to the public in 1950 as a tranquil oasis close to Wenceslas Square. By the entrance is a Gothic portal leading down to a cellar restaurant – U Františkánů (At the Franciscans). In the 1980s several of the beds were replanted with herbs, cultivated by the Franciscans in the 17th century.

# ❹ Museum of Communism

*Národní Muzeum*

Na Příkopě 10. **Map** 3 C4. **Tel** 22 42 12 966. Ⓜ Můstek. **Open** 9am–9pm daily. 🌐 **muzeumkomunismu.cz**

This museum explores how Communism affected various areas of Prague society, such as politics, sports and everyday life, during the totalitarian regime of 1948 to 1989.

On display are original artifacts, gathered from the museum's archive, along with other rare items acquired from public and private collections. These include photos, propaganda material and film footage. There is also a recreation of an interrogation room, complete with a spotlight and a typewriter.

A view of the Church of Our lady of the Snows from the Franciscan gardens

Façade of the State Opera, formerly the New German Theatre

pulled down in 1885 to make way for the present building. This was originally known as the New German Theatre, built to rival the Czechs' National Theatre (see pp156–7). A Neo-Classical frieze decorates the pediment above the columned loggia at the front of the theatre. The figures include Dionysus and Thalia, the muse of comedy. The interior is stuccoed, and original paintings in the auditorium and on the curtain have been preserved. In 1945 the theatre became the city's main opera house.

# ❺ Hotel Europa
*Hotel Evropa*

Václavské náměstí 25. **Map** 4 D5. **Tel** 22 42 15 387. Ⓜ Můstek. 🚋 3, 9, 14, 24. ✉ ♿ 🌐 **evropahotel.cz**

Though a trifle shabby in places, the Europa Hotel is a wonderfully preserved reminder of the golden age of hotels. It was built in highly decorated Art Nouveau style between 1903 and 1906. Not only has its splendid façade crowned with gilded nymphs survived, but many of the interiors on the ground floor have remained virtually intact, including all the original bars, large mirrors, panelling and light fittings.

# ❻ National Museum
*Národní Muzeum*

Václavské náměstí 68. **Map** 6 E1. **Tel** 22 44 97 111. Ⓜ Muzeum. **Closed** until 2015; visit building at Vinohradská 1 from 10am–6pm daily until then. 🌐 **nm.cz**

The vast Neo-Renaissance building at one end of Wenceslas Square houses the National Museum. Designed by Josef Schulz as a triumphal affirmation of the Czech national revival, it was completed in 1890. The entrance is reached by a ramp decorated with allegorical statues. Seated by the door are History and Natural History.
The building is undergoing extensive restoration, which is expected to be complete in 2015. Until then, temporary

exhibitions are housed in a nearby building formerly known as Radio Free Europe. The collections are mainly devoted to mineralogy, archaeology, anthropology, numismatics and natural history. A Pantheon also contains busts and statues of Czech scholars, writers and artists.

# ❼ State Opera
*Státní Opera*

Wilsonova 4/Legerova 75. **Map** 4 E5. **Tel** 22 49 01 866. Ⓜ Muzeum. 🚋 3, 9, 14, 24. **Open** for performances only. *See Entertainment p218 & p220.* 🌐 **opera.cz**

The first theatre built here, the New Town Theatre, was

# ❽ Mucha Museum
*Muchovo Muzeum*

Panská 7. **Map** 4 D4. **Tel** 22 42 16 415. Ⓜ Můstek, Náměstí Republiky. 🚋 3, 9, 14, 24, 26. **Open** 10am–6pm daily. 📷 💻 🌐 **mucha.cz**

The 18th-century Kaunicky Palace is home to the first museum dedicated to this Czech master of Art Nouveau. A selection of more than 100 exhibits include paintings and drawings, sculptures, photographs and personal memorabilia. The central courtyard becomes a terrace for the café in the summer, and there is a museum shop offering exclusive gifts with Mucha motifs.

Main staircase of the National Museum

# Art Nouveau in Prague

The decorative style known as Art Nouveau originated in Paris in the 1890s. It quickly became international as most of the major European cities quickly responded to its graceful, flowing forms. In Prague it was called "Secese" and at its height in the first decade of the 20th century, dying out during World War I, when it seemed frivolous and even decadent. There is a wealth of Art Nouveau in Prague, both in the fine and decorative arts and in architecture. In the New Town and the Jewish Quarter (see pp82–95), entire streets were demolished at the turn of the century and built in the new style.

**Praha House**
This house was built in 1903 for the Prague Insurance Company. Its name is in gilt Art Nouveau letters at the top.

## Architecture

Art Nouveau made its first appearance in Prague at the Jubilee exhibition of 1891. Architecturally, the new style was a deliberate attempt to break with the 19th-century tradition of monumental buildings. In Art Nouveau the important aspect was ornament, either painted or sculpted, often in the form of a female figure, applied to a fairly plain surface. This technique was ideally suited to wrought iron and glass, popular at the turn of the century. These materials were light but strong. The effect of this, together with Art Nouveau decoration, created buildings of lasting beauty.

**Hotel Central**
Built by Alois Dryák and Bedřich Bendelmayer in 1900, the façade of this hotel has plasterwork shaped like tree branches.

**Hlahol Choir Building, 1905**
The architect Josef Fanta embellished this building with mosaics and sculptures by Karl Mottl and Josef Pekárek (see also p142).

**Hotel Meran**
Finished in 1904, this grand Art Nouveau building is notable for its fine detailing inside and out.

Ornate pilasters

Decorative statues

Brass and wrought-iron balustrade

**Hlavní nádraží**
Prague's main railway station was completed in 1901. With its huge interior glazed dome and elegant sculptural decoration, it shows many Art Nouveau features.

## Decorative and Fine Arts

Many painters, sculptors and graphic artists were influenced by Art Nouveau. One of the most successful exponents of the style was the artist Alfons Mucha (1860–1939). He is celebrated chiefly for his posters. Yet he designed stained glass (see p104), furniture, jewellery, even postage stamps. It is perhaps here, in the decorative and applied arts, that Art Nouveau had its fullest expression in Prague. Artists adorned every type of object – doorknobs, curtain ornaments, vases and cutlery – with tentacle- and plant-like forms in imitation of the natural world from which they drew their inspiration.

**Postage Stamp, 1918**
A bold stamp design by Alfons Mucha marked the founding of the Czechoslovak Republic.

**Poster for Sokol Movement**
Mucha's colour lithograph for the sixth national meeting of the Sokol gymnastic movement (1912) is in Tyrš's Museum (Physical Culture and Sports).

### Záboj and Slavoj
These mythical figures (invented by a forger of old legends) were carved by Josef Myslbek for Palacký Bridge in 1895. They are now in Vyšehrad.

**Glass Vase**
This iridescent green vase made of Bohemian glass has relief decoration of intertwined threads. It is in the Museum of Decorative Arts.

**Curtain Ornament and Candlestick**
The silver and silk ornament adorns the Mayor's room of the Municipal House. The candlestick by Emanuel Novák with fine leaf design is in the Museum of Decorative Arts.

### Where to See Art Nouveau in Prague

Detail of doorway, Široká 9, Jewish Quarter

**Architecture**
Apartment Building, Na příkopě 7
Hanavský Pavilion p161
Hlahol Choir Building, Masarykovo nábřeží 10
Hlavní nádraží, Wilsonova
Hotel Central, Hybernská 10
Hotel Evropa p146
Industrial Palace p160 and Four Guided Walks pp178–9
Ministerstvo pro místní rozvoj p69
Municipal House p66
Palacký Bridge (Palackého most)
Praha House, Národní třída 7
Wiehl House p144

**Painting**
Trades Fair Palace pp164–5

**Sculpture**
Jan Hus Monument p72
Vyšehrad Garden and Cemetery p160 and Four Guided Walks pp180–81

**Decorative Arts**
Mucha Museum p147
Museum of Decorative Arts p86
Prague Museum p161

# Street-by-Street: Charles Square

The southern part of the New Town resounds to the rattle of trams, as many routes converge in this part of Prague. Fortunately, the park in Charles Square (Karlovo náměstí) offers a peaceful and welcome retreat. Some of the buildings around the Square belong to the University and the statues in the centre represent writers and scientists, reflecting the academic environment. There are several Baroque buildings and towards the river stands the historic 14th-century Slavonic Monastery.

**The Czech Technical University** was founded here in 1867 in a grand Neo-Renaissance building.

Charles Square Centre

Church of St Wenceslas

RESSLOVA

VÁCLAVSKÁ

KARLO

NA MORÁNI

**⑫ ★ Church of St Cyril and St Methodius**
A plaque and a bullet-scarred wall are reminders of a siege in 1942, when German troops attacked Czech and Slovak paratroopers hiding here after assassinating Nazi Reinhard Heydrich.

To the river

**⑪ ★ Charles Square**
The centre of the square is a pleasant 19th-century park with lawns, formal flowerbeds, fountains and statues.

To metro Karlovo náměstí

Church of St Cosmas and St Damian

VYŠEHRADSKÁ

POD SLOVANY

**⑮ Slavonic Monastery Emauzy**
In 1965 a pair of modern concrete spires by František Černý were added to the church of the 14th-century monastery.

TROJICKÁ

**⑭ Church of St John on the Rock**
This view of the organ and ceiling shows the dynamic Baroque design of Kilian Ignaz Dientzenhofer.

**9 Church of St Ignatius**
The sun rays and gilded cherubs on the side altars are typical of the gaudy decoration in this Baroque church built for the Jesuits.

**Eliška Krásnohorská** was a 19th-century poet who wrote the libretti for Smetana's operas. A statue of her was put up here in 1931.

**Locator Map**
See Central Prague Map pp16–17

JEČNÁ

**A statue of Jan Purkyně** *(1787–1869)*, an eminent physiologist and pioneer of cell theory, was erected in 1961. It is the most recent of the many memorials in the square.

**10 Jesuit College**
Founded in the mid-17th century, this imposing building has been a hospital since the suppression of the Jesuits in 1773 *(see pp32–3)*.

U NEMOCNICE

18th-century Institute of Gentlewomen (now a hospital)

**13 Faust House**
In the 18th century this house was owned by Count Ferdinand Mladota of Solopysky. The chemical experiments he performed reinforced the associations that gave the building its name.

BENÁTSKÁ

0 metres 100
0 yards 100

**16 Botanical Gardens**
Though part of the Charles University, the gardens are open to the public and are known for their profusion of rare plants. They make a pleasant place to relax.

**Key**
— Suggested route

**For key to symbols** see back flap

Sculptures on the façade of the Jesuit College by Tomasso Soldati

# ❾ Church of St Ignatius
*Kostel Sv. Ignáce*

Ječná 2. **Map** 5 C2. **Tel** 22 19 90 200.
🚇 Karlovo náměstí. 🚊 3, 4, 6, 10, 16, 18, 21, 22, 24. **Open** 6am–6:30pm daily. 🕇 6:30am, 7:30am, 5:30pm Mon–Sat, 7am, 9am, 11am, 5:30pm Sun.

With its wealth of gilding and flamboyant stucco decoration, St Ignatius is typical of the Baroque churches built by the Jesuits to impress people with the glamour of their faith. The architects – Carlo Lurago, who started work on the church in 1665, and Paul Ignaz Bayer, who added the tower in 1687 – were also responsible for the adjoining Jesuit College.

The painting on the high altar of *The Glory of St Ignatius* (St Ignatius Loyola, the founder of the Jesuit order) is by Jan Jiří Heinsch.

The Jesuits continued to embellish the interior right up until the suppression of their order in 1773, adding stuccowork and statues of Jesuit and Czech saints.

# ❿ Jesuit College
*Jezuitská Kolej*

Karlovo náměstí 36. **Map** 5 B2.
🚇 Karlovo náměstí. 🚊 3, 4, 6, 10, 14, 16, 18, 21, 22, 24. **Closed** to the public.

Half the eastern side of Charles Square is occupied by the former college of the Jesuit order in the New Town. As in other parts of Prague, the Jesuits were able to demolish huge swathes of the city to put up another bastion of their formidable education system. The college was built between 1656 and 1702 by Carlo Lurago and Paul Ignaz Bayer. The two sculptured portals are the work of Johann Georg Wirch who extended the building in 1770. After the suppression of the Jesuit order in 1773, the college was converted into a military hospital. It is now part of Charles University.

# ⓫ Charles Square
*Karlovo Náměstí*

**Map** 5 B2. 🚇 Karlovo náměstí.
🚊 3, 4, 6, 10, 16, 18, 21, 22, 24.

Since the mid-19th century the square has been a park. Though surrounded by busy roads, it is a pleasant place to sit and read or watch people exercising their dachshunds.

The square began life as a vast cattle market, when Charles IV founded the New Town in 1348. Other goods sold in the square included firewood, coal and pickled herring from barrels. In the centre of the market Charles had a wooden tower built, where the coronation jewels were put on display once a year. In 1382 the tower was replaced by a chapel, from which, in 1437, concessions made to the Hussites by the pope at the Council of Basle were read out to the populace.

# ⓬ Church of St Cyril and St Methodius
*Kostel Sv. Cyrila A Metoděje*

Resslova 9. **Map** 5 B2. **Tel** 22 49 20 686.
🚇 Karlovo náměstí. 🚊 3, 4, 6, 10, 16, 18, 22, 24. **Open** 9am–5pm Tue–Sun (Nov–Mar: Tue–Sat). 🕇 8am Wed, 8am, 5pm Sat, 9:30am Sun. 🚻 ✉ ♿
🌐 pravoslavnacirkev.cz

This Baroque church, with a pilastered façade and a small central tower, was built in the 1730s. It was dedicated to St Charles Borromeo and served as the church of a community of retired priests, but both were closed in 1783. In the 1930s the church was restored and given to the Czechoslovak Orthodox Church, and rededicated to St Cyril and St Methodius, the 9th-century "Apostles to the Slavs" *(see pp22–3)*. In May 1942 parachutists who assassinated Reinhard Heydrich, the Nazi governor of Czechoslovakia, hid in the crypt along with members of the Czech Resistance. Surrounded by German troops, they took their own lives rather than surrender. Bullet holes made by German machine guns during the siege can still be seen below the memorial plaque on the outer wall of the crypt, which now houses a museum of these times.

Main altar in the Church of St Cyril and St Methodius

# ❸ Faust House
*Faustův Dům*

Karlovo náměstí 40, 41. **Map** 5 B3. 🚇 Karlovo náměstí. 🚋 3, 4, 10, 16, 18, 21, 24. **Closed** to the public.

Prague thrives on legends of alchemy and pacts with the devil, and this Baroque mansion has attracted many. There has been a house here since the 14th century when it belonged to Prince Václav of Opava, an alchemist and natural historian. In the 16th century it was owned by the alchemist Edward Kelley. The chemical experiments of Count Ferdinand Mladota of Solopysky, who owned the house in the mid-18th century, gave rise to its association with the legend of Faust.

Baroque façade of Faust House

# ❹ Church of St John on the Rock
*Kostel Sv. Jana Na Skalce*

Vyšehradská 49. **Map** 5 B3. **Tel** 22 19 79 325. 🚋 3, 4, 10, 16, 22, 24. **Open** for services only. ✝ 11am Sun. ♿

One of Prague's smaller Baroque churches, St John on the Rock is one of Kilian Ignaz Dientzen-hofer's most daring designs. Its twin square towers are set at a sharp angle to the church's narrow façade and the interior is based on an octagonal floorplan. The church was completed in 1738, but the double staircase leading up to the west front was not added until the 1770s. On the high altar there is a wooden version of Jan Brokof's statue of St John Nepomuk *(see p137)* which stands on the Charles Bridge.

# ❺ Slavonic Monastery Emauzy
*Klášter Na Slovanech-Emauzy*

Vyšehradská 49. **Map** 5 B3. **Tel** 22 49 17 662. 🚋 3, 4, 10, 16, 18, 21, 24. Monastery church: **Open** 11am–5pm Mon–Fri (also Sat in summer). Cloisters: **Open** by appt. ✝ 10am daily. ♿ 🚫 ♿ **w** emauzy.cz

Both the monastery and its church were almost destroyed in an American air raid in 1945. During their reconstruction, the church was given a pair of modern reinforced concrete spires.

The monastery was founded in 1347 for the Croatian Benedictines, whose services were held in the Old Slavonic language, hence its name "Na Slovanech". In the course of Prague's tumultuous religious history it has since changed hands many times. In 1446 a Hussite order was formed here, then in 1635 the monastery was acquired by Spanish Benedictines. In the 18th century the complex was given a thorough Baroque treatment, but in 1880 it was taken over by some German Benedictines, who rebuilt almost everything in Neo-Gothic style. The monastery has managed to preserve some historically important 14th-century wall paintings in the cloister, though many were damaged in World War II.

Remains of 14th-century wall paintings in the Slavonic Monastery

# ❻ Botanical Gardens
*Botanická Zahrada*

Na slupi 16. **Map** 5 B3. **Tel** 22 19 51 879. 🚋 18, 24. Glasshouses: **Open** 10am–5pm daily (Feb, Mar: to 4pm; Nov–Jan: to 3:30pm). Gardens: **Open** 10am–7:30pm daily (Feb, Mar: to 5pm; Sep, Oct: to 6pm; Nov–Jan: to 4pm). ♿ 🚫 ♿ **w** bz-uk.cz

Charles IV founded Prague's first botanical garden in the 14th century. This is a much later institution. The university garden was founded in the Smíchov district in 1775 but moved here in 1897. The huge greenhouses date from 1938.

Special botanical exhibitions and shows of exotic birds and tropical fish are often held here. One star attraction of the gardens is the giant water lily, *Victoria cruziana,* whose huge leaves can support a small child. During the summer it produces dozens of flowers that only survive for a day.

Entrance to the university's Botanical Gardens

Octagonal steeple of St Catherine's

### ⓱ Church of St Catherine

*Kostel Sv. Kateřiny*

Kateřinská 30. **Map** 5 C3. ⚇ 4, 6, 10, 16, 22. **Closed** to the public.

St Catherine's stands in the garden of a former convent, founded in 1354 by Charles IV to commemorate his victory at the Battle of San Felice in Italy in 1332. In 1420, during the Hussite revolution *(see pp28–9)*, the convent was demolished, but in the following century it was rebuilt by Kilian Ignáz Dientzenhofer as an Augustinian monastery. The monks remained here until 1787, when the monastery closed. Since 1822 it has been used as a hospital. In 1737 a new Baroque church was built, but the slender steeple of the old Gothic church was retained. Its octagonal shape has gained it the nickname of "the Prague minaret".

### ⓲ Chalice Restaurant

*Restaurace U Kalicha*

Na bojišti 12–14. **Map** 6 D3. **Tel** 22 49 12 557. Ⓜ IP Pavlova. ⚇ 4, 6, 10, 16, 22. **Open** 11am–11pm daily (book ahead). ♿ Ⓦ **ukalicha.cz**

This Pilsner Urquell beer hall owes its fame to the novel *The Good Soldier Švejk* by Jaroslav Hašek. It was Švejk's favourite drinking place and the establishment trades on the popularity of the best-known character in 20th-century Czech literature. The staff dress in period costume from World War I, the era of this novel.

### ⓳ Dvořák Museum

*Muzeum Antonína Dvořáka*

Ke Karlovu 20. **Map** 6 D2. **Tel** 22 49 23 363. Ⓜ IP Pavlova. ⚌ 291. **Open** 10am–1:30pm, 2–5pm Tue–Sun and for concerts. 📷 ♿ Ⓦ **nm.cz**

One of the most enchanting secular buildings of the Prague Baroque now houses the Antonín Dvořák Museum. On display are Dvořák scores and editions of his works, plus photographs and memorabilia of the great 19th-century Czech composer, including his piano, viola and desk.

The building is by the great Baroque architect Kilian Ignaz Dientzenhofer *(see p129)*. Just two storeys high with an elegant tiered mansard roof, the house was completed in 1720, for the Michnas of Vacínov and was originally known as the Michna Summer Palace. It later became known as Villa Amerika, after a nearby inn called Amerika. Between the two pavilions flanking the house is a fine iron gateway, a replica of the Baroque original. In the 19th century the villa and garden fell into decay. The garden statues and vases, from the workshop of Matthias Braun, date from about 1735. They are original but heavily restored, as is the interior of the palace. The ceiling and walls of the large room on the first floor are decorated with 18th-century frescoes by Jan Ferdinand Schor.

### ⓴ Church of St Stephen

*Kostel Sv. Štěpána*

Štěpánská. **Map** 5 C2. **Tel** 22 19 90 224. ⚇ 4, 10, 16, 22. **Open** only for services. ⛪ 11am Sun. 📷

Founded by Charles IV in 1351 as the parish church of the upper New Town, St Stephen's was finished in 1401 with the completion of the multi-spired steeple. In the late 17th century the Branberg Chapel was built on to the north side of the church. It contains the tomb of the prolific Baroque sculptor Matthias Braun.

Most of the subsequent Baroque additions were removed when the church was scrupulously re-Gothicized in the 1870s by Josef Mocker. There are several fine Baroque paintings, however, including *The Baptism of Christ* by Karel Škréta at the end of the

Villa Amerika, home of the Dvořák Museum

Gothic pulpit in St Stephen's

left hand aisle and a picture of St John Nepomuk *(see p137)* by Jan Jiří Heinsch to the left of the 15th-century pulpit. The church's greatest treasure is undoubtedly a beautiful Gothic panel painting of the Madonna, known as *Our Lady of St Stephen's*, which dates from 1472.

Impressive façade of the New Town Hall

## ㉑ New Town Hall
*Novoměstská Radnice*

Karlovo náměstí 23. **Map** 5 B1. ☑ Karlovo náměstí. ☐ 3, 4, 6, 10, 16, 18, 21, 22, 24. **Tel** 22 49 48 229. Tower: **Open** 10am–6pm daily. ☑ **nrpraha.cz**

In 1960 a statue of Hussite preacher Jan Želivský was unveiled in front of the New Town Hall. It commemorates the first and bloodiest of many

defenestrations. On 30 July 1419 Želivský led a crowd of demonstrators to the Town Hall to demand the release of some prisoners. When they were refused, they stormed the building and threw the Catholic councillors out of the windows. Those who survived the fall were finished off with pikes.

The Town Hall already existed in the 1300s; the Gothic tower was added in the mid-15th century and contains an 18th-century chapel. In the 16th century it acquired an arcaded courtyard. After the joining-up of the four towns of Prague in 1784, the Town Hall ceased to be the seat of the municipal administration and became a courthouse and a prison. It is now used for cultural and social events.

## ㉒ U Fleků

Křemencova 11. **Map** 5 B1. **Tel** 22 49 34 019. ☑ Národní třída, Karlovo náměstí (closed till 2015). ☐ 3, 4, 6, 9, 10, 16 18, 22, 24. Museum: **Open** 10am–4pm Mon–Fri. ☑ ☑ ☑ ☑ **ufleku.cz**

Records indicate that beer was brewed here as early as 1459. This archetypal Prague beer hall has been fortunate in its owners, who have kept up the tradition of brewing as an art rather than just a means of

making money. In 1762 the brewery was purchased by Jakub Flekovský, who named it U Fleků (At the Fleks). The present brewery, the smallest in Prague, makes a special strong, dark beer. There is also a small museum of Czech brewing history and a restaurant, which is popular with tourists. Note, any welcome drinks will be added to your bill.

U Fleků, beer hall exterior, clock,

## ㉓ Church of St Ursula
*Kostel Sv. Voršily*

Národní 8. **Map** 3 A5. **Tel** 22 49 30 577. ☑ Národní třída (closed till 2015). ☐ 6, 9, 18, 22. ☐ 5pm daily (8am for schools). For tours, call 22 49 30 511. **Concerts** ☑

The delightful Baroque church of St Ursula was built as part of an Ursuline convent founded in 1672. The original sculptures still decorate the façade and in front of the church stands a group of statues featuring St John Nepomuk (1747) by Ignaz Platzer the Elder. The light airy interior has a frescoed, stuccoed ceiling and on the various altars there are lively Baroque paintings. The main altar has one of St Ursula.

The adjoining convent has been returned to the Ursuline order and is now a Catholic school. In the building on the right-hand side of the church is the entrance to the Institute of Endocrinology.

# ㉔ National Theatre

*Národní Divadlo*

This gold-crested theatre has always been an important symbol of the Czech cultural revival. Work started in 1868, funded largely by voluntary contributions. The original Neo-Renaissance design was by the Czech architect Josef Zítek. After its destruction by fire *(see opposite)*, Josef Schulz was given the job of rebuilding the theatre and all the best Czech artists of the period contributed towards its lavish and spectacular decoration. During the late 1970s and early 1980s the theatre was restored and the New Stage was built by architect Karel Prager.

The theatre from Marksmen's Island

★ **Auditorium**
The elaborately painted ceiling is adorned with allegorical figures representing the arts by František Ženíšek.

## KEY

① **The five arcades** of the loggia are decorated with lunette paintings by Josef Tulka, entitled Five Songs.

② **The New Stage auditorium**

③ **Laterna Magika**

④ **A bronze three-horse chariot**, designed by Bohuslav Schnirch, carries the Goddess of Victory.

⑤ **The startling** sky-blue roof covered with stars, is said to symbolize the summit all artists should aim for.

★ **Lobby Ceiling**
This ceiling fresco is the final part of a triptych painted by František Ženíšek in 1878 depicting the *Golden Age of Czech Art.*

**★ Stage Curtain**
This sumptuous gold and red stage curtain, showing the origin of the theatre, is the work of Vojtěch Hynais.

**VISITORS' CHECKLIST**

**Practical Information**
Národní 2, Nové Město.
**Map** 3 A5.
**Tel** 22 49 01 448.
Box office: **Open** 8am–4pm daily.
Auditorium: **Open** only during performances. 🛗

**Transport**
Ⓜ Národní třída, line B. 🚋 6, 9, 17, 18, 21, 22 to Národní divadlo.

**Façade Decoration**
This standing figure on the attic of the western façade is one of many figures representing the Arts sculpted by Antonín Wagner in 1883.

**The President's Box**
The former royal box, lined in red velvet, is decorated with famous historical figures from Czech history by Václav Brožík.

## National Theatre Fire

On 12 August, 1881, just days before the official opening, the National Theatre was completely gutted by fire. It was thought to have been started by metalworkers on the roof. But just six weeks later, enough money had been collected to rebuild the theatre. It was finally opened two years late in 1883 with a performance of Czech composer Bedřich Smetana's opera *Libuše (see p81)*.

# FURTHER AFIELD

Visitors to Prague, finding the old centre packed with sights, tend to ignore the suburbs. It is true that once you start exploring away from the centre, the language can become more of a problem. However, it is well worth the effort, first to escape the crowds of tourists milling around the Castle and the Old Town Square, and second to realize that Prague is a living city as well as a picturesque time capsule. Most of the museums and other sights in the first part of this section are easily reached by Metro, tram or even on foot. If you are prepared to venture a little further, do not miss the grand palace at Troja or the monastery at Břevnov – which was the first in Bohemia, founded in 993, and later rebuilt in Baroque style. The Day Trips *(pp168–71)* include visits to castles close to Prague and the historic spa towns of Marienbad and Karlsbad, which attracted the first tourists to Bohemia during the 19th century.

## Sights at a Glance

**Museums and Galleries**
**5** Prague Museum
**7** National Technical
Museum
**8** *Trade Fair Palace*
*pp164–5*
**12** Villa Müller

**Monasteries**
**13** Břevnov Monastery

**Cemeteries**
**2** Olšany Cemeteries

**Historic Districts**
**1** Vyšehrad
**3** Žižkov
**4** Náměstí Míru

**Historic Sites**
**14** White Mountain and
Star Hunting Lodge

**Historic Buildings**
**10** *Troja Palace pp166–7*

**Parks and Gardens**
**6** Letná Park
**9** Exhibition Ground and
Stromovka Park
**11** Zoo

### Key

| | |
|---|---|
| ▨ | Central Prague |
| ▨ | Greater Prague |
| ▬ | Major road |
| = | Minor road |

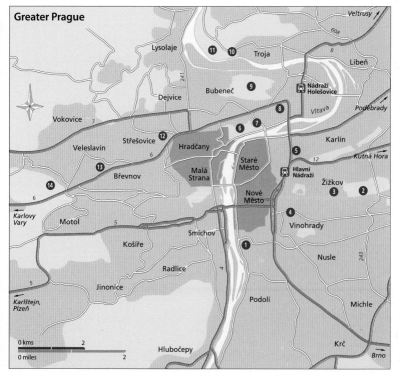

◀ A view of the splendid Imperial Hall in Troja Palace

For map symbols *see back flap*

Vyšehrad Cemetery, where some of Prague's most famous figures are buried

# ❶ Vyšehrad

**Map** 5 B5. Ⓜ Vyšehrad. 🚊 3, 6, 7, 17, 18, 24.

A rocky outcrop above the Vltava, Vyšehrad means "castle on the heights" *(see pp180–81)*. It was fortified in the 10th century and, at times, used as the seat of the Přemyslid princes *(see p22–23)*. The area has great historical and mythological significance, and in the 1870s it became the site of a national cemetery. Many luminaries of Czech culture are buried here, including the composers Antonín Dvořák *(see p154)* and Bedřich Smetana *(see p81)*, who paid tribute to the second seat of the Přemyslid dynasty in his opera *Libuše (see p34)*. Each year,

Well-tended grave in the eastern part of the Olšany Cemeteries

a service is held at Smetana's grave to mark the beginning of the Prague Spring International Music Festival *(see p52)*.

Within the walls of Vyšehrad are many fascinating sights, such as the huge twin-spired Church of St Peter and St Paul, the 11th-century Rotunda of St Martin, the mysterious Devil's Column and the castle walls themselves *(see pp180–81)*. From these walls, there are superb views over the Vltava river and across to Prague, which can be particulary lovely at sunset. Vyšehrad Park, with its tree-lined paths, is ideal for a relaxing stroll.

The streets around the fortress are also worth exploring. There are some fine examples of Cubist houses, built by Josef Chochol, on Rašínovo nábřeží, Libušina and the corner of Přemyslova and Neklanova.

# ❷ Olšany Cemeteries

*Olšanské Hřbitovy*

Vinohradská 153, Jana Želivského. **Tel** 26 73 10 652. Ⓜ Želivského. 🚊 5, 10, 11, 16, 26. **Open** Mar, Apr, Oct: 8am–6pm daily; May–Sep: 8am–7pm daily; Nov–Feb: 8am–5pm daily. .

At the northwest corner of the main cemetery stands the small Church of St Roch (1682), protector against the plague – the first cemetery was founded here in 1679 specifically for the burial of plague victims. In the course of the 19th century, the old cemetery was enlarged and new ones developed, including a Russian cemetery, distinguished

by its old-fashioned Orthodox church (1924–5), and a Jewish cemetery, where Franz Kafka *(see p70)* is buried. Tombs include those of painter Josef Mánes (1820–71) who worked during the Czech Revival movement *(see pp34–5)*, and Josef Jungmann (1773–1847), compiler of a five-volume Czech–German dictionary.

Equestrian statue of Jan Žižka

# ❸ Žižkov

Ⓜ Florenc. National Memorial Vitkov, U památníku 1900. **Tel** 22 27 81 676. 🚌 133, 175. **Open** 10am–6pm Wed–Sun. 🅿 🖥 🆆 **nm.cz**

This quarter of Prague was the scene of a historic victory for the Hussites *(see pp28–9)* over Crusaders sent by the Emperor Sigismund to destroy them. On 14 July 1420 on Vítkov hill, a tiny force of Hussites defeated an army of several thousand well-armed men. The determined, hymn-singing Hussites were led by the one-eyed Jan Žižka.

In 1877 the area around Vítkov was renamed Žižkov in honour of Žižka's victory, and in 1950 a bronze equestrian statue of Žižka by Bohumil Kafka was erected on the hill. About 9m (30 ft) high, this is the largest equestrian statue in the world. It stands in front of the National Memorial, built in 1928–38 in honour of the Czechoslovak legionaries, and rebuilt and extended after World War II. The Memorial later served as a mausoleum for Klement Gottwald and other Communist leaders. Their remains have since been removed and the building was given to the National Museum *(see p147)*, which has a permanent exhibition on Czechoslovak history.

Relief by Josef Myslbek on portal of St Ludmilla in Náměstí Míru

Nearby is a giant television transmitter, 216 m (709 ft) high. Locals are suspicious of the rays emanating from this great tube of reinforced concrete, built in 1985–92.

## 4 Náměstí Míru

**Map** 6 F2. 🚇 Náměstí Míru. 🚃 4, 10, 16, 22. 🚌 135. Church of St Ludmila: **Open** Mar–Oct: 9am–4pm Mon–Sat, noon–4pm Sun. ✝ 4:30pm daily, 9am, 11am & 4:30pm Sun.
🔲 **ludmilavinohrady.cz**

This attractive square, with a well-kept central garden, is the focal point of the mostly residential Vinohrady quarter. At the top of its sloping lawns stands the attractive, brick Neo-Gothic Church of St Ludmila (1888–93), designed by Josef Mocker, architect of the west end of St Vitus's Cathedral *(see pp102–105)*. Its twin octagonal spires are 60 m (200 ft) high. On the tympanum of the main portal is a relief of Christ with St Wenceslas and St Ludmila by the great 19th-century sculptor Josef Myslbek. Leading artists also contributed designs for the stained-glass windows.

The outside of the square is lined with attractive buildings, including the Vinohrady Theatre, a spirited Art Nouveau building completed in 1907. The façade is crowned by two huge winged figures sculpted by Milan Havlíček, symbolizing Drama and Opera.

## 5 Prague Museum
*Muzeum Hlavního Města Prahy*

Na Poříčí 52. **Map** 4 F3. **Tel** 22 48 16 773. 🚇 Florenc. 🚃 3, 8, 24.
**Open** 9am–6pm Tue–Sun. 🖼
🔲 **muzeumprahy.cz**

The collection records the history of Prague from primeval times. A new museum was built to house the exhibits in the 1890s. Its Neo-Renaissance façade is rich with stucco and sculptures, and the interior walls are painted with historic views of the city. Some of the impressive items on display include examples of Prague china and furniture, relics of the medieval guilds and paintings of Prague through the ages. The most remarkable exhibit is the paper and

wood model of Prague by Antonín Langweil. Completed in 1834, it covers 20 sq m (25 sq yards). The scale of the extraordinarily accurate model is 1:500.

## 6 Letná Park
*Letenské Sady*

**Map** 3 A1. 🚇 Malostranská, Hradčanská. 🚃 1, 5, 8, 12, 17, 18, 20, 22, 25, 26.

Across the river from the Jewish Quarter, a large plateau overlooks the city. It was here that armies gathered before attacking Prague Castle. Since the mid-19th century it has been a wooded park.

On the terrace at the top of the granite steps that lead up from the embankment stands a curious monument – a giant metronome built in 1991. It was installed after the Velvet Revolution on the pedestal formerly occupied by the gigantic stone statue of Stalin leading the people, which was blown up in 1962. A far more durable monument is the Hanavský Pavilion, a Neo-Baroque cast iron structure, built for the 1891 Exhibition. It was later dismantled and erected on its present site in the park, where it houses a popular restaurant and café. The park has a popular beer garden in summer at its eastern end.

View of the Vltava and bridges from Letná Park

# 🅐 National Technical Museum

*Národní Technické Muzeum*

Kostelní 42. **Tel** 22 03 99 111. 🚃 1, 5, 18, 25, 26. **Open** 10am–6pm Tue–Sun. 📷 ✉️ 🛍️ ♿ 🆆 **ntm.cz**

Though it tries to keep abreast of all scientific developments, the museum's strength is its collection of machines from the Industrial Revolution to the present day, the largest of its kind in Europe. The History of Transportation section, in the vast central hall, is filled with locomotives, railway carriages, bicycles, veteran motorcars and motorcycles, with aeroplanes and a hot-air balloon suspended overhead.

The photography and cinematography section is well worth a visit, as is the collection of astronomical instruments. The section on measuring time is also popular, especially on the hour, when everything starts to chime at once. In the basement there is a huge reconstruction of a coal mine, with tools tracing the development of mining from the 15th to the 19th century. The museum also features exhibitions on the history of printing, architecture and civil engineering.

# 🅑 Trade Fair Palace

*Veletržní Palác*

See pp164–5.

# 🅒 Exhibition Ground and Stromovka Park

*Výstaviště A Stromovka*

🚃 5, 12, 17. Exhibition Ground: **Open** 10am–11pm daily. 🌳 Stromovka Park: **Open** 24hrs daily. Lapidarium **Tel** 70 20 13 372. **Open** 10am–4pm Wed, noon–6pm Thu–Sun. ♿ 🆆 **nm.cz**

Laid out for the Jubilee of 1891, the Exhibition Ground has a lively funfair and is great for a day out with children. All kinds of exhibitions, sporting events, spectacles and concerts are staged in summer. The large

The Industrial Palace, centrepiece of the 1891 Exhibition Ground

park to the west was the former royal hunting enclosure and deer park, first established in the late 16th century. The name Stromovka means "place of trees". Opened to the public in 1804, the park is still a pleasant wooded area and an ideal place for a walk. The Lapidarium holds an exhibition of 11th- to 19th-century sculpture, including some originals from Charles Bridge *(see pp136–9)*. On display are decorated windows, spouts, fountains, groups of statues and memorials.

# 🅓 Troja Palace

*Trojský Zámek*

See pp166–7.

# 🅔 Zoo

*Zoologická Zahrada*

U trojského zámku 3/120. **Tel** 29 61 12 111. Ⓜ Holešovice, then 🚌 112. **Open** Jun–Aug: 9am–7pm daily; Apr, May, Sep, Oct: 9am–6pm daily; Nov–Feb: 9am–4pm daily; Mar: 9am–5pm daily. 📷 ♿ 🚻 🆆 **zoopraha.cz**

Attractively situated on a rocky slope overlooking the right bank of the Vltava, the zoo was founded in 1924. It now covers an area of 64 hectares (160 acres) and there is a chair lift to take visitors to the upper part.

The zoo's 2,500 animals represent 500 species, 50 of them extremely rare in the wild. It is best known for its breeding programme of Przewalski's horses, the only species of wild horse in the world. It has also enjoyed success in breeding big cats, gorillas and orang-utans. In addition there are two pavilions, one for lions, tigers and other beasts of prey and one for elephants. The zoo also works on reintroducing endangered species to the wild.

Red panda, relative of the famous giant panda, in Prague Zoo

# ⓬ Villa Müller
*Müllerova Vila*

Nad Hradním vodojemem 14. **Tel** 22 43 12 012. 🚇 Hradčanská, then 🚊 1, 2, 18 to Ořechovka. **Open** Apr–Oct: 9am–6pm Tue, Thu, Sat & Sun; Nov–Mar: 10am–5pm Tue, Thu, Sat & Sun. 📷 🎫 Apr–Oct: 9am, 11am, 1pm, 3pm, 5pm; Nov–Mar: 10am, noon, 2pm, 4pm. ♿ 🌐 **mullerovavila.cz**

A severe, white concrete façade, asymmetric windows and a flat roof characterize the Villa Müller. It was designed by Modernist architect Adolf Loos and built in 1928–30 by construction entrepreneur František Müller for himself and his wife Milada, who were leading lights of Czech society at that time. Loos used his innovative spatial theory known as "Raumplan" in the design of both the outside and the inside of the building, so that all the spaces look and feel interconnected. The roof terrace at the top of the house provides a "framed" view of Prague cathedral in the distance.

In contrast to the building's functional exterior, the interiors combine traditional furnishings with vibrant use of marble, wood and silk. The villa fell into disrepair during the 1950s, and in 1995 ownership passed to the city of Prague. A programme of restoration took place between 1997 and 2000, when it was opened to the public as a National Cultural Monument.

# ⓭ Břevnov Monastery
*Břevnovský Klášter*

Markétská 28. **Tel** 22 04 06 111. 🚊 22, 25. 📷 only. On request Mon–Fri (call 22 04 06 270); 10am, 2pm Sat & Sun; also 4pm Apr–Oct. 📷 📹 🌐 **brevnov.cz**

From the surrounding suburban housing, you would never guess that Břevnov is one of the oldest parts of Prague. A flourishing community grew up here around the Benedictine abbey founded in 993 by Prince Boleslav II *(see p22)* and Bishop Adalbert (Vojtěch) – the first monastery in Bohemia. An ancient well called Vojtěška marks the spot where prince and bishop are said to have met and decided to found the monastery.

The gateway, courtyard and most of the present monastery buildings are by the great Baroque architects Christoph and Kilian Ignaz Dientzenhofer *(see p129)*. The monastery Church of St Margaret was completed in 1715, and is based on a floorplan of overlapping ovals, as ingenious as any of Bernini's churches in Rome. In 1964 the crypt of the original 10th-century church was discovered below the choir and is open to the public. Of the other buildings, the most interesting is the Theresian Hall, with a painted ceiling dating from 1727.

Star Hunting Lodge in peaceful surroundings

# ⓮ White Mountain and Star Hunting Lodge
*Bílá Hora A Hvězda*

Obora Hvězda. 🚊 1, 22, 25. Obora Hvězda (game park): **Open** 24hrs daily. Summer House Hvězda: **Tel** 23 53 57 938. **Open** Apr & Oct: 10am–5pm Tue–Sun; May–Sep: 10am–6pm Tue–Sun. 📷 📹

The Battle of the White Mountain *(see p33)*, fought on 8 November 1620, had a very different impact for the two main communities of Prague. For the Protestants it was a disaster that led to 300 years of Habsburg domination; for the Catholic supporters of the Habsburgs it was a triumph, so they built a memorial chapel on the hill. In the early 1700s this chapel was converted into the grander Church of Our Lady Victorious and decorated by leading Baroque artists, including Václav Vavřinec Reiner.

In the 16th century the woodland around the battle site had been a royal game park. The hunting lodge, completed in 1556, survives today. This fascinating building is shaped as a six-pointed star – *hvězda* means star. On site is a small exhibition about the building and its history. Also on show are exhibits relating to the Battle of the White Mountain and temporary exhibitions about Czech culture.

Modernist Villa Müller, seen from the garden

# ❽ Trade Fair Palace

*Veletržní palác*

The National Gallery in Prague opened its museum of 20th- and 21st-century art in 1995, housed in a reconstruction of a former Trade Fair building of 1929. Since 2000 it has also housed a 19th-century collection. Its vast, skylit spaces make an ideal backdrop for the paintings, which range from French 19th-century art and superb examples of Impressionism and Post-Impressionism, to works by Munch, Klimt, Picasso and Miró, as well as a splendid collection of Czech modern art. The collection is subject to rearrangment so the location of artworks may change.

**Grand Meal** (1951–5)
Mikuláš Medek's works range from post-war Surrealism to 1960s Abstraction.

Fourth Floor

**Cubist Bust** (1913–14)
Otto Gutfreund was one of the first artists to apply the principles of Cubism to sculpture, and this work marks his move towards abstract art.

Third Floor

**Cleopatra** (1942–57)
This painting by Jan Zrzavý, a major representative of Czech modern art, took the artist 45 years to complete and is his best- known piece.

**St Sebastian** (1912)
This self-portrait by Bohumil Kubišta takes its inspiration from the martyrdom of St Sebastian, who was persecuted by being bound to a tree and shot with arrows.

**Pomona** (1910)
Aristide Maillol was a pupil of Rodin. This work is part of an exceptional collection of bronzes.

**Key**

- ⬜ Czech Art 1900–1930
- ⬜ 19th- and 20th-century French Art
- ⬜ Czech Art 1930–present day
- ⬜ 20th-century Foreign Art
- ⬜ Temporary exhibition space
- ⬜ Non-exhibition space

★ **Big Dialog** (1966)
Karel Nepraš's sculpture, made from industrial scrap metal held together with wires, was painted red to poke fun at the Communist regime.

## VISITORS' CHECKLIST

**Practical Information**
Veletržní Palác, Dukelských hrdinů 47.
**Tel** 22 43 01 111.
[w] ngprague.cz
**Open** 10am–6pm Tue–Sun (last adm 30 mins before closing).

**Transport**
[M] Vltavská. 12, 14, 15, 17 to Veletržní; 1, 5, 8, 25, 26 to Strossmayerovo náměstí.

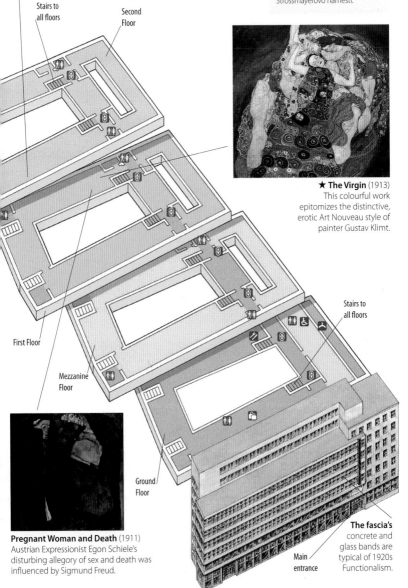

★ **The Virgin** (1913)
This colourful work epitomizes the distinctive, erotic Art Nouveau style of painter Gustav Klimt.

Stairs to all floors

Second Floor

First Floor

Mezzanine Floor

Stairs to all floors

Ground Floor

**Pregnant Woman and Death** (1911)
Austrian Expressionist Egon Schiele's disturbing allegory of sex and death was influenced by Sigmund Freud.

Main entrance

**The fascia's** concrete and glass bands are typical of 1920s Functionalism.

# ⑩ Troja Palace

*Trojský Zámek*

One of the most striking summer palaces in Prague, Troja was built in the late 17th century by Jean-Baptiste Mathey for Count Sternberg, a member of a leading Bohemian aristocratic family. Situated at the foot of the Vltava Heights, the exterior of the palace was modelled on a Classical Italian villa, while its garden was laid out in formal French style. The magnificent interior took over 20 years to complete and is full of extravagant frescoes expressing the Sternberg family's loyalty to the Habsburg dynasty. Troja houses a good collection of 19th-century art.

Terracotta urn on the garden balustrade of Troja Palace

**Defeat of the Turks**
This turbaned figure, tumbling from the Grand Hall ceiling, symbolizes Leopold I's triumph over the Turks.

**★ Garden Staircase**
The two sons of Mother Earth which adorn the sweeping oval staircase (1685–1703) are part of a group of sculptures by Johann Georg Heermann and his nephew Paul, depicting the struggle of the Olympian Gods with the Titans.

## KEY

① Belvedere turret

② Statue of Olympian God

③ Statues of sons of Mother Earth

④ **Chinese Rooms** feature 18th-century murals of Chinese scenes. This room makes a perfect backdrop for a ceramics display.

⑤ Stucco decoration

## VISITORS' CHECKLIST

**Practical Information**
U trojského zámku 1, Prague 7.
**Tel** 28 38 51 614.
ⓦ **ghmp.cz**
**Open** Apr–Oct: 10am–6pm Tue–
Thu, Sat & Sun, 1–6pm Fri.

**Transport**
🚌 *see p55.* Ⓜ Holešovice,
then 🚌 112.

**★ Grand Hall Fresco**
The frescoes in the Grand Hall
(1691–7), by Abraham Godyn,
depict the story of the first
Habsburg Emperor, Rudolph I, and
the victories of Leopold I over the
archenemy of Christianity, the
Sublime Porte (Ottoman Empire).

**Personification
of Justice**
Abraham Godyn's
image of Justice gazes
from the lower east wall
of the Grand Hall.

**★ Landscaped Gardens**
Sloping vineyards were levelled,
hillsides excavated and terraces
built to fulfil the elaborate and
grandiose plans of French
architect, Jean-Baptiste Mathey,
for the first Baroque French-style
formal gardens in Bohemia. The
palace and its geometric
network of paths, terracing,
fountains, statuary and beautiful
terracotta vases, is best viewed
from the south of the garden
between the two orangeries. The
gardens have been carefully
restored according to Mathey's
original plans.

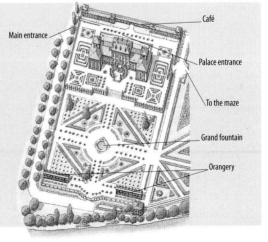

Café

Main entrance

Palace entrance

To the maze

Grand fountain

Orangery

# Day Trips from Prague

The sights that attract most visitors away from the city are Bohemia's picturesque medieval castles. Karlstein, for example, stands in splendid isolation above wooded valleys that have changed little since the Emperor Charles IV hunted there in the 14th century. We have chosen four castles, very varied in character. There are regular organized tours (see p225) to the major sights around Prague, to the historic mining town of Kutná Hora and, if you have more time to spare, to the famous spa towns of Karlsbad and Marienbad in western Bohemia.

## Sights at a Glance

**Castles**
1. Veltrusy
2. Karlstein
3. Konopiště
4. Křivoklát

**Historic Towns**
5. Kutná Hora
6. Karlsbad
7. Marienbad

### Key

= Motorway
= Major road
= Minor road

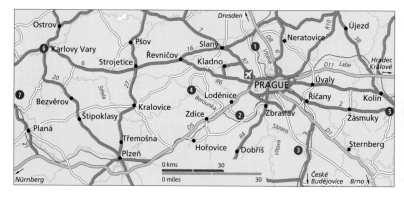

## 1 Veltrusy Château

*Veltruský Zámek*

20 km (12 miles) N of Prague.
**Tel** 31 57 81 146. 🚆 from Masarykovo to Kralupy nad Vltavou, then bus.
**Open** Apr–Oct: 9am–5pm Tue–Sun (last tour 4pm); Nov–Mar: tours can be arranged by calling 602 494 466.
🏷 📷 📬 **w** **zamek-veltrusy.cz**
Park: **Open** dawn to nightfall daily.
Nelahozeves Castle: **Tel** 31 57 09 111.
🚆 from Masarykovo to Nelahozeves – zámek. **Open** Apr–Oct: 9am–5pm Tue–Sun. 🏷 📷 📬 📷
**w** **zamek-nelahozeves.cz**

Veltrusy is a small town beside the Vltava, famous for the 18th-century château built by the aristocratic Chotek family. The building is in the shape of a cross, with a central dome and a staircase adorned with statues representing the months of the year and the seasons.

The estate was laid out as an English-style landscaped deer park, covering an area of 300 hectares (750 acres). Near the entrance there is still an enclosure with a herd of deer. The Vltava flows along one side and

dotted around the grounds are summer houses.

The Doric and Maria Theresa pavilions, the orangery and the grotto date from the late 18th century. The park is planted with some 100 different kinds of tree. The castle was damaged by floods in 2002 and ongoing repairs mean that some rooms may remain closed to the public.

Across the river, and accessible from Veltrusy by bus or train, is

Nelahozeves Castle. This Renaissance castle houses an exhibition entitled "Private Spaces: A Noble Family At Home", depicting the life of the Lobkowicz family over five centuries. Some 12 rooms have been fitted out with period furnishings. On display in the library are the family archives. The family's art treasures are housed in Lobkowicz Palace (see p101). The birthplace of Czech composer Antonín Dvořák is nearby.

Karlstein Castle, built by Emperor Charles IV in the 14th century

## ❷ Karlstein Castle
*Karlštejn*

25 km (16 miles) SW of Prague. **Tel** 31 16 81 617. 🚆 from Smíchov or Hlavní nádraží to Karlštejn (1.5 km/ 1 mile from castle. The uphill walk takes around 40 minutes). **Open** Mar–Oct: 9am–3pm Tue–Sun (to 5:30pm May, Jun & Sep; to 6:30pm Jul & Aug). 🅿 📷 compulsory (book in advance). ✉
**W hradkarlstejn.cz**

View of the castle at Křivoklát, dominated by the Great Tower

The castle was founded by Charles IV as a country retreat, a treasury for the crown jewels and a symbol of his divine right to rule the Holy Roman Empire. It stands on a crag above the River Berounka. The castle is largely a 19th-century reconstruction by Josef Mocker. The original building work (1348–67) was supervised by French master mason Matthew of Arras, and then by Peter Parler. You can still see the audience hall and the bedchamber of Charles IV in the Royal Palace. On the third floor, the Emperor's quarters are below those of the Empress.

The central tower houses the Church of Our Lady, decorated with faded 14th-century wall paintings. A narrow passage leads to the tiny Chapel of St Catherine, the walls of which are adorned with semiprecious stones set into the plaster.

## ❸ Konopiště Castle

40 km (25 miles) SE of Prague. **Tel** 31 77 21 366. 🚆 from Hlavní nádraží to Benešov, then local bus. **Open** Apr, May, Sep: 10am–noon, 1–4pm Tue–Sun (Jun–Aug: to 5pm; Oct & Nov: to 3pm). 🅿 ✉ 📷 💻
**W zamek-konopiste.cz**

Though it dates back to the 13th century, this moated castle is essentially a late 19th-century creation. In between, Konopiště had been rebuilt by Baroque architect František Kaňka and in front of the bridge across the moat is a gate (1725) by Kaňka and sculptor Matthias Braun.

In 1887 Konopiště was bought by Archduke Franz Ferdinand, who later became heir to the Austrian throne. It was his assassination in 1914 in Sarajevo that triggered off World War I. To escape the Habsburg court's disapproval of his wife, he spent much of his time at Konopiště and amassed arms, armour and Meissen porcelain, all on display in the fine furnished interiors. However, the abiding memory of the castle is of the hundreds of stags' heads lining the walls.

Hunting trophies at Konopiště

## ❹ Křivoklát Castle

45 km (28 miles) W of Prague. **Tel** 31 35 58 440. 🚆 from Hlavní nádraží via Beroun or from Masarykovo nádraží via Rakovník (1 km/0.6 miles) from castle). **Open** Apr–Sep: 9am–5pm Tue–Sun (Apr: to 4pm; Jul & Aug: to 6pm); Oct: 10am–4pm Tue–Sun; Nov & Dec: 10am–3pm Sat & Sun; Jan–Mar: 10am–3pm Mon–Sat. 🅿 ✉ 💻
**W krivoklat.cz**

This castle, like Karlstein, owes its appearance to the restoration work of Josef Mocker. It was originally a hunting lodge belonging to the early Přemyslid princes and the seat of the royal master of hounds. In the 13th century King Wenceslas I built a stone castle here, which remained in the hands of Bohemia's kings and the Habsburg emperors until the 17th century.

Charles IV spent some of his childhood here and returned from France in 1334 with his first wife Blanche de Valois. Their daughter Margaret was born in the castle. To amuse his queen and young princess, Charles ordered the local villagers to trap nightingales and set them free in a wooded area just below the castle. Today you can still walk along the "Nightingale Path".

The royal palace is on the eastern side of the triangular castle. This corner is dominated by the Great Tower, 42 m (130 ft) high. You can still see some 13th-century stonework, but most of the palace dates from the reign of Vladislav Jagiello. On the first floor there is a vaulted Gothic hall, reminiscent of the Vladislav Hall in the Royal Palace at Prague Castle *(see pp106–7)*. It has an oriel window and a beautiful loggia, and the chapel has a finely carved Gothic altar. Below the chapel, the Augusta Prison is named for Bishop Jan Augusta of the Bohemian Brethren, imprisoned here in the mid-16th century. The dungeon now houses a grim assortment of torture instruments.

## ❺ Kutná Hora

70 km (45 miles) E of Prague. **Tel** 32 75 12 378 (tourist information). 🚊 from Hlavní nádraží, to Kutná Hora, then bus 1 to Kutná Hora-Město. 🚌 from Florenc. Cathedral of St Barbara: **Open** May–Sep: 9am–5:30pm daily (to 4pm Mon); Oct–Apr: 10am–4pm daily. 🚫 Italian Court: **Open** Mar & Oct: 10am–5pm; Apr–Sep: 9am–6pm; Nov–Feb: 10am–4pm daily. 🚫 Hrádek: **Open** Apr & Oct: 9am–5pm Tue–Sun; May, Jun & Sep: 9am–6pm Tue–Sun; Jul & Aug: 10am–6pm Tue–Sun. 🚫 🎫 Stone House: **Open** as Hrádek. 🆆 **kutnahora.cz**

The town originated as a small mining community in the second half of the 13th century. When rich deposits of silver were found, the king took over the licensing of the mines and Kutná Hora became the second most important town in Bohemia.

In the 14th century five to six tonnes of pure silver were extracted here each year, making the king the richest ruler in Central Europe. The Prague *groschen*, a silver coin that circulated all over Europe, was minted here in the Italian Court (Vlašský; dvůr), so-called because Florentine experts were employed to set up the mint. Strongly fortified, it was also the ruler's seat in the town. In the late 14th century a superb palace with reception

halls and the Chapel of St Wenceslas and St Ladislav, below which lay the royal treasury, were constructed.

When the silver started to run out in the 16th century, the town began to lose its importance; the mint finally closed in 1727. The Italian Court later became the town hall. On the ground floor you can still see a row of forges. Since 1947 a mining museum has been housed in another building, the Hrádek, which was originally a fort. A visit includes a tour of a medieval mine. There is museum in the Stone House (Kamenný dům), a restored Gothic building of the late 15th century.

To the southwest of the town stands the Cathedral of St Barbara, begun in 1380 by the workshop of Peter Parler, also the architect of St Vitus's Cathedral *(see pp102–105)*. The presbytery (1499) has a fine net vault and windows with intricate tracery. The slightly later nave vault is by royal architect Benedikt Ried. The murals show mining scenes. The cathedral, with its three massive and tent-shaped spires rising above a forest of flying

The Italian Court, Kutná Hora's first mint

buttresses, is a wonderful example of Bohemian Gothic.

In Sedlec, a suburb of Kutná Hora, is the Ossuary of All Saints church, where thousands of human bones have been fashioned into furnishings and decorative objects.

## ❻ Karlsbad

*Karlovy Vary*

140 km (85 miles) W of Prague. **Tel** 77 33 78 559. 🚊 from Hlavní nádraží. 🚌 from Florenc. ℹ️ Husovo náměstí 2 (35 53 21 171). 🆆 **karlovyvary.cz**

Legend has it that Charles IV *(see pp26–7)* discovered one of the sources of mineral water that would make the town's fortune when one of his staghounds fell into a hot spring. In 1522 a medical description of the springs was published and by the end of the 16th century over 200 spa buildings had been built there. Today there are 12 hot mineral springs – *vary* means hot springs. The best-known is the Vřídlo (Sprudel), which rises to a height of 12 m (40 ft). At 72°C, it is also the hottest. The water is good for digestive disorders, but you do not have to drink it; you can take the minerals in the form of salts.

The town is also known for its Karlovy Vary china and Moser glass, and for summer concerts

The three steeples of Kutná Hora's great Church of St Barbara

and other cultural events, including an international film festival in early July. The race course is popular with the more sporting invalids taking the waters.

Outstanding among the local historic monuments is the Baroque parish church of Mary Magdalene by Kilian Ignaz Dientzenhofer (1732–6). More modern churches built for foreign visitors include a Russian church (1896) and an Anglican one (1877). The 19th-century Mill Colonnade (Mlýnská kolonáda) is by Josef Zítek, architect of the National Theatre (see pp156–7) in Prague.

## ❼ Marienbad

*Mariánské Lázně*

170 km (105 miles) W of Prague. 🚋 from Hlavní nádraží. 🚌 from Florenc. 🛈 Hlavní 47 (35 46 22 474).
🌐 marianskelazne.cz

The elegance of Marienbad's hotels, parks and gardens has faded considerably since it was the playground of kings and princes at the turn of the century. The area's health-giving waters – *lázně* means bath (or spa) – have been known since the 16th century, but the spa was not founded until the beginning of the 19th century. The waters are used to treat all kinds of disorders; mud baths are also popular.

Most of the spa buildings date from the latter half of the 19th century. The great cast-iron colonnade with frescoes by Josef

Bronze statue of a chamois at Jeleni skok (Stag's Leap), with a view across the valley to the Imperial Sanatorium, Karlsbad

Vylětal is still an impressive sight. In front of it is a "singing fountain", its jets of water now controlled by computer. Churches were provided for visitors of all denominations, including an Evangelical church (1857), an Anglican church (1879) and the Russian Orthodox church of St Vladimír (1902). Visitors can learn the history of the spa in the house called At the Golden Grape (U zlatého

hroznu), where the German poet Johann Wolfgang von Goethe stayed in 1823. Musical visitors during the 19th century included the composers Weber, Wagner and Bruckner, while writers such as Ibsen, Gogol, Mark Twain and Rudyard Kipling also found its treatments beneficial. King Edward VII also came here and in 1905 he agreed to open the golf course (Bohemia's first), despite hating the game.

The cast-iron colonnade at Marienbad, completed in 1889

# FOUR GUIDED WALKS

Prague offers some good opportunities for walking. In the centre of the city, many streets are pedestrianized and the most important sights are confined to quite a small area *(see pp16–17)*. Here are four guided walks of varied character. The first passes through a main artery of the city, from the Powder Gate on the outskirts of the Old Town to St Vitus's Cathedral in Prague Castle, crossing Charles Bridge at its mid-point. This is the Royal Coronation Route, followed for centuries by Bohemian kings. Away from the busy centre, the second and third of the walks take in the peace and tranquillity of two of Prague's loveliest parks – Petřín and the Royal Enclosure. Petřín Park is rewarding for its spectacular views of the city. The Royal Enclosure is outside the centre in the old royal hunting park. The final walk is in Vyšehrad – an ancient fortress which is steeped in history and atmosphere. The views from Vyšehrad of the Vltava and Prague Castle are unparalleled.

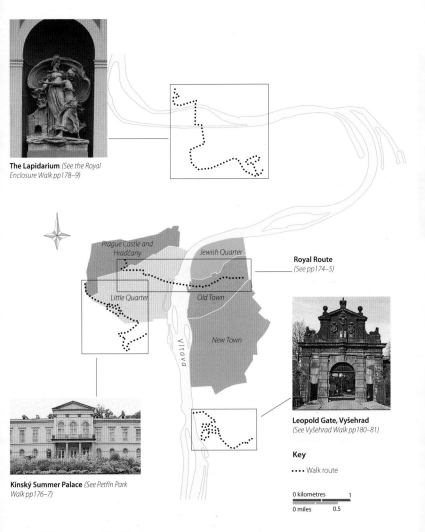

**The Lapidarium** *(See the Royal Enclosure Walk pp178–9)*

Prague Castle and Hradčany

Jewish Quarter

**Royal Route**
*(See pp174–5)*

Little Quarter

Old Town

Vltava

New Town

**Kinský Summer Palace** *(See Petřín Park Walk pp176–7)*

**Leopold Gate, Vyšehrad**
*(See Vyšehrad Walk pp180–81)*

**Key**

•••• Walk route

0 kilometres          1

0 miles          0.5

◀ View of Old Town Square, bustling with tourists

# A 90-Minute Walk along the Royal Route

The Royal Route originally linked two important royal seats: the Royal Court – on the site of the Municipal House and where the walk starts – and Prague Castle, where the walk finishes. The name of this walk derives from the coronation processions of the Bohemian kings and queens who passed along it. Today, these narrow streets offer a wealth of historical and architecturally interesting sights, shops and cafés, making the walk one of Prague's most enjoyable. For more details on the Old Town, the Little Quarter and Hradčany turn to *pages 62–81, 122–41* and *96–121* respectively.

Figural *sgraffito* covers the façade of the Renaissance House at the Minute

### History of the Royal Route

The first major coronation procession to travel along this route was for George of Poděbrady *(see p28)* in 1458. The next large procession took place in 1743, when Maria Theresa was crowned with great pomp – three Turkish pavilions were erected just outside the Powder Gate. September 1791 saw the coronation of Leopold II. This procession was led by cavalry, followed by mounted drummers, trumpeters and soldiers and Bohemian lords. Some 80 carriages came next, carrying princes and bishops. The most splendid were each drawn by six pairs of horses, flanked by servants with red coats and white leather trousers, and carried the ladies-in-waiting. The last great coronation procession along the Royal Route – for Ferdinand V – was in 1836 with over 3,391 horses and four camels.

### From the Powder Gate to Old Town Square

At Náměstí Republiky turn towards the Municipal House *(see p66)* and walk under the Gothic Powder Gate ① *(see p66)*. Here, at the city gates, the monarch and a large retinue of church dignitaries, aristocrats, and foreign ambassadors were warmly welcomed by leading city representatives. The gate leads into one of Prague's oldest streets, Celetná *(see p67)*. It was here the Jewish community and the crafts guilds, carrying their insignia, greeted their king. The street is lined with Baroque and Rococo houses. At house No. 36 was the Mint ②. It moved here after the mint at Kutná Hora *(see p170)* was occupied by Catholic troops in the Hussite Wars *(see pp28–9)*. It minted coins from 1420 to 1784. The House of the Black Madonna ③ contains a museum of Czech Cubist art *(see p67)*. Revellers would watch processions from the taverns At the Spider ④ and At the Vulture ⑤.

At the end of Celetná Street is the Old Town Square ⑥ *(see pp68–71)*. Here, the processions halted beside Týn Church ⑦ *(see p72)* for pledges of loyalty

③ House of the Black Madonna.

⑪ The distinct Baroque façade of the House at the Golden Well in Karlova Street.

from the university. Keep to the left of the square, past No. 17, At the Unicorn ⑧, then No. 20, Smetana House, where the composer began a music school in 1848. Proceed to the Old Town Hall ⑨ (see pp74–6). Here, the municipal guard and a band waited for the royal procession and city dignitaries cheered from the temporary balcony around the hall.

### Along Karlova Street and across Charles Bridge

Walk past the sgraffitoed façade of the House at the Minute and into Malé náměstí ⑩, where merchants waited with members of the various religious orders. Bear left off the square, then turn right into gallery-filled Karlova Street.

considered to be a good omen. But only a few months later he died. Walk under the Old Town Bridge Tower ⑫ and over Charles Bridge ⑬ and then under the Little Quarter Towers ⑭ (see pp136–9).

### The Little Quarter

The walk now follows Mostecká Street. On entering the Little Quarter the mayor handed the city keys to the king and the artillery fired a salute. At the end of this street is Little Quarter Square ⑮ (see p124) and the Baroque church St Nicholas's ⑯ (see pp128–9). The procession passed the church to the sound of its bells.

Leave this picturesque square by Nerudova Street ⑰

ends at the Castle's Matthias Gate (see p50) ⑲. The procession ended with the coronation held at St Vitus's Cathedral.

A decorative house sign in Celetná Street

Beyond Husova Street is an attractive Baroque house, At the Golden Well ⑪. Further on is the 16th-century Clementinum (see p81), where the clergy stood. You then pass into Knights of the Cross Square (see p81). When Leopold II's procession passed through here the clouds lifted, which was

(see p130). Poet and writer Jan Neruda, who immortalized hundreds of Little Quarter characters in books like *Mala Strana Tales*, grew up and worked at No. 47, The Two Suns ⑱. Cross the street, turn sharp right and walk up the Castle ramp, which leads you to Hradčanské Square. The route

### Key

••• Walk route

▬▬ City wall

```
0 metres        300
0 yards         300
```

### Tips for Walkers

**Starting point:** Náměstí Republiky.
**Length:** 2.4 km (1.5 miles).
**Getting there:** Line B goes to Náměstí Republiky metro station. At Hradčany you can get tram 22 back into town.
**Stopping off points:** Rest beneath the sunshades of the outdoor cafés on Old Town Square or Karlova Street in the summer. There are plenty of cafés and restaurants on Malostranské náměstí, as well as along Nerudova Street.

Coronation procession passing through the Knights of the Cross Square

**For additional map symbols** *see back flap*

# A Two-Hour Walk through Petřín Park

Part of the charm of this walk around this large and peaceful hillside park are the many spectacular views over the different areas of Prague. The Little Quarter, Hradčany and the Old Town all take on a totally different aspect when viewed from above. The tree-covered gardens are dotted with châteaux, pavilions and statues and crisscrossed by winding paths leading you to secret and unexpected corners. For more on the sights of Petřín Hill see pages 140–41.

⑤ One of the gateways in the Hunger Wall.

③ Interior of the Church of St Michael.

### Kinský Square to Hunger Wall

The walk starts at náměstí Kinských in Smíchov. Enter Kinský Garden through a large enclosed gateway. This English-style garden was founded in 1827 and named after the wealthy Kinský family, supporters of Czech culture in the 19th century.

Take the wide cobbled and asphalt path on your left to the Kinský Summer Palace ①. This 1830s pseudo-classical building was designed by Jindřich Koch and its façade features Ionic columns terminating in a triangular tympanum. Inside the building is a large hall of columns with a triple-branched staircase beautifully decorated with statues. The Ethnographical Museum, housed here, holds a permanent exhibition of folk art.

Next to the museum is a 1913 statue of the actress Hana Kvapilová.

About 50 m (150 ft) above the palace is the lower lake ②, where a small waterfall trickles into a man-made pond. Keep going up the hill until you reach the Church of St Michael ③, on your left. This 18th-century wooden folk church was moved here from a village in the Ukraine.

Follow the path up the hill for about 20 m (60 ft), then go to the top of the steps to a wide asphalt path known as the Observation Path for its beautiful views of the city. Turn right and further on your left is the small upper lake ④ with a 1950s bronze statue of a seal at

Sunbathers on Petřín Hill

its centre. Keep following the Observation Path; ahead of you stands a Neo-Gothic gate. This allows you to pass through the city's old Baroque fortifications.

### Hunger Wall to Observation Tower

Continue along the path to the Hunger Wall ⑤ *(see pp140–41)*. This was a major part of the Little Quarter's fortifications; the wall still runs from Újezd Street across Petřín Hill and up to

Strahov Monastery. Passing through the gate in the wall brings you to Petřín Park. Take the wide path to the left below the wall and walk up the hill beside the wall until you cross the bridge which spans the funicular railway *(see p141)*. Below on your right you can see the Nebozízek restaurant *(see p201)* famed for its views. On either side of the path are small sandstone rockeries. Most are entrances to reservoirs, built in the 18th and 19th centuries, to bring water to Strahov Monastery; others are left over from the unsuccessful attempts at mining the area. Walk up to the summit of the hill. On your right is the Mirror Maze ⑥ *(see p140)*. Facing the maze is the 12th-century St Lawrence's Church ⑦ *(see p140)*, renovated in 1740 in the Baroque style.

### Observation Tower to Strahov Monastery

A little further on stands the Observation Tower ⑧ *(see p140)*. This steel replica of the Eiffel Tower in Paris is 60 m (200 ft) high. Opposite the tower is the main gate of the Hunger Wall. Pass through, turn left and follow the path to the Rose Garden ⑨.

The garden was planted by the city of Prague in 1932, and features a number of attractive sculptures. When you look down to the far end of the garden you can see Štefánik's Observatory *(see p140)*. This was rebuilt from a municipal building in 1928 by the Czech Astronomical Society and was then modernized in the 1970s. It now houses a huge telescope and is open in the evenings to the public.

Returning to the Observation Tower, follow the wall on the left, passing some chapels of the Stations of the Cross dating from 1834. Then pass through a gap in the Hunger Wall, turn right, and walk past a charming Baroque house. About 50 m (150 ft) beyond this, you pass through another gap in the Hunger Wall on your right. Turn left into a large orchard above Strahov Monastery ⑩ *(see pp120–21)* for spectacular views of the city. Leave by the same hole in the wall that you came in by, turn right, and walk downhill along the wall, through the orchard and past tennis courts to the Strahov

⑦ Sgraffitoed façade of the Calvary Chapel next to the Church of St Lawrence.

Monastery courtyard. You can catch tram 22 from here, or linger in the peaceful monastery grounds. If you feel energetic you can walk back down the hill.

### Tips for Walkers

**Starting point:** náměstí Kinských in Smíchov.
**Length:** 2.7 km (1.7 miles). The walk includes steep hills.
**Getting there:** The nearest metro station to the starting point is Anděl. Trams 6, 9, 12 and 20 go to náměstí Kinských (Kinský Square).
**Stopping off points:** There is a restaurant, Nebozízek, half way up Petřín Hill and in the summer a few snack bars are open at the summit of the Hill near the Observation Tower.

**Key**

••• Walk route

— Hunger wall

Hradčany and the Little Quarter from the summit of Petřín Hill

# A 90-Minute Walk in the Royal Enclosure

The royal enclosure, more popularly called Stromovka, is one of the largest parks in Prague. It was created around 1266 during the reign of Přemysl Otakar II, who fenced the area in and built a small hunting château in the grounds. In 1804 it was opened to the public and became Prague's most popular recreational area. The large park of Troja Palace and the zoological garden are on the opposite river bank.

⑥ A bust on the Academy of Fine Arts.

## The Exhibition Ground (Výstaviště)

From U Výstaviště ① pass through the gate to the old Exhibition Ground. This was created for the 1891 Jubilee Exhibition. Since the late 19th century it has been used for exhibitions and entertainment.

The large Lapidarium of the National Museum ② is on your right. This Neo-Renaissance exhibition pavilion was rebuilt in 1907 in the Art Nouveau style, and decorated with reliefs of figures from Czech history. Many architectural monuments and sculptures from the 11th to the 19th centuries are also housed here.

② The Art Nouveau Lapidarium.

Facing you is the Industrial Palace ③, a vast Neo-Renaissance building constructed of iron which was partially destroyed by fire in 2008. Walk to the right of the building and you will come to Křižík's Fountain ④. This was restored in 1991 in honour of the Czechoslovakia Exhibition. It was designed by the great inventor František Křižík (1847–1941), who established Prague's first public electric lighting system. During summer the fountain is illuminated at night by computer-controlled lights which synchronize with the music (see p53). Behind the fountain there is a permanent fairground.

**Key**

••• Walk route

═══ Railway line

⑩ The summer palace created from a medieval Hunting Château.

On the left of the Industrial Palace is a circular building which houses Marold's Panorama ⑤. This was painted by Luděk Marold in 1898 and depicts the Battle of Lipany. As you walk back to the Exhibition Ground entrance, you pass the Academy of Fine Arts ⑥, decorated with 18 busts of artists. On leaving the Exhibition Ground, turn sharp right. Following the outer edge of the Ground you will pass the Planetarium ⑦ on your left, which has interactive exhibitions; walk straight ahead, take the road down the slope, then turn left into a wide avenue of chestnut trees.

### The Royal Enclosure
Continue for some way along the avenue until you reach a simple building among trees, on your left. Behind this is the Rudolph Water Tunnel ⑧, a grand monument of the age of Rudolph II *(see pp30–31)*. Hewn into rock, the aqueduct is over 1,000 m (3,000 ft) long. Now

⑭ The grand façade of Troja Palace *(see pp166–7)*.

sadly defaced by graffiti, it was built in 1584 to carry water from the Vltava to Rudolph's newly constructed lakes in the Royal Park.

Continue along the path until you reach the derelict Royal Hall ⑨. Built in the late 17th century, it was converted into a restaurant, then rebuilt in 1855 in Neo-Gothic style. Beyond the Royal Hall, at the bend in the main path, take a steep left fork up through woods to the former Hunting Château ⑩. This medieval building was built for the Bohemian kings who used the park as a hunting reserve. The Château was then later enlarged, and in 1805 was changed again by Jiří Fischer into a Neo-Gothic summer palace. Until 1918, this was a residence of the Governor of Bohemia. Today it is used to house the extensive library of newspapers and magazines of the National Museum. Retrace your steps to the main path, walk

ahead and take the first small path on the right which will lead you into a pleasant late-16th- century formal garden ⑪. Return to the main path and turn right. At the fork, take the path which bends to the right along the railway embankment then turn left under the railway line to a canal ⑫.

Walk over the bridge, turn left along the canal, then right across the island. Cross the Vltava ⑬ and turn left into Povltavská Street where a wall marks the medieval boundary of Troja Park. Carry along to the south entrance of the gardens of Troja Palace ⑭ *(see pp166–7)*, and then wander through them up to the palace itself.

### Tips for Walkers

**Starting point:** U Výstaviště in Holešovice.
**Length:** 5 km (3 miles). The walk goes up a very steep incline to the former Hunting Château.
**Getting there:** Trams 5, 12, 14, 15 and 17 run to the starting point. The nearest metro stations are Vltavská or Nádraží Holešovice on line C, ten minutes walk away. At the end of the walk you can get on bus No. 112 at Troja to Nádraží Holešovice metro station.
**Stopping off points:** There are a number of restaurants and kiosks in the Exhibition Ground. All the gardens are tranquil spots in which to rest. If you feel like a boat trip down the Vltava, there are often trips starting from the bridge over the canal to Palacký Bridge *(see p57)*.

⑦ Prague Planetarium, the largest in the Czech Republic.

For additional map symbols *see back flap*

# A 60-Minute Walk in Vyšehrad

According to ancient legend, Vyšehrad was the first seat of Czech royalty. It was from this spot that Princess Libuše is said to have prophesied the future glory of the city of Prague (see pp22–3). However, archaeological research indicates that the first castle on Vyšehrad was not built until the 10th century. The fortress suffered a turbulent history and was rebuilt many times. Today, it is above all a peaceful place with parks and unrivalled views of the Vltava valley and Prague. The fascinating cemetery is the last resting place of many famous Czech writers, actors, artists and musicians.

⑤ Decorative sculpture on the Baroque Leopold Gate.

⑩ The ruin of Libuše's Baths on the cliff face of Vyšehrad Rock.

## V Pevnosti

From Vyšehrad metro ① take the exit for the Congress Centre Prague ②, walk up the steps and continue straight ahead with views of Prague Castle to your right. Go down the incline and straight ahead into the quiet street Na Bučance. Cross the road, turn right at the end, and you find yourself on V Pevnosti, facing the brick walls of the original Vyšehrad Citadel.

Ahead of you is the west entrance to the fortress, the mid-17th-century Tábor Gate ③. Through the gate on the right are the ruins of the 14th-century fortifications built by Charles IV. Further on are the ruins of the original Gothic gate, Špička ④. Past that is the sculpture-adorned Leopold Gate ⑤, one of the most impressive parts of these 17th-century fortifications. It adjoins the brick walls ⑥ that were widened during the French occupation of 1742.

## K rotundě to Soběslavova Street

Turn right out of the gate and just after St Martin's Rotunda, turn left into K rotundě. A

few metres on your left, almost concealed behind high walls, is the New Deanery ⑦. Situated at the corner of K rotundě and Soběslavova streets is the Canon's House ⑧. Turn left down Soběslavova to see the excavations of the foundations of the Basilica of St Lawrence ⑨. This was built by Vratislav II, the first Bohemian king, in the late 11th century, but was destroyed by the Hussites (see pp28–9) in

### Key

- •••  Walk route
- —  Castle wall

| 0 metres | 200 |
|---|---|
| 0 yards | 200 |

18th-century engraving by I G Ringle, showing Vyšehrad and the Vltava

1420. About 20 m (65 ft) past the basilica, turn right on to the fortified walls for a stunning view of Prague.

### Vyšehrad Rock

The wooded outcrop of rock on which Vyšehrad was built drops in the west to form a steep rock wall to the river – a vital defensive position. On the summit of the rock are the Gothic ruins of the so-called Libuše's Baths ⑩. This was a defence bastion of the medieval castle. To the left of the bastion is a grassy patch where the remains of a 14th-century Gothic palace ⑪ have been found.

⑭ The elaborate memorial to the composer Antonín Dvořák in Vyšehrad Cemetery.

### Vyšehrad Park

The western part of Vyšehrad has been transformed into a park. Standing on the lawn south of the Church of St Peter and St Paul are four groups of statues ⑫ by the 19th-century sculptor Josef Myslbek. The works represent figures from early Czech history – including the legendary Přemysl and Libuše (see pp22–3). The statues were originally on Palacký Bridge, but were damaged during the US bombardment of February 1945. After being restored, they were taken to Vyšehrad Park. The park was the site of a Romanesque palace, which was connected to the neighbouring church by a bridge. Another palace was built here in the reign of Charles IV (see pp26–7).

### The Church of St Peter and St Paul

This twin-spired church ⑬ dominates Vyšehrad. It was founded in the latter half of the 11th century by Vratislav II and was enlarged in 1129. In the mid-13th century it burned down and was replaced by an Early Gothic church. Since then it has been redecorated and restored many times in a variety of styles. In 1885, it was finally rebuilt in Neo-Gothic style, the twin steeples being added in 1902. Note the early 12th-century stone coffin, thought to be of St Longinus, and a mid-14th-century Gothic panel painting *Our Lady of the Rains* on the altar in the third chapel on the right.

### Vyšehrad Cemetery and the Pantheon

The cemetery ⑭ was founded in 1869 as the burial place for some of the country's most famous figures, such as Bedřich Smetana (see p81). Access is through a gate at the front. On the east side of the cemetery is the Slavín (Pantheon) – built in 1890 for the most honoured citizens of the Czech nation, including the sculptor Josef Myslbek.

Leave the cemetery by the same gate and return down K rotundě. On your left is the Devil's Columafadn ⑮, said to be left by the devil after losing a wager with a priest. At the end is St Martin's Rotunda (see p46) ⑯, a small Romanesque church built in the late 11th century and restored in 1878. Turn left, walk down hill to Cihelná (Brick) Gate ⑰, built in 1741 and home to a small museum that houses six of the original statues from Charles Bridge. Go down Vratislavova Street to Výtoň tram stop on the Vltava Embankment.

⑫ Statue of Přemysl and Princess Libuše by Josef Myslbek in Vyšehrad Park.

### Tips for Walkers

**Starting point:** Vyšehrad metro station, line C.
**Length:** 1.5 km (1 mile).
**Getting there:** The walk starts at Vyšehrad metro station and ends at Výtoň tram stop. Trams 3, 7, 17 and 21 go back to the city centre.
**Stopping-off points:** Relax in the park next to the church of St Peter and St Paul. There is a café in front of the Basilica of St Lawrence and more outdoor cafés in the summer.

# TRAVELLERS' NEEDS

Where to Stay                184–191
Where to Eat and Drink       192–209
Shopping in Prague           210–215
Entertainment in Prague      216–221

# WHERE TO STAY

Since the "Velvet Revolution" of 1989, Prague has become one of the most visited cities in Europe. Thanks to investment in new hotels, helped by huge injections of foreign capital, Prague has developed enough accommodation to meet every tourist need. Many old hotels have been rebuilt, while others have been fully refurbished. It may be hard to find inexpensive accommodation in the city, however, there are a good number of hotels offering surprisingly reasonable rates as competition grows intense. Several are centrally located and even feature designer touches, as well as good service. Cheaper hotels tend to be old-fashioned places in the centre of the city, or smaller, pension-type hotels located in the suburbs. Staying in a flat or a room in a private home can also save you money. This type of accommodation is usually booked through an agency *(see p186)*. Hostels and campsites offer other budget options *(see p187)*.

The Ungelt hotel *(see p189)*

## Where to Look

As Prague is such a small city, it is best to stay near the centre, close to all the main sights, restaurants and shops. Many hotels are found around Wenceslas Square. Here you are at the hub of everything, and the prices of some (but not all) of the hotels reflect this. Other popular areas include the nearby Náměstí Republiky, and the area around Old Town Square, a few minutes' walk from Charles Bridge. Hotels here include large, international establishments, old-fashioned Czech places, and some small, much more exclusive hotels.

To the south, in the New Town, there are several cheaper hotels only a few metro stops from Old Town Square. But the area is less picturesque, and some of the streets suffer from heavy volumes of traffic. For a view of the river Vltava, stay in the Jewish Quarter, although most hotels here are expensive. There are also a few botels (floating hotels)

moored along the embankments away from the city centre. These can be a good option for budget travellers and make for an unusual stay.

Over Charles Bridge, in the Little Quarter, you will find a handful of interesting hotels in delightful surroundings, but there are far fewer by Prague Castle in Hradčany. Further north of this area, there are some large and particularly unappealing hotels.

Two areas close to the centre worth considering are Vinohrady and Anděl. Quality facilities, plus a variety of restaurants makes these neighbourhoods interesting options. The city's suburbs too, have a number of rather nondescript places. These may have good facilities, but they can be as expensive as their equivalents in the centre, with the added inconvenience of travelling time and cost – bear in mind that the metro stops at midnight, and taxis can become costly. Parking can be difficult; if you have a car make sure the hotel you book has parking places available. It's usually better to find a hotel slightly out of the centre if you you plan to drive, as these are more likely to have available parking.

## How to Book

To reserve a room you can telephone, email or book online (the best deals are often

Interior, Riverside Praha *(see p190)*

◀ The quaint café in Hotel Europa *(see p147)*

found online). It is advisable to get confirmation of your booking in writing or via email and bring it with you when you check in as it can save you some time on arrival. Most hotel receptionists speak English, so you can always ring them for advice; otherwise ask your tour operator for help. A number of UK operators specialize in Prague (see p187).

## Facilities

Following the large investment in many of Prague's hotels, most rooms now have en suite WC and shower or bath, Internet, telephone and TV, which may also offer movie and satellite channels. Many hotels offer a reasonably priced laundry service, and the larger hotels usually have 24-hour room service and mini bars. Guests are expected to vacate rooms by midday, but most hotels are happy to keep luggage safe if you are leaving later.

Czech staff generally speak good English so you should encounter few communication problems (see p224).

## Discount Rates

The price structure for hotels in Prague is fairly flexible. One way to get a cheap rate is to check the hotel's website for Internet-only deals and special rates for weekends, which are quite common. The popular seasons are Christmas, New Year and Easter, as well as summer, when rooms are often hard to find and more expensive.

## Hidden Extras

All hotels include tax (currently at 20%) and service charges in their tariff, but do check these details when you book. Telephone charges can be a shock when you receive your bill, so be aware of the mark-up rate. A few surviving telephone boxes in the city take phone cards and some take credit cards but it may be more practical to use roaming facilities on your mobile phone

Hotel Paříž is a protected monument (see p191)

if your plan is affordable (see p232). Some expensive hotels charge an extra fee for breakfast, others include a continental breakfast, but hot dishes cost extra. Buffet-style continental breakfasts are popular, and usually offer fresh fruit, cereals, yogurt, cold meat and cheese, juice and jugs of coffee and tea.

The modern Hilton Prague hotel dominates the area (see p191)

Tipping is common and is expected in many hotels. As in most countries, single travellers receive no favours. There are few single rooms, particularly in newer hotels, and a supplement is charged for single occupancy of a double room; you'll pay about 70–80% of the standard rate.

## Disabled Travellers

Most of the newer hotels in Prague have wheelchair access (see p228). For information on accommodation suitable for the disabled, contact **Accessible Prague** or the Embassy of the Czech Republic in your country.

## Travelling with Children

Children are accommodated by most hotels, either in family rooms or with extra beds. Reliable baby-sitting services are sometimes available in high-end establishments or small inns. Highchairs are readily available. It is worth asking if there are discounts, or if children can stay free in parents' rooms.

Hotel in a quiet street of a historic neighbourhood

## Private Rooms and Self-Catering Apartments

Over the past few years, the number of private rooms to rent in Prague has grown enormously. Although cheap and popular, they may be some distance from the city centre. Private rooms in homes start at about Kč1,000 per person per night, usually with breakfast. There are also self-contained apartments – a fairly central one-bedroom apartment costs about Kč2,000 per night. Most agencies that offer private rooms also rent out apartments (see Directory opposite).

To book a room or apartment, tell the agency exactly what you want, for how many, when and in which area. The agency will then suggest places. Find out the exact location and the

nearest metro before accepting; if you are in Prague, see it yourself. Make sure you receive written or emailed confirmation of a booking to take with you. On arrival in Prague, pay the agency in cash; they give you a voucher to take to the room or apartment (sometimes you can pay the owner directly). If the agency requires advance payment by banker's draft go direct to the accommodation with your receipt. Agencies may ask for a deposit on bookings from abroad, or charge a registratration fee payable in Prague.

## Hostels

There are many hostels in Prague offering cheap beds year-round. Useful websites include www.hostels.com, www.hostelbookers.com, www.bed.cz, and www.hostelprague.com.

A few hostels operate curfews, so it's worth checking this before you book. It is rarely necessary to bring your own sleeping bag as most hostels tend to provide bed sheets and blankets for free. Sometimes it can be better value to choose a hostel further away from the city centre, as even with the addition of transport costs, these can be cheaper than some of the more central establishments, which can cost just as much as a cheap hotel.

If you are visiting between June and mid-September,

it's worth investigating the thousand or so very basic student rooms available to the public in the summer holidays at Charles University's dormitories (Tel: 22 49 30 010). These are an excellent option for the budget traveller. Locations do vary; some are in the city centre, while others are on the outskirts. However, all have good public transport links. Some other Czech colleges also offer a similar service.

## Camping

Most campsites in or near Prague are closed from November to the start of April. They are very cheap with basic facilities, but are well served by transport. The largest site is at **Camp Dana Troja**, 3 km (1.5 miles) north of the city centre. **Aritma Džbán**, 4 km (2.5 miles) west, is open all year for tents, and **Intercamp Hostel Kotva** is 6 km (4 miles) south of the city on the banks of the Vltava.

## Pensions

In the Czech Republic, pensions, or guesthouses, are a cosy, inexpensive type of accommodation. They offer guests reasonably priced standard rooms with en suite bathrooms, and most include breakfast in the price. Look out for their signs along the roads approaching Prague – the word pension is usually in green. Pensions tend to be located outside the city centre and are therefore most convenient for visitors who are arriving by car.

## Luxury

Prague has many luxury hotels, including well known international chains such as Four Seasons, Hilton, Intercontinental and Radisson Blu. These establishments are known for the quality of their services and amenities.

Most upmarket hotels have a concierge who can help guests with theatre tickets and dinner

Hotel entrance on a Little Quarter street

reservations. A concierge with connections may be able to find you good seats for a show or secure a reservation at one of the best restaurants in Prague. You can also turn to your hotel concierge for help when making travel arrangements and sightseeing plans, and if you need to make use of local services or deal with an emergency. It is polite to tip a

concierge who has helped during your stay.

## Recommended Places to Stay

Our accommodation is divided up into five categories: Luxury, Boutique/Design, Hotels with Character, Budget and Apartments. The list should satisfy all budgets and combines location with

amenities and service. The descriptions highlight the unique aspects of the property to help narrow down your decision. Any establishment highlighted as a DK Choice offers a special experience – either superlative service, beautiful interiors and rooms, top-notch amenities, an excellent on-site restaurant, superb views, or a combination of these.

# DIRECTORY

## Disabled Travellers

**Accessible Prague**
Moravanů 51, Praha 6.
**Tel** 608 531 753.
w accessible prague.com

**Embassy of the Czech Republic**
26–30 Kensington Palace Gardens, London W8 4QY.
**Tel** 020 7243 1115.
w mzv.cz/london

## UK and Czech Agencies

**Cresta Holidays**
Thomas Cook Business Park, Conningsby, Peterborough PE3 8SB.
**Tel** 0844 879 8036.
w crestaholidays.co.uk

**ČSA Holidays**
V Celnici 5. **Map** 4 D3.
**Tel** 22 01 04 704.
w holidayscsa.cz

**Czech Tourist Authority**
13 Harley Street, London W1G 9QG.
**Tel** 020 7631 0427.
w czechtourism.com

**Osprey City Holidays**
5 Thistle Street, Edinburgh EH2 1DF.
**Tel** 0131 243 8098.
w osprey holidays.com

**Page & Moy Ltd**
Compass House, Rockingham Rd, Market Harborough, Leicestershire, LE16 7QD.
**Tel** 0844 567 6633.
w pageandmoy.co.uk

**Prospect Cultural Tours Ltd**
79 William St, Herne Bay, Kent CT6 5NR.
**Tel** 01227 743 307.
w prospecttours.com

**Thomson**
Pre Travel Services, TUI UK, Columbus House, Westwood Business Park, Westwood Way, Coventry CV4 8TT.
**Tel** 0871 231 4691.
w thomson.co.uk

## US Agencies

**Czech Tourist Authority**
1109 Madison Avenue, NY 10028.
**Tel** 212 288 0830.
w usa.czechtourism.com

## Private Rooms and Self-Catering Apartments

### IN UK

**Regent Holidays**
Mezzanine Suite, Froomsgate House, Rupert Street, Bristol BS1 2QJ.
**Tel** 0117 921 1711.
w regent-holidays.co.uk

### IN PRAGUE

**Akasi**
Jungmannovo náměstí 771/9. **Map** 3 C5.
**Tel** 22 22 43 067.

**American Express Business Travel Centre**
Na Příkopě 19. **Map** 3 C4.
**Tel** 22 28 00 100.
w american express.cz

**Apartmentplan.cz**
U Demartinky 1347/3.
**Tel** 60 66 88 970
w apartmentplan.cz

**Autoturist**
Na Strži 1837/9.
**Tel** 26 11 04 401.

**AVE Ltd**
Pod Barvířkou 6.
**Tel** 25 15 51 011.
w praguehotel locator.com

**Čedok**
Na Příkopě 18.
**Map** 4 D4.
**Tel** 800 112 112.
w cedok.com

**Estec**
Vaníčkova 5, Prague 6.
**Tel** 23 31 07 511.
w praha-hotel-operator.cz

**hotel.cz**
Žitná 52.
**Map** 6 D2.
**Tel** 22 25 39 539.
w hotel.cz

**PCA (Prague City Apartments)**
Divadelní 24.
**Tel** 800 800 722 (CZ); 0808 120 2320 (UK); 1 877 744 1222 (US).
w praguecity-apartments.cz

**Prague Information Service (PIS)**
Staroměstské náměstí 1.
**Map** 3 B3.
**Tel** 22 17 14 444.

Rytířská 31.
**Map** 3 C4.

Hlavní nádraží (main station).
**Map** 4 E5.
w praguewelcome.cz

**Travel Agency of Czech Railways**
Na Příkopě 31.
**Map** 3 C4.
**Tel** 97 22 43 053.
w cdtravel.cz

## Hostels

**Hostel Jednota**
Opletalova 38.
**Map** 4 D5.
**Tel** 22 42 30 038.
w alfatourist.cz

**Traveller's Hostel**
Dlouhá 33.
**Map** 3 C3.
**Tel** 22 48 26 662.
w travellers.cz

## Camping

**Aritma Džbán**
Nad Lávkou 5, Praha 6.
**Tel** 23 53 58 554.
w campdzban.eu

**Camp Dana Troja**
Trojská 129, Troja.
**Tel** 28 38 50 482.
w campdana.cz

**Intercamp Hostel Kotva**
U ledáren 55, Braník, Praha 4.
**Tel** 24 44 61 712.
w kotvacamp.cz

# Where to Stay

## Apartments

### Little Quarter

**Hunger Wall Residence** Ⓚ
*Plaská 615/8, Praha 5*
**Tel** *25 74 04 040* **Map** 2 E5
🅦 prague-rentals.com
Well-furnished apartments and
exemplary service.

**Appia Hotel Residence** ⓀⓀ
*Šporkova 3/322, Praha 1*
**Tel** *25 72 15 819* **Map** 2 D3
🅦 appiaresidencesprague.cz
A historic hotel with apartments
for up to four people.

**Armour Hotel Residence** ⓀⓀ
*Malostranské nám. 5, Praha 1*
**Tel** *25 75 35 578* **Map** 2 E3
🅦 amourresidencesprague.cz
Gorgeous rooms with
kitchenettes and helpful staff.

### New Town

**Elysee Apartments** ⓀⓀ
*Václavské náměstí 43, Praha 1*
**Tel** *22 14 55 111* **Map** 4 D5
🅦 elyseeapartmentsprague.cz
Compact, well-equipped
apartments. On-site parking.

### Further Afield

**Prague Classic Rental** Ⓚ
*Záhřebská 37, Praha 2*
**Tel** *22 25 16 466*
🅦 pragueclassicrental.cz
Eight buildings with a range of
apartments. Opt to stay here for a
taste of true Prague living.

## Boutique/Design

### Old Town

**Barcelo** ⓀⓀ
*Celetná 29, Praha 1*
**Tel** *22 23 37 111* **Map** 4 D3

🅦 barcelo.com
Housed in a restored 17th-century
building. Comfortable air-
conditioned rooms and free Wi-Fi.

### Prague Castle and Hradčany

**Domus Henrici** ⓀⓀ
*Loretánská 11, Praha 1*
**Tel** *22 05 11 369* **Map** 1 C3
🅦 domus-henrici.cz
A good value, quiet historic hotel
equipped with modern amenities.

**Hotel Hoffmeister** ⓀⓀ
*Pod Bruskou 7, Praha 1*
**Tel** *25 10 17 111* **Map** 2 F2
🅦 hoffmeister.cz
The imposing Hoffmeister has
airy rooms, lovely outdoor spaces
and an excellent spa.

### Little Quarter

**Domus Balthasar** ⓀⓀ
*Mostecká 5, Praha 1*
**Tel** *25 71 99 499* **Map** 2 E3
🅦 domus-balthasar.cz
Bright, cosy rooms combine
stylish design with traditional
touches at the Domus Balthasar.

### New Town

**Hotel Pav** ⓀⓀ
*Kremencova 13, Praha 1*
**Tel** *22 15 02 111* **Map** 5 B1
🅦 hotel-pav.cz
A reliable hotel with elegantly
furnished rooms, good service
and free Wi-Fi access.

**Hotel Sovereign** ⓀⓀ
*Politických vězňů 16, Praha 1*
**Tel** *22 11 11 000* **Map** 4 D5
🅦 sovereignhotel.cz
Rooms are simple and clean
at this relaxing hotel. There is
an on-site sauna, steam bath
and gym.

**Price Guide**
Prices are based on one night's stay in
high season for a standard double room,
linclusive of service charges and taxes.

Ⓚ     up to Kč3000
ⓀⓀ    Kč3000–6000
ⓀⓀⓀⓀⓀ over Kč6000

**Majestic Plaza** ⓀⓀ
*Štěpánská 33, Praha 1*
**Tel** *22 14 86 100* **Map** 5 C1
🅦 hotel-majestic.cz
Both Art Deco and Biedermeier-
style rooms feature at this popular
hotel. Great views from the
seventh floor.

**Maria Prague** ⓀⓀ
*Opletalova 21, Praha 1*
**Tel** *22 22 11 229* **Map** 4 E5
🅦 falkensteiner.com
A mix of Neo-Classical style and
innovatively decorated rooms.
Wellness spa in the basement.

**Metropol** ⓀⓀ
*Národní 33, Praha 1*
**Tel** *24 60 22 100* **Map** 3 B5
🅦 metropolhotel.cz
Sleek hotel with nine floors of
glass-walled design. Rooms are
comfortable, though small.

**Noir** ⓀⓀ
*Legerova 35, Praha 2*
**Tel** *22 41 04 111* **Map** 6 D3
🅦 hotelnoir.cz
Black and white designer rooms.
There is also a cosy garden café.

### Further Afield

**Ametyst** ⓀⓀ
*Jana Masaryka 11, Praha 2*
**Tel** *22 29 21 921*
🅦 hotelametyst.com
Townhouse-style hotel with
comfortable rooms featuring
wall art that is up for sale.

**Andel's Hotel** ⓀⓀ
*Stroupežnického 21, Praha 5*
**Tel** *29 68 89 688*
🅦 andelshotel.com
Well-equipped rooms featuring
contemporary designs. Offers a
great breakfast buffet.

**Angelo** ⓀⓀ
*Radlická 1, Praha 5*
**Tel** *23 48 01 111*
🅦 angelohotel.com
A colourful design concept
dominates the rooms, which
offer additional work space.

**Art Hotel Praha** ⓀⓀ
*Nad Královskou oborou 53, Praha 7*
**Tel** *23 31 01 331*
🅦 arthotel.cz

Charming exterior of Hotel Hoffmeister, near Prague Castle

Rooms feature contemporary art. The lobby area is as impressive as the private garden.

### Mövenpick Ⓚ
*Mozartova 1, Praha 5*
**Tel** *25 71 51 111*
Ⓦ movenpick-prague.com
Spacious rooms. Take a cable car to the popular on-site restaurant, which offers beautiful views.

### Red and Blue Design Hotel Ⓚ Ⓚ
*Holečkova 13, Praha 5*
**Tel** *22 09 90 100*
Ⓦ redandbluehotels.com
Good-sized rooms with bathrooms decorated in either red or blue.

## Budget

## Old Town

### Černý Slon Ⓚ
*Týnská 1, Praha 1*
**Tel** *22 23 21 521* **Map** 3 C3
Ⓦ hotelcernyslon.cz
Luxurious and historic hotel. Individually designed rooms with great views. Welcoming staff.

### Prague Square Hostel Ⓚ
*Melantrichova 10, Praha 1*
**Tel** *22 42 40 859* **Map** 3 B4
Ⓦ praguesquarehostel.com
This hostel is clean, offers free breakfast and has attentive staff. Excellent location

### U Červené Židle Ⓚ
*Liliová 4, Praha 1*
**Tel** *29 61 80 018* **Map** 3 B4
Ⓦ redchairhotel.com
Rooms are modern and roomy, with charming touches. Beautiful lobby and great staff.

### Modrá Růže Ⓚ Ⓚ
*Rytířská 403/16, Praha 1*
**Tel** *22 44 04 100* **Map** 3 C4
Ⓦ hotelmodraruze.cz
Basic rooms, including a few romantic attic rooms with views.

### U Medvídků Ⓚ Ⓚ
*Na Perštýně 7, Praha 1*
**Tel** *22 42 11 916* **Map** 3 B5
Ⓦ umedvidku.cz
Connected to a historic brewery, this hotel has charming rooms with Gothic rafters and Renaissance painted ceilings.

### Ungelt Ⓚ Ⓚ
*Štupartská 646/7, Praha 1*
**Tel** *22 27 45 900* **Map** 3 C3
Ⓦ ungelt.cz
A mix of apartments and spacious suites with all the latest conveniences.

Imposing mosaic-tiled façade of the Mosaic House

## Jewish Quarter

### Travellers' Hostel Ⓚ
*Dlouhá 33, Praha 1*
**Tel** *22 48 26 662* **Map** 3 C2
Ⓦ travellers.cz
Popular hostel and pension. Great place to meet other travellers and located close to several pubs and clubs.

## Little Quarter

### Little Town Hotel Ⓚ
*Malostranské náměstí 11, Praha 1*
**Tel** *24 24 06 964* **Map** 2 E3
Ⓦ littletownhotel.cz
Stark but modern; a great budget option for the Little Quarter.

### Pension Dientzenhofer Ⓚ
*Nosticova 2, Praha 1*
**Tel** *25 73 11 319* **Map** 2 E4
Ⓦ dientzenhofer.cz
A famous pension, with large, shabby chic rooms. Garden offers river views.

### Dům u Velké Boty Ⓚ Ⓚ
*Vlašská 30/333, Praha 1*
**Tel** *25 75 32 088* **Map** 2 D3
Ⓦ dumuvelkeboty.cz
Homey charm, period furnishings and friendly owners make for a personalized stay.

### Hotel Kampa Ⓚ Ⓚ
*Všehrdova 16, Praha 1*
**Tel** *25 74 04 444* **Map** 2 E5
Ⓦ praguekampahotel.com
Hidden location close to Kampa Park; the rooms feature historical touches.

## New Town

### Jerome House Ⓚ
*V Jirchářích 13, Praha 1*
**Tel** *22 49 33 207* **Map** 5 B1
Ⓦ hoteljeromehouse.cz
Good value for the location, with basic but comfortable rooms; the Jerome House is a little stark but convenient.

### DK Choice

### Mosaic House Ⓚ
*Odborů 4, Praha 2*
**Tel** *22 15 95 350* **Map** 5 B1
Ⓦ mosaichouse.com
An environmentally conscious hotel with trendy rooms ranging from dorms to four-star. A bustling bar and restaurant with friendly and attentive staff make this a welcoming place for travellers of all ages.

### Pension Museum Ⓚ
*Mezibranská 15, Praha 1*
**Tel** *29 63 25 186* **Map** 6 D1
Ⓦ pension-museum.cz
Large rooms, simply but tastefully furnished. An in-room fridge and a delicious breakfast are extra bonuses.

### 987 Prague Hotel Ⓚ Ⓚ
*Senovážné náměstí 15, Praha 1*
**Tel** *25 57 37 200* **Map** 4 E4
Ⓦ 987-praguehotel.com
This great-value hotel has well-decorated rooms and suites.

## Further Afield

### Anna Ⓚ
*Budečská 17, Praha 2*
**Tel** *22 25 13 111*
Ⓦ hotelanna.cz
Rooms have Art Nouveau interiors at this excellent value hotel, with a beautiful breakfast room. Lovely quiet location.

### Czech Inn Ⓚ
*Francouzská 76, Praha 2*
**Tel** *26 72 67 612*
Ⓦ czech-inn.com
A hip hostel with private rooms, a good bar and lots of events.

### Dahlia Inn Ⓚ
*Lípová 1444/20, Praha 2*
**Tel** *22 25 17 518*
Ⓦ dahliainn.com
A small hotel with charming and comfortable rooms. Friendly staff.

### Diplomat Ⓚ
*Evropská 15, Praha 6*
**Tel** *29 65 59 111*
Ⓦ diplomathotel.cz
Close to the airport and town centre, Diplomat has two restaurants and a café.

### Plaza Alta Ⓚ
*Ortenovo nám. 22, Praha 7*
**Tel** *22 04 07 082*
Ⓦ plazahotelalta.com
An eco-friendly hotel, with an on-site Mexican restaurant.

**For more information on types of hotels** *see page 187*

## Hotels with Character
### Old Town

**Hotel Aurus** ⓚ
*Karlova 3, Praha 1*
**Tel** *22 22 20 262*          **Map** 3 A4
Ⓦ hoteltaurus.cz
Small family hotel exuding old-world charm. Rooms are distinctive and have antique furnishings.

**U Zlatého Stromu** ⓚ
*Karlova 6, Praha 1*
**Tel** *22 22 20 441*          **Map** 3 A4
Ⓦ zlatystrom.com
Impressive 18th-century decor. Individually designed rooms equipped with updated amenities.

**Unitas** ⓚ
*Bartolomějská 9, Praha 1*
**Tel** *22 42 30 533*          **Map** 3 B5
Ⓦ unitas.cz
A former convent with enormous rooms and splendid bathrooms.

### DK Choice

**Hotel Josef** ⓚⓚ
*Rybná 20, Praha 1*
**Tel** *22 17 00 111*          **Map** 3 C3
Ⓦ hoteljosef.com
This all-white and glass designer hotel with bright touches and great service has an interesting layout. Two buildings are connected by a courtyard and offer unique design elements. The lobby is a showpiece in itself. Enroll for a morning sightseeing jog through the city.

### Jewish Quarter

**Maximilian** ⓚⓚ
*Haštalská 14, Praha 1*
**Tel** *22 53 03 118*          **Map** 3 C2
Ⓦ maximilianhotel.com
A designer hotel decorated with muted colours and Art Deco touches. Try the superb breakfast.

### Prague Castle and Hradčany

**Lindner Hotel Prague Castle** ⓚⓚ
*Strahovská 128, Praha 1*
**Tel** *22 60 80 000*          **Map** 1 B4
Ⓦ lindner.de/en/hotel_prague_castle
Located behind Prague Castle, this beautifully reconstructed former stable is a must-visit.

### Little Quarter

**Charles Hotel** ⓚⓚ
*Josefská 1, Praha 1*
**Tel** *21 11 51 300*          **Map** 2 E3
Ⓦ hotel-charles.cz

Spacious and cosy bathroom, U Zlaté Studně

Just off Charles Bridge, this hotel has charming and historic rooms.

### DK Choice

**Icon** ⓚⓚ
*V Jámě 6, Praha 1*
**Tel** *22 16 34 100*          **Map** 5 C1
Ⓦ iconhotel.eu
Hip hotel with efficient staff and wonderful rooms in a bustling location. Facilities include a spa, a fashionable lounge and a bar. In-room iPod connections and all-day breakfast are just a few of the bonuses.

**Palace Road Hotel** ⓚⓚ
*Nerudova 7, Praha 1*
**Tel** *25 75 31 941*          **Map** 2 D3
Ⓦ palaceroad.com
Conveniently located near many attractions, this hotel has uniquely decorated rooms in a number of buildings.

**Sax** ⓚⓚ
*Jánský vršek 328/3, Praha 1*
**Tel** *25 75 31 268*          **Map** 2 D3
Ⓦ hotelsax.cz
Decked out in 50s, 60s, and 70s decor, this colourful hotel makes for a memorable stay. Simple yet cosy rooms.

### DK Choice

**U Zlaté Studně** ⓚⓚ
*Zlaté studně 166/4, Praha 1*
**Tel** *25 70 11 213*          **Map** 2 E2
Ⓦ goldenwell.cz
Situated beneath Prague Castle, in the maze of the Little Quarter streets, the "Golden Well" offers lovely rooms with interesting views. The hotel also houses one of the city's top restaurants.

**Augustine Hotel** ⓚⓚⓚ
*Letenská 12/33, Praha 1*
**Tel** *26 61 12 233*          **Map** 2 F3
Ⓦ theaugustine.com
A former monastery with Cubist-style rooms and a cellar brewery.

### New Town

### DK Choice

**Fusion** ⓚ
*Panská 9, Praha 1*
**Tel** *22 62 22 800*          **Map** 4 D4
Ⓦ fusionhotels.com
The stripped down, industrial chic-style rooms here feature contemporary decor. A six-person bed is just one of its unique features. There is a bar and a restaurant and staff are committed to ensuring that guests have a good time.

**Hotel Yasmin** ⓚⓚ
*Politických vězňů 12, Praha 1*
**Tel** *23 41 00 100*          **Map** 4 D5
Ⓦ hotel-yasmin.cz
Close to Wenceslas Square, Yasmin offers comfortable rooms with fresh, contemporary decor.

### Further Afield

**U Blaženky** ⓚ
*U Blaženky 1, Praha 5*
**Tel** *25 15 64 532*
Ⓦ ublazenky.cz
Delightful, cosy villa with a wonderful ambience and attentive staff.

**Moods** ⓚⓚ
*Klimentská 28, Praha 1*
**Tel** *420 222 330 100*
Ⓦ hotelmoods.com
A Czech children's story painted on the rooms' walls, a moss wall in the lobby and all-day breakfast make staying here an enjoyable and whimsical experience.

**Riverside Praha** ⓚⓚ
*Janáčkovo nábřeží 15, Praha 5*
**Tel** *22 59 94 611*
Ⓦ mamaison.com
A historic hotel with a fairytale exterior and an exquisite location on the banks of the Vltava. The rooms are sophisticated, with touches of elegance, and feature modern amenities.

**Key to prices** *see page 188*

# Luxury
## Old Town

### Grand Hotel Praha
*Staroměstské náměstí 22, Praha 1*
**Tel** *420 221 632 556* **Map** 3 C3
w grandhotelpraha.cz
Located opposite the Astronomical Clock, this Baroque palace has rooms decorated with murals and antique furnishings.

### Ventana
*Celetná 7, Praha 1*
**Tel** *420 221 776 600* **Map** 3 C3
w ventana-hotel.net
Experience Art Nouveau luxury in enormous rooms and suites with amazing Old Town views.

### Hotel Paříž
*U Obecního domu 1, Praha 1*
**Tel** *420 222 195 195* **Map** 4 D2
w hotel-paris.cz
Beautiful rooms and excellent decor make for a luxurious stay. Don't miss the stunning staircase.

### Pachtuv Palace
*Karolíny Světlé 34, Praha 1*
**Tel** *420 234 705 111* **Map** 3 A4
w mamaison.com/pachtuvpalace
Frescoes, chapel ceilings and architectural gems dominate the interiors of this palace.

## Jewish Quarter

### Four Seasons
*Veleslavínova 2a/1098, Praha 1*
**Tel** *22 14 27 000* **Map** 3 A3
w fourseasons.com
Superbly located on the banks of the Vltava river, this hotel offers classic Four Seasons luxury.

### Intercontinental
*Pařížská 30, Praha 1*
**Tel** *29 66 31 111* **Map** 3 B2
w icprague.com
Comfortable rooms and a variety of dining options are available at the Intercontinental.

### President
*Nám. Curieových 100, Praha 1*
**Tel** *23 46 14 111* **Map** 3 B2
w hotelpresident.cz
Bright, fabulously furnished rooms and a well-regarded restaurant.

## Prague Castle and Hradčany

### Savoy
*Keplerova 6, Praha 1*
**Tel** *420 224 302 430* **Map** 1 B3
w goldentulipsavoyprague.com
A bit dated, but still lovely, this place offers a complimentary minibar.

## Little Quarter

### Alchymist
*Tržiště 19, Praha 1*
**Tel** *420 257 286 011* **Map** 2 D3
w alchymisthotel.com
Royally furnished rooms, individually decorated and distinct from one another. Facilities include a great spa.

### Aria
*Tržiště 9, Praha 1*
**Tel** *420 225 334 111* **Map** 2 E3
w ariahotel.net
Musically themed rooms dedicated to a style of music or a famous composer, such as Mozart or Puccini. Guests have private access to Prague Castle's garden.

### Mandarin Oriental
*Nebovidska 459/1, Praha 1*
**Tel** *420 233 088 888* **Map** 2 E4
w mandarinoriental.com
Reconstructed from parts of a former monastery, each of this hotel's rooms boasts a distinct design.

## New Town

### Boscolo Prague
*Senovážné náměstí 13, Praha 1*
**Tel** *22 45 93 111* **Map** 4 E4
w prague.boscolohotels.com
Close to the main train station, this hotel boasts Italian opulence and an impressive spa.

### Prague Inn
*28. října 378/15, Praha 1*
**Tel** *22 60 14 444* **Map** 3 C4
w hotelpragueinn.cz
Spacious rooms with stylish furnishings and comfortable beds.

### DK Choice
**Radisson Blu Alcron**
*Štěpánská 40, Praha 1*
**Tel** *22 28 20 000* **Map** 6 D1
w radissonblu.com/hotel-prague
A historic Art Deco hotel with high ceilings and period furnishings combined with excellent amenities and good service. Its Alcron restaurant boasts one of the country's top chefs, and there is a lobby cocktail bar as well.

### Sheraton Prague Charles Square Hotel
*Žitná 8, Praha 2*
**Tel** *22 59 99 999* **Map** 5 C1
w sheratonprague.com
A hip lobby, sleek rooms and sophisticated dining venues.

## Further Afield

### Corinthia Hotel Prague
*Kongresová 1, Praha 4*
**Tel** *26 11 91 111*
w corinthia.com
Close to the Prague Congress Centre, the Corinthia is ideal for business travellers.

### Hilton Prague
*Pobřežní 1, Praha 8*
**Tel** *22 48 41 111*
w hiltonprague.com
All Rooms are modern and spacious; some have views over the river. Classic Hilton service.

### Kempinski Hotel Hybernska
*Hybernská 12, Praha 1*
**Tel** *22 62 26 111*
w kempinski-prague.com
Beautifully reconstructed hotel with a gorgeous garden.

### Le Palais
*U Zvonarky 1, Praha 2*
**Tel** *420 234 634 111*
w palaishotel.cz
A *belle époque* hotel with brightly coloured rooms. Great spa.

### Prague Marriott
*V celnici 8, Praha 1*
**Tel** *420 222 888 888*
w marriott.com
Spacious and well-equipped rooms and a good on-site restaurant.

Homey yet elegant interiors of Kempinski Hotel Hybernska

**For more information on types of hotels** *see page 187*

# WHERE TO EAT AND DRINK

Restaurants in Prague, just like the tourist economy, have improved in recent years. For decades, state-licensed eating and drinking establishments had little incentive to experiment or progress. But attitudes have changed. New restaurants are opening constantly, many of them foreign-owned, offering the discerning eater ever-increasing choice. The restaurants described in this section reflect the change, though many only serve a limited range of standard Western dishes in addition to the staple Czech meals. *Recommended Restaurants* on pages 198–205 summarizes the key features of the restaurants and cafés listed in this guide, which are organized by area. Information on pubs, beer halls and bars appears on pages 206–7. Compared to Western European prices, eating out in Prague is still cheap.

## Tips on Eating Out

Because of the huge influx of tourists, eating out has changed in character. The lunch hour can be any time from 11am to 3pm, and for most Czechs the normal time for the evening meal is around 7pm. However, many of the restaurants stay open late and it is possible to get a meal at anytime from 10am until 11pm. Kitchens close 30 minutes to one hour earlier than stated closing times.

During spring and summer, the large numbers of visitors tend to put a strain on many of Prague's more popular restaurants. To be certain of a table, especially in the very well-known restaurants, it is advisable to book in advance.

The city centre is full of restaurants, and there are several off the normal tourist track. Prices also tend to be lower the further you go from the centre.

## Places to Eat

The importance of a stylish yet comfortable setting, and food which is inspired rather than just prepared, is slowly beginning to trickle down to Prague's better and more innovative restaurants. The places which follow this maxim are generally the best.

One of the simplest places to eat is the sausage stand, a utilitarian establishment that is very common in Central Europe. The sausages can either be eaten standing at the counter or taken away cold. For a late-night meal your best bet is often a *gyros* (kebab) or pizza served from a street stand.

For greater comfort, head for a café (*kavárna*). Cafés range from loud, busy main street locations to quieter bookstore establishments. All have fully stocked bars and many serve a variety of food from simple pastries and sandwiches to full-blown meals. Opening hours differ widely, but many open early in the morning and are good for a quick, if not quite a Western-style, breakfast.

Brunch buffets, complete with champagne and jazz, are

Outside dining in a pretty coutyard

available at a number of the city's fine-dining establishments. Brunch costs no more than Kč600, so it is a great option for those who want to experience high quality food without breaking the bank.

A restaurant is called a *restaurace*; a *vinárna* specializes in wine and may have small snacks to match the drinks.

Plain Czech food is normally available at the local beer hall (*pivnice*) or pub (*hospoda*), though the emphasis at this type of place is normally on drinking rather than eating.

## Reading the Menu

Never judge a restaurant by the standard of its menu translations – mistakes are common in every class of restaurant. Many menus still list the weight of meat served. Typically, you'll need to order main meal accompaniments like potatoes, rice or dumplings separately, unless the menu specifically includes it. The same applies to salads and other side dishes (*see pp194–5 for The Flavours of Prague*).

La Truffe (*see p199*)

Tourists eating at the outdoor cafés in the Old Town Square

## Extra Costs

In some restaurants or bars the waiter may bring nuts to your table. Yes, they are for you to eat, but at a price equal to, or higher than, an appetizer. You will not insult anybody by telling the waiter to take them away. The same applies to appetizers brought round by the waiter.

You may notice extra charges you don't recognize when you check your bill. But they may well be legitimate, as cover charges (usually Kč10–25) might include such items as milk, ketchup, bread and butter might be charged for. Finally, a 17.5% tax is normally included in the menu.

## Etiquette

You don't have to wait to be seated in snack bars and smaller eateries. It is also quite normal

Fine dining amid stained-glass Art Deco splendour

for others to join your table if there is any room. No restaurant has an official dress code, but people tend to dress up when dining in upmarket restaurants.

## Payment and Tipping

The average price for a full meal in the centre of Prague ranges from about Kč250 to Kč1,100 per person and more, depending on the type of establishment. In some restaurants the waiter may write your order on a piece of paper and then leave it on your table for the person who comes around when you are ready to pay. Generally a 10 per cent tip is appropriate. Add the tip to the bill, do not leave the money on the table. Most restaurants accept major credit cards, but ask before the meal to make sure. Travellers' cheques are not accepted.

## Vegetarians

The situation for vegetarians in Prague is improving as awareness increases. Fresh vegetables are available throughout the year, and numerous restaurants offer vegetarian and vegan options. Nevertheless, even when a dish is described as meatless, it's always worth double-checking. Vegetarians should particularly beware of menu sections called *bez masa* as, whilst the literal translation of this word is "without meat", its actual meaning is that meat is not the main ingredient in the dishes listed.

## Disabled Travellers

Many restaurants still do not cater specifically for the disabled. The staff will almost always try and help, but Prague's ubiquitous stairs and basements will defeat all but the most determined.

## Reservations

There is generally no need to reserve a table at lunchtime or on weekday evenings in Prague. If you are planning to eat dinner on a Friday or Saturday evening, however, particularly in Prague's better known restaurants, it is advisable to book in advance. Reservations can be done in person, by telephone or online. Alternatively, online booking companies will make a free reservation for you. Your booking is confirmed by email and you pay as usual at the restaurant.

## Recommended Restaurants

Prague offers an astonishing array of cuisines, from French and Asian to traditional and modern Czech fare (*see Flavours of Prague pp194–5*). Traditional Czech involves dishes with lots of meat, potatoes or dumplings, while modern Czech is where enterprising chefs are taking the old recipes and making them fresher and lighter.

Our restaurants are divided into six geographical areas: Old Town, Jewish Quarter, Prague Castle and Hradčany, Little Quarter, New Town and Further Afield. We've selected the best from across the city, and encourage you to move out of the centre and explore some other neighbourhoods for more variety and cheaper prices. The specially recommended restaurants, marked as DK Choice, have been chosen because they offer a special experience – either for the superb cuisine, for enjoying a traditional Czech dining night out, for the excellent value, or a combination of these.

# The Flavours of Prague

While few visitors come to Prague for the food, there is far more to contemporary Czech cuisine than the Central European norm of meat, potatoes and rice. Czech food remains based on seasonally available ingredients, while a simple, no-fuss approach allows natural flavours to dominate most dishes. The staples of Czech cooking are pork, beef, game and carp, which tend to be served grilled or roasted, accompanied by a light sauce and vegetables. They are also used in sour soups, known as *polévky*. It is unlikely that you will leave Prague without tasting *knedlíky* (dumplings), either savoury or sweet.

Blueberries

Atmospheric U Pinkasů cellar bar and restaurant *(see p203)*

## Meat

The Czech favourite is pork *(vepřové)*. It appears in countless dishes, including soups, goulash and sausages, or can be served on its own, either grilled or (more commonly) roasted and served with sliced dumplings and sweet-sour cabbage *(Vepřo-knedlozelo)*. It also appears in other forms, notably as Prague ham *(Pražska šunka)*, a succulent,

lightly smoked meat usually eaten with bread at breakfast or with horseradish as a starter at suppertime.

Veal, occasionally served in the form of breadcrumbed, fried Wiener schnitzel *(smažený řízek)*, is popular.

Beef in the region has never been up to international standards, and needs to be prepared well to be edible. The

Prague favourite is *Svíčková*, sliced, roast sirloin, served in a cream sauce with dumplings and sliced lemon. If cooked well it can be tender and delicious. Beef is also used in goulash and stews. Most of the beef served in top restaurants is likely to be imported. Czech lamb *(jehněčí)* is not the best in the world, either, though for a short period from mid-March to mid-May there is

Apple strudel  Trdelník (sweet pastry)
Honzova buchta (fruit buns)
Čokoládový řez (chocolate cake)
Český koláč (plu... jam bun)
Bublanina (... crumble...)

Selection of typical Czech cakes and pastries

## Local Dishes and Specialities

*Knedlíky* (dumplings), either savoury (špekové) in soups or sweet (ovocné) with fruits and berries, are perhaps Bohemia's best-known delicacy. Once a mere side dish they have now become a central feature of Czech cuisine, as Postmodern chefs rediscover their charms and experiment with new and different ways of cooking and serving them. Other specialities of the region include *Dršťková polévka*, a remarkably good tripe soup, which – although an acquired taste – has also seen something of a revival in recent years as better restaurants add it to their menus. Duck and pheasant remain popular in Prague and, with the city surrounded by fine hunting grounds, such game is always of top quality. Pork, though, is the city's (and the nation's) most popular food, served roasted on the bone, with red cabbage.

Stuffed eggs

**Polévka s játrovými knedlíčky**
Soup with liver dumplings is a common dish in the Czech Republic.

Wild chanterelle mushrooms from the forests around the city

good lamb available in Prague's markets, where it is usually sold whole, complete with the head which is used to make soup.

## Game

There is a wide variety of game to be found in the forests around Prague. Depending on the season (the best time is autumn) you will find duck, pheasant, goose, boar, venison, rabbit and hare on many menus. Duck is probably the most popular game dish, usually roasted with fruits, berries or sometimes with chestnuts, and served with red cabbage. Small pheasants, roasted whole with juniper and blueberries or cranberries, are also popular, while venison is often served grilled with mushrooms. Rabbit and hare are usually presented in spicy, goulash-style sauces.

## Vegetables

Fresh vegetables are becoming more popular as an accompaniment to meals. Note, however, that Czechs tend to boil their vegetables into oblivion. While more and more imported, out-of-season produce is finding its way into supermarkets, many

Fresh vegetables on a Prague market stall

Czechs are unwilling to pay the higher prices these goods demand. As a result, the hardy cabbage remains the country's top vegetable, used in numerous different ways, such as raw as a salad, or boiled as an accompaniment to roast meats. The Czech version of *sauerkraut*, *kyselé zelí*, is ubiquitous. Mushrooms, too, are well liked, and find their way in to many sauces, especially those served with game.

### BEST LOCAL SNACKS

**Sausages** Street stalls and snack bars all over the city sell traditional sausages (*klobásy* and *utopence*), frankfurters (*párky*) or bratwurst, served in a soft roll with mustard.

**Chlebíčky** Open sandwiches on sliced baguette are found in any delicatessen or snack bar in Prague. Toppings are usually ham, salami or cheese, always accompanied by a gherkin (*nakládaná okurka*).

**Pivní sýr** Beer cheese is soaked in ale until it becomes soft. It is served spread on bread and eaten with pickles or onions.

**Nakládaný hermelín** This whole round cheese is pickled in oil with onions and paprika. A firm favourite in pubs.

**Palačinky** Pancakes are filled with ice cream and/or fruits and jam, and are topped with lashings of sugar.

**Pečený kapr s kyselou omáčkou** Carp with sour cream and lemon is popular, especially at Christmas.

**Vepřové s křenem** Pork is served roasted, on the bone, with red cabbage and either sauerkraut or horseradish.

**Ovocné knedlíky** Sweet dumplings are filled with fruits or berries, usually blueberries or plums.

# What to Drink in Prague

Czech beers are famous around the world, but nowhere are they drunk with such appreciation as in Prague. The Czechs take their beer *(pivo)* seriously and are very proud of it. Pilsner and its various relations originate in Bohemia. It is generally agreed that the best Pilsners are produced close to Pilsen – and all the top producers are not far from Prague. Beers can be bought in cans, in bottles, and best of all, on draught. Canned beer is made mostly for export, and no connoisseur would ever drink it. The Czech Republic also produces considerable quantities of wine, both red and white, mainly in Southern Moravia. Little of it is bottled for export. Mineral water can be found in most restaurants; Mattoni and Dobrá voda (meaning good water) are the two most widely available brands.

Gambrinus, legendary King of Beer, and trademark of a popular brand of Pilsner

Traditional copper brew-kettles in Plzeň

## Pilsner and Budweiser

The best-known Czech beer is Pilsner Urquell. Clear and golden, with a strong flavour of hops, Pilsner is made by the lager method: bottom-fermented and slowly matured at low temperatures. The word "Pilsner" (now a generic term for similar lagers brewed all over the world) is derived from Plzeň (in German, Pilsen), a town 80 km (50 miles) southwest of Prague, where this type of beer was first made in 1842. The brewery that developed the beer still makes it under the name Plzeňský prazdroj (original source), better known abroad as Pilsner Urquell. A slightly sweeter beer, Budweiser Budvar is brewed 150 km (100 miles) south of Prague in the town of České Budějovice (in German, Budweis). The American Budweiser's first brewer adopted the name after a visit to Bohemia in the 19th century.

Budweiser logo

Pilsner Urquell logo

## Types of Czech Beer

Originally, Czech beers were divided into draft, lager and special beers, according to the concentration of malt they contained (known as original gravity). However, in 1997 a new system was introduced that is more in line with EU practices. Czech beer now falls into one of four main groups according to colour – light *(světlé)*, semi-dark *(polotmavé)*, dark *(tmavé)* and cut *(řezané)*. Within these groups are a further 11 sub-groups categorized by measures of alcohol, sugar, wheat and yeast content, as well as the method of final adjustment of the beer. Confusingly, pubs still use the old system of categorization by original gravity.

Kozel beer label

## Beer and Beer Halls

| Staropramen | Gambrinus | Velkopopovický kozel | Budweiser Budvar | Plzeňský prazdroj (Pilsner Urquell) |

The real place to enjoy Czech beer is a pub or beer hall *(pivnice)*. Each pub is usually supplied by a single brewery *(pivovar)*, so only one brand of beer is available, but several different types are on offer. The major brands include Pilsner Urquell and Gambrinus from Plzeň, Staropramen from Prague, and Velkopopovický Kozel from Velké Popovice, south of Prague. The usual drink is draught light beer *(světlé)*, but a number of beer halls, including U Fleků *(see p155)* and U Kalicha *(see p154)* also serve special, strong dark lagers (ask for *tmavé*).

A half litre of beer (equivalent to just under a pint) is called a *velké* (large), and a third of a litre (larger than a half pint) is called a *malé* (small). The waiters bring beers and snacks to your table and mark everything you eat and drink on a tab. You should be aware that in some pubs there is a tacit

assumption that all the customers want to go on drinking until closing time, so don't be surprised if more beers arrive without you having ordered them. If you don't want them, just say no. The bill is only totted up when you are ready to leave.

People enjoying a drink in one of Prague's beer gardens

## Wines

Czech wine producers have not yet emulated the success of other East European wine-makers. The main wine-growing region is in Moravia, where most of the best wine is produced for local consumption. Some wine is also made in Bohemia, around Mělník, just north of Prague. The whites are made mostly from Riesling, Müller-Thurgau or Veltliner grapes (*polosuché* is demi-sec and *suché* is sec). Rulandské (Pinot) is an acceptable dry white. The reds are slightly better, the main choices being Frankovka and

Rulandské, white and red

Vavřinecké. In the autumn, a semi-fermented young, sweet white or red wine called *burčák* is sold and drunk across the capital.

## Czech Spirits and Liqueurs

In every restaurant and pub you'll find Becherovka, a bitter-sweet, amber herbal drink served both as an aperitif and a liqueur. It can also be diluted with tonic (called Beton). Other local drinks include Borovička, a juniper-flavoured spirit, and plum brandy or Slivovice. The latter is clear, strong and an acquired taste. Imported spirits and cocktails are more expensive.

Becherovka

# Where to Eat and Drink

## Old Town

**Bohemia Bagel**
American **Map** 3 C3
*Masná 2, Praha 1*
**Tel** *22 48 12 560*
Great breakfast place, but also has wholesome sandwiches and burgers. Free refills of coffee make this a popular spot. High-speed Internet at reasonable rates throughout the day.

**Country Life**
Vegetarian **Map** 3 B4
*Melantrichova 15, Praha 1*
**Tel** *22 42 13 366* **Closed** *Sat*
Best bargain lunch in town. The self-serve buffet has freshly made hot and cold vegetarian dishes; pay by weight. Also try the excellent sandwiches, salads, soups and desserts.

**Kabul**
Afghan **Map** 3 A5
*Karolíny Světlé 14, Praha 1*
**Tel** *22 42 35 452*
An eclectic menu, welcoming staff and a local feel – Kabul offers reasonable, but hearty Afghan dishes and pizza. Expect crowds at lunchtime.

**Las Adelitas**
Mexican **Map** 3 B4
*Malé náměstí 13, Praha 1*
**Tel** *22 22 33 247*
Go around the corner from the Astronomical Clock to savour authentic Mexican food at this neighbourhood eatery. Try the freshly prepared *burritos*, *enchiladas* and *quesadillas*. Also check out the interesting array of Mexican beers and tequilas.

### DK Choice

**Lehká Hlava**
Vegetarian **Map** 3 A4
*Boršov 2/280, Praha 1*
**Tel** *22 22 20 665*
The best vegetarian restaurant in Prague has a creative take on international cuisine and trippy, cool interiors. The extensive menu ranges from Asian to Mexican to Lebanese. The Thai red curry with tofu is a treat, and the *burrito* will force you to skip dessert. There are many vegan offerings as well.

**Maitrea**
Vegetarian **Map** 3 C3
*Týnská ulička 6/1064, Praha 1*
**Tel** *22 17 11 631*
Beautiful restaurant with a well-designed menu that includes Asian and Mexican dishes. Great lunch specials are also available.

**Století**
International **Map** 3 A5
*Karolíny Světlé 21/320, Praha 1*
**Tel** *22 22 20 008*
Prompt service and delicious food is offered at this often missed, though centrally located, restaurant. The Czech dishes on the menu are creatively named and prepared.

**U Provaznice**
Czech **Map** 3 C4
*Provaznická 3, Praha 1*
**Tel** *22 42 32 528*
Cheerful pub in an excellent location with a reasonably priced menu. Be prepared to find it packed with locals at lunchtimes.

### Price Guide

Prices are based on a three-course meal per person, with a half-bottle of house wine, including tax and service.

Ⓚ under Kč500
ⒾⓀ Kč500–800
ⓀⓀⓀⓀⓀ over Kč800

**U Tří růží**
Czech **Map** 3 B4
*Husova 10/232, Praha 1*
**Tel** *60 15 88 287/2*
This brew house makes its own beer and serves classic Czech dishes. Six fresh beers are always on tap.

**Caffrey's**
Irish **Map** 3 C3
*Staroměstské nám. 10, Praha 1*
**Tel** *22 48 28 031*
This Pub on Old Town Square has amazing food and plenty of TVs all around. A great place to meet travellers and expats.

**Divinis**
Italian **Map** 3 C3
*Týnská 21, Praha 1*
**Tel** *22 23 25 440* **Closed** *Sun*
This wine bar serves typical northern Italian favourites in a private and elegant space. The top-notch wine selection is primarily from Italy.

**Kogo**
Italian **Map** 3 C4
*Havelská 499/27, Praha 1*
**Tel** *22 42 14 543*
A good location makes this eatery an ideal spot for lunch or dinner. Savour solid Italian cuisine in spacious and lovely surroundings.

**Le Saint-Tropez**
French **Map** 3 C3
*Týnska ulička 606/3, Praha 1*
**Tel** *22 48 10 750*
Sample well-presented regional French cuisine and exquisite wine in this pretty cellar space. There's a summer garden as well.

**Parnas**
Czech-International **Map** 3 A5
*Smetanovo nábřeží 1012/2, Praha 1*
**Tel** *22 42 39 604*
Art Deco-style restaurant next to the Vltava river, and close to Charles Bridge, with a fresh take on Czech cuisine. Be sure to check out the list of creative international dishes.

**Pizza Nuova**
Italian **Map** 4 D2
*Revoluční 1/655, Praha 1*
**Tel** *22 18 03 308*

Elegantly designed interiors at Lehká Hlava, Prague's finest vegetarian restaurant

Opulent Art Nouveau decor with colourful tile mosaics at Plzeňská

One of the best pizzerias in town, this place is known for its thin-crust pizza. Fresh fish, pasta and other Italian specialities are also on the menu, and there's an antipasto bar.

### Platina
Czech    ⓀⓀ   Map 3 A5
*Karolíny Světlé 323/27, Praha 1*
**Tel** *23 90 09 244*
Relish modern Czech cuisine with an inventive touch at this eatery. The menu changes seasonally and the focus is on using local ingredients. Barbeque on the terrace in summer.

### Plzeňská
Czech    ⓀⓀ   Map 4 D3
*Náměstí republiky 5, Praha 1*
**Tel** *22 20 02 770*
A fun evening is in store at Plzeňská, with its fabulous Art Nouveau interiors, friendly staff and extensive menu of Czech dishes.

### Red Pif
International    ⓀⓀ   Map 3 A5
*Betlémská 9, Praha 1*
**Tel** *22 22 32 086*    **Closed** *Sun*
This industrial-chic restaurant and wine shop offers a small but delicious menu and a great wine list. Beautifully designed interiors.

### School Restaurant & Lounge
Czech-International    ⓀⓀ   Map 3 A4
*Smetanovo nábř. 22, Praha 1*
**Tel** *22 22 22 173*
Well-prepared modern Czech and international cuisine is served in a large, modern dining space with views across the Vltava. Efficient staff.

### U Závoje
International    ⓀⓀ   Map 3 B4
*Havelská 500/25, Praha 1*
**Tel** *60 22 57 640*
The menu here is designed to complement the extensive list of French wines. The cellar space is cosy and inviting.

### VinodiVino
Italian    Ⓚ   Map 3 C3
*Štupartská 769/18, Praha 1*
**Tel** *22 23 11 791*
This restaurant and wine bar features specialities from southern Italy. The small menu is well-designed, with signature offerings.

### Ambiente Brasileiro
Brazilian    ⓀⓀⓀ   Map 3 B3
*U Radnice 8, Praha 1*
**Tel** *22 42 34 474*
Choose from a variety of dishes at this all-you-can-eat buffet. Brazilian *churrasco* is paraded around the restaurant on skewers.

### Bellevue
International    ⓀⓀⓀ   Map 3 A4
*Smetanovo nábř. 18, Praha 1*
**Tel** *22 22 21 443*
Come here for a unique dining experience, where you design your own multi-course meal. Ingredients are carefully chosen and staff will suggest suitable wines. Excellent views of Prague Castle.

### Buddha Bar
Asian    ⓀⓀⓀ   Map 3 C3
*Jakubská 8, Praha 1*
**Tel** *22 17 76 400*    **Closed** *Sun & Mon*
Over-the-top dining room overlooked by a massive Buddha. Imaginative Asian cuisine. There's also a separate bar/lounge.

### Francouzská Restaurace
French    ⓀⓀⓀ   Map 4 D3
*Náměstí republiky 5, Praha 1*
**Tel** *22 20 02 784*
Delicious dishes almost over-shadowed by the Art Nouveau interiors. They also serve Czech and international cuisine. Strong wine list.

### La Truffe
French    ⓀⓀⓀ   Map 3 C3
*Týnská 633/12, Praha 1*
**Tel** *60 83 08 574*    **Closed** *Sun*
Beautiful interiors with lots of cosy nooks and frescoed walls. The menu is dedicated to the truffle.

### Le terroir
French-International    ⓀⓀⓀ   Map 3 B4
*Vejvodova 1, Praha 1*
**Tel** *60 28 89 118*
**Closed** *Sun & Mon*
One of Prague's top gastronomic experiences, and the best place for wine lovers. The food is equally good and well prepared.

### Mlýnec
Czech    ⓀⓀⓀ   Map 3 A4
*Novotného lávka 9, Praha 1*
**Tel** *27 70 00 777*
Focuses on using locally sourced meat and fish and serves a nice selection of meals. Roast lunch every Sunday.

### Sarah Bernhardt
French-Czech    ⓀⓀⓀ   Map 4 D3
*U Obecního domu 1, Praha 1*
**Tel** *22 21 95 900*
Fresh and light Czech and French dishes in a beautiful setting; this place serves an enjoyable meal.

### V Zátiší
International    ⓀⓀⓀ   Map 3 B4
*Liliová 1, Praha 1*
**Tel** *22 22 21 155*
For a memorable dining experience with excellent food and service, reserve a table at V Zátiší. Expert staff add to the pleasure.

### Zdenek's Oyster Bar
Seafood    ⓀⓀⓀ   Map 3 C3
*Malá Štupartská 636/5, Praha 1*
**Tel** *72 59 46 250*
Serious seafood restaurant with an intriguing oyster bar. Try the generous platters of oysters and clams. Don't miss the lobster roll, the most authentic example in Prague.

Entrance to the upscale La Truffe, great for authentic French fare

**For more information on types of restaurants** *see page 193*

# Jewish Quarter

## DK Choice
**Lokál** ⓚ
Czech **Map** 3 C2
*Dlouhá 33, Praha 1*
**Tel** *22 23 16 265*
Fun, old-style Czech pub with
well-done Czech classics and
lots of fresh Pilsner Urquell beer.
Modern lighting, long tables and
wooden chairs create a cosy
ambience. Service is excellent
and the food is tasty.

**Mistral Café** ⓚ
International **Map** 3 B3
*Valentinská 56/11, Praha 1*
**Tel** *22 23 17 737*
A casual place near the Old Town,
Mistral offers good food in a
bright and welcoming setting.

**Aldente Trattoria Vineria** ⓚⓚ
Italian **Map** 3 C2
*Vězeňská 4, Praha 1*
**Tel** *22 23 13 185*
Try the fresh seasonal dishes at
this casual and calming *trattoria*.
Specials change weekly. Good
selection of Italian wines
and spirits.

**Bílkova 13** ⓚⓚ
Italian-International **Map** 3 B2
*Bílkova 13, Praha 1*
**Tel** *22 48 29 254*
Simple but creative Italian fare
served in a lovely open dining
space. There's also a café with
a smaller snack menu.

**Cartouche** ⓚⓚ
French-International **Map** 3 C2
*Bílkova 14, Praha 1*
**Tel** *22 23 17 103*
This place specializes in
grilled meats, but the ambience
dominates the dining experience.
Romantic, with a 16th-
century vibe.

Sophisticated interiors at Barock, known
for its excellent Asian cuisine

Understated elegance at the highly praised La Degustation

## DK Choice
**Grosseto Marina** ⓚⓚ
Italian **Map** 3 A3
*Alšovo nábřeží, Praha 1*
**Tel** *60 54 54 020*
Enjoy superb service, beautiful
river views over Prague Castle
and excellent Italian food – on
a boat. The top deck is a great
place to have a drink, with or
without descending below
deck for a lovely dinner of pasta,
fish, meat, or even pizza. An
early evening visit is best to
watch the sun set and the
city lights glow.

**La Belle Epoque** ⓚⓚ
American **Map** 3 A3
*Křížovnická 8, Praha 1*
**Tel** *22 23 21 926*
Tex-Mex specialities, with an
emphasis on steak, served in
a rustic setting. Argentinian beef
and New Zealand lamb feature
prominently on the menu.

**La Veranda** ⓚⓚ
Italian-French **Map** 3 B2
*Elišky Krásnohorské 10/2, Praha 1*
**Tel** *22 48 14 733* **Closed** Sun
Bright and homey interiors
greet guests at La Veranda.
Chefs use a variety of organic
and locally sourced products in
their dishes.

**La Vita e Bella** ⓚⓚ
Italian **Map** 3 B2
*Elišky Krásnohorské 5, Praha 1*
**Tel** *22 23 10 039* **Closed** Sun
Trendy restaurant with fresh fish
and seafood. Homemade pastas
and gnocchi are also on offer.
The dining space is as beautiful
as the food.

**Barock** ⓚⓚ
Japanese-International **Map** 3 B2
*Pařížská 24, Praha 1*
**Tel** *22 23 29 221*
Casual but modern interiors
are a backdrop to a tasty menu
of international dishes. Japanese
and Thai food feature heavily.

**Chagall's** ⓚⓚⓚ
International **Map** 3 C2
*Kozí 5, Praha 1*
**Tel** *73 90 02 347*
A well-regarded, modern take on
Central European cuisine, great
service and welcoming interiors.
Chagall's convenient location is
great for lunch or dinner.

**CottoCrudo** ⓚⓚⓚ
Italian **Map** 3 A3
*Veleslavinova 1098/2a, Praha 1*
**Tel** *22 14 26 880*
Browse the meat and cheese
bars or feast on excellent Italian
cuisine at your table. Great
interiors and a fun concept.
Indecisive diners may be
challenged here.

**King Solomon** ⓚⓚⓚ
Jewish **Map** 3 B3
*Široká 8, Praha 1*
**Tel** *22 48 18 752*
Traditional Kosher Jewish
cooking with a Czech touch. Veal,
deer and lamb are sourced locally.
Bread is made on site and offered
alongside hummus and tahini.

**La Casa Argentina** ⓚⓚⓚ
Argentinian **Map** 3 C2
*Dlouhá 35/730, Praha 1*
**Tel** *22 23 11 512*
The swinging seats at the bar are
just one feature of the jungle-like
interiors at this eatery, which is
usually full with guests enjoying
dinner or drinks.

## DK Choice
**La Degustation** ⓚⓚⓚ
Czech-International **Map** 3 C2
*Haštalská 18, Praha 1*
**Tel** *22 23 11 234*
For the ultimate Czech
dining experience step, into La
Degustation. Six or 11 courses
of fresh, flavourful food are
paired with wines. Chefs prepare
each tiny dish with considerable
care for ingredients and design,
and are supported by knowledg-
eable and pleasant staff.

**La Finestra in Cucina** ⓚⓚⓚ
Italian **Map** 3 B3
*Platnéřská 90/13, Praha 1*
**Tel** *22 23 25 325*
La Finestra in Cucina's small menu offers Italian favourites cooked to perfection. Beautiful surroundings and delicious food. Great service and wine list.

**Zlatá Praha** ⓚⓚⓚ
Czech-International **Map** 3 B2
*Pařížská 30, Praha 1*
**Tel** *29 66 30 914*
Sit at the top of the Old Town and munch on locally sourced seasonal specialities. Don't miss the popular Sunday brunch.

## Prague Castle and Hradčany

**Host** ⓚⓚ
Czech-International **Map** 1 C3
*Loretánská 15, Praha 1*
**Tel** *60 38 17 633*
Good, fair-priced food in a major tourist hub. Classic Czech food is well done at this eatery. Modern interiors with great views.

**Villa Richter** ⓚⓚ
International **Map** 2 F2
*Staré zámecké schody 6/251, Praha 1*
**Tel** *25 72 19 079*
Two restaurants in one. Terra offers well-priced Czech cuisine, while Piano Noble serves Central European dishes with a modern touch.

## Little Quarter

**Bar Bar** ⓚ
International **Map** 2 E5
*Všehrdova 17, Praha 1*
**Tel** *25 73 12 246*
Fun, casual neighbourhood place with an intriguing interior. Large selection of dishes on the menu and a good choice of wines.

### DK Choice

**Café Lounge** ⓚ
International **Map** 2 E5
*Plaská 615/8, Praha 1*
**Tel** *25 74 04 020*
Beautiful interiors with a secret courtyard, delicious fresh soup, great coffee and a creative evening menu make this a go-to place from morning till night. There's a special coffee and wine each week, and the pastry chefs are extremely talented at making imaginative desserts.

The ambience is relaxed thanks to the restful interiors and the welcoming staff.

**Café Savoy** ⓚ
Czech-French **Map** 2 F5
*Vítězná 5, Praha 1*
**Tel** *25 73 11 562*
This charming and bustling spot serves lovely coffee, light lunches and gourmet meals.

**Kočár z Vídně** ⓚ
Austrian **Map** 2 F4
*Saská 520/3, Praha 1*
**Tel** *77 70 43 793*
For authentic Austrian food in Prague, stop by this eatery. Try the well done *wiener schnitzel* (veal coated in breadcrumbs). Extensive Austrian wine list.

**Luka Lu** ⓚ
Balkan **Map** 2 E4
*Újezd 33, Praha 1*
**Tel** *25 72 12 388*
Unique interiors, friendly service and well-prepared fish, pasta and barbeque specialities. There is streetside and outdoor seating in the courtyard.

**Malostranská beseda** ⓚ
Czech-International **Map** 2 E3
*Malostranské náměstí 21, Praha 1*
**Tel** *25 74 09 112*
Traditional Czech food and beer served in an elegant building in the heart of the Little Quarter. A buzzing place for lunch.

**Nebozízek** ⓚ
International **Map** 2 D5
*Petřínské sady 411, Praha 1*
**Tel** *25 73 15 329*
One of the city's best park restaurants, offering indoor and outdoor dining with a view. Standard fare at decent prices.

**U Malého Glena** ⓚ
International **Map** 2 E4
*Karmelitská 23, Praha 1*
**Tel** *25 75 31 717*
Well-executed burgers, ribs, Tex-Mex and a small selection of Czech dishes at this casual eatery. Tiny jazz club in the cellar.

**Café de Paris** ⓚⓚ
French **Map** 2 E4
*Maltézské náměstí 4, Praha 1*
**Tel** *60 31 60 718*
Considered one of the best French brasseries in Prague. Family-run, small dining room with an excellent menu featuring their speciality "Entrecôte Café de Paris" – a steak served with a special sauce made from a secret recipe.

**Cowboys** ⓚⓚ
Steakhouse **Map** 2 D3
*Nerudova 40, Praha 1*
**Tel** *29 68 26 107*
A modern restaurant with tasty beef specialities. Cowboys "favourite combi-nations" are a good choice. Unforgettable view from the garden.

**Gitanes** ⓚⓚ
Mediterranean **Map** 2 E3
*Tržiště 7, Praha 1*
**Tel** *25 75 30 163*
With meals from a number of regional countries, as well as a top-notch wine list, Gitanes is a welcome find in the Little Quarter find.

**Konírna** ⓚⓚ
Czech **Map** 2 E4
*Maltézské náměstí 10, Praha 1*
**Tel** *25 75 34 121*
Traditional Czech cooking with a modern twist. Konírna's menu has old recipes not found in many restaurants.

Vibrant and cheerful dining room at Luka Lu

**For more information on types of restaurants** *see page 193*

Outstanding view from the rooftop terrace, Terasa U Zlaté Studně

**U Malířů** ⓀⓀ
Czech-International **Map** 2 E4
*Maltézské náměstí 11, Praha 1*
**Tel** *25 75 30 318*
Gorgeous historic interiors and an interesting menu featuring modern Czech cuisine. An excellent place for a quiet dinner. Friendly and helpful staff.

**Alchymist** ⓀⓀⓀ
International **Map** 2 E4
*Nosticova 1, Praha 1*
**Tel** *25 73 12 518*
**Closed** *Sun & Mon*
A wild interior and a menu featuring French and Lebanese touches. The summer garden is a delightful bonus.

**Coda** ⓀⓀⓀ
International **Map** 2 E3
*Tržiště 9, Praha 1*
**Tel** *22 5334 761*
Elegant, musically themed interiors and a rich menu featuring unique flavours and a special Czech section. The rooftop terrace is ideal for an afternoon drink.

**Essensia** ⓀⓀⓀ
Czech-Asian **Map** 2 E4
*Nebovidská 459/1, Praha 1*
**Tel** *23 30 88 888*
This place offers classic Asian and local Czech dishes. Try the *Kulajda* (creamy Czech soup), or the salmon poached in orange oil. The Oriental themed interior has vaulted ceilings.

**Terasa U Zlaté Studně** ⓀⓀⓀ
International **Map** 2 E2
*U Zlaté studně 4, Praha 1*
**Tel** *25 75 33 322*
Also known as "At the Golden Well", this neighbourhood restaurant offers a beautiful interior and stunning views. The menu is perfectly prepared and served. In the summer, dine on the rooftop terrace.

**The Sushi Bar** ⓀⓀⓀ
Japanese **Map** 2 F5
*Zborovská 49, Praha 5*
**Tel** *60 32 44 882*
Modern interiors and a huge menu of well-prepared sushi. This was the first sushi bar in Prague and it's still one of the best.

# New Town

**Bresto** Ⓚ
French-Italian **Map** 3 C1
*Štěpánská 31, Praha 1*
**Tel** *22 22 12 810*
**Closed** *Sun*
Creative cooking and a great wine list. Wide choice of coffees. Perfect for a full meal or a snack break.

**Café Louvre** Ⓚ
Czech-International **Map** 3 B5
*Národní 22, Praha 1*
**Tel** *22 49 30 949*
A Czech institution, Café Louvre offers a good variety and quality of food, including an excellent selection of cakes, pastries and coffees. Play a game of pool in the on-site billiards room.

**Café Slavia** Ⓚ
Czech-International **Map** 3 A5
*Národní 1, Praha 1*
**Tel** *22 42 18 493*
Traditional Prague café with a full menu, lovely Art Deco interiors and pretty windows. The wonderful cake selection makes for a lovely afternoon break. There is often live music in the evenings.

**Dynamo** Ⓚ
International **Map** 5 A1
*Pštrossova 29, Praha 1*
**Tel** *22 49 32 020*
Dynamo is a design gem with good vegetarian options, a few Czech dishes and a pasta selection.

**Fama** Ⓚ
Czech **Map** 3 C5
*Vladislavova 18, Praha 1*
**Tel** *22 49 49 305* **Closed** *Sun*
Creative, well-presented dishes on a diverse menu served in a modern dining room. Lots of Pilsner Urquell to accompany the food.

**Home Kitchen** Ⓚ
International **Map** 5 C1
*Jungmannova 8, Praha 1*
**Tel** *73 47 14 227* **Closed** *Sun*
Casual, homey place that's great for a quick lunch. The menu changes seasonally and features daily soups, small salads and sandwiches.

**Klub Cestovatelů** Ⓚ
Lebanese **Map** 5 A1
*Masarykovo nábřeží 22, Praha 1*
**Tel** *22 49 30 390*
Tasty food, good service and relaxing interiors – this is an enjoyable spot for lunch or dinner with a convenient New Town riverside location.

**Miss Saigon** Ⓚ
Vietnamese-Japanese **Map** 5 B1
*Myslíkova 26, Praha 2*
**Tel** *22 25 60 328*
Great sushi and pho (noodle soup) along with a wide range of other specialities – all well-prepared and served in a relaxed dining space.

## DK Choice

**Nota Bene** Ⓚ
Czech **Map** 6 D2
*Mikovcova 4, Praha 2*
**Tel** *72 12 99 131* **Closed** *Sun*
A fascinating, rotating beer list and locally sourced Czech specialities make Nota Bene one of the hottest places around. There is also a beer hall in the basement that only serves beer and snacks. Book in advance.

**Novoměstský Pivovar** Ⓚ
Czech-International **Map** 5 C1
*Vodičkova 20, Praha 1*
**Tel** *22 22 32 448*
Classic Czech dishes served in a working brewery. Novoměstský Pivovar is a great place to expand your knowledge of beer.

**Renommé** Ⓚ
Czech-French **Map** 5 A1
*Na sturze 1, Praha 1*
**Tel** *22 49 34 109*
Around the corner from the National Theatre, this small and elegant family-run restaurant serves seasonal meals with an emphasis on foie gras and fish.

### Solidní Jistota
International  Ⓚ  Map 5 A1
*Pštrossova 21, Praha 1*
**Tel** *72 59 84 964*  **Closed** *Mon*
Hearty fare including burgers, steak and chicken wings are served at this casual place, which also has an on-site night club. Prices are good and the food is satisfying. Open till late.

### U Pinkasů
Czech  Ⓚ  Map 3 C5
*Jungmannovo nám. 15/16, Praha 1*
**Tel** *22 11 11 150*
Beloved beer hall with typical interiors, food and beer. U Pinkasů could be considered a tourist trap, but it still attracts the locals.

### Universal
French-International  Map 5 B1
*V Jirchářích 6, Praha 1*
**Tel** *22 49 34 416*
Casual French bistro with a classic menu and interiors that match the relaxed vibe.

### Žofín
International  Ⓚ  Map 5 A1
*Slovanský Ostrov, Praha 1*
**Tel** *77 47 74 774*
Lovely garden restaurant located on one of the Vltava river's islands. Excellent family spot with enjoyable food.

### Alcron
International  Ⓚ Ⓚ  Map 6 D1
*Štěpánská 40, Praha 1*
**Tel** *22 28 20 410*  **Closed** *Sun*
This intimate, Michelin-starred restaurant has a small, fascinating menu with some of the most creative dishes in Prague.

### Čestr
Czech  Ⓚ Ⓚ  Map 6 E1
*Legerova 75/57, Praha 1*
**Tel** *22 27 27 851*
The specialty here is beef cooked in a variety of ways. The meat is locally sourced and the menu

Cream-coloured walls with an array of unusual objects, Universal

lists over 20 different cuts. The beer list is extensive. An excellent place for meat lovers.

### Cicala
Italian  Ⓚ Ⓚ  Map 6 D1
*Žitná 43, Praha 1*
**Tel** *22 22 10 375*  **Closed** *Sun*
This *trattoria* offers a taste of Italy in its brick-lined cellar space and modern ground floor restaurant. *Bucatini all'amatriciana* (pasta with a tomato and pancetta sauce) is one of the house specialties. Service is friendly.

### Como
Mediterranean  Ⓚ Ⓚ  Map 4 D5
*Václavské náměstí 818/45, Praha 1*
**Tel** *22 22 47 240*
A good dining option on Wenceslas Square is hard to find, but this place offers tasty dishes, served by friendly staff. Try the beautifully cooked leg of lamb.

### El Emir
Lebanese  Ⓚ Ⓚ  Map 3 C4
*Václavské náměstí 1, Praha 1*
**Tel** *22 42 81 099*
Extensive, flavourful menu featuring fresh fish and lots of mezze. Oriental-style decor and a pleasant atmosphere.

### Le Patio
Asian  Ⓚ Ⓚ  Map 3 B5
*Národní 22, Praha 1*
**Tel** *77 45 39 301*
Creative, Asian dishes are served by cheerful staff. Try the Jungle duck (roasted duck in a Thai curry sauce), or the Indonesian beef. The interior is beautiful. Live music is performed on weekends.

### Miyabi
Japanese  Ⓚ Ⓚ  Map 5 C1
*Navrátilova 10, Praha 1*
**Tel** *29 62 33 102*
**Closed** *Sun*
Miyabi is one of the oldest Japanese restaurants in town and offers

The wood-panelled interiors of Le Patio

delicious and expert cooking. Excellent sushi and stylish interiors.

### Pagana
Italian  Ⓚ Ⓚ  Map 3 B5
*Spálená 14, Praha 1*
**Tel** *22 40 56 300*  **Closed** *Sat & Sun*
Pagana serves classic Italian dishes to discerning diners. Fabulous interiors decorated with hand-painted images. Reservations are recommended.

### Rotisserie
Czech  Ⓚ Ⓚ  Map 3 B5
*Mikulandská 121/6, Praha 1*
**Tel** *73 42 09 228*
Classic and contemporary Czech food is served, with seasonal changes to the menu. Their motto is "good taste counts." Pretty dining space.

### Suterén
Czech-Central European  Ⓚ Ⓚ  Map 5 A1
*Masarykovo nábřeží 26, Praha 1*
**Tel** *22 49 33 657*  **Closed** *Sun*
Housed in an Art Nouveau building, this place specializes in game and poultry. It also has a good seafood selection.

### Ultramarin
Thai-International  Ⓚ Ⓚ  Map 3 B5
*Ostrovní 32, Praha 1*
**Tel** *22 49 32 249*
Stylish restaurant with a good selection of dishes including grilled meats. There's an on-site night club, which serves cocktails.

### Celeste
French  Ⓚ Ⓚ Ⓚ  Map 5 A2
*Rašínovo nábř. 80, Praha 2*
**Tel** *22 19 84 160*  **Closed** *Sun*
Located atop the famed Dancing House. Modern French food is served in gorgeous interiors. Amazing views.

**For more information on types of restaurants** *see page 193*

Cosy and comfortable dining area, U Emy Destinnové

## DK Choice

**U Emy Destinnové** Ⓚ Ⓚ Ⓚ
International **Map** 5 C2
*Kateřinská 7, Praha 2*
**Tel** *22 49 18 425* **Closed** *Sun*
Well-cooked, creative food
is served here, along with
excellent wine and service.
U Emy Destinnové does Black
Angus beef and seafood expertly
well. Table-side cooking and a
tank from which to choose your
own lobster and crab add to
the entertainment value. Staff
are passionate about what
they are doing.

**Zvonice** Ⓚ Ⓚ Ⓚ
Czech-International **Map** 4 D4
*Jindřišská věž, Praha 1*
**Tel** *22 42 20 009*
A wide variety of dishes are
served here. The specialities are
boar and venison. Located in an
old Gothic belfry, this restaurant
is hard to beat for atmosphere.

## Further Afield

**Hanil** Ⓚ
Japanese
*Slavíkova 24, Praha 3*
**Tel** *420 222 715 867*
Excellent sushi and friendly
service make Hanil a place to
seek out. The house speciality is
the popular Korean dish, *bulgogi*.
Portions are hearty.

**Hybernia** Ⓚ
Czech-International
*Hybernská 7/1033, Praha 1*
**Tel** *22 42 26 004*
Traditional Czech cuisine with a
modern twist is served here. The
Hybernia is very popular through-
out the day. There is a large bar
area and outdoor terrace seating.

**Kofein** Ⓚ
Czech-International
*Nitranská 9, Praha 3*
**Tel** *27 31 32 145*
Czech-inspired tapas and a range
of internationally leaning mains;
their daily specials are always
recommended. Cosy non-
smoking dining area.

**Mash Hana** Ⓚ
Japanese
*Badeniho 3, Praha 6*
**Tel** *22 43 24 034* **Closed** *Sun & Mon*
Excellent Japanese food in a
warm, welcoming ambience. The
chef is the first person guests see
on entering this bright restaurant.

**Olympus** Ⓚ
Greek
*Kubelíkova 9, Praha 3*
**Tel** *22 27 22 239*
A large variety of well-prepared
Greek dishes are served at this
eatery. Don't miss the special
Greek cheeses. The relaxed atmos-
phere makes it easy to while away
an afternoon or evening here.

**Pho Vietnam Tuan & Lan** Ⓚ
Vietnamese
*Slavíkova 1657/1, Praha 2*
**Tel** *77 36 88 689*
For authentic Vietnamese cuisine
stop by this eatery, which is
constantly overflowing with folks
crazy for its quality dishes and
great prices. Try the spring rolls.

**Aromi** Ⓚ Ⓚ
Italian
*Mánesova 1442/78, Praha 2*
**Tel** *22 27 13 222*
The Italian chef here creates a
small but tasty menu of classic
favourites. Daily specials based
on fresh seasonal ingredients.

**Café Imperial** Ⓚ Ⓚ
Czech-International
*Na Poříčí 15, Praha 1*
**Tel** *24 60 11 440*
Creative cooking is served at this
eatery, which also offers a special
Czech menu selection, breakfast
and daily lunch specials.

**Červená tabulka** Ⓚ Ⓚ
International
*Lodecká 4, Praha 1*
**Tel** *22 48 10 401*
The homey interior belies the
high quality of the dishes, most
of which have Italian leanings.

**Kolkovna** Ⓚ Ⓚ
Czech
*V Kolkovně 8, Praha 1*
**Tel** *22 48 19 701*
Popular Pilsner brewery restaurant.
Guests will find fresh beer,
speedy service and big plates
of Czech cooking.

**La Boca** Ⓚ Ⓚ
International
*Truhlářská 10, Praha 1*
**Tel** *22 23 12 073*
Cosy restaurant in a busy

Art Noveau ceramic wall tiling and mosaic ceiling, Café Imperial

Sumptuous dining room in one of Prague's most stylish restaurants, SaSaZu

neighbourhood. The menu includes tapas, fresh pasta, and savoury desserts. There is also a children's menu.

### DK Choice

**La Terrassa** &#9424;&#9424;
Spanish
*Janáčkovo nábřeží - Dětský ostrov, Praha 5*
**Tel** *60 43 00 300*
Enjoy tapas and other freshly made Spanish specialities on a beautifully renovated boat on the Vltava. The staff are perfectly attentive and knowledgable about the wine list. The food and service are so good that guests will want to come again, even if they have to sit below deck. Highly recommended for summer dining.

**Mailsi** &#9424;&#9424;
Pakistani
*Lipanská 1, Praha 3*
**Tel** *22 27 17 783*
A one-of-a-kind restaurant in Prague, Mailsi's simple interior belies the authentic and flavourful food coming out of the kitchen.

**Mozaika** &#9424;&#9424;
International
*Nitranská 13, Praha 3*
**Tel** *22 42 53 011*
With a mixed-up menu of flavours, leaning towards Asian, Mozaika offers solid cooking in a trendy setting.

**Na Kopci** &#9424;&#9424;
International
*K Závěrce 2774/20, Praha 5*
**Tel** *25 15 53 102*
Modern Czech cuisine plus some French dishes are on the menu

here. They are particularly proud of their beef tartar and seasonal specialities. Service is friendly.

**Občanská Plovárna** &#9424;&#9424;
Thai
*U Plovárny 8, Praha 1*
**Tel** *25 75 31 451*
Set on the banks of the Vltava, this restaurant has a modern interior and excellent Thai food, especially the spicy curries.

**Olivia** &#9424;&#9424;
Mediterranean
*Plavecká 404/4, Praha 2*
**Tel** *22 25 20 288*          **Closed** *Sun*
Lovely, family-run restaurant with a focus on fresh, creative cooking. Dishes are carefully sourced and expertly prepared and served.

**Osteria De Clara** &#9424;&#9424;
Italian
*Mexicka 7, Praha 10*
**Tel** *27 17 26 548*          **Closed** *Sun*
Out of the way, but worth the trip. Serves excellent, simply prepared dishes and has a good wine list.

**Sahara Café** &#9424;&#9424;
International
*Náměstí Míru 6, Praha 2*
**Tel** *22 25 14 987*          **Closed** *Sun*
Roomy, beautiful café with a variety of small, Middle Eastern-style dishes as well as mains ranging from pasta to grilled meat and fish.

### DK Choice

**Sansho** &#9424;&#9424;
International
*Petrská 25, Praha 1*
**Tel** *22 23 17 425*
**Closed** *Sun & Mon*
With no set menu, Sansho

prepares everything daily, based on what they source from local farmers. The dining room is family-style, and almost looks unfinished, but the casual approach includes an open kitchen and extends to the friendly staff. Chefs place a premium on the quality of their meat cuts, but there's always something on the menu for vegetarians.

**The Pind** &#9424;&#9424;
Indian
*Korunní 1151/67, Praha 3*
**Tel** *22 25 16 085*
Excellent Indian food with a spicy kick. The Pind has a lovely dining area and welcoming staff.

**Aureole** &#9424;&#9424;&#9424;
Asian-fusion
*Hvězdova 1716/2b, Praha 4*
**Tel** *22 27 55 380*
This is the highest restaurant in Prague and it has a stunning interior. The menu features sushi and curry.

### DK Choice

**SaSaZu** &#9424;&#9424;&#9424;
Asian
*Bubenské nábřeží 306, Praha 7*
**Tel** *28 40 97 455*
This restaurant, awarded a Michelin Bib Gourmand, offers excellent food from Indonesia, Thailand and Vietnam. The opportunity to experiment with a variety of flavours does not happen often, but guests will be rewarded throughout with innovative dishes. Don't rush – this is a meal to savour.

**For more information on types of restaurants** *see page 193*

# Pubs, Beer Halls and Bars

Prague has somewhere to suit practically everyone's taste, from sophisticated cocktail bars to traditional Czech cellar pubs. One particular breed of pub, the themed Irish, English or sports bar, caters mainly to the large number of young English men who travel to Prague on stag weekends. The real charm of drinking in Prague is that it's possible to stroll around the Old Town and find places to drink and fraternize with Czechs and expatriates alike. If you sit at an empty table, don't be surprised if others join you. In some traditional Czech pubs a waiter will automatically bring more beer as soon as you appear close to finishing, unless you indicate otherwise. It pays to expect the unexpected in Prague – in some supposedly upmarket places, the waiters' attitude can be surly and unhelpful, while in the humblest pub you may find service to be efficient and courteous.

## Traditional Pubs and Beer Halls

Traditionally, Czech pubs either serve food or are large beer halls dedicated to the mass consumption of beer. The words *hostinec* and *hospoda* used to indicate a pub with food, whereas a *pivnice* served only beer, but over time the distinctions have faded.

Recommended for the brave, **U Zlatého tygra** (The Golden Tiger) is a loud Czech literati pub, wall-to-wall with mostly male regulars. (This is where the Czech president, Vaclav Havel took Bill Clinton to show him local beer culture.) **U Fleků** has brewed their unique beer, Flekovské, since 1499. For authenticity, and Budvar, try **U Medvídků** which is not far away from the National Theatre (see pp156–7) and the Old Town Square. **U Vejvodů** is a former traditional Czech pub which has embraced tourism, with large tables and waiters who understand English. You lose something in authenticity but the beer is good, the food decent and there's usually a place to sit. The traditional *hospoda* scarcely comes more so than **U Pinkasů**, hidden behind Wenceslas Square in a quaint courtyard.

## Cocktail Bars

Prague now has almost more cocktail bars than you could shake a swizzle stick at, but there are some that stand out. On Pařížská, Prague's Fifth Avenue, you'll find **Bugsy's**. This bar has even printed their own cocktail bible, though towards the end of the week it does become somewhat overtaken by burly men in long coats. That fate has yet to befall the neighbouring **Barock**, a cocktail bar and restaurant with a noticeably chic clientele. In **Beer Factory** you can tap your own beer, sample cocktails or just listen or dance to music.

## Irish Pubs and Theme Bars

Prague now has theme bars in all shapes and sizes, with still the most common being the ubiquitous Irish pub. **Caffreys** is one of Prague's most popular – and pricier – Irish bars, located off the Old Town Square. **Rocky O'Reilly's** is the biggest Irish pub in town, and a rowdy place, packed to the rafters if there is a big football match on the television. **Jáma** is a lively pub with great bar food that serves Prague's best burger, among other attributes. Just a stone's throw away from Charles Bridge is possibly the only Irish-Cuban hybrid pub anywhere, the noisy and fun **O'Che's**.

There is karaoke at **Molotow Cocktail Bar**, while **La Casa Blu** is a South American bar where the Chilean, Peruvian, Mexican and Czech staff create a carnival-type atmosphere.

## Bohemian Hangouts

Not only in the geographical heart of Bohemia, these bars also represent the unconventional side of Prague city-life. **Al Capone's** is one of the most famous, not to say notorious, drinking dens in the Old Town, host to a parade of visitors and locals. **Chapeau Rouge** is a rowdy college joint that is a guaranteed all-nighter, with a street-level bar that's loads of fun and a downstairs club that's hopping most of the night. Over the Vltava in the Castle district you'll find **U Malého Glena** which translates roughly to "at Little Glen's", and is one of the longest surviving expatriate bars in the city. Not far away is **Jo's Bar & Garáž**, which has also stood the test of time as an expat hangout. It's a small, cavernous pub, Mexican eatery and disco, and becomes quickly packed. **Jet Set** embodies the winning combination of a great bar and a delicious eatery.

## Sports Bars

Sports bars have taken off in Prague, with places like **Zlatá Hvězda**, with its deck of TV screens. Two popular sports bars further from the city centre are **Abyss Bar** in Michle and **Club Velbloud** in Žižkov.

## Café Society

The city is embedded in café society, ranging from old-fashioned smoky joints to cafés within bookstores, boutiques and billiard halls. Some are restaurants, others focus on drinking, but all serve alcohol. Located inside the Cubist House of the Black Madonna (see p67) is **Grand Café Orient**. Other places to see and be seen are **Ebel** in the Old Town and **Slavia**, by the river opposite the National Theatre. For a perfect meeting place, try the **Grand Café Praha** opposite the clock tower in Old Town Square. **Globe** café and bookstore is a legend among Prague's expatriate community and is said to serve the best cappuccino.

# DIRECTORY

## Traditional Pubs and Beer Halls

**Kolkovna-Olympia**
Vítězná 7.
**Map** 2 E5.
**Tel** 25 15 11 080.
w kolkovna.cz

**Monastery Brewery**
Strahovské nádvoří 301/10. **Map** 1 B4.
**Tel** 23 33 53 155.
w klasterni-pivovar.cz

**The Beer House**
*Pivovarský Dům*
Lípová 15.
**Map** 5 C2.
**Tel** 29 62 16 666.
w gastroinfo.cz/pivodum

**The Black Bull**
*U Černého Vola*
Loretánské nám 1.
**Map** 1 B3.
**Tel** 22 05 13 481.

**The Golden Tiger**
*U Zlatého Tygra*
Husova 17. **Map** 3 B4.
**Tel** 22 22 21 111.
w uzlatehotygra.cz

**The Shot Out Eye**
*U Vystřeleného Oka*
U Božích bojovníků 3.
**Tel** 22 25 40 465.

**U Fleků**
Křemencova 11.
**Map** 5 B1.
**Tel** 22 49 34 019.
w ufleku.cz

**U Kalicha**
Na Bojišti 12–14.
**Map** 6 D3.
**Tel** 29 61 89 600.
w ukalicha.cz

**U Medvídků**
Na Perštýně 7.
**Map** 3 B5.
**Tel** 22 42 11 916.
w umedvidku.cz

**U Pinkasů**
Jungmannovo náměstí 15/16. **Map** 3 C5.
**Tel** 22 11 11 150.
w upinkasu.cz

**U Vejvodů**
Jilská 4. **Map** 3 B4.
**Tel** 22 42 19 999.
w restauraceuvejvodu.cz

## Cocktail Bars

**Bar Hush**
Lublaňská 39. **Map** 6 E3.
**Tel** 22 42 41 448.
w hushcafe.cz

**Barock**
Pařížská 24. **Map** 3 B2.
**Tel** 22 23 29 221.
w barockrestaurant.cz

**Beer Factory**
Václavské náměstí 58.
**Map** 6 D1. **Tel** 23 41 01 117. w beer-factory.cz

**Bugsy's**
Pařížská 10. **Map** 3 B2.
**Tel** 840 284 797.
w bugsysbar.com

**Coyotes Prague**
Malé náměstí 2.
**Map** 3 B4.
**Tel** 22 42 16 000.
w coyotesprague.cz

**Sherlock's Pub**
Bartolomějská 11.
**Map** 3 B5.
**Tel** 22 42 40 588.
w sherlockspub.cz

**Zanzibar**
Lázeňská 6. **Map** 2 E4.
**Tel** 25 75 30 762.
w zanzi.cz

## Irish Pubs and Theme Bars

**Black Angels**
Staroměstské nám. 29.
**Map** 3 B3.
**Tel** 22 42 13 807.
w blackangelsbar.cz

**Caffreys**
Staroměstské nám. 10.
**Map** 3 B3. **Tel** 22 48 28 031. w caffreys.cz

**George & Dragon**
Staroměstské nám. 11.
**Map** 3 B3.
w georgeanddragonprague.com

**Jáma (The Hollow)**
V jámě 7. **Map** 5 C1.
**Tel** 22 29 67 081.
w jamapub.cz

**James Joyce**
U Obecního dvora 4.
**Map** 4 D3.
**Tel** 22 48 18 851.
w jamesjoyceprague.cz

## J.J. Murphy's

Tržiště 4.
**Map** 2 E3.
**Tel** 25 75 35 575.
w jjmurphys.cz

**La Casa Blu**
Kozí 15. **Map** 3 C2.
**Tel** 22 48 18 270.
w lacasablu.cz

**Merlin**
Bělehradská 68A.
**Map** 6 E2.
**Tel** 22 25 22 054.
w merlin-pub.cz

**Molotow Cocktail Bar**
Karlovo náměstí 31.
**Map** 5 B2.

**O'Che's**
Liliová 14. **Map** 3 C3.
**Tel** 22 22 21 178.
w oches.com

**Rocky O'Reilly's**
Štěpánská 32.
**Map** 3 A5.
**Tel** 22 22 31 060.
w rockyoreillys.cz

## Bohemian Hangouts

**Al Capone's**
Bartolomějská 3.
**Map** 3 B5.
**Tel** 22 42 41 040.
w alcapone.cz

**Chapeau Rouge**
Jakubská 2.
**Map** 3 C3.
**Tel** 22 23 16 328.
w chapeaurouge.cz

**Duende**
Karolíny Světlé 30.
**Map** 3 A4.
**Tel** 77 51 86 077.
w barduende.cz

**Jet Set**
Radlická 1c, Prague 5.
**Tel** 25 73 27 251.
w jetset.cz

**Jo's Bar & Garáž**
Malostranské nám 7.
**Map** 2 E3.
**Tel** 25 75 31 422.
w josbar.cz

**U Malého Glena**
Karmelitská 23.
**Map** 2 E4.
**Tel** 25 75 31 717.
w malyglen.cz

## Sports Bars

**Abyss Bar**
Michelská 2, Praha 4.
**Tel** 73 15 10 612.

**Club Velbloud**
Hraniční 3, Praha 3.
**Map** 6 D1.
**Tel** 73 99 36 696.

**Zlatá Hvězda**
Ve smečkách 12.
**Map** 6 D1.
**Tel** 29 62 22 292.
w sportbar.cz

## Café Society

**Café Imperial**
Na Poříčí 15.
**Map** 4 D3.
**Tel** 24 60 11 440.
w cafeimperial.cz

**Ebel Coffee**
Řetězová 9.
**Map** 3 B4.
**Tel** 603 823 665.
w ebelcoffee.cz

**Globe**
Pštrossova 6.
**Map** 5 A1.
**Tel** 22 49 34 203.
w globebookstore.cz

**Grand Café Orient**
Dům U Černé Matky Boží
Ovocný trh 19.
**Map** 3 C3.
**Tel** 22 42 24 240.
w grandcafeorient.cz

**Grand Café Praha**
Staroměstské nám. 22.
**Map** 3 B3.
**Tel** 22 16 32 522.
w grandcafe.cz

**Hotel Evropa Café**
Václavské náměstí 25.
**Map** 3 C5.
**Tel** 22 42 15 387.
w evropahotel.cz

**Neo Palladium Café**
Palladium, Náměstí Republiky 1.
**Map** 4 D3.
**Tel** 22 23 14 638.
w neopalladiumcafe.cz

**Slavia**
Smetanovo nábř 2.
**Map** 3 A5.
**Tel** 22 42 18 493.
w cafeslavia.cz

# Nightlife

Nightlife in Prague is as lively as in other European cities. A constant stream of visitors and a spirited local crowd has seen to that. Cheap drink, cutting-edge performers, liberal gambling and prostitution laws all help pull in the crowds. Prague is also now firmly established as a tour-stop for major American and UK pop and rock acts, with venues such as the Tipsport and O2 arenas playing host to big names at least once a month.

On a more local level, Prague's club scene is a proven testing ground for up-and-coming bands, and its dance/music events, which are heavily influenced by nearby Berlin, are renowned for being experimental. Prague's gay and lesbian scene is buzzing, and the local population is among the most tolerant in mainland Europe.

## Discos and Nightclubs

The biggest club in the city is the **Lucerna Music Bar**, which offers a varied programme – either live local bands or a DJ playing classic hits – in an unusual basement ballroom in the beautiful, but run down, Lucerna building. It fills up quickly however, so make sure you get there early. **Karlovy Lázně** is another large club, which sometimes has live bands. **Zlatý Strom** offers techno/house together with 1970s, 1980s and 1990s dance tunes until 5am in a spectacular medieval cellar setting.

The trendier clubs, more likely to be playing cutting-edge music, include **Nebe** and **Radost FX**, where the city's most affluent are attracted by a constant diet of house music and plush decor, together with **XT3** and **SaSaZu.** The **Double Trouble** is popular with visiting stag parties, which means it can get quite rowdy. For enthusiasts looking for genuinely experimental and original hardcore house and techno music, the best place to go is **Roxy**, where sets are often accompanied by art-house video projections. Roxy regularly hosts live rock bands, including a number of big-name bands.

If it is cabaret you are after, try **Tingl Tangl**, a club well known for its lively transvestite shows.

## Rock and Pop Clubs

Lovers of live rock music are well served in Prague. One school of thought feels that the anarchic influence of Prague's pioneering 1980s rock bands helped – however inadvertently – bring down the communist regime. There are today a large number of popular rock venues – generally small clubs and cafés – which host a variety of different groups. The indigenous scene continues to thrive – Prague's own rock bands play both their own compositions as well as cover versions of more famous numbers, many singing in English. Higher-profile, more internationally renowned Western bands play in Prague regularly, usually at the **Tipsport Arena** or **O2 Arena**.

The **Rock Café** and the **UZI Rock Bar**, both very popular venues, offer regular concerts followed by discos. Other venues include the **Futurum Music Bar**, open till the early hours. **Palác Akropolis** in Žižkov is great for visiting foreign bands. The Lucerna Music Bar and Roxy also host regular bands.

## Jazz

The roots of jazz in Prague can be traced not only to the American tradition but also to the pre-war heyday of Prague's famous jazz players, such as Jaroslav Ježek. Even during the communist period, Prague was an internationally renowned centre of jazz, never failing to attract the biggest names. Dizzy Gillespie, Stan Getz, Duke Ellington and Buddy Rich all played in Prague during the 1960s and 1970s.

Today, Prague's many jazz clubs play all forms, from Dixieland to swing. One of the leading and most popular jazz venues in the city is the **Jazz Club Reduta**, which has daily jazz concerts at around 9pm. When former US President Bill Clinton asked his Czech counterpart Vaclav Havel if he could play some jazz during a state visit to Prague in January 1994, the Czech president took him to the Jazz Club Reduta. The **Jazz Boat** is a great way to see the sights from the river and relax to local jazz. At the **AghaRTA Jazz Centrum**, you can hear a high standard of playing. **U Malého Glena** has regular live blues, jazz and funk, as does **Jazz Republic**, with performances every night from 9pm. For serious enthusiasts, the International Jazz Festival (various venues) and the Bohemia Jazzfest in Old Town Square, both held every few years, attract talent from all over the world. **Blues Sklep** is a relative newcomer to Prague's jazz scene and offers an inventive schedule, showcasing acts from jazz, blues and other genres.

## Gay and Lesbian Venues

With even mainstream clubs such as **Radost FX** holding regular gay nights, it is no wonder that Prague is considered one of Europe's hottest gay destinations. The scene is liberal and diverse. Clubs are split into various categories, with **Termix** being a loud and lively disco, and always packed. **Drake's Club** is a less in-your-face venue, and popular with visitors, while the city's most famous gay venue, **Friends**, is a cocktail bar. Friends has a steady following among expat and local men who are less interested in cruising than in just having a drink with like-minded folks. **Temple**, a gay centre, features a bar, disco, sex shop and hotel on the same premises.

The website www.prague.gayguide.net is a valuable resource for all things gay in Prague, including gay-friendly hotels, guesthouses and groups and associations.

## Adult Prague

Like it or not, Prague has seen itself become the sex tourism capital of Europe since 1989, partly thanks to ubiquitous cheap beer and the mistaken assumption that prostitution is legal in the Czech Republic. The law is, in fact, deliberately opaque. While locals may seem fairly tolerant towards the sex industry and associated nightlife, and some clubs and venues hosting prostitution have a veneer of respectability, visitors are well advised to steer clear.

# DIRECTORY

## Discos and Nightclubs

**Double Trouble**
Melantrichova 17.
**Map** 3 B4.
**Tel** 22 16 32 414.
w doubletrouble.cz

**Karlovy Lázně**
Novotného lávka,
Smetanovo nábřeží 198.
**Map** 3 A4.
**Tel** 22 22 20 502.
w karlovylazne.cz

**Lucerna Music Bar**
Vodičkova 36.
**Map** 3 C5.
**Tel** 22 42 17 108.
w musicbar.cz

**Misch Masch**
Veletržní 61, Praha 7.
w mischmasch.cz

**Nebe**
V Celnici 4. **Map** 4 D3.
**Tel** 777 662 081.
Václavské Náměstí 56.
**Map** 6 D1.
**Tel** 608 129 535.
Křemencova 10.
**Map** 5 B1.
w nebepraha.cz

**Radost FX**
Bělehradská 120.
**Map** 6 E2.
**Tel** 22 42 54 776.
w radostfx.cz

**Roxy**
Dlouhá 33. **Map** 3 C3.
w roxy.cz

**SaSaZu**
Bubenské náměstí 13,
Praha 7. **Tel** 28 40 97 455.
w sasazu.com

**Tingl Tangl**
Karolíny Světlé 12.
**Map** 3 A5.
**Tel** 22 42 38 278.
w tingltangl.cz

**Újezd**
Újezd 18.
**Map** 2 E5.
**Tel** 25 15 10 873.
w klubujezd.cz

**XT3**
Rokycanova 29,
Praha 3.
**Tel** 22 27 83 463.
w xt3.cz

**Zlatý Strom**
Karlova 6.
**Map** 3 A4.
**Tel** 22 22 20 441.
w zlatystrom.cz

## Rock and Pop Clubs

**Futurum Music Bar**
Zborovská 7, Praha 5.
**Map** 2 F5.
**Tel** 25 73 28 571.
w futurum.musicbar.cz

**Klub Lávka**
Novotného lávka 1.
**Map** 3 A4.
**Tel** 22 10 82 299.
w lavka.cz

**O2 Arena**
See p221.

**Palác Akropolis**
Kubelíkova 27.
**Tel** 29 63 30 911.
w palacakropolis.cz

**Rock Café**
Národní 20.
**Map** 3 B5.
**Tel** 22 49 33 947.
w rockcafe.cz

**Tipsport Arena**
See p221.

**UZI Rock Bar**
Legerova 44.
**Map** 6 D3.
**Tel** 777 637 989.
w demon.barr.cz/uzi

## Jazz Clubs

**AghaRTA Jazz Centrum**
Železná 16.
**Map** 3 C4.
**Tel** 22 22 11 275.
w agharta.cz

**Blues Sklep**
Liliová 10.
**Map** 3 B4.
**Tel** 22 14 66 138.
w bluesklep.cz

**Jazz Boat**
Boat: Kotva Gate No. 5,
under Čechův Bridge,
Dvořákovo Nábřeží.
**Map** 3 B2.
**Tel** 73 11 83 180.
w jazzboat.cz

**Jazz Club U Staré Paní**
Michalská 9.
**Map** 3 B4.
**Tel** 602 148 377.
w jazzstarapani.cz

**Jazz Club Reduta**
Národní 20.
**Map** 3 B5.
**Tel** 22 49 33 487.
w redutajazzclub.cz

**Jazz Republic**
28. října 1. **Map** 3 C5.
**Tel** 22 42 82 235.
w jazzrepublic.cz

**U Malého Glena**
Karmelitská 23.
**Map** 2 E4.
**Tel** 25 75 31 717.
w malyglen.cz

## Gay and Lesbian Venues

**Drake's Club**
Zborovská 50, Praha 5.
**Map** 2 F5
**Tel** 25 73 26 828.
w drakes.cz

**Escape**
V jámě 8.
**Map** 5 C1.
w escapeprague.eu

**Fenoman Club**
Belgická 28, Praha 2.
**Map** 6 F3.
**Tel** 22 27 11 458.
w fenomanclub.cz

**Friends**
Bartolomějská 11.
**Map** 3 B5.
**Tel** 22 62 11 920.
w friendsprague.cz

**Heaven**
Gorazdova 11.
**Map** 5 A3.
**Tel** 22 49 21 282.
w heaven.cz

**ON Club**
Vinohradská 40.
**Map** 6 F1.
**Tel** 724 384 464.
w onclub.cz

**Temple**
Seifertova 3, Praha 3.
**Tel** 22 27 10 773.

**Termix**
Třebízského 4a.
**Tel** 22 27 10 462.

# SHOPPING IN PRAGUE

With its wide, pedestrianized streets, classy shopping malls, souvenir shops and antiques *bazars*, Prague is established as one of Europe's leading shopping destinations. Almost all of the major US and Western European retailers have established outlets in the city. The quality of goods manufactured in the Czech Republic is always of a high standard. Most of Prague's best shopping areas are in the centre of the city, and you can spend a whole day just diving in and out of small speciality shops and large department stores. For a different shopping experience, the few traditional markets in the city offer everything from vegetables and fresh fruit to imported Russian caviar, toys, clothes, furniture, Czech crafts and electrical parts. Large malls are dispersed further out on the outskirts of Prague but are easily accessible by car or metro.

## Opening Hours

Most of Prague's shops open from 10am to 6pm Monday to Friday and from 9am to 1pm on Saturdays, although supermarkets are open for much longer, from 7am until 9 or 10pm.

Food stores open earlier too, most of them at 7am – reflecting the early working day of many locals – and close at around 9pm. Some Chinese, Vietnamese and Pakistani supermarkets are open 24 hours (you can find one at Národní and two close to I.P. Pavlova metro station). Department stores and the big shopping centres and malls are open daily between 8am and 9pm, with their supermarkets starting an hour earlier and closing an hour later. All are open on Sundays. Some Tesco supermarkets (Skalka, Novodvorská Plaza and Nový Smíchov) open at 6 or 7am and close at midnight, while three others (at Avion Shopping Park, OC Letňany and NC Eden) are open round the clock.

In the centre, around Old Town Square and Celetná and Karlova streets, many shops rely almost entirely on tourists for their trade, so have adapted their opening hours accordingly. They are usually open daily from 10am until late evening. Some close at 11pm. All the shops are at their most crowded on Saturdays, and for stress-free shopping, it's often better to wander around them during the week. Prague's

The antique shop in Bridge Street in the Little Quarter

market in Havelská is open daily, while River Town market is open Monday to Saturday. Opening times for both are from 7am until the evening.

## How to Pay

Most staple goods, such as food, are cheaper than comparable items in the West, as long as they do not need to be imported. However, with more and more multinationals, such as Boss and Pierre Cardin, moving into the city, prices are slowly starting to rise.

The total price of goods should always include Value Added Tax (this is 20 per cent of the total price, depending on what is being sold). Cash payments can usually only be made in Czech crowns, though some shops now take euros. The exchange rate in supermarkets such as Tesco, Billa and Albert can sometimes be even better than in the exchange offices. Smaller shops appreciate it if you pay the exact amount and at times may refuse to accept banknotes of Kč1,000 and above. All major credit and charge cards are widely accepted (*see p230*).

Global Refund is a programme for non-EU residents that allows tax-free shopping for purchases exceeding Kč2,000. When you make a purchase at a shop displaying the Global Refund sign, ask at the cash till for a tax-free cheque. On leaving the country, show your items, receipts and cheques to customs officials, who will stamp the cheques, and you will get your VAT back. For more details, go to the Global Refund website (www. globalrefund.com).

## Sales and Bargains

Following the examples of the Western stores, sales are becoming more popular. As a result, it is now quite normal for clothes to be sold off cheaper at the end of each season. There is also an increasing number of post-Christmas sales in the shops found around Old Town Square, Wenceslas Square, Na Příkopě and 28. října.

If you want vegetables, fruit, meat or other perishable produce, buy them at the beginning of the day, when the best quality goods are still on sale. There is no point in waiting till the end of the day in the hope of getting bargains, as is the case in Western shops that reduce prices to get rid of perishable items.

## Where to Shop

Most of Prague's best shops are conveniently located in the city centre, especially in and around Wenceslas Square, though the souvenir shops lining Nerudova on the way up to the castle are also well worth your time. Many of these shopping areas have been pedestrianized, making for leisurely window-shopping, although they can get rather crowded. There are a number of department stores which sell an eclectic range of Czech and Western items, with more opening all the time. The well-known department store **Kotva** (The Anchor), lies in the centre of the city. It was built in

1975 and its four storeys offer a wide range of Western goods, particularly fashion and electronics, with the bonus of an underground car park. But compared to Western department stores, Kotva has a smaller selection of goods than you may be accustomed to, and is now struggling to compete with the newer and more glamorous **Palladium** shopping mall across the square. Prices for some of the more luxurious items on sale, such as perfumes, can often be equivalent to the Western ones.

Another popular store is **Tesco**. This has a good selection of Czech and Western products in a bland 1970s building on Národní třída. The city's oldest department store is **Bílá Labuť** (The White Swan) in Na Poříčí. It was opened shortly before the occupation of Czechoslovakia in 1939 and was the first building in Prague to have an escalator. It has since fallen on hard times and its future as a department store is uncertain.

**Debenhams**, another famous name from Western Europe, has opened an enormous store on Wenceslas Square, and its home furnishings department on the third floor is very popular with locals.

The outskirts of Prague are now home to massive shopping parks, with large hypermarkets. Tesco has several hypermarkets, including in

Nový Smíchov, in OC Letňany and at Zličín, next to the equally enormous IKEA.

## Markets and Malls

Prague city centre is not blessed with a great market for most of the year, though the Christmas Gift Market in Old Town Square is worth visiting. The city's major central market, **Havelská tržnice** *(see p215)*, sells mainly fresh produce and cheap souvenirs. Another large market is **Pražská tržnice** in Holešovice (take the metro to Vltavská). The best of Prague's flea markets is **Buštěhrad Collector's Market** *(see p215)*, a glorified car-boot sale close to Lidice. Various markets – farmer's, Christmas and Easter – are organized in front of Arkády Pankrác building *(see p215)*.

Western-style shopping malls are common in Prague. Na Příkopě – between Náměsti Republiky and Václavské náměstí – is home to five: **Palladium, Slovanský dům, Myslbek, Černá růže** and **Koruna Palace** *(see p215)*. Further out, but close to metro stations, are **Arkády Pankrác, Nový Smíchov** and **Flora** *(see p215)*. There are also other malls on the outskirts of Prague, all with huge car parks.

### DIRECTORY

#### Department Stores

**Bílá Labuť**
Na Poříčí 23.
**Map** 4 E3.
**Tel** 22 48 11 364.

**Debenhams**
Václavské náměstí. 21.
**Map** 4 D5.
**Tel** 22 10 15 047.

**Kotva**
Náměstí Republiky 8.
**Map** 4 D3.
**Tel** 22 48 01 111.

**Palladium**
Náměstí Republiky 1.
**Map** 4 D3.
**Tel** 22 57 70 250.
W palladiumpraha.cz

**Tesco**
Národní 26.
**Map** 3 B5.
**Tel** 22 20 03 111.

A second-hand bookshop in Prague

# What to Buy in Prague

There is a huge selection of goods available in Prague's shops. Prague's more traditional products, such as Bohemian crystal, china, wooden toys and antiques, make great souvenirs, and there are still some real bargains to be picked up, though you will need to shop around. Increasingly popular are the more unusual, though less authentic, goods which are sold by many of Prague's street shops. These include Soviet army medals, Red Army uniforms and Russian dolls. Lovely Czech gems are also worth investigating, particularly garnets.

## Glass and China

Bohemian glass and china have always been ranked among the finest in the world. From huge, decorative vases to delicate glass figurines, the vast selection of glass and china items for sale is daunting. Crystal, glass and china can be quite different depending on where they are made. Lead crystal ranges in lead content from 14 to 24 per cent, for example. Always make sure you are fully aware of what you are buying.

Some of the best glass and china in Bohemia is produced at the Moser glassworks at Karlovy Vary and sold at **Moser**.

The blood-red Bohemian garnet, the national stone of the Bohemian people, is highly popular and can be purchased as jewellery in many stores, including **Crystal Direct**, **Celetná Crystal** and **Erpet Bohemia Crystal**. Another great store to visit is **Artěl**, which sells mouth-blown glassware designed by Karen Feldman.

However, prices for certain goods, especially classically designed vases, decanters and bowls are starting to reflect the increasing popularity of Bohemian crystal. The days when such goods could be purchased in Prague for half the Western European price are over. Yet, value for money remains high, and you can still pick up bargains if you shop around carefully. Remember that many of the modern pieces are just as lovely and much cheaper.

Bohemian porcelain, while not as celebrated as Bohemian crystal, also makes an excellent gift or souvenir. **Český Porcelán**, the country's most famous factory, is in Dubí, close to the town of Teplice, an hour's drive towards the German border from Prague, and its factory shop offers wonderful bargains. Český Porcelán also has a shop in Prague. Other names worth looking out for include Royal Dux Bohemia, Haas & Czjzek, A. Ruckl & Sons and Toner.

Because of the fragile nature of the goods, many shops will pack anything you buy there. But if you go for a more expensive piece, it is worth looking into insurance before you leave Prague.

## Antique Shops

Given its history as a major city in the Hapsburg empire, Prague is a great place to hunt for antiques. Hidden treasures seemingly lurk around every corner, and prices are still generally lower than in the West. Most of the city's shopping districts have a large number of antique shops: Old Town is full of them, as is the Royal Route from the castle. Look out for Bohemian furniture, glass and porcelain, as well as military and Soviet memorabilia.

Antique shops that are well worth exploring include **Dorotheum**, **Starožitnosti pod Kinskou** and **Pražské Starožitnosti**. **Military Antiques** is a haven for all army fanatics. For goods over Kč1,000, check with the shop whether you will need a licence to export them. You should watch out for an increasing number of fakes which are now appearing in the market.

Prague also has several *bazar* shops which stock a range of items at cheaper prices. Items are often unusual and good bargains can be found. **Bazar Nekázanka** is a small, popular shop full of second-hand goods. For furniture bargains, **Antik Bazar** is well worth a visit.

## Traditional Crafts

The traditional manufacture of high-quality, hand-crafted goods still survives in modern-day Prague. The variety of the merchandise available in the shops – hand-woven carpets, wooden toys, table mats, beautifully painted Easter eggs, baskets, figurines in folk costumes and ceramics – are all based on Czech and Moravian folk crafts and then enriched with modern elements. You can buy traditional craft items from many market stalls as well as a fair number of shops.

Making items from clay is an ancient craft in the Czech Republic. Česká Keramika has a long tradition of manufacturing ceramics.

A jewellery shop known for using only the best Czech garnets mounted in stylish, contemporary settings is **Studio Šperk**. You should also look out for a chain of shops called **Manufaktura** (Handmade), which sells goods made only in the Czech Republic and has a huge choice of hand-carved decorative items, as well as original cosmetics.

A number of street vendors around Old Town Square also sell handmade items including jewellery and puppets. Czech wooden items are of the highest quality (*see* Speciality Shops, *pp214–15*).

## Books

There are numerous bookshops in Prague, reflecting its literary heritage, and many sell

English-language books. One of the main bookshops is **Big Ben Bookshop**, where you'll find a range of English-language books (including quite a few Czech works which have been translated into English). **Palác knih–Neo Luxor** offers a great selection of books on its three floors. There are several branches scattered around the city.

Maps and guides to Prague in English can be bought at **Knihkupectví Academia**. Other specialist bookshops include **Fišer's Bookshop** and **Kanzelsberger**, with locations around the city. **Franz Kafka Bookshop** sells editions of the author's works in a variety of languages. Prague also has second-hand bookshops. **Antikvariát Dlážděná** is one of the best and has a vast selection. **Antikvariát Ztichlá Klika** deals in antiquarian books as well as 20th-century avant-garde works.

The legendary **Globe** café and bookstore has been a good place to find second-hand English books and enjoy the city's best cappuccino since 1993, when the shop was opened in a poorer part of the capital by five entrepreneurial Americans. Now relocated to the city centre, the Globe hosts regular literary events and art exhibitions, as does the newer **Shakespeare & Sons**, another great English bookstore, which also holds film nights and poetry readings.

# DIRECTORY

## Glass and China

**Artěl**
Celetná 29 (entrance at Rybná 1).
**Map** 3 C3.
**Tel** 22 48 15 085.

U lužického semináře.
**Map** 2 F3.
**Tel** 25 15 54 008.
W **artelshop.com**

**Celetná Crystal**
Celetná 15.
**Map** 3 C3.
**Tel** 22 23 27 987.
W **czechcrystal.com**

**Český Porcelán**
Perlová 1.
**Map** 3 B4.
**Tel** 22 42 10 955.
W **cesky.porcelan.cz**

**Crystal Direct**
Karlova 24.
**Map** 3 A4.
**Tel** 22 22 20 126.

**Dana-Bohemia**
*Glass, China, Crystal*
Národní 43.
**Map** 3 A5.
**Tel** 22 42 14 655.
W **danabohemia.cz**

**Erpet Bohemia Crystal**
Staroměstské náměstí 27.
**Map** 3 C3.
**Tel** 22 42 29 755.
W **erpetcrystal.cz**

**Moser**
Na příkopě 12.
**Map** 3 C4.
**Tel** 22 42 11 293.

Staroměstské náměstí 15.
**Map** 3 C3.
**Tel** 22 18 90 891.
W **moser-glass.com**

## Antique Shops

**Antik Bazar**
Pobřežní 42, Praha 8.
**Tel** 60 34 80 904.
W **antik-bazar.cz**

**Bazar Nekázanka**
Nekázanka 17. **Map** 4 D4.
**Tel** 22 42 10 550.
W **nekazanka.cz**

**Dorotheum**
Ovocný trh 2. **Map** 3 C4.
**Tel** 22 42 22 001.
W **dorotheum.cz**

**Military Antiques**
Charvátova 11. **Map** 3 C5.
**Tel** 22 53 79 724.

**Pražské Starožitnosti**
*Zdeněk Uhlíř*
Mikulandská 8.
**Map** 3 B5.
**Tel** 22 49 30 572.

**Starožitnosti pod Kinskou**
Náměstí Kinských 7.
**Tel** 25 73 11 245.
W **antique-shop.cz**

## Gifts and Souvenirs

**Česká Keramika**
Celetná 4.
**Map** 3 C3.
**Tel** 22 42 11 896.

**Manufaktura**
Karlova 26.
**Map** 3 A4.
**Tel** 22 16 32 480.

Melantrichova 17.
**Map** 3 B4.
**Tel** 22 16 32 480.
W **manufaktura.biz**
Two of several branches.

**Studio Šperk**
Dlouhá 19.
**Map** 3 C3.
**Tel** 22 48 15 161.
W **drahonovsky.cz**

## Books

**Antikvariát Dlážděná**
Dlážděná 7.
**Map** 4 E4.
**Tel** 22 22 43 911.
W **adplus.cz**

**Antikvariát Ztichlá Klika**
Betlémská 10–14.
**Map** 3 A5.
**Tel** 22 22 21 561.
W **ztichlaklika.cz**

**Big Ben Bookshop**
Malá Štupartská 5.
**Map** 3 C3.
**Tel** 22 48 26 565.
W **bigben bookshop.com**

**Fišer's Bookshop**
*Fišer Knihkupectví*
Kaprova 10.
**Map** 3 B3.
**Tel** 22 23 20 730.

**Franz Kafka Bookshop**
Staroměstské náměstí 12.
**Map** 3 B3.
**Tel** 22 23 21 454.

**Globe**
Pštrossova 6.
**Map** 5 A1.
**Tel** 22 49 34 203.
W **globebookstore.cz**

**Kanzelsberger**
Václavské náměstí 42.
**Map** 4 D5.
**Tel** 22 42 17 335.
W **dumknihy.cz**

**Knihkupectví Academia**
Václavské náměstí 34.
**Map** 4 D5.
**Tel** 22 42 23 511.
W **academia.cz**

**Palác knih – Neo Luxor**
Václavské náměstí 41.
**Map** 4 D5.
**Tel** 29 61 10 370
One of several branches.

**Shakespeare & Sons**
U Lužického semináře 10.
**Map** 2 F3.
**Tel** 25 75 31 894.
W **shakes.cz**

# Markets, Malls and Speciality Shops

Take your pick – super-modern mall or traditional market. Prague has them both, although do remember that Prague's main market is at some distance from the city centre at Holešovice. Malls are springing up everywhere in the city, and Prague has made a name for itself as a leading place to find all sorts of odd bits and pieces in any number of speciality stores. From Fabergé eggs to Jewish *yarmulkas*, you'll find it in Prague.

## Markets

Prague's markets offer a vast range of goods, although most are aimed at locals, offering fruit and vegetables, cheap clothing and electronics. The largest market in the city, **River Town** (**Holešovická tržnice**), was converted from a former slaughter-house. The market now sells fresh fruit and vegetables, and all kinds of poultry, as well as fish, textiles, flowers, electronics, antiques, toys and furniture. These are all sold in several large halls and in outdoor stalls. The market is generally open from Monday to Saturday, 7am to 8pm.

In Havelská, right in the centre of the city, is **Havelská tržnice**, which mainly sells fruit, vegetables and cheap souvenirs. It is open daily, 7am–7pm).

You will also enjoy foraging through the junk, antiques, furniture and military memorabilia (none of which comes with a promise of a refund or guarantee) at the out-of-town **Buštěhrad Collectors Market**, allegedly the third-largest market of its kind in Europe. You can get there by public transport, taking a bus from Dejvická or Zličín metro stations. The market is only open on the second and fourth Friday and Saturday of the month, from 6am to noon. Another flea market worth visiting, Bleší trhy Praha, is at Kolbenova metro station, and is open 6am–1:30pm at weekends.

Old Town Square plays host to an excellent and very popular Christmas Market from the end of November through the New Year's holiday. Besides the stalls selling gifts and toys, there are others selling hot wine and sausages, and there is also a small children's play area. The Square also hosts the city's Christmas tree and a number of open-air winter concerts.

## Malls

There is an increasing number of Western-style shopping malls in Prague, which are more popular and often much better than the old department stores, offering better value and a greater range of high-quality goods. In the very centre of town on Náměstí Republiky (on metro B), **Palladium** has hundreds of shops and restaurants on five levels. Just down the street, on Na příkopě, the upmarket **Myslbek**, **Černá růže** and **Koruna Palace** (metro A and B) are home to a great number of chic boutiques and jewellery stores. In addition, at **Slovanský dům**, there is a multiplex cinema as well as a fabulous Kogo restaurant.   You can also take the metro to visit three-storey galleries **Arkády Pankrác** (metro C) and **Palác Flora** (metro B). **Nový Smíchov** at Anděl (metro B) is home to a two-storey Tesco, as well as multiplex Palace Cinemas and Cinestar (*see p219*) nearby.

Very popular is the huge **Centrum Chodov** (metro C), with 200 shops. **Galerie Harfa**, close to the O2 Arena, has an ice-skating rink on the roof, which is free for public use (Českomoravská, metro B). At the furthest outskirts of the city, at both ends of metro line B, there are many hypermarkets and malls, including **Metropole Zličín**, which also has a multiplex cinema. The largest mall in the country, **OC Letňany** (metro line C and shuttle bus) is close to the D8 motorway. **Šestka** can be useful for last-minute shopping, as it is situated just next to the airport and served by bus Number 119 between Dejvická and Ruzyně Airport.

## Street Stalls

Street stalls and wandering vendors are not officially allowed to operate in most areas of Prague, though a number of vendors are permitted to sell souvenirs around Charles Bridge. Street stalls are allowed near the entrance to the Old Jewish Cemetery in the Jewish Quarter, and they also line the Old Castle Steps from Malostranská metro station up to the castle's eastern gate.

As most of these sellers are well vetted, the goods on sale tend to be reasonably good quality, though you are unlikely to find any real bargains, and much of what is on sale can be bought cheaper in souvenir stores.

## Speciality Shops

Bohemia and Moravia have long been known for their fine wooden toys. You will find a number of shops selling them throughout the city, especially in Old Town, but beware cheap imports. You can be sure of the genuine article at **Hračky Traditional Toys** near the castle, Beruška in New Town and **Sparky's House of Toys**, just off Na Příkopě, a treasure trove for children of all ages. Older children might also like **Games & Puzzles** on Wenceslas Square, which specializes in all sorts of mind teasers, including hand-made wooden labyrinths.

If you are looking for something a little quirky, but very Czech, try **Botanicus** near Old Town Square, which sells all-natural and all-Czech health and beauty products, from soap to massage oil. Another popular store is **Qubus**, which sells anything and everything, as long as it is the height of modern design.

Most of the weird and wonderful things on sale were designed by young Czechs. There are a number of other weird and wonderful stores in Prague. The **Spanish Synagogue Gift Shop** sells torah pointers, *yarmulkas*, watches and other Jewish gifts. **Le Patio** on Národní is a shop specializing in original illuminations and candelabra, as well as top-quality restored furniture imported from India, and tables and chairs made by some outstanding Czech blacksmiths. Another favourite for design fans is **de.fakto**, an upmarket version of IKEA, in the centre of the city. **Art Deco Galerie** is an upmarket junk shop with gorgeous period-pieces, glass, accessories, home furnishings and second-hand clothing. The prize for most bizarre shop in Prague must go to **Original Stoves by Trakal**, a store specializing in the restoration of historic stoves.

## Food and Delicatessens

Prague's supermarkets are well stocked with the basic foodstuffs. **Delicacies-lahůdky** is a small shop with meat and fish counters. A specialist food shop, selling smoked sausage, cheeses and other local delicacies, is **Jan Paukert**. For freshly baked bread visit the bakers around Wenceslas Square and Karmelitská Street. **Paneria Pekařství** shops sell a good selection of patisseries and sandwiches.

For the best selection of local and international delicacies, however, try **Bakeshop** on Kozí just off Old Town Square. You'll find excellent breads and baked goods, as well as brownies, cookies and delicious sandwiches and salads. It's great for a snack, an informal lunch or to pick up supplies for a picnic.

# DIRECTORY

## Markets and Malls

**Arkády Pankrác**
Na Pankráci 86, Pankrác.
**Map** 6 F1.
**Tel** 22 51 11 100.
W arkady-pankrac.cz

**Buštěhrad Collectors Market**
Bleší trhy, Buštěhrad.
**Tel** 602 335 834.
W bustehradantik.cz

**Centrum Chodov**
Roztylská 19, Chodov.
**Tel** 27 21 73 600.
W centrumchodov.cz

**Černá růže**
Na příkopě 12.**Map** 3 C4.
**Tel** 22 10 14 111.
W cernaruze.cz

**Galerie Harfa**
Českomoravská 2420,
Praha 9. **Tel** 26 60 55 600.
W galerieharfa.cz

**Havelská tržnice**
Havelský trh. **Map** 3 C3.

**Koruna Palace**
Václavské náměstí 1.
**Map** 3 C5.
**Tel** 22 42 19 526.
W koruna-palace.cz

**Metropole Zličín**
Zličín. **Tel** 22 60 81 540.
W metropole.cz

**Myslbek**
Na příkopě 19–21 &
Ovocný trh 8.
**Map** 3 C4.
**Tel** 22 42 39 550.
W ngmyslbek.cz

**Nový Smíchov**
Plzeňská 8.
**Tel** 25 15 11 151.
W novysmichov.eu

**OC Letňany**
Veselská 663, Praha 9.
**Tel** 22 17 41 111.
W oc-letnany.cz

**Palac Flora**
Vinohradská 151.
**Map** 6 F1.
**Tel** 25 57 41 712.
W palacflora.com

**Palladium**
Náměstí Republiky 1.
**Map** 4 D3.
**Tel** 22 57 70 250.
W palladiumpraha.cz

**River Town**
(Holešovická tržnice)
Bubenské nábřeží 13.
Praha 7.
**Tel** 22 08 00 592.
W holesovicka
trznice.cz

**Slovanský dům**
Na příkopě 22.
**Map** 3 C4.
W slovanskydum.com

**Šestka**
Fajtlova 1090/1, Praha 6.
**Tel** 22 50 23 100.
W sestka.cz

## Speciality Shops

**Art Deco Galerie**
Michalská 21.
**Map** 3 B4.
**Tel** 22 42 23 076.
W artdecogalerie-
mili.com

**Botanicus**
Týn 3.
**Map** 3 C3.
**Tel** 23 47 67 446.
W botanicus.cz

**de.fakto**
Vejvodova 3.
**Map** 3 B4.
**Tel** 22 42 33 815.
W defakto.cz

**Games & Puzzles**
Václavské náměstí 38.
**Map** 6 D1.
**Tel** 22 49 46 506.
W hras.cz

**Hračky Traditional Toys**
Loretánské náměstí 3.
**Map** 1 B3.
**Tel** 60 35 15 745.

**Le Patio**
Národní 22.
**Map** 3 A5.
**Tel** 22 49 34 402.
W lepatiolifestyle.com

**Original Stoves by Trakal (Stará Kamna)**
Karmelitská 21.
**Map** 2 E4.
**Tel** 25 75 34 203.
W starakamna.cz

**Qubus**
Rámová 3.
**Map** 3 C2.
**Tel** 22 23 13 151.
W qubus.cz

**Spanish Synagogue Gift Shop**
Věžeňská 1.
**Map** 3 B2.

**Sparky's House of Toys**
Havířská 2.
**Map** 3 C4.
**Tel** 22 42 39 309.
(one of several branches.)
W sparkys.cz

## Foods and Delicatessens

**Bakeshop**
Kozí 1.
**Map** 3 C2.
**Tel** 22 23 16 823.
W bakeshop.cz

**Delicacies-lahůdky**
Zlatý Kříž
Jungmannovo náměstí
19.
**Map** 3 C5.
**Tel** 22 25 19 451.

**Jan Paukert**
Národní 17.
**Map** 3 B5.
**Tel** 22 42 22 615.
W janpaukert.cz

**Paneria Pekařství**
Kaprova 3.
**Tel** 23 50 10 101.
W paneria.cz
Also at: Nekázanka 19.
**Map** 4 D4; Vodičkova 33.
**Map** 3 C5.
(several branches.)

# ENTERTAINMENT IN PRAGUE

Prague offers a wide variety of entertainment for its visitors, with something for every taste and interest. Whether you prefer opera to jazz or mini-golf to a football match, there is plenty to choose from. Movie buffs can choose from many of the latest Hollywood blockbusters, a lot of them in English with subtitles. For the adventurous, mime and fringe theatre are both thriving. Prague has a superb musical tradition, which includes symphony orchestras, opera, musicals, jazz and folk music. Concerts are performed throughout the year, in venues which range from Baroque palaces to public parks and gardens. Even if you don't speak Czech, you can still enjoy the city's cultural offerings. Some plays can be seen in English, and for many types of entertainment, music, dance and sport, a knowledge of the language isn't necessary at all.

## Practical Information

The best place to look for information about what's on and where in Prague is in the English-language newspaper *The Prague Post (see p233)*. This provides details of the best entertainment and cultural events which will be of interest to an English-speaking audience. Those events that are in English or have translation facilities are marked. Other sources of information are the leaflets and City Guides given out at the ticket agencies in the city, such as **Ticketpro** or **Ticketportal**. In addition, there are two online bulletin boards in English, www.expats.cz and http://prague.tv, aimed at expats and visitors. You can also buy a booklet called *Přehled*, printed in English and available from any PIS office. For a comprehensive rundown of events, buy *Culture in Prague*, a detailed monthly publication listing information on a variety

A performance of *Cosí Fan Tutte* at the Mozart Festival

of local exhibitions, concerts and theatre.

## Booking Tickets

Tickets can be bought in advance from the box office at most venues. You can also book tickets in advance by writing to, or ringing, the venue. Remember that many of the city's box offices may not have any English speakers available. Tickets for the **opera** or for any of the performances at the **National Theatre** can also be booked online. The more popular events tend to become heavily booked up in advance by tour groups – particularly during the summer – and by season-ticket holders. However, standby tickets are usually available about an hour before the show. If this isn't practical and you want to be sure of a ticket on a particular day, it is better to buy them at a booking agency. The drawback to using agencies, however, is that commission on these tickets can be high,

## Puppet Theatre

Puppetry has a long tradition in Prague and is still strongly represented. The most famous puppet show in the city is held at the **Spejbl and Hurvínek Theatre** *(see p219)*. The show revolves around Daddy Spejbl and his reprobate son Hurvínek. Other puppet theatres include the **National Marionette Theatre** *(see p219)*, known for its entertaining puppet rendition of Mozart's *Don Giovanni*. The Theatre in the Old Town *(see p219)* and the **Puppet Empire** *(see p219)* also put on puppet shows occasionally. Check listings *(see pp224–5)*.

Theatre puppets

sometimes doubling the original price. Your hotel receptionist may also be able to get you tickets.

### Ticket Prices

Ticket prices are cheap compared to Western prices, except for certain performances, most notably during the Prague Spring Music Festival (see p52). Prices range from around Kč100 for a small fringe production to up to Kč3,000 for a performance by an internationally famous orchestra. Paying by credit card is usually only acceptable at ticket agencies.

The Neo-Classical Estates Theatre (Stavovské divadlo)

A view of the Rudolfinum auditorium (see p221)

### Ticket Touts

There has been a spate of counterfeit tickets on sale, especially for the larger rock concerts. To be safe, always buy your tickets at reputable agencies or at the venue itself.

### Late-night Transport

Prague's metro (see pp242–3) stops running shortly after midnight, while the normal bus and tram service also ends around midnight. Then the city's extensive night bus and tram service takes over. Timetables are displayed at each stop. Night trams and buses are regular and efficient and it is likely that there will be a tram or bus stop near your

hotel. Taxis provide the most certain form of late-night transportation, but beware of unscrupulous drivers trying to overcharge you (see p240). It is often a good idea to try to walk a little way from the theatre before you hail a cab; the fare will probably be a lot cheaper. Ask at your hotel before you go out to find out what the best transport options are.

### Music Festivals

The most famous music festival of all is the Prague Spring Music Festival, held between May and June (see p52). Hundreds of international musicians come to Prague to take part in the celebrations. Other music festivals include the Mozart Festival (see p52), held in the summer, and the Musica International Music Fair (see p54) that takes place in the autumn.

Sparta Stadium (see p221)

## DIRECTORY

### Booking Agents

**Bohemia Ticket**
Malé náměstí 13.
**Map** 3 B4.
**Tel** 22 42 27 832.

Also at: Na Příkopě 16.
**Map** 4 D4.
**Tel** 22 42 15 031.
W ticketsbti.cz

**National Theatre tickets**
**Tel** 22 49 01 448.
W narodni-divadlo.cz

**Prague Information Service (PIS)**
Staroměstské náměstí 1.
**Map** 3 B3.
**Tel** 22 17 14 444.
W praguewelcome.cz

**Ticket Art**
Politických vězňů 9.
**Map** 4 D5.
**Tel** 22 28 97 552.
W ticket-art.cz

**Ticketpro**
Štěpánská 61.
**Map** 5 C1.
**Tel** 23 47 04 204.
W ticketpro.cz

**Ticket Portal**
Politických vězňů 15.
**Map** 4 D5.
**Tel** 22 22 46 283.
W ticketportal.cz

**Ticket Stream**
Koubková 8.
**Map** 6 E3.
**Tel** 22 42 63 049.
W ticketstream.cz

# The Performing Arts and Film

Prague has always been known for its artistic heritage. Theatre has played an important role in the city's cultural development, and in recent decades the range of entertainment has expanded considerably. Even during the communist period Prague remained a centre of experimental theatre, not least with the emergence of Black Light Theatre in the 1960s. Today, this tradition continues, with new theatre groups emerging all the time, ever more experimental. In general, the theatre season runs from September to June. During the summer, open-air performances are given in Prague's gardens and parks. For those who prefer to dance till dawn, relax to the sound of jazz or take in a movie – you will find plenty to entertain you in this city.

## English-language Performances

Many theatres in Prague have started to stage a number of English-language productions, especially in the summer months. Even if the play is not performed in English, some venues use supertitles to provide a translation. For details, check the listings (see Listings and Tickets pp224–5).

## Major Theatres

Prague's first permanent theatre was built in 1738, but the city's theatrical tradition dates from the Baroque and Renaissance periods.

The National Theatre (see pp156–7) is Prague's main venue for opera, ballet and plays. The neighbouring New Stage is another important venue. It is also the main stage for the multimedia **Laterna Magika** company, which is one of Prague's best-known theatre groups as well as being at the forefront of European improvisational theatre.

Other major theatres in the city include the **Comedy Theatre** and the "stone theatres." These gained importance during the 19th century and include the **Vinohrady Theatre** and the **Estates Theatre** (see p67) – one of the most respected in Prague. The Prague Municipal Theatre is an acting company whose plays appear in turn at the **ABC Theatre** and the **Rokoko Studio of Drama**. The **Kolowrat Theatre** is based in the Kolowrat Palace.

## Fringe Theatres

These originated during the 1960s and won renown for their fight against the status quo. The groups are still very innovative and largely experimental. They perform in small theatres, and many of Prague's best actors and actresses have developed their skills while working for some of these companies.

Fringe theatres include the **Dramatic Club**, well known for its supporting ensemble; the **Ypsilon Studio**, with one of the finest acting companies in the city; **Theatre Na Fidlovačce**, which stages a mix of musicals and straight drama; the large **Theatre Below Palmovka**, renowned for its mix of classical and modern plays; and the **Theatre in Celetná**. One of Prague's most spectacular theatrical and music venues is **Křižík's Fountain**, at the Exhibition Ground, where classical concerts are held and full orchestras perform to stunning lightshows. The **Semafor Theatre** is the home of the tremendously popular comedian, Jiří Suchý.

## Pantomime, Mime and Black Light Theatre

Some of the most popular theatre entertainment in Prague is Black Light Theatre, where black-clad actors move objects against a dark stage without being seen – a stunning visual spectacle, pantomime and mime. None of the three requires any understanding of Czech and all are strongly represented.

**Jiří Srnec's Black Light Theatre** is one of the major venues for Black Light Theatre performance. **Ta Fantastika** is another. These and others are listed in the directory (see p219).

## Dance

In Prague, opera and ballet companies traditionally share the National Theatre, where the Czech Republic's best permanent ballet company is based. The **Prague State Opera** also has a resident ballet ensemble that is keen to usurp the reputation of **National Theatre** company as the city's best. The tickets for the ballet at both major venues are even lower than for opera performances. You can also watch ballet performances at the **Estates Theatre**. **Ponec** is an experimental performance dance space dedicated to modern dance, and hosts the annual Tanec Praha international festival of contemporary dance and movement theatre in June.

## Cinemas

Although Prague doesn't show all the latest Hollywood blockbusters, more than 80 per cent of the films shown are recent US productions, most of them in English with Czech subtitles. Multiplex cinemas are now big business. The largest of these multiplexes are **Cinema Cities**, which can be found in Flóra, Zličin, Háje, Anděl, Letňany, Hostivař, and one in the centre in **Slovanský Dům** – boast eight to ten screens. **Světozor** is great for catching Czech films with English subtitles. **Bio Oko** is an art house cinema with a great café and an ambitious repertoire of contemporary Czech films as well as classics. **Lucerna** is a lovely cinema to visit, with a beautiful interior. Other cinema options are listed in the directory.

# DIRECTORY

## Theatres

**ABC Theatre**
Divadlo Abc
Vodičkova 28.
**Map** 3 C5.
**Tel** 22 42 15 943.
🌐 mestskadivadla
prazska.cz

**Animato Black Light Theatre**
Černe Divadlo Animato
Na příkopě 10.
**Map** 3 C4.
**Tel** 22 51 13 311.
🌐 blacklighttheatre
prague.cz

**Broadway**
Na příkopě 31.
**Map** 3 C4.
**Tel** 22 51 13 311.
🌐 divadlo-
broadway.cz.

**Comedy Theatre**
Divadlo Komedie
Jungmannova 1.
**Map** 5 B1.
**Tel** 22 42 22 734.
🌐 divadlokomedie.cz

**Dramatic Club**
Činoherní Klub
Ve Smečkách 26.
**Map** 6 D1.
**Tel** 29 62 22 128.
🌐 cinoherniklub.cz

**Estates Theatre**
Stavovské Divadlo
Ovocný trh 6.
**Map** 3 C3.
**Tel** 22 49 01 448.
🌐 narodni-divadlo.cz

**Jiří Srnec's Black Theatre**
Černé Divadlo
Jiřího Srnce
U Lékárny 597, 15600
Praha 5.
**Tel** 25 79 21 835.
🌐 blacktheatresrnec.cz

**Kolowrat Theatre**
Divadlo Kolowrat
Ovocný trh 6.
**Map** 3 C3.
**Tel** 22 49 01 448.
🌐 narodni-divadlo.cz

**Křižík's Fountain**
Křižíkova Fontána
Výstaviště, Praha 7.
**Tel** 723 665 694.
🌐 krizikovafontana.cz

## Laterna Magika
Národní 4.
**Map** 3 A5.
**Tel** 224 931 482.
🌐 laterna.cz

**National Marionette Theatre**
Národní Divadlo Marionet
Žatecká 1.
**Map** 3 B3.
**Tel** 22 48 19 322.
🌐 mozart.cz

**National Theatre**
Národní Divadlo
Národní 2.
**Map** 3 A5.
**Tel** 22 49 01 448.
🌐 narodni-divadlo.cz

**Puppet Empire**
Říše Loutek
Žatecká 1.
**Map** 3 B3.
**Tel** 22 23 24 565.
🌐 riseloutek.cz

**Reduta Theatre**
Divadlo Reduta
Národní 20. **Map** 3 B5.
**Tel** 22 49 33 487.
🌐 redutajazzclub.cz

**Rokoko Studio of Drama**
Divadlo Rokoko
Václavské náměstí 38.
**Map** 4 D5.
**Tel** 22 42 17 113.
🌐 rokoko.cz

**Semafor Theatre**
Divadlo Semafor,
Dejvická 27.
**Tel** 23 39 01 384.
🌐 semafor.cz

**Spejbl and Hurvínek Theatre**
Divadlo Spejbla A Hurvínka
Dejvická 38, Praha 6.
**Tel** 22 43 16 784.
🌐 spejbl-hurvinek.cz

**Ta Fantastika**
Karlova 8.
**Map** 3 A4.
**Tel** 22 22 21 366.
🌐 tafantastika.cz

**Theatre Below Palmovka**
Divadlo Pod Palmovkou
Zenklova 34, Praha 8.
**Tel** 283 011 127.
🌐 divadlopod
palmovkou.cz

## Theatre in Celetná
Divadlo V Celetne
Celetná 17.
**Map** 3 C3.
**Tel** 22 23 26 843.
🌐 divadlovceletne.cz

**Theatre in the Old Town**
Divadlo V Dlouhé
Dlouhá 39.
**Map** 3 C3.
**Tel** 22 17 78 629.
🌐 divadlovdlouhe.cz

**Theatre Na Fidlovačce**
Divadlo Na Fidlovačce
Křesomyslova 625.
**Map** 6 E5.
**Tel** 24 14 04 040.
🌐 fidlovacka.cz

**Vinohrady Theatre**
Divadlo Na Vinohradech
Náměstí Míru 7.
**Map** 6 F2.
**Tel** 22 42 57 601.
🌐 dnv-praha.cz

**WOW**
Václavské náměstí 56.
**Map** 3 C5.
**Tel** 22 40 32 172.
🌐 wow-wow.com

**Ypsilon Studio**
Studio Ypsilon
Spálená 16.
**Map** 3 B5.
**Tel** 22 49 47 119.
🌐 ypsilonka.cz

## Dance

**National Theatre**
Národní Divadlo Balet
Národní 2.
**Map** 3 A5.
**Tel** 22 49 01 448.
🌐 narodni-divadlo.cz

**Ponec**
Husitská 24a/899, Praha 3.
**Tel** 22 48 17 886.
🌐 divadloponec.cz

**Prague State Opera**
Státní Opera Praha
Wilsonova 4.
**Map** 6 E1.
**Tel** 22 42 27 266.
🌐 opera.cz

## Cinemas

**Bio Oko**
Františka Křížka 15,
Praha 7.
**Tel** 23 33 82 606.
🌐 biooko.cz

**Cinema City Flóra**
Vinohradská 151,
Praha 3.
**Tel** 25 57 42 021.

**Cinema City Galaxie**
Arkalycká 3/951,
Háje, Praha 4.
**Tel** 26 79 00 567.
🌐 cinemacity.cz

**Cinema City Nový Smíchov**
Plzeňská 8.
**Tel** 25 57 42 021.
🌐 palacecinemas.cz

**Cinema City Slovanský Dům**
Na Příkopě 22.
**Map** 3 C4.
**Tel** 25 57 42 021.
🌐 palacecinemas.cz

**Cinema City Zličín**
Řevnická 1, Praha 5.
**Tel** 25 79 51 966.
🌐 cinemacity.cz

**Cinestar Anděl**
Radlická 1, Praha 5.
**Tel** 25 11 15 111.

**Cinestar Černý Most**
Chlumecká 8, Praha 9.
**Tel** 26 67 90 999.
🌐 cinestar.cz

**Evald**
Národní 28.
**Map** 3 B5.
**Tel** 22 11 05 225.
🌐 evald.cz

**Lucerna**
Vodičkova 36.
**Map** 3 C5.
**Tel** 22 42 16 972.
🌐 lucerna.cz

**Mat**
Karlovo náměstí 19.
**Map** 5 B2.
**Tel** 22 49 15 765.
🌐 mat.cz

**Světozor**
Vodičkova 41.
**Map** 3 C5.
**Tel** 22 49 46 824.
🌐 kinosvetozor.cz

# Music and Sport

Prague may not match the vibrancy of Vienna or Budapest, but it certainly can hold its own among Europe's leading cultural destinations. During the holiday season, concerts of classical and Baroque music are held in churches and palaces around the city. Another great attraction for music lovers are Prague's music festivals *(see pp52–4)*.

Sports fans are well served too, with top-class ice hockey and Champions League football.

## Opera

Since Richard Wagner's *The Mastersingers of Nurnburg* officially opened Prague's State Opera House on 5 January 1888, Prague has been a centre of operatic excellence. Today, two highly competitive world-class opera companies give opera top billing on Prague's cultural calendar. And while the low Soviet-era prices of yore are now long gone, top-price seats range from Kč1,000 to 1,200, which makes opera in Prague more accessible than most cities in Europe.

The two major companies, the National and the State, both perform exclusively in their own theatres – the National Opera Company in the **National Theatre** *(see pp156–7)*; the State Opera Company at the **Prague State Opera**. The latter presents a predominantly classical Italian repertoire, always in the orginal language, and performances are always popular. Tickets should be bought in advance. The National Opera Company has a more experimental repertoire, and most of its operas are performed in Czech.

To view a Czech opera, by Czech composers such as Smetana or Dvořák, the National Theatre is your best opportunity. A branch of the National Theatre, the **Estates Theatre** *(see p219)*, performs mainly classical, Italian operas in the original language.

## Classical Music

The Czech Philharmonic Orchestra (CPO) has been based at the magnificent **Rudolfinum** *(see p86)* since giving its first concert there in January 1896, when it was conducted by no less a personality than Anton Dvořák, whose name the Rudolfinum's grand hall now carries. Finding immediate success with the public in Prague and abroad (the Philharmonic travelled to London on tour as early as 1902), the orchestra is today recognised by music lovers as one of the finest in the world.

The post of chief conductor of the CPO is one of the most revered appointments in classical music; currently the post is filled by Eliahu Inbal. Almost all contemporary Czech music, including the celebrated 2000 work *Requiem* by Milan Slavický, premiered at the Rudolfinum. The programme is varied, however, and the works of Czech composers share the limelight with those of their foreign counterparts.

Besides the Rudolfinum, the main concert venue for classical music is the Smetana Hall, found in the **Municipal House** *(see p66)*. Other permanent concert halls include the **Atrium in Žižkov**, a converted chapel, the **Clementinum** and the imposing **Congress Centre Prague**. **Bertramka** is a venue with the added attraction of being the place where Mozart stayed when he was in Prague. He composed the overture for *Don Giovanni* here.

## Music in Churches and Palaces

Concerts performed in the numerous churches and palaces around Prague are extremely popular. Many of these buildings are normally closed to the public, so this is the only chance to see them from inside. Major churches include the **Church of St James** *(see p67)*;

the **Church of St Giles** *(see p77)*; the **Church of St Nicholas** *(see pp128–9)* in the Little Quarter; the **Church of St Nicholas** *(see p72)* in the Old Town; the **Church of St Francis** in Knights of the Cross Square *(see p81)*; **St Vitus's Cathedral** *(see p100)* and **St George's Basilica** *(see p100)*. Other important venues are the **Lobkowicz Palace** *(see p101)* and the **Sternberg Palace** *(see pp112–13)*. It's worth checking the listings magazines *(pp224–5)* for the specific dates and timings of concerts.

## World Music

A small number of clubs and bars in Prague offer ethnic music. The **Palác Akropolis** hosts diverse performances daily in an atmospheric, converted 1920s-theatre building. The Akropolis has hosted the likes of Ani Difranco, Apollo 440 and Transglobal Underground. A variety of bands can be seen from around the world in an unusual setting, at the **House of Culture**. Some of the better jazz clubs *(see pp208–9)* also feature world musicians and bands on a regular basis. Another place worth checking out is **La Bodequita del Medio**, a Cuban restaurant that features Cuban performers some weekend evenings.

## Sports

Czechs are crazy about most sports, and given their habit of winning international competitions in any number of events on a regular basis, it is not surprising. The biggest spectator sports are ice hockey and football, in that order of importance.

The main Czech ice hockey league is the best in Europe after the Russian league (KHL), and both US NHL and KHL rosters are filled with Czech players. Prague has two teams in the top division, Sparta and Slavia. Sparta plays its home games at the **Tipsport Arena**, where tickets cost from Kč80 onwards. Slavia play at the **O2 Arena**, built for the 2004 Ice Hockey World Championship, held in, but surprisingly not won by, the Czech Republic. Tickets here cost Kč100 and up. There are three games a week throughout the season, from September to May, so you should be able to catch a game.

Czech football has long been admired throughout the world, and the national team has been among the world's best for some time. The domestic league is less admired, as many of the country's top stars play in richer leagues elsewhere in Europe. The country's leading team, Sparta Prague, however, is a perennial

qualifier for the European Champions League, which guarantees a procession of big-name opponents. Tickets for Champions League games (played September to December, depending on Sparta's progress) sell out quickly. Home matches of the Czech Republic are also played at **Generali Arena**, also known as the Sparta Stadium.

If you want to get active yourself, you may have to travel a little further out of town, as sports facilities are not extensive in central Prague. Squash, however, is very popular, and there are a number of courts in the city centre, including **ASB** on Wenceslas Square. Mini-golf is on

offer at the **Motel**. The **Czech Lawn Tennis Club** on Štvanice Island also offers 14 clay courts and six indoor courts that can be rented by the general public all day at the weekends and until 3pm on weekdays.

**Aquapalace Praha** is the largest water park in Central Europe, with many pools, a health centre and the large Sauna World, which has a wide range of Finnish saunas and a Roman spa. During the summer, various sports can be performed on two beaches at Vltava River – **Smíchov Beach** and **Žluté lázně**. **Fun Island** is a sports and relaxation centre at Císařská louka (Imperial Meadow) island.

# DIRECTORY

## Music Venues

**Academy of Music**
*Hudební Fakulta Amu*
Malostranské náměstí 13.
**Map** 2 E3.
**Tel** 23 42 44 111.
W hamu.cz

**Atrium in Žižkov**
*Atrium Na Žižkově*
Čajkovského 12, Praha 3.
**Tel** 22 27 21 838.
W atriumzizkov.cz

**Bertramka**
*Bertramka Muzeum W A Mozarta*
Mozartova 169, Praha 5.

**Church of St Francis**
*Kostel Sv. Františka*
Křižovnické náměstí.
**Map** 3 A4.

**Church of St Giles**
*Kostel Sv. Jiljí*
Husova 8.
**Map** 3 B4.
**Tel** 22 42 20 235.
W kostel-praha.cz

**Church of St James**
*Kostel Sv. Jakuba*
Malá Štupartská.
**Map** 3 C3.

**Church of St Nicholas (Old Town)**
*Kostel Sv. Mikuláše*
Staroměstské náměstí.
**Map** 3 B3.

**Church of St Nicholas**
*Kostel Sv. Mikuláše*
Malostranské náměstí.
**Map** 2 E3.

**Church of Sts Simon and Jude**
Kostel Sv. Šimona A Judy
Dušní ulice.
**Map** 3 B2.
W fok.cz

**Clementinum**
Zrcadlová Síň Klementina
Mariánské náměstí 5.
**Map** 3 B3.

**Congress Centre Prague**
Kongresové Centrum Praha
5. května 65, Prague 4.
**Tel** 26 11 71 111.
W kcp.cz

**Lobkowicz Palace**
Lobkovický Palác
Jiřská 3, Pražský hrad.
**Map** 2 E2.
**Tel** 23 33 12 925.
W lobkowicz.cz

**Music Theatre in Karlín**
Hudební Divadlo Karlín
Křižíkova 10. **Map** 4 F3.
**Tel** 22 18 68 666.
W hdk.cz

**Prague State Opera**
Státní Opera Praha
Wilsonova 4. **Map** 6 E1.
**Tel** 22 42 27 266.
W opera.cz

**Rudolfinum – Dvořák Hall**
*Rudolfinum – Dvořákova Síň*
Alšovo nábřeží 12.
**Map** *3 A3.*
**Tel** *22 70 59 227.*
W ceskafilharmonie.cz

**St George's Basilica**
*Bazilika Sv. Jiří*
Jiřské náměstí,
Pražský hrad.
**Map** 2 E2.

**St Vitus's Cathedral**
*Katedrála Víta*
Pražský hrad.
**Map** 2 D2.

**Sternberg Palace**
*Šternberský Palac*
Hradčanské náměstí 15.
**Map** 1 C3.
**Tel** 23 30 90 570.

## World Music

**House of Culture**
*Kulturní Dům Vltavská*
Bubenská 1,
Praha 7.
**Tel** 22 08 78 455.
W vltavska.cz

**La Bodeguita del Medio**
Kaprova 5.
**Map** 3 B3.
**Tel** 22 48 13 922.
W bodeguita.cz

**Palác Akropolis**
Kubelíkova 27.
**Tel** 29 63 30 911.
W palacakropolis.cz

## Sporting Venues

**Aquapalace Praha**
Commercial Zone
Průhonice.
**Tel** 27 11 04 111.
W aquapalace.cz

**ASB Squash**
Václavské náměstí 13–15.
**Tel** 22 42 32 752.

**Czech Lawn Tennis Club**
Štvanice 38,
Praha 7.
**Tel** 22 23 33 444.

**Fun Island**
Císařská louka,
Praha 5.
**Tel** 72 41 09 198.
W fun-island.cz

**Generali Arena**
Milady Horákové 98,
Praha 7.
**Tel** 29 61 11 400.
W sparta.cz

**Minigolf Motol**
Nad Hliníkem,
Praha 5.
**Tel** 77 72 94 668.

**O2 Arena**
Českomoravská 17,
Praha 9.
**Tel** 26 61 21 122.
W O2arena.cz

**Smíchov Beach**
*Smíchov Pláž*
Smíchov, Praha 3.

**Tipsport Arena**
Za Elektrárnou 419,
Praha 7.
**Tel** 26 67 27 443.
W hcsparta.cz

**Žluté lázně**
Podolské nábřeží,
Praha 4.
**Tel** 22 44 63 777.

# SURVIVAL GUIDE

Practical Information        224–233

Getting to Prague           234–237

Getting Around Prague       238–243

# PRACTICAL INFORMATION

Since the fall of the Iron Curtain in the late 1980s, the Czech Republic has not only joined the European Union, but has also held its presidency. In that time, Prague has transformed into a true European capital city, and today all facilities – hotels, banks, restaurants and information centres – are of a high standard. Even so, a little forward planning remains worthwhile. Researching a sight to check when it is open and how best to get there can save a lot of time and inconvenience. Prague's transport system is straightforward, and most of the city's sights are located within walking distance of one another. In general, prices are not as low as they once were, making hunting out bargains in the less touristy parts of the city a worthwhile exercise. Prague is a safe city for tourists, but pick-pocketing is rife, as are scams involving taxis, restaurants in the city centre and money changers.

## When to Go

One of the best times to visit Prague is during the summer when the weather is warm, although the city can be rather crowded then. Other busy times of the year for the Czech capital are Easter and major Catholic festivals (see pp52–5). The main sights, such as the Old Town Square, are always packed during these periods, but the crowds give Prague a carnival atmosphere. Street entertainers, buskers and stalls spring up around the most popular attractions.

Be sure to bring a raincoat in the summer, warm clothes in winter when temperatues regularly drop below freezing, and sturdy shoes all year round. Climate and rainfall charts can be found on pages 53–5.

## Visas and Passports

A valid passport or, where applicable, an ID card is needed when entering the Czech Republic from countries outside the Schengen Zone.

British nationals must have a valid passport, but visas are not required. Visitors from the United States, Canada, Australia and New Zealand need a valid passport with a minimum of 90 days remaining on it, and they can stay for up to three months without a visa. As visa requirements do change, visitors are advised to contact the Czech embassy or consulate, or check details with their travel agent to confirm what is required before travelling. If you require a

visa, you can obtain one from your nearest Czech embassy or consulate.

## Customs Information

For non-EU visitors, customs allowances per person are 2 litres (3.6 pints) of wine, as well as 1 litre (1.8 pints) of spirits and 200 cigarettes. The maximum value of currency that can be brought into or taken out of the Czech Republic is €10,000. Sums in excess of this must be declared to the customs authority. To export authentic antiques, you need to obtain a special licence (see Shopping p212).

VAT (value added tax) can be claimed back on items totalling Kč1,000 or more that are taken out of the country within 30 days of the date of purchase.

A branch of the Prague Information Service in Staroměstské náměstí

## Tourist Information

There are a number of tourist information offices and specialized agencies in Prague that provide advice on anything from accommodation and travel to restaurants and guided tours.

The efficient **Prague Information Service (PIS)** is the city's best source of tourist information. It has three offices in the city centre and one at the airport, and provides visitors with advice, maps and listings (see pp216–17) in English, German, Russian, French, Czech, Spanish, Italian, Japanese and Chinese. If you want similar information on the rest of the country, visit the **Czech Republic Information Centre** or **Čedok**, the country's largest tour operator.

## Language

Czechs are now as likely to speak Italian, Spanish and French as English and German, so booking a room, ordering a meal or buying a ticket has become much easier. However, be aware that the level of customer service does vary.

## Listings and Tickets

There are hundreds of galleries, museums, clubs and theatres scattered throughout the city, and to find out what's on it is best to consult a listings paper. The English-language newspaper The Prague Post gives detailed listings of most events and exhibitions. Available from

Entry tickets for some of
Prague's major tourist sights

newsstands in the city centre, it
also gives tips for the visitor and
has informative articles on
Prague, its politics and its people.
Online, listings can be found on
the PIS website and at www.
expats.cz and www.prague.tv.
The comprehensive Czech-
language listings book *Přehled*
is best explained by a friendly
PIS worker.

The price of admission to
museums varies widely, from
Kč30 to around Kč300. Most
churches are free, with a
collection box for donations at
the door. Tickets for
entertainment events can be
bought from booking agencies
or at the venue itself
(*see pp216–17*). Some hotels can
also book tickets for you;
alternatively, try a large travel
agent in the city centre.

## Opening Hours

This guide lists the opening
hours for individual museums,
galleries and churches. Most of
the city's major sights can be

visited throughout the year,
but many of Prague's gardens
and the castles outside the city
are open only from 1 April to
31 October. Visiting hours are
normally from 9am to 5pm
daily, but during the summer
months opening times are
extended to 6pm. Note that
final admission times can
often be as much as an hour
earlier. Gardens stay open
until 8pm in July and August.
Most museums and several
castles are closed on Monday.
The National Museum is closed
on the first Tuesday of the
month, and the Jewish
Museum is closed on Saturday.
Museum Night in June is an
opportunity to visit collections
for free between 7pm and
1am. A free transport service
between the museums
also operates.

Opening hours of Prague's
shops vary widely. Many
businesses are open between
7am and 6pm Monday to Friday,
and 8am to noon on Saturday.
Department stores generally stay
open until be-tween 7 and 9pm
on Saturday and Sunday. Prague
does not have a standard day for
late-night shopping, although
many of the more expensive
tourist shops stay open until
around 10pm on most nights.

Banks are open from 8am to
5pm Monday to Friday.
Restaurants, cafés and bars all
have varied opening hours
(*see pp193–3*). Most bars open
from 10am and, with no
licensing laws, often stay open
until everyone leaves.

A person taking photographs of one of Prague's many picturesque sights

Children riding the miniature train at Prague Zoo

## Travellers with Special Needs

Facilities for the disabled are slowly increasing in Prague. The prevalence of narrow streets and uneven paving, especially in the centre, do contribute to problems, but ramps are being added to allow easier access into buildings. Hotels are introducing facilities for travellers with special needs, and transport options have also improved, with low access on Prague's trams and lifts installed in many metro stations. Visit the Prague Public Transport Company website at www.dpp.cz to plan your journey using wheelchair-accessible metro stations, trams and buses, and three special bus lines for wheelchair-users. Timetables at tram stops indicate which services are wheelchair-accessible.

The PIS (see p225) distributes a superb booklet, *Accessibility Atlas for People with Impaired Mobility*. Published by the **Prague Organization for Wheelchair Users**, it contains all the information you need to make the most out of your stay in Prague. The PIS also provides maps and guides in Braille in various languages.

Between the PIS office and the Astronomical Clock is a 24-hour wheelchair-accessible toilet. Press the buzzer by the wheelchair logo for access.

## Travelling with Children

Czechs are tremendously family-oriented and love well-behaved children. When travelling on public transport, it is not unusual for strangers to offer to help – for example by vacating seats for parents with young children. If you have a pram, indicate this clearly to tram drivers, and they will allow extra time for you to get on board. Children are welcome in bars and restaurants, but remember that the Czech Republic has not introduced a smoking ban yet. However, there are a number of non-smoking restaurants with kids' areas, and Pizza Nuova (see p201) even offers on-site baby-sitting at weekends.

**Bohemia Bagel** is another restaurant with a dedicated kids' area. Baby-changing facilities are free in any branch of McDonald's, **Mothercare** and Marks & Spencer, while public toilets often cost Kč5–10. Breast-feeding in public is not very common but perfectly acceptable. Staying in an apartment may be a better option than a hotel if you have children.

Modern playgrounds abound in Prague – try the ones at Letná (Map 3 A1) and Riegrovy Sady (Map 6 F1). The zoo (see p162) and the adjacent **Botanical Garden** make an excellent day out, as do the bobsleigh track at **Bobsled Prague**, **The Museum of Miniatures**, **Choco Story Museum** and, in the summer, **Aquapalace Praha** (see p221) or **Podolí Pool**. For more ideas visit www.kidsinprague.com.

## Senior Travellers

Many international hotels, car-hire firms and airlines offer discounts for seniors with proof of pensioner status. *Důchodce/Důchodkyně* means "pensioner" in Czech, so keep an eye out for this word at ticket offices, although museums, concert halls and sights may offer a discount only to Czech pensioners. The public transport system allows discounts only to Czech seniors. However, public transport in Prague is among the cheapest in Europe.

## Student Travellers

If you are entitled to an International Student Identity Card (ISIC), it is worth getting one before travelling to Prague. Admission charges to most of Prague's major attractions, such as museums, galleries, castles and other historic buildings, are up to 50 per cent cheaper on production of a valid ISIC card (for example, admission to Prague Castle is half the price of the full entrance

International Student Identity Card

fee). Students can also get cheaper coach and train travel. If you are looking for somewhere low-cost to stay, many youth hostels in the centre of the city offer student discounts (see Where to Stay, pp186–7). Some restaurants, such as **Pizzeria Einstein**, offer discounts as well.

## Time

Prague is on Central European time, which is Greenwich Mean Time (GMT) plus 1 hour. Summer time runs effectively from the end of March up until the end of October – this is GMT plus 2 hours. New York is 6 hours behind Prague, and Los Angeles is 9 hours behind. Sydney is 9 hours ahead (10 in summer), while Moscow and Johannesburg are 2 and 1 hours ahead respectively.

## Electricity

The electricity supply in Prague is 230V AC, and two-pin plugs are used. For British or US plugs, an adaptor is needed. Adaptors can be purchased in any large electrical shop such as Dat Art or Electro World in malls *(see p215)*

## Conversion Chart

**Imperial to Metric**
1 inch = 2.54 centimetres
1 foot = 30 centimetres
1 mile = 1.6 kilometres
1 ounce = 28 grams
1 pound = 454 grams
1 pint = 0.6 litre
1 gallon = 4.6 litres

**Metric to Imperial**
1 millimetre = 0.04 inch
1 centimetre = 0.4 inch
1 metre = 3 feet 3 inches
1 kilometre = 0.6 mile
1 gram = 0.04 ounce
1 kilogram = 2.2 pounds
1 litre = 1.8 pints

## Responsible Tourism

Czechs are great nature-lovers and, therefore, fairly green. Large municipal recycling bins are prevalent across the city, encouraging the recycling of books, clothes, furniture and other items. Organic food and clothing are becoming popular. **Country Life** operates an organic farm and bakery to supply its own and others' shops and restaurants, while **Evergreen Butik** is Prague's first organic fashion store, with clothes designed in London and handmade in Kathmandu. **Manufaktura** sells handmade wooden ornaments, toys and utensils, recycled paper and more. In supermarkets, try to buy Czech products to support the local economy. Look out for Kubík juices, Kofola (the Czech-Slovak alternative to Coca-Cola), Mattoni, Dobrá voda and Korunní still and sparkling water, and Orion and Opavia biscuits and sweets. Seasonal markets are also good for local produce.

Look out for the EU Ecolabel flower logo on various products and services. **Adria Hotel** and **Hotel Adalbert** have earned this endorsement by conserving water and energy, and recycling and decreasing waste.

Ecotourism is another aspect of the Czech Republic's commitment to environmental sustainability. **Greenways**, a local NGO, publishes maps and guides for cycling to and around the country, while the **European Centre for Eco Agro Tourism** offers a Green *Holiday Guidebook* to the Czech Republic in various languages.

EU Ecolabel logo

---

## DIRECTORY

### Travellers with Special Needs

**Czech Association of Persons with Disabilities**
Karlínské náměstí 12.
**Map** 5 B2.
**Tel** 22 23 17 489.

**Prague Organization for Wheelchair Users**
Benediktská 6. **Map** 4 D3.
**Tel** 22 48 27 210.

### Travelling with Children

**Bobsled Prague**
Prosecká 34b.
**Tel** 28 48 40 520.
W bobovadraha.cz

**Bohemia Bagel**
Masná 2. **Tel** 22 48 12 560.

**Botanical Garden**
Nádvorní 134.
**Tel** 23 41 48 111.
W botanicka.cz

**Choco Story Museum**
Celetná 10. **Map** 3 C3.
**Tel** 22 42 42 953.
W choco-story-praha.cz

**Mothercare**
Na Příkopě 19–21. **Map** 3
C4. W mothercare.com

**The Museum of Miniatures**
Strahov Monastery.
**Map** 1 B4. **Tel** 23 33 52 371.
W muzeumminiatur.com

**Podolí Pool**
Podolská 74.
**Tel** 24 14 33 952.

**Public Transport Museum**
Patočkova 4, Praha 6. **Tel** 29
61 28 900. W dpp.cz

### Student Travellers

**Pizzeria Einstein**
Rumunská 25. **Map** 6 D3.
**Tel** 22 25 22 635.

### Responsible Tourism

**Adria Hotel**
Václavské náměsti 26.
**Map** 4 D5. **Tel** 22 10 81 111.
W adria.cz

**Country Life**
Melantrichova 15. **Map** 3
B3. **Tel** 22 42 13 366.

**European Centre for Eco Agro Tourism**
W eceat.org

**Evergreen Butik**
Uruguayská 6, Praha 2.
**Tel** 72 57 40 615.
W etique.cz

**Greenways**
W greenways.cz

**Hotel Adalbert**
Břevnovský klášter,
Markétská 1. **Tel** 22 04 06
170. W hoteladalbert.cz

**Manufaktura**
Melantrichova 17.
**Map** 3 B4.

### Religious Services

**Anglican**
St. Clement's, Klimentská 5.
**Map** 3 C2. **Tel** 22 33 10
266. W anglican.cz

**Baptist**
International Baptist
Church of Prague,
Vinohradská 68. **Map** 6 F1.
**Tel** 731 778 735.
W ibcp.cz

**Hussite Church**
Church of St Nicholas,
Staroměstské náměstí.

**Map** 3 C3. **Tel** 23 47 60
058. W husiti.cz

**Interdenominational**
International Christian,
Peroutkova 57. **Tel** 29 63
92 338. W icprague.cz

**Jewish**
Various synagogues.
**Tel** 22 48 00 849.
W kehilaprag.cz
Old-New Synagogue
*(see pp88–9).*
Jerusalem Synagogue,
Jeruzalémská 7. **Map** 4 E4.

**Methodist-Evangelical**
Malostranské náměstí.
**Map** 2 E3.
W praguefellowship.cz

**Muslim**
Islamic Foundation Praha,
Blatská 1491. **Map** 5 C2.
**Tel** 28 19 18 876.
W praha.muslim.cz

**Roman Catholic**
Various churches.
W apha.cz
Church of the Infant Jesus
of Prague, Karmelitská 9.
**Map** 2 E4. **Tel** 25 75 33 646.
W pragjesu.info

# Personal Security and Health

Compared to many Western cities, Prague is relatively safe. Even if you do not need emergency help from the police, you should feel free to approach them at any time for advice of any kind – they are generally helpful to the tourist population. If you should need emergency medical care during your stay in Prague, it will be given free. An increasing number of English-speaking services are available, including health centres, pharmacies and dentists (see p229).

A Prague police station sign

## The Police and Security Services

In Prague you will come across several kinds of policemen and -women and members of various security services. Report any problems to a uniformed state police officer at a police station. The main stations are marked on the Street Finder maps (see pp244–55). The state police carry guns and can arrest a suspect. They patrol the streets on foot or drive grey, blue and yellow patrol cars. The municipal police, the other main security force, is divided into different sections. Special mobile police stations are set up during tourist high season in locations such as the Old Town Square. They are staffed by multilingual officers to enable tourists to

Municipal police badge

State police badge

report crimes and seek on-the-spot advice. The **Tourist Police Station** is where you should go to report any losses and thefts. The office is manned 24 hours a day, seven days a week. For lost property, it is worth trying the **Ztráty a nálezy** (lost-and-found office) on Karolíny Světlé. The traffic police regulate parking, including clamping and issuing fines (see p241), speeding and drink-driving. It is illegal to drive with any alcohol in your bloodstream, and if you are caught the penalties are severe. If you have a serious traffic accident, you must immediately ring the state police. It is against the law to move anything before the police get there. You will also see private security guards. These are called

sekuriťáci, or "black sheriffs" (many actually wear black uniforms) and tend to guard banks and be used as security at football matches. They are armed with truncheons.

## What to be Aware of

Prague is a safe and unthreatening city to walk around. Violence and robberies are rare in the city centre. Crimes against tourists are usually limited to petty pilfering from cars and hotels, and the only really prevalent issue – pickpockets. Using your common sense should help you to avoid trouble. Always remember to keep your bag in sight and avoid carrying your passport, wallet and valuables in your back pocket or in an open bag. Thieves tend to operate in busy areas such as crowded trams, metro cars and popular sights. Be careful when watching the hourly movements of the Astronomical Clock, for instance. Pickpockets are skilled and use very clever diversionary tactics. Be aware and keep everything safe and close. It is very unlikely that anything stolen will ever be recovered. Never leave anything of value in your car and try to park in an underground car park.

It is always advisable to take out adequate insurance before you arrive in Prague since it is difficult to arrange once there. Report any thefts to the state or municipal police for future insurance claims.

Prague is generally safe for women travelling on their own. However, one place that is advisable to avoid at night if you are a woman alone is

A male state police officer

A municipal police officer

A female state police officer

A "black sheriff"

Wenceslas Square, because local men might assume that you are one of the city's prostitutes.

Prague has some less-than-reputable bars and cafés that stay open into the early hours. Bars with the words "non-stop" and "herna" are synonymous with shady characters gambling on slot machines. See the bars and cafés listings on *pp206–7* for recommended venues to visit. Be aware that the more touristy restaurants and many taxi drivers have a tendency to overcharge. It is best to take a taxi from a Fair Place taxi rank *(see p240).* Keep all of your receipts.

Before you travel, take photocopies of all essential documents, including your passport. Place your passport in your hotel safe and carry the photocopy with you when you are out and about. You are expected to have your passport with you only when driving.

### In an Emergency

Your hotel should be able to put you in touch with a local doctor if necessary, but if you need immediate help, Prague's emergency services are available 24 hours a day. Non-Czech speakers should call 112; an English-speaking operator will translate via a three-way conversation to the service you

need. Hospitals with casualty units are marked on the Street Finder maps *(see pp244–55).*

### Health Care and Pharmacies

All EU nationals are entitled to free health care in the Czech Republic. To claim medical treatment, visitors must have a European Health Insurance Card (EHIC card), which should be presented to the physician along with a valid form of identification. Not all treatments are covered by the card, so additional medical insurance is definitely advisable.

Pharmacy sign

Medical tourism is increasingly popular; **Health Centre Prague** offers cheaper procedures than in the rest of Europe.

There are also 24-hour pharmacies *(lékárna)* with staff who are qualified to give advice and administer simple remedies. If you want an English-speaking doctor, visit the **Diplomatic Health Centre** for foreigners at Na Homolce. Alternatively, try the privately run **Canadian Medical Center** or, for dental care, **Elite Dental Prague**. You will need to take a passport and a means of payment with you.

Those with respiratory problems should be aware that between October and March sulphur dioxide levels in Prague occasionally exceed the World Health Organization's accepted levels. With increasing car ownership in the city and a lack of funding for alternative fuels, this situation seems unlikely to improve, so if you think you may be affected by fumes, be sure to take any medication you might need with you on your trip.

Municipal police patrol car

Ambulance

## DIRECTORY

### Emergency Numbers

**Emergency Operator**
Tel 112 (in English).

**Ambulance**
Tel 155.

**Police**
Tel 158 (state)/156 (municipal).

**Fire**
Tel 150.

### Police

**Tourist Police Station**
Jungmannovo náměstí 9.
**Map** 3 C5.

### Lost Property Bureau

**Lost and Found
(Ztráty a nálezy)**
Karoliny Světlé 5.
**Map** 3 A5.
**Tel** 22 42 35 085.
**Open** 8am–4pm Mon–Fri (to 5:30pm Mon & Wed; to 2pm Fri).

### Medical Centres

**Canadian Medical Center**
Veleslavínská 1.
**Tel** 72 43 00 301 (24 hours).
**Open** 8am–6pm Mon–Fri (to 8pm Tue & Thu), 9am–2pm Sat.
W cmcpraha.cz

**Diplomatic Health Centre
(Nemocnice Na Homolce)**
Roentgenova 2.
**Tel** 25 72 71 111.
**Open** 24 hours a day.
W homolka.cz

**Elite Dental Prague**
Vodičkova 5. **Map** 3 C3.
**Tel** 22 25 10 888.
**Open** 8am–8pm Mon–Thu, 8am–4pm Fri.
W elitedental.cz

**Health Centre Prague**
Vodičkova 28, 3rd entrance, 2nd floor.
**Map** 3 C5.
**Tel** 60 34 33 833 (24 hrs).
**Open** 8am–5pm Mon–Fri.
W doctor-prague.cz

### 24-Hour Pharmacies

**Lékárna Palackého**
Palackého 5. **Map** 3 C5.
**Tel** 22 49 46 982.

**Lékárna u Sv. Ludmily**
Belgická 37. **Map** 6 F3.
**Tel** 22 25 13 396.

# Banking and Local Currency

With its increasingly international profile, Prague is becoming more expensive, although residential sections of the city remain cheaper than the tourist centre. Banks now have international desks staffed by multilingual cashiers, and ATMs dot the city streets. Credit cards are widely accepted, although in smaller outlets it is wise to ask first, while traveller's cheques can be changed only in banks. It is worth bearing in mind that bureaux de change usually take some commission regardless of their "zero" claims.

## Banks and Bureaux de Change

The large, modern banks generally found in the city centre all open between 9am and 5pm or 6pm Monday to Friday. Hundreds of bureaux de change are found in tiny shops throughout the city. However, despite sometimes offering better exchange rates than the banks, their commission charges (often hidden in the small print) are huge, often as high as 12%. Compare this to the 1–5% charged by banks, along with a minimum commission of Kč20–50. The only advantage of these exchange offices is their convenience. Many are open late every day, some offer a 24-hour service and queues are rare.

Most of the larger hotels will also change foreign currency for you, but again commission rates may be very high. If you have some Czech currency left over from your stay, you can reconvert your money. All banks will reconvert your extra crowns for a small commission. Finally, never change your money on the black market. As well as being illegal, the rate is not any higher than banks or

exchanges, and it is guaranteed you will be given notes that are not legal tender.

Traveller's cheques are a safe alternative to carrying cash. It is recommended that you take well-known brands – such as American Express or Thomas Cook for example – although it is unlikely that the major banks will refuse any. Traveller's cheques are not accepted as currency by any shops or restaurants, and they must be changed at banks or bureaux de change.

An automatic teller machine (ATM) for dispensing cash

## ATMs

There are ATMs (bankomats) all over the centre of Prague, and this is the easiest method to get your Czech currency. Many ATMs are in the entrance to banks, but they are accessible even if the branch is closed. They accept most major credit and debit cards, and information is available in English, German, French and Czech. Be aware that you will probably be charged an overseas transaction fee each time you use your card so check with your bank how much this fee is.

## Credit Cards

Paying by credit card is becoming more popular in Prague – not only in hotels and restaurants, but also in supermarkets and shops. Even if an outlet displays a credit card sign, do not assume they will accept all types of card as payment. In a restaurant it is better to ask before ordering your meal to avoid difficulties later. The cards most often accepted are American Express, VISA and MasterCard. Most banks will allow cash advances (up to your limit) on your card.

## DIRECTORY

### Banks

**Česká Národní Banka**
Na příkopě 28. **Map** 3 C4.
**Tel** 22 44 11 111. **W** cnb.cz

**Česká Spořitelna**
Rytířská 29. **Map** 3 C4.
**Tel** 800 207 207. **W** csas.cz

**Československá Obchodní Banka**
Na příkopě 18. **Map** 3 C4.
**Tel** 800 300 300. **W** csob.cz

**GE Money Bank**
Hybernská 20. **Map** 4 D3.
**Tel** 22 14 90 611.
**W** gemoney.cz

**Komerční Banka**
Václavské náměstí 42.
**Map** 4 D5. **Tel** 955 545 111.
**W** kb.cz

**UniCredit Bank**
Revoluční 7. **Map** 4 D2.
**Tel** 844 11 33 55.
**W** unicreditbank.cz

### Bureaux de change

**Eurochange**
Opletalova 30. **Map** 4 E5.
**Tel** 22 42 43 614.

**Exchange**
Náměstí Franze Kafky 2.
**Map** 3 B3.
**Tel** 800 225 588.

**Inter Change**
Rytířská 26. **Map** 3 C4.
**Tel** 22 42 21 757.
One of several branches.
**W** interchange.cz

Façade of the Česká Spořitelna bank

## Currency

The currency in Prague and the Czech Republic is the Czech crown (*koruna*), which is abbreviated as Kč (the international abbreviation is CZK). *Hellers* (of which there are 100 to the crown) have been phased out.

The Czech crown is the best and usually the only possible currency to use when making payments in cash. Some hotels and shops accept payment in euros, but the exchange rate may not always be favourable. Tesco accepts euros and gives change in Czech crowns at the going bank rate, as does Marks & Spencer, where they accept pounds sterling as well.

## Banknotes

*Czech banknotes are available in the denominations Kč100, Kč200, Kč500, Kč1,000, Kč2,000 and Kč5,000.*

Kč5,000 note

Kč2,000 note

Kč1,000 note

Kč500 note

Kč200 note

Kč100 note

1 crown (Kč1)

2 crowns (Kč2)

## Coins

*Coins come in the following denominations: Kč1, Kč2, Kč5, Kč10, Kč20 and Kč50. All the coins have the Czech emblem, a lion rampant, on one side.*

5 crowns (Kč5)

10 crowns (Kč10)

20 crowns (Kč20)

50 crowns (Kč50)

# Communications and Media

The main Czech telephone service is called Telefónica O2 Czech Republic. O2 provides a comprehensive digital network of phones across the country and, along with Vodafone and T-Mobile, constitutes the Czech mobile market. Wi-Fi zones and Internet cafés can be found all over Prague; the latter are often in courtyards or on the first floor of buildings. Česká Pošta remains an efficient postal service within the Czech Republic and overseas.

O2 phone boxes in Prague

## Public Telephones

Despite the growing use of mobile phones, there are still many public phones in the Czech Republic; indeed, there are more phone boxes here than in most European countries.

O2 public phones accept cash (euros and Czech crowns), credit cards and phonecards. Depending on which phone you find, you can send a text message and an email as well as make a call. In hotels, you can usually get a direct line, but commission charges on the

calls are often exorbitant. Remember also that international calls can be extremely expensive, no matter what time of day you phone. The cheapest way to call abroad is via an international call office, such as the **Call Point Internet**. You can buy phonecards *(telefonní karta)* from tobacconists *(tabáks)* and newsstands, and from post offices, supermarkets and petrol stations. Two popular cards are Karta X, a pre-paid calling card that allows you to make national and international calls from any phone; and Trick, a multi-functional card that can be used to pay for telephone calls and Internet services.

On all phones in the country, the dialling tone is a short note followed by a long one; the ringing tone consists of long regular notes, and the engaged signal has short and rapid notes. All Czech phone numbers have nine digits, and Prague numbers start with a 2.

## Mobile Phones

Czech mobile phones operate on a GSM band of 900/ 1800 MHz, the same standard in use throughout Europe, but different from that used in the United States. US cell phones will work provided they are tri-band phones and that the service provider allows for international roaming. To avoid high roaming fees, you can obtain local pay-as-you-go SIM cards, which give you a temporary telephone number and allow you to make calls and send text messages on the local network.

Pay-as-you-go cards are very well priced. You pay for credit but the SIM card is free. The three main mobile-phone operators are Telefónica O2 (www.cz.o2.com), Vodafone (www.vodafone.cz) and T-Mobile (www.t-mobile.cz). Czech mobile numbers start with a 6 or 7.

## Internet Access

Most hotels offer guests some form of in-room Internet access, through either a wireless or a LAN connection. Wireless connections may not be reliable, depending on how far your room is from the router. If Internet access is important to you, it's best to mention this at the hotel reception when checking in and request a room with a strong wireless signal. Most hotels will usually also have a public computer terminal for guests to surf the Internet or, failing that, they will allow guests to quickly check their emails on the hotel computer. The receptionist should know the location of the nearest Internet café.

Internet cafés are relatively common in Prague. Rates are reasonable, at Kč1–2 per minute. Just because the word "café" is part of the name, do not assume they will serve coffee or that the coffee will be drinkable if they do. It is also worth bearing in mind that more and more cafés, bars and restaurants are offering customers with laptops free wireless access;

## Reaching the Right Number

- Czech directory enquiries and operator 1180
- International directory enquiries and to make a collect call 1181
- International call followed by the country code 00
- In case of emergencies (Police) 158
- Emergency operator (English) 112

If you have problems getting through to a number in Prague, it is likely that the number has changed due to the modernization of the phone system. To check, ring the directory enquiries number and ask for an English-speaker.

look for the Wi-Fi sticker. Connections are usually straightforward and pretty fast. If there's a password, the staff will tell you what it is.

Post office sign

## Postal Services

There are a number of post offices in Prague (see Street Finder Maps on pp244–55). The best and largest one is the **Main Post Office** in Jindřišská, just off Wenceslas Square. It has a huge variety of services, including a large phone room where you can make international calls. This service operates from 7am to 11pm. The Main Post Office offers easy-access information in English, and swift and efficient service. Take a ticket when you enter the building, then wait until the electronic display indicates which booth you should go to. If you want to buy some of the Czech Republic's attractive stamps, go to window 29 (no ticket required).

The Main Post Office on Jindřišská is open from 2am to midnight. Most other post offices offer more regular business hours, from 8am to 6pm or 7pm Monday to Friday, and from 8am until noon on Saturday.

There is no first- or second-class mail in the Czech Republic, but the majority of letters usually arrive at their destination within a few days. If you want to send something more valuable through the post, use the

registered mail service, which is reliable and efficient.

Postcards and letters can be posted in the many orange post boxes scattered around Prague. Both take around five working days to arrive in the UK and about a week to get to the USA. Stamps can be bought from post offices, newsagents or tabáks – they will also tell you what stamps you need. All parcels and registered letters need to be handed in at a post office.

For emergency parcels and packages that need to arrive quickly, you can use an international courier service, such as **DHL**, rather than the post office.

Post restante letters are delivered to the Main Post Office in Jindřišská Street. Go to window 1 or 2 (open 7am to 8pm Monday to Friday and 7am to noon Saturday) with your passport or other official identification.

## Newspapers

Prague has a number of newspapers, including an English-language one, The Prague Post. This provides informative pieces on Prague, its people and politics, and it also includes a good leisure supplement, Night & Day. For a Czech daily newspaper translated into English, go to www.ceskenoviny.cz/news. Other online resources on Prague are www.expats.cz, www.prague.tv and www. praguemonitor.com.

Most of the newsstands located around Wenceslas Square and other popular tourist spots sell the main quality European newspapers such as The Times, The Guardian, El País and Die Zeit, as well as US papers such as the International Herald Tribune.

## TV and Radio

Czech television dubs everything, so local TV is not much use to non-Czech speakers. However, most hotels have freeview news channels, and the larger chains have packages that include film channels.

You can listen to the BBC World Service on 101.1FM; it is also possible to listen to the BBC online, by logging on to www. bbc.co.uk. One of the most popular local stations is Radio 1 (91.9MHz), which has an English-language show, High Fidelity (8–11pm Fri). Another weekly English- language show, The Friday Ripple (5–7pm Fri), is on Radio Wave (www.wave.cz).

Copy of The Prague Post

## DIRECTORY

### Internet Cafés and Call Shops

**Bohemia Bagel**
Holešovice, Dukelských hrdinů 48 (across from Parkhotel).
**Tel** 22 08 06 541.
**Open** 10am–midnight daily.

**Call Point Internet**
Myšák Gallery, Vodičkova 31.
**Map** 3 C5.
**Open** 10am–8pm daily.

**Káva Káva Káva**
Národní 37. **Map** 3 B5.
**Tel** 22 42 28 862.
**Open** 7am–10pm daily (from 9am Sat & Sun).
w kava-coffee.cz

### Postal Services

**DHL**
Václavské náměstí 47. **Map** 4 D5.
**Tel** 840 103 000/ 22 03 00 111.
w dhl.cz

**Main Post Office**
Jindřišská 14. **Map** 4 D5.
**Tel** 84 01 11 244/22 11 31 111.
w cpost.cz

Tobacconist's, where you can also buy stamps and phonecards

# GETTING TO PRAGUE

Prague is located right at the heart of Europe and enjoys good transport connections with the rest of the continent. There are direct flights every day from most of Europe's major cities and, via Delta Airlines and ČSA, from selected cities in the USA. There are no direct flights from Australia, however. International coach transport is efficient and inexpensive, but

journey times can be off-putting. Prague is well served by international railways, but as this is a popular means of getting to Prague trains tend to get booked up early, especially in the summer. The main train station (Hlavní nádraží) is close to Wenceslas Square and the city centre and, except for the airport, other major points of arrival are also fairly central.

## Travelling by Air

Prague has good flight connections to most major European cities. More than 40 international airlines fly to Prague Airport (Letiště Praha Ruzyně). If you are travelling from the United States, **Delta Airlines** operates a limited number of non-stop flights from Atlanta and New York. There are no Australian or New Zealand carriers flying direct to Prague, although you can fly **British Airways** with a stop in London. Other major airlines include **KLM**, **Air France**, **Lufthansa**, **Emirates** and **Czech Airlines (ČSA)**. It takes about 1 hour and 50 minutes to fly from London to Prague, and about 9 hours from the east coast of North America.

## Tickets and Fares

Prague has become increasingly popular with budget carriers, both as a hub and a destination. Both **easyJet**

and **Jet2.com** fly regularly between Prague and several cities in the UK; **Ryanair** also flies direct to Brno, the Czech Republic's second city. **Smart Wings**, **Wizz Air** and **German Wings** are popular budget carriers that connect Prague to destinations in the rest of Europe. Booking online or by phone as early as possible will get you the best prices from these budget airlines, and taking only cabin luggage keeps the price down too.

APEX (advanced purchase) tickets can be a cheap option, but they have stringent conditions attached to them. These include having to book your ticket at least a month in advance and severe penalties if you cancel your flight.

If you ring well in advance, airlines will quote you the standard fare, but the price may be lowered nearer the time if seats remain unsold – this is rarely the case in the summer months, however, as Prague is

Sign for passport control

such a popular destination. You may get a better deal in winter (except over the Christmas and New Year period when prices rise again). Students and regular business travellers may be able to get discounts at any time of year. Children under two who do not occupy a separate seat usually pay 10 per cent of the adult fare. If you do get a cheap deal, ensure that you will get a refund if your travel agent goes out of business.

## Prague Airport

Prague's only international airport is at Ruzyně, 15 km (9 miles) northwest of the city centre. The airport is modern, clean, efficient and functional. It offers all that you would expect from an international airport: ATMs and 24-hour exchange facilities; car rental offices; a duty-free shop; a post office and a left-luggage office.

The airport was thoroughly modernized at the start of the millennium, including the addition of a new terminal. Terminal 1 is used for inter-continental flights, including those to the UK, North America, the Middle East, Africa and Asia. All domestic flights and flights to destinations within the EU and other Schengen countries are served by Terminal 2. The two terminals are connected and

Departures board in Terminal 2 at Prague Airport

are only a short walk apart. There is also a business- class lounge and catering facility, as well as a shopping centre within the Marriott Courtyard Hotel, just across the airport forecourt.

Terminal 3, also known as the South Terminal, is further away and used only for general aviation and private planes.

## Transport from the Airport to the City

Getting to and from Prague airport is easy, relatively fast and economical, unless you fall victim to one of Prague's infamous taxi scams *(see p240)*. Allow at least 60 minutes to reach the airport by road from the city centre at rush hour, though on a good day it could take as little as 30 minutes. Travelling by a combination of the metro and standard bus takes about 45 minutes depending on connections.

The airport is linked to the city centre by a regular mini-bus service run by **CEDAZ**. For the return trip to the airport, there is a bus stop at V Celnici street, a short distance from Náměstí Republiky. Buses leave every 30 minutes from 7:30am to 7pm, and tickets cost Kč130 per person.

For a service on demand to and from the airport, **AAA Radiotaxi** are a reliable option

CEDAZ bus operating between the airport and the city

and offer a 47 per cent discount on a return trip. They can take you to addresses outside the city, and they can even be used to tour the rest of the Czech Republic.

A regular public bus service runs to the airport from Dejvická metro (bus 119) and from Zličín metro (bus 100). Between midnight and 5am, the 510 night bus will take you into the city every half hour for the standard Kč32 public transport ticket. The Airport Express bus stops at Dejvická, Masarykovo nádraží, Náměstí Republiky and Hlavní nádraží; it runs every half-hour between 5:45am and 9:15pm and costs Kč60.

Alternatively, there are always taxis waiting in front of the terminal. Taxis provided by **AAA** and 1.1.1 Radiocab Taxi offer a fixed price. The prices are comparable, but it should not cost more than Kč600 to get to the city centre.

The airport forecourt, from which buses and taxis can be taken into town

## DIRECTORY

### Airport Information

**Airport Praha Ruzyně**
Tel 22 01 11 888. W prg.aero

### Main Airline Offices

**Air France**
Tel 23 30 90 933.
W airfrance.com

**British Airways**
Tel 23 90 00 299. W ba.com

**Czech Airlines (ČSA)**
V Celnici 5. Map 4 D3.
Tel 23 90 07 007. W csa.cz

**Delta Airlines**
Tel 23 30 90 933. W delta.com

**EasyJet**
W easyjet.com

**Emirates**
W emirates.com

**German Wings**
W germanwings.com

**Jet2.com**
W jet2.com

**KLM**
Tel 23 30 90 933. W klm.com

**Lufthansa**
Tel 23 40 08 234.
W lufthansa.com

**Ryanair**
W ryanair.com

**Smart Wings**
W smartwings.com

**Wizz Air**
W wizzair.com

### Airport Bus

**CEDAZ**
Tel 22 01 16 758. W cedaz.cz

### Taxi Transfers

**AAA Radiotaxi**
Tel 22 11 11 111. W aaataxi.cz

The façade of Hlavní nádraží

## Travelling by Train

Rail travel is an enjoyable and environmentally friendly way to travel to and from Prague. Prague is connected by rail to all the major capitals of Europe. International trains have dining cars and couchettes, but tickets are often more expensive than budget air fares. Buy well in advance to ensure a seat and get the best possible deal.

The railways in the Czech Republic are run by České Dráhy (ČD). There are several types of train run by ČD. These include the *rychlík* (express) trains; the *osobní* (passenger) trains, which form a local service and stop at all stations; the EX, or national express, for longer distances; the SC (Supercity), which is the fastest and most comfortable train service between Prague, Brno and Ostrava; and the EC (Eurocity), or international express. Alternatively, Regiojet makes for a cheaper and more comfortable option to Pardubice and Ostrava. More lines are expected in the near future.

Tickets can be bought in advance. If you want to buy a ticket just before your train leaves, be warned that queues at ticket booths can be long, especially on Fridays and Sundays. First-class carriages exist on most trains and guarantee you a seat. In the timetable, an "R" in a box by a train number means you must have a seat reserved on that train. An "R" without a box means a reservation is recommended. If you are caught in the wrong carriage, you have to pay an on-the-spot fine.

## Train Stations

The biggest and busiest railway station in Prague is Hlavní nádraží, which is only a 5-minute walk from Wenceslas Square. The thorough renovation of the Art Nouveau station is progressing well, and the gleaming interior now has shops, restaurants, a pub and even a jeweller's. As well as shops, the lower ground floor has an inexpensive left-luggage facility, a tourist office (open 9am–7pm Mon–Sat and 9am–5pm Sun) and the central ticket office (open 3:30am–00:30am). In this ticket hall there is also a **ČD Travel Agency**, where all international rail tickets, including those for Eurostar, are sold by multilingual station staff. Many international trains also stop at Nádraží Holešovice.

Prague's oldest train terminal, Masarykovo nádraží, serves mainly Prague's suburbs and a few other domestic routes. Similarly, many domestic routes are served from Smíchov.

## Travelling by Coach

Coach connections from Prague to many of the major European cities have improved immeasurably, and tickets tend to sell out quickly. Some Czech towns – such as Karlovy Vary, Hradec Králové, Český Krumlov and Terezín – are much easier to reach by coach than train.

The city's main bus terminal is Florenc, on the northeastern edge of the New Town. There is also a smaller station at Anděl called Na Knížecí. The Florenc terminal stays open from 4am until midnight and offers food outlets, information kiosks, inexpensive left-luggage facilities and tickets sales from such companies as **Eurolines** and **Student Agency** to name just two.

During the summer months, there are hundreds of coach trips to all the major coastal resorts in southern Europe. These get booked up quickly by Czechs, so buy your ticket well in advance and be sure to reserve a seat.

## Travelling by Car

To drive a car in the Czech Republic you must be at least 18 years of age. Most foreign driving licences, including Canadian, US and EU ones, are recognized. New Zealand and Australian drivers, however, should get an International Driving Licence before leaving home.

If you bring your own car to Prague, by law you must carry the following with you at all times: a

A uniformed railway employee

A Eurolines long-haul coach

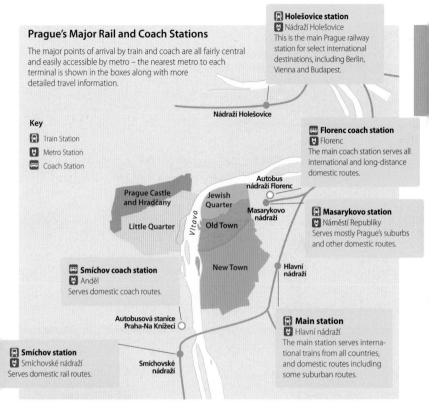

## Prague's Major Rail and Coach Stations

The major points of arrival by train and coach are all fairly central and easily accessible by metro – the nearest metro to each terminal is shown in the boxes along with more detailed travel information.

**Key**

🚉 Train Station

Ⓜ Metro Station

🚌 Coach Station

**Holešovice station**
Ⓜ Nádraží Holešovice
This is the main Prague railway station for select international destinations, including Berlin, Vienna and Budapest.

Nádraží Holešovice

**Florenc coach station**
Ⓜ Florenc
The main coach station serves all international and long-distance domestic routes.

**Masarykovo station**
Ⓜ Náměstí Republiky
Serves mostly Prague's suburbs and other domestic routes.

**Main station**
Ⓜ Hlavní nádraží
The main station serves international trains from all countries, and domestic routes including some suburban routes.

Prague Castle and Hradčany

Jewish Quarter

Little Quarter

Old Town

Vltava

Autobus nádraží Florenc

Masarykovo nádraží

New Town

Hlavní nádraží

**Smíchov coach station**
Ⓜ Anděl
Serves domestic coach routes.

Autobusová stanice Praha-Na Knížecí

**Smíchov station**
Ⓜ Smíchovské nádraží
Serves domestic rail routes.

Smíchovské nádraží

---

A Czech motorway sign

valid driver's licence; vehicle registration card; a hire certificate or, if you are borrowing the car, a letter signed by the owner and authorized by a recognized body, such as the AA or RAC, giving you permission to drive it; and a Green Card (an international motoring certificate for insurance).

If you drive on the motorway, you will also need to display a special highway sticker available at the border, petrol stations and post offices. Other items you have to carry at all times are a set of replacement bulbs, red warning triangles, a first-aid kit and a safety vest. You also have to display a national identification sticker. Headlights must be used at all times, even during daylight hours. It is compulsory to wear seat belts if fitted, and children under 12 years of age are not allowed in the front seat. When you are driving, it is strictly forbidden to have any alcohol in your blood or to use a mobile phone.

There are good motorway connections to all the major cities in the Czech Republic, including Plzeň and Brno, and many more are under construction.

The speed limit on motorways is 130 km/h (81 mph); on dual and single carriageways, 90 km/h (56 mph); and in urban areas, 50 km/h (31 mph). The traffic police patrolling the roads are very vigilant, and any infringements are dealt with harshly. There are also occasional road blocks to catch drunken drivers. Visit www. motorway.cz for more details on driving on Czech motorways.

## DIRECTORY

### Train Travel

**ČD Travel Agency**
Praha Hlavní nádraži, Wilsonova 8.
**Map** 4 E5. **Tel** 840 112 113.
🌐 **cd.cz**

### Coach Travel

**Eurolines**
Florenc Coach Station. **Map** 4 F3.
🌐 **elines.cz**

**Student Agency**
Florenc Coach Station. **Map** 4 F3.
**Tel** 841 101 101.
🌐 **studentagency.cz**

### Car Travel

**Budget**
Prague Airport, main station.
**Map** 4 E5. **Tel** 23 53 25 713.
🌐 **budget.cz**

**Car Breakdown/Service/ Accidents**
**Tel** 1230/1240.

# GETTING AROUND PRAGUE

The centre of Prague is conveniently small, and most of the sights can be reached comfortably on foot. However, to cross the city quickly, or to visit a more remote sight, the public transport is efficient, clean and cheap. It is based on trams, buses and the underground (metro) system, all of which are run by the Prague Public Transport Company (Dopravní podnik hlavního města Prahy). Throughout this guide, the best method of transport is given for each sight. The metro and trams serve the city centre, while buses are used to reach the suburbs. The entire system is simple to use – only one ticket is needed for all three forms of transport. Bus, tram and metro routes are found on city maps, available at most city centre tabáks, bookshops and newsagents; or refer to the map on the inside back cover of this guide.

## Green Travel

Prague has a fantastic public transport system. Buses serve the outer suburbs, thereby decreasing congestion on central streets, where trams, cars, bikes, pedestrians and even horses jostle for space. Comprehensive and 24-hour public transport means that driving a car is unnecessary.

Prague is also wonderfully compact, so walking between sights is not just possible but preferable. Cycling is another good way of getting around. Renting a bike is easy (see p241).

The World Carfree Network (www.worldcarfree.net) has its headquarters in Prague. The group is responsible for organizing World Carfree Day (22 September), which usually involves a mass bike ride in many cities worldwide. The last Thursday of each month sees the Auto*Mat Critical Mass bike ride, which sets off from Jiřího z Podebrad square at 6pm.

Cycling around the city

## The Transport System

The best way of getting around the city centre by public transport is by tram or metro. Prague's rush hours are between 6am and 8am and 3pm and 5pm, Monday to Friday. However, more trains, trams and buses run at these times, so crowding is not usually a problem. Some bus routes to the suburbs only run during peak hours.

## Tickets

Prague's transport network relies on the honour system. Be aware that periodic checks are carried out by plain-clothes ticket inspectors who levy a large on-the-spot fine if you don't have a valid ticket. Transfer tickets cover the entire system and allow 30 or 90 minutes of travel after validation. Buy the ticket before you travel and validate it in the machines provided, or you will be travelling illegally.

Tickets are available for Kč24 (for 30 minutes of travel including transfers) or Kč32 (for 90 minutes), and can be used on all forms of public transport, including the funicular railway that runs from Újezd up Petřín Hill; the boat service (lines P1–6); and the railway network (lines R and S). For shorter journeys around the city centre, the 30-minute transfer ticket will usually suffice.

Longer-term tickets are often more convenient and a good idea if you are planning on seeing many tourist sights

24-hour ticket

30-minute ticket

around the city. They offer unlimited rides for a number of days – a one-day ticket costs Kč110 and a three-day ticket is Kč330.

Children aged between 6 and 15 pay reduced prices – they pay half the fare on Kč24, Kč32 and Kč110 tickets.

Tickets may be purchased from the automatic machines at the entrance of all metro stations, at some tram or bus stops, and at tabáks (tobacconists), newsagents and some shops. For more information on transport routes, maps and tickets, visit the Prague Transport Information website or one of the information offices listed below.

## DIRECTORY

**Prague Public Transport Information Centres**
Muzeum metro station.
**Open** 7am–9pm daily.

Ruzyně Airport, Terminals 1 & 2.
**Open** 7am–9pm daily.

Holešovice train station, Anděl.
**Open** 7am–9pm Mon–Fri,
9:30am–5pm Sat.

**Prague Transport Information**
**Tel** 29 61 91 817. **W** dpp.cz

A busy tram on the streets of Prague

## Travelling by Tram

Trams are Prague's oldest method of public transport. Horse-drawn trams appeared on the streets in 1879, but by 1891 the first electric tram was in operation. The metro may be faster in terms of travelling distances, but when you factor in descending to and ascending from stations, the tram system is actually the most efficient, not to mention pleasant, way of getting around the city. Some lines operate only in the rush hour, and there are several night trams, all of which pass by Lazarská in the New Town.

The tram system is run by the **Prague Public Transport Company**. Tram tickets are also valid for the metro and buses (see Tickets opposite). You have to buy your ticket before you board a tram. Once you have entered, you will see a small, yellow punching machine on

two or three metal poles just inside the doors. Insert your ticket, and it will be validated automatically. If you do not punch your ticket, it is not valid, and if you are caught by a ticket inspector, you will have to pay an on-the-spot fine. Make sure you buy the correct ticket for your desired journey. Each tram stop has a timetable – the stop underlined is where you are standing. The stops below that line indicate where that tram is heading.

Trams run every 4 to 20 minutes. Doors either open and close automatically or by pushing a button. The current stop and the next stop are announced in Czech. The metro closes shortly after midnight. A small number of night trams run every 30 minutes. These trams (numbers 51–59) are marked by white numbers on a dark background at the stop.

## Tram Signs

*These are found at every tram stop and tell you which trams stop there, and in what direction each tram is going.*

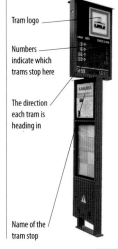

Tram logo

Numbers indicate which trams stop here

The direction each tram is heading in

Name of the tram stop

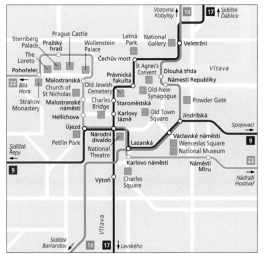

## Useful Tram Routes

This map shows the best tram routes for sight-seeing in Prague. The locations of major sights are marked, as well as the nearest useful tram stop. Sights should then only be a short walk away.

**Key**

- Major sight
- Tram route
- Tram stop
  (selected stops only)

A typical public bus in Prague

## Travelling by Bus

Most visitors to Prague are likely to use a bus only to travel to and from the airport *(see p235)* and the zoo. By law, buses are not allowed in the city centre because they produce noxious fumes and the streets are too narrow. Instead, they are used to transport people from the suburbs to tram and metro stops outside the centre.

Unless you have enough small change, you must purchase a ticket before you board a bus. Tickets are available from the vending machines at the entrance of metro stations, *tabáks* (tobacconists) and all the usual agents *(see p238)*.

You must validate your ticket in the punching machine on the bus. When buying a ticket, choose either a Kč24 transfer ticket allowing 30 minutes of travel, or a Kč32 ticket, which is valid for 90 minutes. You have to push a button to open the doors on most buses, though some open automatically. There is a high-pitched warning signal when doors are about to close. You are expected to give up your seat for the elderly, the disabled and people with small children.

Bus timetables are located at every stop. They have the numbers of all the buses that stop there and the timetable for each route. The frequency of buses varies considerably. In the rush hour there may be 12 to 15 buses an hour; at other times, as few as three.

There are more than 25 buses that run during the night, serving the outer areas not covered by the tram and metro system. These buses are numbered in the 500s and 600s.

## Travelling by Taxi

Taxis in Prague are a useful but frustrating form of transport. All taxis are privately owned, and there are many unscrupulous drivers who are out to charge as much as they can get away with. Never take a taxi from outside a hotel or tourist sight, as these are most likely to be operated by drivers who fall into this category; the only taxis safe to hail on the street are Fair Place taxis (www.prague-taxi. co.uk/taxi-fair-place.htm). Drivers in the Fair Place scheme guarantee a fair price, a safe ride, a professional approach and high standards. There are around 50 Fair Place taxi ranks across Prague.

Official taxis have a roof lamp and the company name, registration number and basic price list must be displayed on both front doors. Prices currently are Kč40 boarding fee, Kč28/km travel and Kč6/minute waiting. After the journey, the driver is obliged to print an official receipt. To get an idea of taxi prices in Prague, look at one of the Fair Place price leaflets, available for free in hotels and train stations.

If you think you have been scammed by a taxi driver, take their name and number so you can report them to the police *(see pp228–9)*. The best way not to be taken advantage of is to use a Fair Place taxi or have your hotel or restaurant call another reputable firm.

Unless your Czech pronunciation is good, always have your destination written down in Czech.

| | |
|---|---|
| Pedestrian zone | Pedestrian crossing |

Street or square name and Prague district

Street number — City registration number

## Prague on Foot

Walking around Prague is the most enjoyable way to see the city. Some pedestrian crossings are controlled by traffic lights, but be sure to cross only when the green man is showing, and even then, check the road carefully before you do so. It is now illegal for drivers to ignore pedestrian crossings, but for years they were allowed to do so, and old habits die hard. Be especially careful at crossings that do not have traffic lights.

Bear in mind that trams do have priority at pedestrian crossings, which can be confusing. They also travel at high speeds, occasionally coming upon you with little warning. Considering the uneven cobbled streets, the steep hills and the mass of tram lines, flat, comfortable shoes for walking are strongly recommended.

Yellow AAA taxis at a Fair Place taxi rank

## Cycling in Prague

One of the greenest and best ways of getting around Prague is by bike. First-timers will benefit from taking a tour first to get the lay of the land since bike lanes are rare. Renting a bike is easy, and most rental places, such as **Praha Bike**, also arrange good tours. Bike paths line both sides of the Vltava, and there is a series of biking/hiking trails linking Prague to Vienna (www. pragueviennagreenways.org).

A boat tour on the Vltava run by Prague Venice Boats

## Driving a Car

Most visitors are better off not driving around the centre of Prague. The city's complex web of one-way streets, the pedestrianized areas around the historic core of the city and a severe shortage of parking spaces make driving very difficult. Prague's public transport system is a much more efficient way of travelling around the city.

If you do decide to drive, be aware that on-the-spot fines for traffic violations are common. You must drive on the right, and the law states that both driver and front- and back-seat passengers should wear seat belts. The speed limit in the city is 50 km/h (31 mph) unless a sign indicates otherwise.

Parking spaces in the centre are scarce, and the penalties for illegal parking are harsh. Meter parking from 8am to 6pm costs Kč30–40 per hour. Orange zones allow parking for two hours and green zones for six; blue zones are reserved for residents. To use the meter, insert coins for the amount of time you need and display your receipt prominently on the dashboard.

Unfortunately, car theft is rife, and expensive Western cars are a favourite target. Try to park in an official – preferably underground – car park (see the Street Finder maps pp244–55).

Better yet, park at one of the guarded car parks (look for the "P+R" symbol) at the edge of the city and use public transport to get in.

If you are towed, call the police (Tel 156) to locate your car. The maximum fine is Kč1,300 (Kč850 if you stop them in the process), plus Kč150 parking fee, and Kč200 for each subsequent day. If you get clamped, a sticker lists the number to call to have the clamp removed.

One-way traffic and No stopping except for supply lorries

## Sightseeing Tours

Many firms offer trips around Prague's major sights, as well as outings to castles such as Karlstein and Konopiště (see pp168–9). Tours usually start from Náměstí Republiky (Republic Square) and from the upper part of Wenceslas Square. These trips can be expensive, but prices vary, so check what's on offer before you make a booking. The Jewish Museum (see p89) organizes trips around the Jewish Quarter. For those on a tight budget, the PIS (see p225) offers some of the cheapest tours in town. Tours can also be booked through Čedok (see p227).

A trip on tram 91, run by the Museum of Municipal Mass Transport, is one of the cheapest and best city-centre tours. It starts off at the Exhibition Ground (see pp178–9) and travels around the Old Town, the New Town and the Jewish Quarter. This service runs from Easter to the middle of November every weekend and public holiday. Tickets can be bought on board. Tram 22 will take you from the city up to the castle.

Sightseeing tours in horse-drawn carriages are run from the Old Town Square. Walking and bike tours give a level of detail to Prague unseen from speedier modes of transport, while boat tours (see also pp56–9) allow for fantastic views of major sights.

## DIRECTORY

### Sightseeing Tour Operators

**Martin Tour Praha**
Main Office: Štěpánská 61.
**Map** 5 C1. **Tel** 22 42 12 473.
**W** martintour.cz

**Prague Walking Tours**
Dlouhá 37. **Map** 4 D2.
**Tel** 77 53 69 121.
**W** praguer.com

**Praha Bike**
Dlouhá 24. **Map** 3 C3.
**Tel** 73 23 88 880.
**W** prahabike.cz

**Precious Legacy**
Kaprova 13. **Map** 3 B3.
**Tel** 22 23 21 954.
**W** legacytours.net

**Premiant City Tour**
Na Příkopě 23. **Map** 4 D4.
**Tel** 60 66 00 123.
**W** premiant.cz

**Private Prague Guide**
Blanická St. 922/25.
**Map** 6 F2. **Tel** 73 10 31 02.
**W** private-prague-guide.com

# Travelling by Metro

The underground railway, known as the metro, is the quickest (for longer journeys) and most comfortable form of transport in Prague. It is managed by the Prague Public Transport Company, and its construction began in 1967. It has three lines, A, B and C. The straightforward layout and clear signs make finding your way around the system very easy. Trains run between 5am and midnight.

The metro sign for
Můstek metro station

### Finding Your Way Around the Metro

Metro entrances are not always easy to spot. Look for a sign displaying the letter "M" within an upside-down triangle *(see right)*. The colour of the sign (green, yellow or red) indicates which line the station is on. The street entrance will normally lead you down a flight of steps.

Once you have purchased your ticket and passed through the unmanned ticket barriers – you must validate your ticket here – continue down the escalators to the trains. At the bottom of each escalator is a long central corridor with a platform on either side for trains travelling in either direction. Signs suspended from the ceiling indicate the direction of the trains *(see opposite page)*. The edges of the platforms are marked with a white, broken line that should not be crossed until the train stops. You may have to push a button to open the train doors, which play a recorded warning message when they are about to close. During the journey the name of the next station is announced in Czech.

Line A (green) is the most useful for tourists, because it covers all the main areas of the city centre – Prague Castle, the Little Quarter, the Old Town and the New Town – as well as the main shopping area around Wenceslas Square.

Displayed above some seats are disabled signs. These seats should be given up for the elderly, the disabled and those with small children.

The spacious interior of Můstek metro station

### Automatic Ticket Machines

You can buy transport tickets at designated ticket sellers *(see p238)* or at the yellow automatic ticket machines in the metro station. The ticket machines, and tickets themselves, may vary in design and colour, but they are still applicable to all forms of transport. The machines offer a choice of tickets at varying prices – for adults and children – as well as a choice of languages (either Czech or English).

**1** Check which price band is the right one to meet your requirements, then press the appropriately labelled button. Once validated, a transfer ticket is valid for 30 or 90 minutes (Kč24 or Kč32 respectively).

**2** If you want more than one ticket – whether of the same price band or another – press the relevant buttons; the total amount owed will be displayed on screen.

**3** If you are sure of your choice of ticket, insert coins into this slot. Most machines give change.

**4** Collect your ticket, plus any change that may be due to you, from the large slot at the base of the machine.

## Making a Journey by Metro

**1** To decide which line to take, find your destination and its nearest metro station on the Street Finder *(see pp246–57)*, then plot your route on a metro map. The Prague metro is fairly straightforward to use; Line A is green, line B is yellow and line C is red. Metro maps can be obtained free of charge at most metro stations. A metro map has also been included at the end of this book.

The central corridor with platforms either side and signs indicating the direction of trains

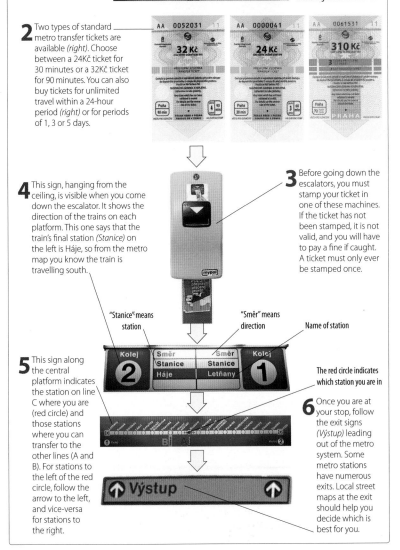

**2** Two types of standard metro transfer tickets are available *(right)*. Choose between a 24Kč ticket for 30 minutes or a 32Kč ticket for 90 minutes. You can also buy tickets for unlimited travel within a 24-hour period *(right)* or for periods of 1, 3 or 5 days.

**4** This sign, hanging from the ceiling, is visible when you come down the escalator. It shows the direction of the trains on each platform. This one says that the train's final station *(Stanice)* on the left is Háje, so from the metro map you know the train is travelling south.

**3** Before going down the escalators, you must stamp your ticket in one of these machines. If the ticket has not been stamped, it is not valid, and you will have to pay a fine if caught. A ticket must only ever be stamped once.

"Stanice" means station

"Směr" means direction

Name of station

**5** This sign along the central platform indicates the station on line C where you are (red circle) and those stations where you can transfer to the other lines (A and B). For stations to the left of the red circle, follow the arrow to the left, and vice-versa for stations to the right.

The red circle indicates which station you are in

**6** Once you are at your stop, follow the exit signs *(Výstup)* leading out of the metro system. Some metro stations have numerous exits. Local street maps at the exit should help you decide which is best for you.

Kolej **2** — Směr / Stanice / Háje — Směr / Stanice / Letňany — Kolej **1**

Výstup

# STREET FINDER

The map references given for all the sights, hotels, restaurants, bars, shops and entertainment venues described in this book refer to the maps in this section only. A complete index of street names and all the places of interest marked, can be found on the following pages. The key map (right) shows the area of Prague covered by the *Street Finder*. This map includes sightseeing areas, as well as districts for hotels, restaurants, pubs and entertainment venues. In keeping with Czech maps, none of the street names in the index or on the Street Finder have the Czech word for street, *ulice*, included (though you may see it on the city's street signs). For instance, Celetná ulice appears as Celetná in both the index and the Street Finder. The numbers preceding some street names are dates. In our index we ignore the numbers, so that 17. listopadu (17 November), is listed under "L".

### Key

- Major sight
- Place of interest
- Other building
- Ⓜ Metro station
- 🚆 Train station
- 🚌 Coach station
- 🚊 Tram stop
- 🚡 Funicular railway
- ⛴ River boat boarding point
- ℹ Tourist information office
- ✚ Hospital with casualty unit
- 🚓 Police station
- ✝ Church
- ✡ Synagogue
- ══ Railway line
- ── City wall
- ▪▪▪ Pedestrian street

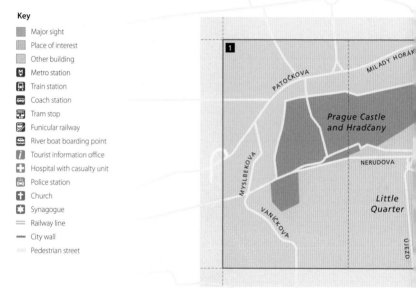

### Scale of Map Pages

| 0 metres | 200 |
|---|---|
| 0 yards | 200 |

1:8,400

Aerial view of the Baroque Church of St Nicholas in the Old Town Square

The imposing twin towers of the Church of
St Peter and St Paul on top of Vyšehrad rock

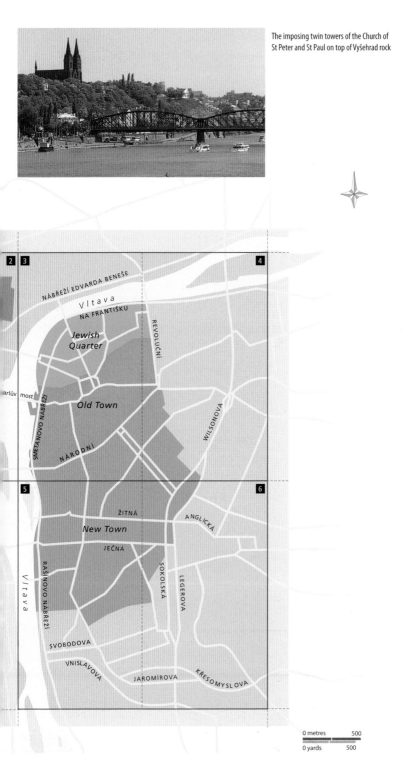

2 3 4

NÁBŘEŽÍ EDVARDA BENEŠE

V l t a v a

NA FRANTIŠKU

Jewish
Quarter

REVOLUČNÍ

arlův most

SMETANOVO NÁBŘEŽÍ

Old Town

WILSONOVA

NÁRODNÍ

5 6

ŽITNÁ

ANGLICKÁ

New Town

JEČNÁ

RAŠÍNOVO NÁBŘEŽÍ

SOKOLSKÁ

LEGEROVA

V l t a v a

SVOBODOVA

VNISLAVOVA

JAROMÍROVA

KŘESOMYSLOVA

0 metres    500
0 yards    500

# Street Finder Index

The order of the names in the index is affected by the *háček*, the accent like an inverted circumflex (*háček* means "little hook"). In the Czech alphabet, **č**, **ř**, **š** and **ž** are treated as separate letters. Street names beginning with **ř**, for example, are listed after those beginning with **r** without an accent.

Churches, buildings, museums and monuments are marked on the Street Finder maps with their English and Czech names. In the index, both forms are listed. However, English names for streets and squares, such as Wenceslas Square, do not appear on the maps. Where they are listed in the index, the Czech name is given in brackets in the form that appears on the map.

**Useful Words**

| | |
|---|---|
| **dům** | house |
| **hrad** | castle |
| **kostel** | church |
| **klášter** | convent, monastery |
| **most** | bridge |
| **nábřeží** | embankment |
| **nádraží** | station |
| **náměstí** | square |
| **sady** | park |
| **schody** | steps |
| **třída** | avenue |
| **ulice** | street |
| **ulička** | lane |
| **zahrada** | garden |

## A

| | |
|---|---|
| Albertov | 5 C4 |
| Alšovo nábřeží | 3 A3 |
| Americká | 6 F3 |
| Anenská | 3 A4 |
| Anenské náměstí | 3 A4 |
| Anežská | 3 C2 |
| Anglická | 6 E2 |
| Anny Letenské | 6 F1 |
| Apolinářská | 5 C4 |
| Archbishop's Palace | 2 D3 |
| Arcibiskupský palác | 2 D3 |
| At St Thomas's | 2 E3 |
| At the Three Ostriches | 2 F3 |
| autobusové nádraži Praha, Florenc | 4 F3 |
| autobusová zast. Hradčanská | 2 D1 |

## B

| | |
|---|---|
| Badeniho | 2 F1 |
| Balbínova | 6 E2 |
| Bartolomějská | 3 B5 |
| Barvířská | 4 E2 |
| Bazilika sv. Jiří | 2 E2 |
| Bělehradská | 6 E2 |
| Belgická | 6 F3 |
| Bělohorská | 1 A4 |
| Belvedér | 2 E1 |
| Belvedere | 2 E1 |
| Benátská | 5 B3 |
| Benediktská | 4 D3 |
| Besední | 2 E5 |
| Bethlehem Chapel | 3 B4 |
| Betlémská | 3 A5 |
| Betlémská kaple | 3 B4 |
| Betlémské náměstí | 3 B4 |
| Bílkova | 3 B2 |
| Biskupská | 4 E2 |
| Biskupský dvůr | 4 E2 |
| Blanická | 6 F2 |
| Bolzanova | 4 E4 |

| | |
|---|---|
| Boršov | 3 A4 |
| Botanical Gardens | 5 B3 |
| Botanická zahrada | 5 B3 |
| Botič | 6 D5 |
| Botičská | 5 B4 |
| Boženy Němcové | 6 D4 |
| Bridge Street (Mostecká) | 2 E3 |
| Bruselská | 6 E3 |
| Brusnice | 1 C2 |
| Břehová | 3 A2 |
| Břetislavova | 2 D3 |

## C

| | |
|---|---|
| Capuchin Monastery | 1 B2 |
| Carolinum | 3 C4 |
| Celetná | 3 C3 |
| Chaloupeckého | 1 B5 |
| Chalice Restaurant | 6 D3 |
| Charles Bridge (Karlův most) | 2 F4 |
| *continues* | 3 A4 |
| Charles Square (Karlovo náměstí) | 5 B2 |
| Charles Street (Karlova) | 2 A4 |
| *continues* | 3 B4 |
| Charvátova | 3 B5 |
| Chodecká | 1 A5 |
| Chotkova | 2 E1 |
| Chotkovy sady | 2 F1 |
| Chrám sv. Víta | 2 D2 |
| Church of Our Lady before Týn | 3 C3 |
| Church of Our Lady beneath the Chain | 2 E4 |
| Church of Our Lady of the Snows | 3 C5 |
| Church of Our Lady Victorious | 2 D4 |
| Church of St Castullus | 3 C2 |

| | |
|---|---|
| Church of St Catherine | 5 C3 |
| Church of St Cyril and St Methodius | 5 B2 |
| Church of St Gall | 3 C4 |
| Church of St Giles | 3 B4 |
| Church of St Ignatius | 5 C2 |
| Church of St James | 3 C3 |
| Church of St John on the Rock | 5 B3 |
| Church of St Lawrence | 1 C5 |
| Church of St Martin in the Wall | 3 B5 |
| Church of St Nicholas (Little Quarter) | 2 D3 |
| Church of St Nicholas (Old Town) | 3 B3 |
| Church of St Simon and St Jude | 3 B2 |
| Church of St Stephen | 5 C2 |
| Church of St Thomas | 2 E3 |
| Church of St Ursula | 3 A5 |
| Church of the Holy Ghost | 3 B3 |
| Cihelná | 2 F3 |
| Clam-Gallas Palace | 3 B4 |
| Clam-Gallasův palác | 3 B4 |
| Clementinum | 3 A4 |
| Cubist Houses | 3 B2 |
| Cukrovarnická | 1 A1 |

## Č

| | |
|---|---|
| Čechův most | 3 B2 |
| Čelakovského sady | 6 E1 |
| *continues* | 6 D1 |
| Černá | 5 B1 |
| Černín Palace | 1 B3 |
| Černínská | 1 B2 |
| Černínský palác | 1 B3 |
| Čertovka | 2 F4 |
| Červená | 3 B3 |

## D

| | |
|---|---|
| Dalibor Tower | 2 E2 |
| Daliborka | 2 E2 |
| Dělostřelecká | 1 A1 |
| Diskařská | 1 A5 |
| Dittrichova | 5 A2 |
| Divadelní | 3 A5 |
| Dlabačov | 1 A4 |
| Dlážděná | 4 E4 |
| Dlouhá | 3 C3 |
| Dražického | 2 F3 |
| Dražického náměstí | 2 E3 |
| Dřevná | 5 A3 |
| Dům pánů z Kunštátu | 3 B4 |
| Dům U Dvou zlatých medvědů | 3 B4 |
| Dušní | 3 B2 |
| Dvořák Museum | 6 D2 |
| Dvořákovo nábřeží | 3 A2 |

## E

| | |
|---|---|
| Elišky Krásnohorské | 3 B2 |
| Estates Theatre | 3 C4 |

## F

| | |
|---|---|
| Faust House | 5 B3 |
| Faustův dům | 5 B3 |
| Florenc (metro) | 4 F3 |
| Franciscan Garden | 3 C5 |
| Francouzská | 6 F2 |
| Františkánská zahrada | 3 C5 |
| Fričova | 6 E5 |
| Fügnerovo náměstí | 6 D3 |
| Funicular Railway | 2 D5 |

## G

| | |
|---|---|
| Gogolova | 2 F1 |
| Golden Lane (Zlatá ulička) | 2 E2 |
| Golz-Kinský Palace | 3 C3 |
| Gorazdova | 5 A3 |

Grand Priory Square
(Velkopřevorské
náměstí) 2 E4

## H

Hálkova 6 D2
Harantova 2 E4
Haštalská 3 C2
Haštalské náměstí 3 C2
Havelská 3 B4
Havelská ulička 3 C4
Havířská 3 C4
Havlíčkova 4 E3
Helénská 4 F5
Hellichova 2 E4
Helmova 4 E2
High Synagogue 3 B3
Hládkov 1 A3
Hladová zed' 1 B4
Hlávkův most 4 F1
Hlavní nádraží 4 E5
Hlavní nádraží
(metro) 4 E4
Hlavova 5 C4
Hlavsova 3 B4
Horská 5 C5
Hotel Europa 4 D5
Hotel Evropa 4 D5
House at the Two
Golden Bears 3 B4
Hradčanská
(metro) 2 E1
Hradčanské
náměstí 1 C3
Hradební 4 D2
Hroznová 2 F4
Hunger Wall 1 B4
Husitská 4 F4
Husova 3 B4
Hvězdárna 2 D5
Hybernská 4 D3

## I

Ibsenova 6 F2
Italian Street (Vlašská) 2 D3
Italská 4 F5
continues 6 E2

## J

Jáchymova 3 B3
Jakubská 3 C3
Jalovcová 3 B4
Jan Hus Monument 3 B3
Jana Masaryka 6 F4
Jánská 2 D3
Jánský vršek 2 D3
Jaromírova 6 D5
Ječná 5 C2
Jelení 1 B2
Jenštejnská 5 A2
Jeruzalémská 4 E4
Jesuit College 5 B2

Jewish Town Hall 3 B3
Jezuitská kolej 5 B2
Jilská 3 B4
Jindřišská 4 D5
Jiráskovo náměstí 5 A2
Jiráskův most 5 A2
Jiřská 2 E2
Jižní zahrady 2 D3
Josefská 2 E3
Jugoslávská 6 E2
Jungmannova 3 C5
continues 5 C1
Jungmannovo
náměstí 3 C5

## K

K Brusce 2 E1
K Haštalu 4 D2
K Rotundě 5 B5
Kampa 2 F4
Kamzíková 3 C4
Kanovnická 1 C2
Kaprova 3 B3
Kapucínská 1 C3
Kapucínský klášter 1 B2
Karlova 3 A4
Karlovo náměstí 5 B2
Karlovo náměstí
(metro) 5 A3
Karlův most 2 F4
continues 3 A4
Karmelitská 2 E4
Karolinum 3 C4
Karoliny Světlé 3 A4
Katedrála Sv. Víta 2 D2
Kateřinská 5 C3
Ke Hradu 2 D3
Ke Karlovu 6 D2
Ke Štvanici 4 F2
Keplerova 1 B2
continues 1 B3
Klárov 2 F2
Klášter sv. Anežky 3 C2
Klášter sv. Jiří 2 E2
Klášterská 3 C2
Klausen Synagogue 3 B2
Klausová synagóga 3 B2
Klementinum 3 A4
Klimentská 4 D2
Knights of the Cross
Square (Křižovnické
náměstí) 3 A4
Konviktská 3 A5
Koperníkova 6 F4
Korunní 6 F2
Kosárkovo nábřeží 3 A2
Kostečná 3 B3
Kostel Panny Marie
pod řetězem 2 E4
Kostel Panny Marie
před Týnem 3 C3
Kostel Panny Marie
Sněžné 3 C5

Kostel Panny Marie
Vítězné 2 E4
Kostel sv. Cyrila
a Metoděje 5 B2
Kostel sv. Ducha 3 B3
Kostel sv. Havla 3 C4
Kostel sv. Haštala 3 C2
Kostel sv. Ignáce 5 C2
Kostel sv. Jakuba 3 C3
Kostel sv. Jana
na Skalce 5 B3
Kostel sv. Jiljí 3 B4
Kostel sv. Kateřiny 5 C3
Kostel sv. Martina
ve zdi 3 B5
Kostel sv. Mikuláše 2 D3
Kostel sv. Mikuláše 3 B3
Kostel sv. Tomáše 2 E3
Kostel sv. Vavřince 1 C5
Kostel sv. Voršily 3 A5
Kostel sv. Šimona
a Judy 3 B2
Kostel sv. Štěpána 5 C2
Koubkova 6 E3
Kozí 3 C2
Kožná 3 C4
Krakovská 6 D1
Králodvorská 4 D3
Královská zahrada 2 D2
Královský palác 2 D2
Krocínova 3 A5
Křemencova 5 B1
Křesomyslova 6 E5
Křižíkova 4 F3
Křižovnická 3 A4
Křižovnické náměstí 3 A4
Kubistické domy 3 B2
Kuňětická 4 F5

## L

Ladova 5 A4
Lanová dráha 2 D5
Lazarská 5 B1
Lázeňská 2 E4
Ledebour Garden 2 E2
Ledeburská zahrada 2 E2
Legerova 6 D2
Letenská 2 F3
Letenské sady 3 A1
Letenský tunel 3 C1
Libušina 5 A5
Lichnická 4 F5
Liliová 3 B4
Linhartská 3 B4
Lípová 5 C2
listopadu, 17. 3 B2
Little Quarter Square
(Malostranské
náměstí) 2 E3
Lobkovická zahrada 1 C4
Lobkovický palác 2 E2
Lobkowicz Palace 2 E2
Lodecká 4 E2

Lodní mlýny 4 E2
Londýnská 6 E2
Loreta 1 C3
Loretánská 1 B3
Loretánské náměstí 1 B3
Loreto, the 1 C3
Lublaňská 6 E2

## M

Magdalény
Rettigové 5 B1
Macharovo náměstí 1 A1
Máchova 6 F3
Maisel Synagogue 3 B3
Maiselova 3 B3
Maiselova synagóga 3 B3
Malá Klášterská 3 C2
Malá Štěpánská 5 C2
Malá Štupartská 3 C3
Malé náměstí 3 B4
Malostranská
(metro) 2 F2
Malostranské
nábřeží 2 F5
Malostranské
náměstí 2 E3
Maltese Square
(Maltézské
náměstí) 2 E4
Maltézské
náměstí 2 E4
Mánesova 6 E1
Mánesův most 3 A3
Mariánské
hradby 2 D2
Mariánské
náměstí 3 B3
Martinic Palace 1 C2
Martinický
palác 1 C2
Martinská 3 B5
Masarykovo
nábřeží 5 A2
Masarykovo
nádraží 4 E3
Masná 3 C3
Melantrichova 3 B4
Melounová 6 D2
Mezibranská 6 D1
Mickiewiczova 2 F1
Michalská 3 B4
Michna Palace 2 E4
Michnův palác 2 E4
Mikovcova 6 D2
Mikulandská 3 B5
Milady Horákové 1 C1
Mirror Maze 1 C4
Mišeňská 2 F3
Mlynářská 4 E2
Morstadtova 1 A3
most Legií 2 F5
continues 3 A5

| | |
|---|---|
| most M. R. Štefánika | 4 D1 |
| Mostecká | 2 E3 |
| Municipal House | 4 D3 |
| Museum of Decorative Arts | 3 A3 |
| Můstek (metro) | 3 C4 |
| *continues* | 4 D5 |
| Muzeum (metro) | 6 D1 |
| Muzeum Antonína Dvořáka | 6 D2 |
| Muzeum Bedřicha Smetany | 3 A4 |
| Myslbekova | 1 A3 |
| Myslíkova | 5 A1 |

## N

| | |
|---|---|
| Na baště sv. Jiří | 2 E1 |
| Na baště sv. Ludmily | 2 F1 |
| Na baště sv. Tomáše | 2 F1 |
| Na bojišti | 6 D3 |
| Na Děkance | 5 B4 |
| Na Fidlovačce | 6 F5 |
| Na Florenci | 4 E3 |
| Na Folimance | 6 E5 |
| Na Františku | 3 B2 |
| Na Hrádku | 5 B3 |
| Na Hrobci | 5 A4 |
| Na Hubálce | 1 A2 |
| Na Kampě | 2 F4 |
| Na Kleovce | 6 F4 |
| Na Libušince | 5 A5 |
| Na Moráni | 5 A3 |
| Na Můstku | 3 C4 |
| Na náspu | 1 B2 |
| Na Opyši | 2 E2 |
| Na Ořechovce | 1 A1 |
| Na ostrůvku | 6 F5 |
| Na Panenské | 1 A3 |
| Na Perštýně | 3 B5 |
| Na poříčí | 4 D3 |
| Na poříčním právu | 5 A3 |
| Na Příkopě | 3 C4 |
| Na rejdišti | 3 A2 |
| Na Rybníčku | 5 C2 |
| Na Salvátorská | 3 B3 |
| Na Slovanech | 5 B3 |
| Na slupi | 5 B4 |
| Na Smetance | 6 F1 |
| Na struze | 5 A1 |
| Na valech | 2 D1 |
| Na výtoni | 5 B4 |
| Na zábradlí | 3 A4 |
| Na zbořenci | 5 B2 |
| Na Zderaze | 5 B2 |
| Nábřeží Edvarda Beneše | 3 A2 |
| Nábřeží kpt. Jaroše | 4 D1 |

| | |
|---|---|
| Nábřeží Ludvíka Svobody | 4 D2 |
| Nad Octárnou | 1 A2 |
| Nad Panenskou | 1 A4 |
| Nad Petruskou | 6 F4 |
| Nad Vojenským hřbitovem | 1 A3 |
| Náměstí Bratří Synků | 6 F5 |
| Náměstí Curieových | 3 B2 |
| Náměstí F. Kafky | 3 B3 |
| Náměstí I. P. Pavlova | 6 D2 |
| Náměstí Jana Palacha | 3 A3 |
| Náměstí Míru | 6 F2 |
| Náměstí Míru (metro) | 6 F2 |
| Náměstí Pod Emauzy | 5 B3 |
| Náměstí Republiky | 4 D3 |
| Náměstí Republiky (metro) | 4 E3 |
| Náplavní | 5 A2 |
| Náprstek museum | 3 B4 |
| Náprstkova | 3 A4 |
| Náprstkovo Muzeum | 3 A4 |
| Národní | 3 A5 |
| Národní divadlo | 3 A5 |
| *continues* | 5 A1 |
| Národní muzeum | 6 E1 |
| Národní třída (metro) | 3 B5 |
| National Museum | 6 E1 |
| National Theatre | 3 A5 |
| *continues* | 5 A1 |
| Navrátilova | 5 C1 |
| Nebovidská | 2 E4 |
| Nekázanka | 4 D4 |
| Neklanova | 5 B5 |
| Nerudova | 2 D3 |
| New Town Hall | 5 B1 |
| New World (Nový Svět) | 1 B2 |
| Nezamyslova | 6 D5 |
| Nosticova | 2 E4 |
| Nové mlýny | 4 D2 |
| Novoměstská radnice | 5 B1 |
| Novomlýnská | 4 D2 |
| Novotného lávka | 3 A4 |
| Nový Svět | 1 B2 |
| Nuselská | 6 F5 |
| Nuselský most | 6 D5 |

## O

| | |
|---|---|
| Odborů | 5 B1 |
| Obecní dům | 4 D3 |
| Obrazárna Pražského hradu | 2 D2 |
| Observation Tower | 1 C4 |
| Old Jewish Cemetery | 3 A2 |
| Old Town Hall | 3 C3 |

| | |
|---|---|
| Old Town Square (Staroměstské náměstí) | 3 B3 |
| Old-New Synagogue | 3 B2 |
| Oldřichova | 6 D5 |
| Olivova | 4 D5 |
| Olympijská | 1 B5 |
| Omladinářů | 5 B1 |
| Opatovická | 5 B1 |
| Opletalova | 4 D5 |
| Ostrčilovo náměstí | 5 C5 |
| Ostrov Štvanice | 4 F1 |
| Ostrovní | 3 B5 |
| *continues* | 5 A1 |
| Otakarova | 6 F5 |
| Otevřená | 1 A2 |
| Ovocný trh | 3 C3 |

## P

| | |
|---|---|
| Palác Golz-Kinských | 3 C3 |
| Palace of the Lords of Kunštát | 3 A4 |
| Palackého | 3 C5 |
| Palackého most | 5 A3 |
| Palackého náměstí | 5 A3 |
| Panská | 4 D4 |
| Parléřova | 1 A3 |
| Pařížská | 3 B2 |
| Patočkova | 1 A3 |
| Pavlova, I. P. (metro) | 6 D2 |
| Pelclova | 2 E4 |
| Perlová | 3 B4 |
| Perucká | 6 F4 |
| Petrská | 4 E2 |
| Petrské náměstí | 4 E2 |
| Petřín Park | 2 D5 |
| Petřínské sady | 2 D5 |
| Pevnostní | 1 B1 |
| Picture Gallery of Prague Castle | 2 D2 |
| Pinkas Synagogue | 3 A3 |
| Pinkasova synagóga | 3 A3 |
| Plaská | 2 E5 |
| Platnéřská | 3 B3 |
| Plavecká | 5 A4 |
| Pobřežní | 4 F2 |
| Pod baštami | 2 E1 |
| Pod Bruskou | 2 F2 |
| Pod hradbami | 1 B1 |
| Pod Karlovem | 6 E4 |
| Pod Nuselskými schody | 6 E4 |
| Pod Slovany | 5 B4 |
| Pod Větrovem | 5 C3 |
| Pod Zvonařkou | 6 E4 |
| Podskalská | 5 A3 |
| Pohořelec | 1 B3 |
| Politických vězňů | 4 D5 |
| Polská | 6 F1 |
| Pomník Jana Husa | 3 B3 |
| Powder Gate | 4 D3 |

| | |
|---|---|
| Powder Tower | 2 D2 |
| Prašná brána | 4 D3 |
| Prašná věž | 2 D2 |
| Prokopská | 2 E4 |
| Provaznická | 3 C4 |
| Průchodní | 3 B5 |
| Přemyslova | 5 B5 |
| Příběnická | 4 F4 |
| Příčná | 5 C1 |
| Pštrossova | 5 A1 |
| Purkyňova | 3 B5 |
| Půtova | 4 E2 |

## R

| | |
|---|---|
| R Street NE | 4E1 |
| R Street NW | 1B1 |
| R Street NW | 3A1 |
| Randolph Place NW | 4D1 |
| Reservoir Road NW | 1A1 |
| Rhode Island Avenue NW | 3A2 |
| Ridge Place NW | 4D2 |
| Riggs Place NW | 2F1 |
| Riggs Place NW | 3A1 |
| Riggs Street NW | 2F1 |
| Rock Creek and | 2D3 |
| Rolfe Street | 1A3 |
| Radnické schody | 1 C3 |
| Rámová | 3 C2 |
| Rašínovo nábřeží | 5 A2 |
| Rejskova | 6 E5 |
| Resslova | 5 B2 |
| Restaurace U Kalicha | 6 D3 |
| Revoluční | 4 D2 |
| Riegrovy sady | 6 F1 |
| Rohanské nábřeží | 4 F1 |
| Royal Garden | 2 D2 |
| Royal Palace | 2 D2 |
| Rozhledna | 1 C4 |
| Rubešova | 6 E1 |
| Rudolfinum | 3 A3 |
| Rumunská | 6 E2 |
| Růžová | 4 D4 |
| Růžový sad | 1 C5 |
| Rybná | 3 C2 |
| Rytířská | 3 B4 |

## Ř

| | |
|---|---|
| Řásnovka | 3 C2 |
| Řetězová | 3 B4 |
| Řeznická | 5 C1 |
| Říční | 2 E5 |
| října, 28. | 3 C5 |
| Římská | 6 E1 |

## S

| | |
|---|---|
| St Agnes's Convent | 3 C2 |
| St George's Basilica | 2 E2 |
| St George's Convent | 2 E2 |
| St Vitus's Cathedral (Katedrála Sv. Víta) | 2 D2 |

| | | | | | | |
|---|---|---|---|---|---|---|
| Salmovská | 5 C2 | Strahovská zahrada | 1 B4 | U nemocnice | 5 B3 | Vojan Park | 2 F3 |
| Samcova | 4 E2 | Strahovský klášter | 1 B4 | U Obecního domu | 4 D3 | Vojanovy sady | 2 F3 |
| Sarajevská | 6 E5 | Strmá | 1 B1 | U obecního dvora | 3 C2 | Vojtěšská | 5 A1 |
| Saská | 2 E4 | Střelecký ostrov | 2 F5 | U Písecké brány | 2 E1 | Voršilská | 3 B5 |
| Sázavská | 6 F3 | Střešovická | 1 A2 | U plovárny | 3 A2 | Votočkova | 5 C4 |
| Schönbornská | | Stříbrná | 3 A4 | U Prašné brány | 4 D3 | Vozová | 4 F5 |
| zahrada | 2 D4 | Studničkova | 5 C4 | U Prašného mostu | 2 D1 | Vratislavova | 5 B5 |
| Schwarzenberg | | Svatoplukova | 6 D5 | U půjčovny | 4 D4 | Vrchlického sady | 4 E4 |
| Palace | 2 D3 | Svatovítská | 1 C1 | U radnice | 3 B3 | Vrtba Garden | 2 D4 |
| Schwarzenberský | | Svobodova | 5 A4 | U Sovových | | Vrtbovská zahrada | 2 D4 |
| palác | 2 D3 | | | mlýnů | 2 F5 | Všehrdova | 2 E5 |
| Seifertova | 4 F4 | **Š** | | U staré školy | 3 B2 | Východní | 1 A1 |
| Sekaninova | 6 D5 | | | U starého hřbitova | 3 B2 | Vysoká synagóga | 3 B3 |
| Seminářská | 3 B4 | Šafaříkova | 6 E3 | U Sv. Tomáše | 2 E3 | Vyšehradský | |
| Seminářská | | Šeříková | 2 E5 | U Tří pštrosů | 2 F3 | hřbitov | 5 B5 |
| zahrada | 2 D4 | Široká | 3 B3 | U Zlaté studně | 2 E2 | | |
| Senovážná | 4 D4 | Šítkova | 5 A1 | U Zvonařky | 6 E4 | **W** | |
| Senovážné náměstí | 4 E4 | Školská | 5 C1 | U železné lávky | 2 F2 | | |
| Sezimova | 6 F5 | Škrétova | 6 E1 | Uhelný trh | 3 B5 | Wallenstein Palace | 2 E3 |
| Sibeliova | 1 A2 | Špálova | 1 A1 | Újezd | 2 E4 | Washingtonova | 4 E5 |
| Skořepka | 3 B4 | Španělská | 4 F5 | Uměleckoprůmyslové | | continues | 6 D1 |
| Slavojova | 5 C5 | continues | 6 E1 | muzeum | 3 A2 | Wenceslas Square | |
| Slavonic House | 4 D4 | Španělská | | Uruguayská | 6 F3 | (Václavské | |
| Slavonic Monastery | 5 B3 | synagóga | 3 C2 | Úvoz | 1 B3 | náměstí) | 3 C5 |
| Slezská | 6 F2 | Šporkova | 2 D3 | | | continues | 6 D1 |
| Slovanský dům | 4 D4 | Štěpánská | 5 C1 | **V** | | Wenzigova | 6 D4 |
| Slovanský ostrov | 5 A1 | Šternberský palác | 1 C2 | | | Wilsonova | 4 E5 |
| Slunná | 1 A1 | Štupartská | 3 C3 | V celnici | 4 D3 | continues | 6 E1 |
| Smetana Museum | 3 A4 | Šubertova | 6 F2 | V cípu | 4 D4 | | |
| Smetanovo nábřeží | 3 A5 | | | V jámě | 5 C1 | **Z** | |
| Sněmovní | 2 E3 | **T** | | V jirchářích | 5 B1 | | |
| Sokolovská | 4 F2 | | | V kotcích | 3 B4 | Za Haštalem | 3 C2 |
| Sokolská | 6 D2 | Templová | 3 C3 | V pevnosti | 5 B5 | Za Hládkovem | 1 A3 |
| Soukenická | 4 D2 | Těšnov | 4 F2 | V tůních | 6 D2 | Za Pohořelcem | 1 A4 |
| South Gardens | 2 D3 | Těšnovský tunel | 4 E1 | Václavská | 5 B2 | Za Poříčskou bránou | 4 F2 |
| Spálená | 3 B5 | Thunovská | 2 E3 | Václavské náměstí | 3 C5 | Záhořanského | 5 A2 |
| continues | 5 B1 | Tomášská | 2 E3 | continues | 6 D1 | Záhřebská | 6 F3 |
| Spanish Synagogue | 3 C2 | Trojanova | 5 A2 | Valdštejnská | 2 E2 | Zámecká | 2 E3 |
| Spartakiadní | | Trojická | 5 B3 | Valdštejnská zahrada | 2 E3 | Zámecké schody | 2 D3 |
| Stadion | 1 B5 | Truhlářská | 4 D3 | Valdštejnské náměstí | 2 E3 | Závišova | 6 E5 |
| Spytihněvova | 6 E5 | Tržiště | 2 E3 | Valdštejnský palác | 2 E3 | Zborovská | 2 F5 |
| Staré zámecké | | Tychonova | 2 E1 | Valentinská | 3 B3 | Zbrojnická | 1 A1 |
| schody | 2 E2 | Tylovo náměstí | 6 E2 | Vaníčkova | 1 A4 | Zítkovy sady | 5 A3 |
| Stárkova | 4 E2 | Týnská | 3 C3 | Varšavská | 6 F3 | Zlatá | 3 B4 |
| Staroměstská | | Týnská ulička | 3 C3 | Ve Smečkách | 6 D1 | Zlatá ulička | 2 E2 |
| (metro) | 3 B3 | Tyršova | 6 D3 | Vejvodova | 3 B4 | Zlatnická | 4 E2 |
| Staroměstská | | | | Veleslavínova | 3 A3 | Zrcadlové bludiště | 1 C4 |
| radnice | 3 C3 | **U** | | Velkopřevorské | | | |
| Staroměstské | | | | náměstí | 2 E4 | **Ž** | |
| náměstí | 3 B3 | U Bruských kasáren | 2 F2 | Vězeňská | 3 C2 | | |
| Staronová | | U Brusnice | 1 B2 | Vikářská | 2 D2 | Žatecká | 3 B3 |
| synagóga | 3 B2 | U Bulhara | 4 F4 | Vinařického | 5 B4 | Železná | 3 C4 |
| Starý židovský | | U divadla | 4 E5 | Viničná | 5 C3 | Železniční most | 5 A5 |
| hřbitov | 3 A2 | U Dobřenských | 3 A4 | Vinohradská | 6 E1 | Židovská radnice | 3 B3 |
| State Opera | 4 E5 | U Fleků | 5 B1 | Vítězná | 2 E5 | Žitná | 5 C1 |
| continues | 6 E1 | U kasáren | 1 C3 | Vladislavova | 3 C5 | | |
| Státní opera | 4 E5 | U laboratoře | 1 A1 | continues | 5 C1 | | |
| continues | 6 E1 | U lanové dráhy | 2 E5 | Vlašská | 1 C4 | | |
| Stavovské divadlo | 3 C4 | U letohrádku | | Vltava | 3 A2 | | |
| Štefánik's Observatory | 2 D5 | královny Anny | 2 E1 | continues | 5 A3 | | |
| Sternberg Palace | 1 C2 | U lužického | | Vnislavova | 5 A5 | | |
| Strahov Monastery | 1 B4 | semináře | 2 F3 | Vocelova | 6 E2 | | |
| Strahovská | 1 B4 | U milosrdných | 3 B2 | Vodičkova | 3 C5 | | |
| | | U nemocenské | | continues | 5 C1 | | |
| | | pojišťovny | 4 D2 | | | | |

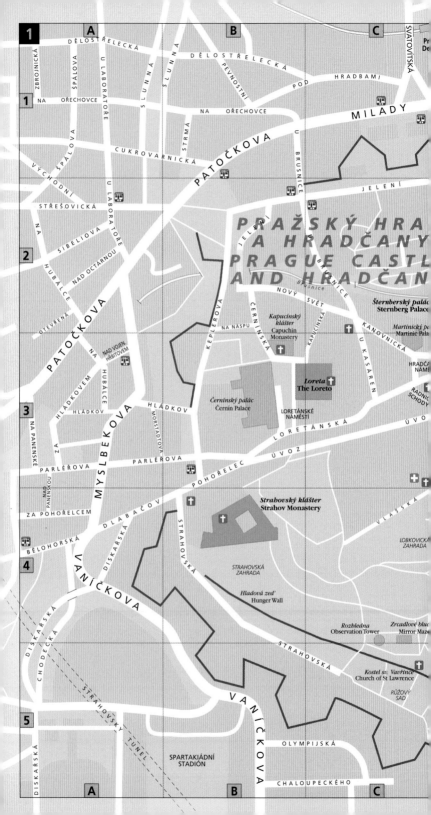

**1**

A     B     C

SVATOVÍTSKÁ

Pr
De

DĚLOSTŘELECKÁ

ZBROJNICKÁ

SPÁLOVA

U LABORATOŘE

SLUNNÁ

DĚLOSTŘELECKÁ

PEVNOSTNÍ

POD HRADBAMI

NA   OŘECHOVCE

MILADY

1

ORECHOVCE

NA

SLUNNÁ

STRMÁ

NA OŘECHOVCE

CUKROVARNICKÁ

VÝCHODNÍ

SPÁLOVA

U LABORATOŘE

PATOČKOVA

U BRUSNICE

JELENÍ

STŘEŠOVICKÁ

ŠIBELIOVA

NAD OCTÁRNOU

NA

HUBÁLCE

JELENÍ

**PRAŽSKÝ HRA
A HRADČANY
PRAGUE CASTL
AND HRADČAN**

2

OTEVŘENÁ

BRUSNICE

NOVÝ SVĚT

ČERNÍNSKÁ

**Šternberský palác
Sternberg Palace**

PATOČKOVA

NA NÁSPU

KEPLEROVA

NA VOJEN
HŘBITOVEM

NAD

HUBÁLCE

HLÁDKOVEM

*Kapucínský
klášter*
Capuchin
Monastery

✝

KAPUCÍNSKÁ

U KASÁREN

KANOVNICKÁ

*Martinický pa*
Martinic Pala

HRADČA
NÁMĚ

3

NA PANENSKÉ

ZA

HLÁDKOV

HLÁDKOV

MORSTADTOVA

*Černínský palác*
Černín Palace

*Loreta*
The Loreto

✝

LORETÁNSKÉ
NÁMĚSTÍ

RADNIC
SCHODY

MYSLBEKOVA

PARLÉŘOVA

NAD
PANENSKOU

PARLÉŘOVA

POHOŘELEC

LORETÁNSKÁ

ÚVOZ

ÚVOZ

ÚVO

✝ ✝

ZA POHOŘELCEM

DLÁBAČOV

✝

**Strahovský klášter
Strahov Monastery**

VLAŠSKÁ

4

BĚLOHORSKÁ

DISKAŘSKÁ

STRAHOVSKÁ

✝

*STRAHOVSKÁ
ZAHRADA*

*LOBKOVICK
ZAHRADA*

VANÍČKOVA

DISKAŘSKÁ

CHODECKÁ

*Hladová zeď*
Hunger Wall

STRAHOVSKÝ TUNEL

*Rozhledna*
Observation Tower

*Zrcadlové blu*
Mirror Maze

STRAHOVSKÁ

*Kostel sv. Vavřince*
Church of St Lawrence

*RŮŽOVÝ
SAD*

5

DISKAŘSKÁ

VANÍČKOVA

OLYMPIJSKÁ

*SPARTAKIÁDNÍ
STADIÓN*

CHALOUPECKÉHO

A     B     C

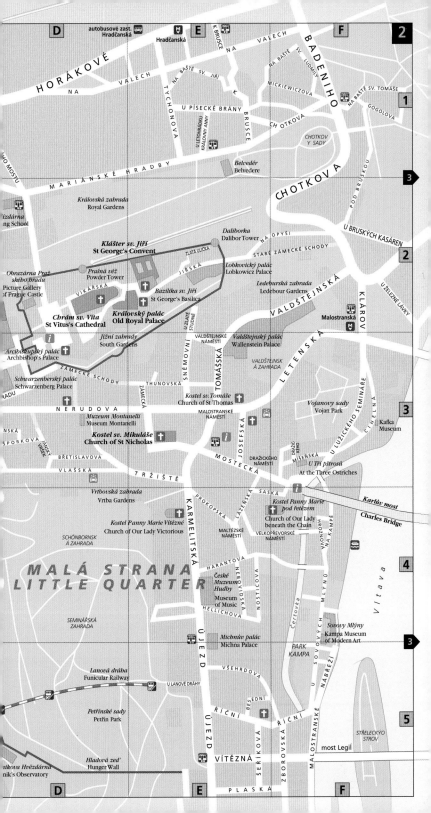

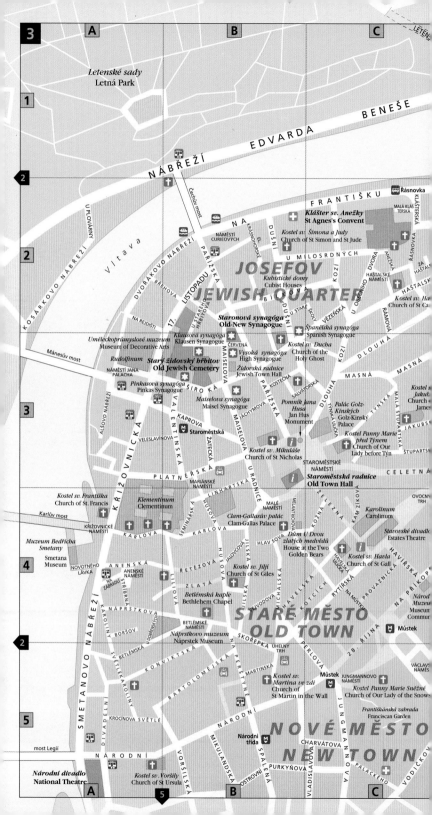

**3**

**A**     **B**     **C**     LETEN...

Letenské sady
Letná Park

**1**

BENEŠE

EDVARDA

NÁBŘEŽÍ

**2**

Čechův most

Řásnovka

Vltava

NÁMĚSTÍ
CURIEOVÝCH

FRANTIŠKU

MALÁ KLÁŠTERSKÁ

**2**

NA KŘIŽOVNICKÉ

DUŠNÍ

U MILOSRDNÝCH

*Klášter sv. Anežky*
**St Agnes's Convent**

U PLOVÁRNY

KOSÁRKOVO NÁBŘEŽÍ

DVOŘÁKOVO NÁBŘEŽÍ

BŘEHOVÁ

PAŘÍŽSKÁ

LISTOPADU

NA

*Kostel sv. Šimona a Judy*
Church of St Simon and St Jude

ANEŽSKÁ

DVOŘÁ

ZA HAŠT...

VĚZEŇSKÁ

KOZÍ

KONVY

17.

**JOSEFOV**

U STARÉHO HŘBITOVA

BÍLKOVA

*Kubistické domy*
Cubist Houses

HAŠTALSKÉ
NÁMĚSTÍ

HAŠTALSKÁ

NA REJDIŠTI

**JEWISH QUARTER**

*Kostel sv. Ha...*
Church of St Ca...

RÁMOVÁ

Mánesův most

*Uměleckoprůmyslové muzeum*
Museum of Decorative Arts

*Klausová synagóga*
Klausen Synagogue

ČERVENÁ

*Staronová synagóga*
**Old-New Synagogue**

*Španělská synagóga*
Spanish Synagogue

U STARÉ ŠKOLY

DLOUHÁ

*Rudolfinum*

*Vysoká synagóga*
High Synagogue

*Kostel sv. Ducha*
Church of the
Holy Ghost

KOZÍ

MASNÁ

MASNÁ

NÁMĚSTÍ JANA
PALACHA

*Starý židovský hřbitov*
**Old Jewish Cemetery**

MAISELOVA

*Židovská radnice*
Jewish Town Hall

KOSTEČNÁ

*Kostel s...
Jakub...*
Church
James...

ALŠOVO NÁBŘEŽÍ

*Pinkasova synagóga*
Pinkas Synagogue

ŠIROKÁ

PAŘÍŽSKÁ

DLOUHÁ

TÝNSKÁ

MALÁ ŠTUPARTSKÁ

JAKUBSKÁ

VALENTINSKÁ

*Maiselova synagóga*
Maisel Synagogue

JÁCHYMOVA

SALVÁTORSKÁ

*Palác Golz-
Kinských*
Golz-Kinský
Palace

TÝNSKÁ ULIČKA

ŠTUPARTS...

**3**

KAPROVA

VELESLAVÍNOVA

*Pomník Jana
Husa*
Jan Hus
Monument

*Kostel Panny Marie
před Týnem*
Church of Our
Lady before Týn

KŘIŽOVNICKÁ

MAISELOVA

ŽATECKÁ

Staroměstská

PLATNÉŘSKÁ

*Kostel sv. Mikuláše*
Church of St Nicholas

STAROMĚSTSKÉ
NÁMĚSTÍ

CELETNÁ

*Kostel sv. Františka*
Church of St. Francis

MARIÁNSKÉ
NÁMĚSTÍ

U RADNICE

LINHARTSKÁ

*Staroměstská radnice*
**Old Town Hall**

MALÉ
NÁMĚSTÍ

ŽELEZNÁ

KAM ZIKOVA

OVOCNÝ
TRH

Karlův most

*Klementinum*
Clementinum

HUSOVA

SEMINÁŘSKÁ

*Clam-Gallasův palác*
Clam-Gallas Palace

MELANTRICHOVA

*Karolinum*
Carolinum

KŘIŽOVNICKÉ
NÁMĚSTÍ

KARLOVA

*Stavovské divadlo*
Estates Theatre

*Muzeum Bedřicha
Smetany*
Smetana
Museum

NOVOTNÉHO
LÁVKA

*Dům U Dvou
zlatých medvědů*
House at the Two
Golden Bears

JILSKÁ

HLAVSOVA

*Kostel sv. Havla*
Church of St Gall

HAVÍŘSKÁ

**4**

ANENSKÁ

ŘETĚZOVÁ

*Kostel sv. Jiljí*
Church of St Giles

JALOVCOVÁ

MICHALSKÁ

RYTÍŘSKÁ

U MŮSTKU

PROVAZNICKÁ

NA PŘÍKOPĚ

NA ZÁBRADLÍ

STŘÍBRNÁ

LILIOVÁ

ZLATÁ

*Betlémská kaple*
Bethlehem Chapel

SKOŘEPKA

VODIČKOVA

KONVIKTSKÁ

*Náprstkovo muzeum*
Náprstek Museum

**STARÉ MĚSTO**
**OLD TOWN**

*Národní
Muzeu...*
Museum
Commu...

BARTOLOMĚJSKÁ

KAROLÍNY SVĚTLÉ

NÁPRSTKOVA

BETLÉMSKÉ
NÁMĚSTÍ

Můstek

SMETANOVO NÁBŘEŽÍ

BORŠOV

DOBROVSKÉHO

SVĚTLÉKAROLÍNY

PERLOVA

**2**

28. ŘÍJNA

UHELNÝ
TRH

Můstek

VÁCLAVSKÉ
NÁMĚS...

MARTINSKÁ

*Kostel sv.
Martina ve zdi*
Church of
St Martin in the Wall

JUNGMANNOVO
NÁMĚSTÍ

*Kostel Panny Marie Sněžné*
Church of Our Lady of the Snows

PERŠTÝNĚ

SPÁLENÁ

DIVADELNÍ

KROCÍNOVA SVĚTLÉ

NÁRODNÍ

MIKULANDSKÁ

OSTROVNÍ

*Františkánská zahrada*
Franciscan Garden

JUNGMANNOVA

**5**

most Legii

*Národní divadlo*
**National Theatre**

NÁRODNÍ

*Kostel sv. Voršily*
Church of St Ursula

VORŠILSKÁ

Národní
třída

CHARVÁTOVA

PURKYŇOVA

VLADISLAVOVA

SPÁLENÁ

**NOVÉ MĚSTO**
**NEW TOWN**

PALACKÉHO

VODIČKO...

**A**     **5**     **B**     **C**

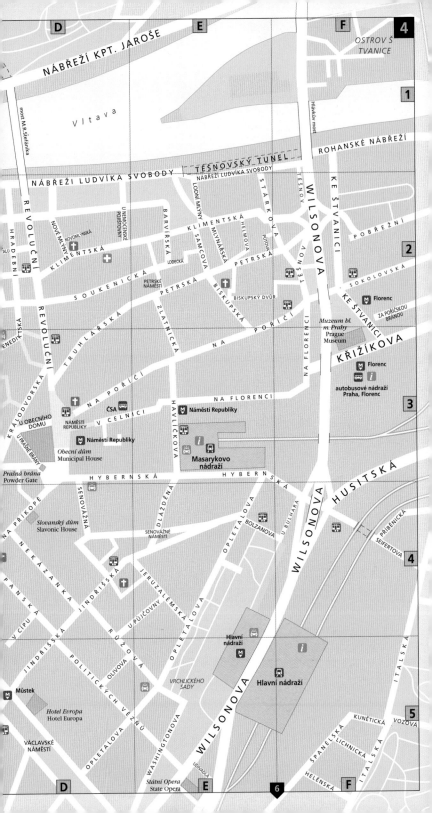

D    E    F    4

OSTROV Š
TVANICE

1

NÁBŘEŽÍ KPT. JAROŠE

most M.R.Štefánika

V l t a v a

Hlávkův most

NÁBŘEŽÍ LUDVÍKA SVOBODY

TĚŠNOVSKÝ TUNEL

NÁBŘEŽÍ LUDVÍKA SVOBODY

ROHANSKÉ NÁBŘEŽÍ

REVOLUČNÍ

HRADEBNÍ

NOVÉ MLÝNY

NOVOMLÝNSKÁ

KLIMENTSKÁ

U NEMOCENSKÉ POJIŠŤOVNY

BARVÍŘSKÁ

LODECKÁ

KLIMENTSKÁ

SAMCOVA

LODNÍ MLÝNY

MLYNÁŘSKÁ

HELMOVA

ŠTÁRKOVA

PUTOVÁ

TĚŠNOV

WILSONOVA

KE ŠTVANICI

POBŘEŽNÍ

2

SOKOLOVSKÁ

Florenc

SOUKENICKÁ

PETRSKÉ NÁMĚSTÍ

PETRSKÁ

BISKUPSKÁ

BISKUPSKÝ DVŮR

ZA PORÍČSKOU BRANOU

BENEDIKTSKÁ

REVOLUČNÍ

TRUHLÁŘSKÁ

ZLATNICKÁ

NA PORÍČÍ

TĚŠNOV

NA FLORENCI

Muzeum hl. m. Prahy
Prague Museum

KE ŠTVANICI

KŘIŽÍKOVA

Florenc

i

autobusové nádraží
Praha, Florenc

3

KRÁLODVORSKÁ

U OBECNÍHO DOMU

NÁMĚSTÍ REPUBLIKY

ČSA

V CELNICI

NA PORÍČÍ

NA FLORENCI

Náměstí Republiky

HAVLÍČKOVA

Náměstí Republiky

U PRAŠNÉ BRÁNY

Obecní dům
Municipal House

i

Masarykovo
nádraží

Prašná brána
Powder Gate

HYBERNSKÁ

HYBERNSKÁ

NA PŘÍKOPĚ

Slovanský dům
Slavonic House

SENOVÁŽNÁ

DLÁŽDĚNÁ

SENOVÁŽNÉ NÁMĚSTÍ

OPLETALOVA

BOLZANOVA

U BULHARA

WILSONOVA

HUSITSKÁ

PŘÍBĚNICKÁ

SEIFERTOVA

4

NEKÁZANKA

PANSKÁ

JINDŘIŠSKÁ

JERUZALÉMSKÁ

U PŮJČOVNY

OPLETALOVA

V CÍPU

JINDŘIŠSKÁ

RŮŽOVÁ

POLITICKÝCH VĚZŇŮ

OLIVOVA

Hlavní
nádraží

i

ITALSKÁ

Hlavní nádraží

WILSONOVA

VRCHLICKÉHO SADY

Můstek

Hotel Evropa
Hotel Europa

OPLETALOVA

V JÁMĚ

KUNĚTICKÁ

VOZOVÁ

5

VÁCLAVSKÉ NÁMĚSTÍ

OPLETALOVA

WASHINGTONOVA

WILSONOVA

DIVADELNÍ

ŠPANĚLSKÁ

LICHNICKÁ

ITALSKÁ

Státní Opera
State Opera

HELÉNSKÁ

D    E    6    F

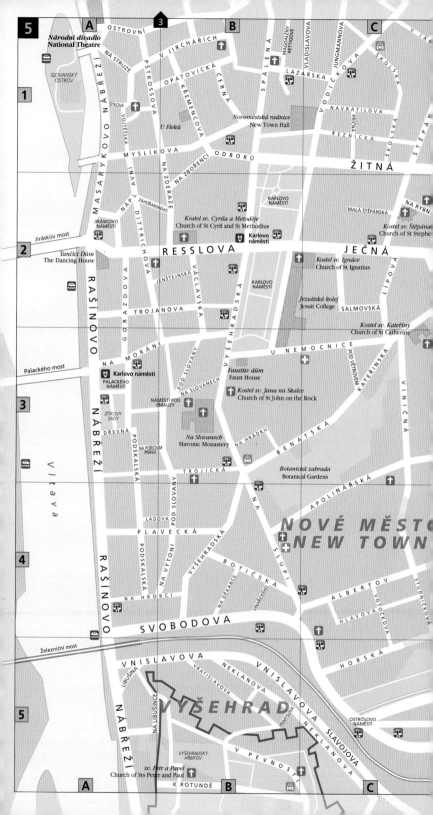

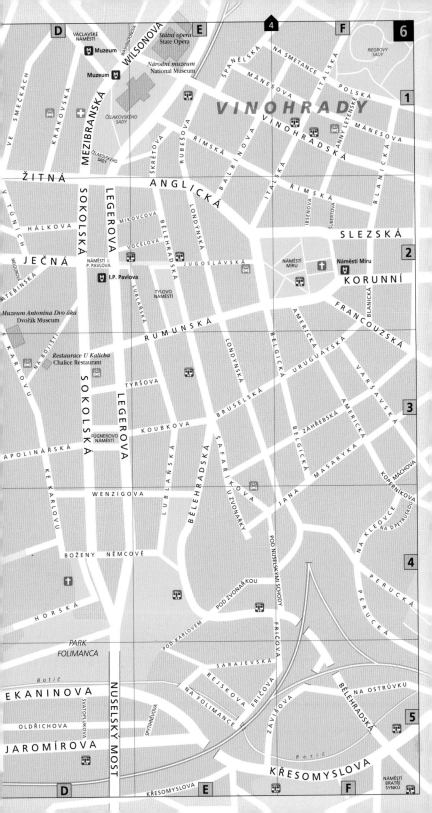

256 | GENERAL INDEX

# General Index

Page numbers in **bold** type refer to main entries

## A

Academy of Fine Arts 179
Adalbert, St 23, 24, 136, 140, 163
*Adam and Eve* (Cranach) 114
Adria Palace 144
Agencies (accommodation) 187
Agnes, St 25, 37, 46, 94
Air pollution 229
Air travel 234–5
Airport (Ruzyn ) 234–5
Aleš, Mikuláš
　National Theatre murals 35
　Old Town Hall decorations 75
　Štorch house 64, 70
　U Rotta decorations 64
　Wiehl House 144
All Saints' Chapel (Royal Palace)
　106, 107
*The Allegory of Night* (Braun) 111
Alliprandi, Giovanni Battista
　110, 135
American Express 230
Anglican Church 227
Ann, St 138
Anne, Empress 110
*The Annunciation of Our Lady*
　(Master of the Vyšší Brod
　Altarpiece) 94
Anthony of Padua, St 71, 137
Antiques
　customs regulations 224
　shops 212, 213
Aostalli, Ottavio 127, 141
Apartments (self-catering) 186,
　187, 188
*Apostles* (Sucharda) 76
Archbishop's Palace 48, **111**
Arcibiskupský Palác 111
Arcimboldo, Giuseppe
　*Rudolph II* 30
Art Nouveau 42, 148–9
Asam, Kosmas Damián 73
Assicurazioni Generali Building 145
At the Black Sun 65
At the Fleks 155
At the Golden Grape (Marienbad)
　171
At the Golden Horseshoe 123
At the Golden Scales 124
At the Golden Snake 80
At the Golden Unicorn (Little
　Quarter) 132
At the Golden Unicorn (Old
　Town) 70
At the Golden Well 80, 175
At the Haláneks 77
At the Minute 175

At the Ox 71
At the Poor Wretch's 70
At the Red Fox 71
At the Spider 174
At the Stone Bell 68
At the Stone Madonna 70
At the Stone Ram 70
At the Three Golden Bells 134
At the Three Little Fiddles 124
At the Three Ostriches 133, **134**
At the Three Red Roses 130
At the Two Golden Bears 31, **73**
　Street-by-Street map 64
At the Two Suns 130
At the Unicorn 175
At the Vulture 174
ATMs 230
Augusta, Bishop Jan 169
Augusta Prison (Křivoklát Castle)
　169
Augustine, St 137
Augustinians 115, 127, 154
Austerlitz, Battle of (1805) 34
Australian Consulate 225

## B

Ball Game Hall 31, 111
Balšánek, Antonín 66
Bambino di Praga 131
Banknotes 231
Banks 230
Baptist Church of Prague 227
Barbara, St 139
Baroque architecture 32–3, 46,
　47, 50–51
Bars 206–7, 225
Basle, Council of 152
Bassano, Jacopo 115
Bassevi, Hendela 89
Bayer, Paul Ignaz
　Church of St Ignatius 152
　Jesuit College 152
Bazilika sv. Jilí 100–101
BBC World Service 233
B chovice 54
Beck, Moses 88
Beer 196–7
Beer halls 192, 197, 206–7
Beethoven, Ludwig van 52, 80,
　132
Belvedér 110–11
Belvedere 30, 31, **110–11**
　Prague's Best 48, 50
Bendelmayer, Bedřich 148
Bendl, Jan 81
Benedictines 72, 92, 153, 163
Beneš, Edvard 21, 36
Benzi, St Philip 136
Bernard, St 139
Bernini, Gian Lorenzo 138, 163

Bertramka 33
　concerts 53
Bethlehem Chapel 13, **77**
　history 27, 28, 29
　Prague's Best 46
　Street-by-Street map 79
Betlémská kaple 77
*Big Dialog* (Nepraš) 165
Bílá Hora a Hv zda 163
Black Light Theatre 218
"Black sheriffs" 228
Blaeu, William 121
Blanche de Valois 169
Boats
　Vltava river trips 52
Bohemia Brethren 93
Bohemian Chancellery 107
Bohemian Diet 106
Boleslav I, Prince 19, 20, 22
Boleslav II, Prince 20, 22
　Břevnov Monastery 163
　Church of St Lawrence 140
　tomb of 101
Book shops 212–13
Borgia, St Francis 138
Bořiat, Jaroslav 116
Bořivoj, Prince 22, 97, 100, 106
Bořivoj II, Prince 24
Borromeo, St Charles 152
Borromini, Francesco 128
Bossi, CG 68
Botanical Gardens **153**
　Prague's Best 51
　Street-by-Street map 149
Botanická zahrada 153
Botels (floating hotels) 184
Bourdon, Sébastien 115
Brahe, Tycho 31, 43, 116, 117
　tomb of 69, 72
Brandl, Petr 42, 67, 100
　*The Holy Family* 132
Braque, Georges 115
Braun, Antonín 49, 110
　*The Allegory of Night* 111
　St Nicholas (Old Town) 72
Braun, Matthias 169
　Dvořák Museum 154
　Grand Priory 131
　Hercules statues 49, 80
　Konopišt Castle gate 169
　portrait 138
　*St Luitgard* 137
　Schönborn Palace caryatids 125
　Thun-Hohenstein Palace 124
　tomb of 154
　Vrtba Garden statues 130
Breakfast, in hotels 185
Břetislav I, Prince 20
Břetislav II, Prince 24
Břevnov Monastery 23, **163**

Břevnovský Klášter 163
Brick Gate 181
Bridge Street 12, **134**
  Street-by-Street map 132
Brokof, Ferdinand
  *Calvary* 93
  Charles Bridge statues 136
  Church of St Gall statues 73
  *St Francis Borgia* 33
  *St John the Baptist* 131
  *St John Nepomuk* 85, 92, 153
  statue of 138
  tomb of Count Vratislav of
    Mitrovice 67
Bronzino, Agnolo
  *Eleanor of Toledo* 115
Brothers of Mercy 93
Broník, Václav 147, 157
  *Defenestration (of 1618)* 107
Bruckner, Anton 171
Brüderle, Jan 119
Brueghel, Jan 31
Brueghel, Pieter the Elder 42
Budweiser Budvar 196
Buquoy Palace 131
Bureaux de change 230
Buses 240

## C

Cafés 192
  opening hours 225
Cajetan, St 137
Call shops 233
Calvary Chapel 177
Calvinists 102
Camping 186, 187
Canadian Embassy 225
Canaletto 115
Canon's House 180
Capuchin Monastery 46, 47,
  **116–17**
*Cardinal Cesi's Garden* (van Cleve)
  112
Carlone, Carlo 80
Carmelites 51, 130–31, 135, 146
Carolinum 12, 13, **67**
  history 26, 27
  Street-by-Street map 65
Cars 228
  driving in Prague 236–7, 241
Caruso, Enrico 127
Castles
  Karlstein Castle 12, 26, 27, **168–9**
  Konopišt Castle 114, **169**
  Křivoklát Castle 169
  Nelahozeves Castle 168
  Veltrusy Château 168
  *see also* Prague Castle
Cathedral *see* St Vitus's Cathedral
Cathedral Čechův Bridge 56

Čedok 224, 225
*Celebration of the Holy Trinity*
  (Palko) 129
Celetná Street 13, **67**, 174
  Street-by-Street map 65
Cemeteries
  Old Jewish 12, 13, 43, 83, 84,
    **88–9**
  Olšany 160
  Vyšehrad 181
Černín Palace 51, **117**, 135
Černínský Palác 117
Černý, František 148
Čertovka 58, 131, 133
České Budějovice 196
České Dráhy (ČD) 236
Chalice Restaurant 154
Chapel of Elijah 135
Chapel of St Catherine 169
Chapel of St Theresa 135
Chapel of St Wenceslas, St Vitus's
  Cathedral 26, 44
Charles I, Emperor 21
Charles IV, Emperor 19, 20, 153, 154
  art collection 42
  Carolinum 65, 67
  Charles Square 152
  Church of Our Lady of the
    Snows 48, 146
  churches 46
  Hunger Wall 140–41
  Karlsbad 170
  Karlstein Castle 169
  Křivoklát Castle 169
  Na Slovanech Monastery 59
  New Town 143
  Prague Castle 97
  Royal Palace 106, 107
  St Vitus's Cathedral 102
  statue of 81, 139
  tomb of 105
  Vyšehrad 180
Charles VI, Emperor 21
Charles Bridge 12, 13, 123, 175
  history 27, 87
  Little Quarter Side 136–7
  Old Town Side 138–9
  statues 33, 42, 136–9
  Street-by-Street map 133
  Visitors' Checklist 139
Charles Square 13, **152**
  Street-by-Street map 148–9
Charles Street 12, 13, **80**
Charnel House 85
Charter flights 234
Charter 77 37
Chemists *see* Pharmacies
Children 185, 226, 227, 234
China shops 212, 213
Chrám sv. Víta 102–5

*Christ on Clouds* (Czech Master) 85
Christopher, St 138
*Christ's Entry into Jerusalem* 114
Churches (general)
  Baroque architecture 32–3
  music in 220
  Prague's Best 44–7
  services 227
Churches (individual)
  Holy Ghost 85, **92**
  Holy Rood 98
  Holy Rood Rotunda 46
  Holy Saviour (Clementinum) 47,
    78, **81**
  Holy Saviour (St Agnes's
    Convent) 95
  Holy Trinity 130
  of the Infant Jesus 227
  Loreto, The 44, 47, **118–19**
  of the Nativity 119
  Our Lady (Capuchin) 116
  Our Lady (Karlstein) 169
  Our Lady (Prague Castle) 100
  Our Lady (Strahov) 120
  Our Lady before Týn 12, 13, 45,
    46, 64, 69, 71, **72**, 174
  Our Lady beneath the Chain
    132, **134**
  Our Lady of the Snows 46, 144,
    **146**
  Our Lady of Unceasing Succour
    130
  Our Lady Victorious 47, **130–31**,
    132, 163
  St Barbara (Kutná Hora) 159, 170
  St Castullus 85, **93**
  St Catherine **154**
  St Clement 33, 227
  St Cosmas and St Damian 150
  St Cyril and St Methodius 13, 53,
    148, **152**
  St Francis 80–81
  St Gall 12, **73**
  St George's Basilica 12, 13, 44,
    46, 99, **100–101**
  St Giles **77**, 79
  St Ignatius 149, **152**
  St James 45, 65, **67**
  St John on the Rock 47, 148,
    **153**
  St Joseph 132
  St Lawrence (Petřín) 16, **140**,
    177
  St Lawrence (Vyšehrad) 180
  St Longinus's Rotunda 46
  St Ludmilla 47, 161
  St Margaret (Břevnov
    Monastery) 163
  St Martin in the Wall 77
  St Martin's Rotunda 46, 180

Churches (cont.)
  St Nicholas (Little Quarter) 12, 13, 125, 127, **128–9**
  St Nicholas (Old Town) 68, 71, **72–3**, 175, 227
  St Peter and St Paul 45, 47, 59, 160, 181
  St Roch (Olšany Cemeteries) 160
  St Roch (Strahov Monastery) 47
  St Simon and St Jude 85, **93**
  St Stephen 154–5
  St Thomas 44, 47, 115, 125, **127**
  St Ursula 155
  St Vladimír (Marienbad) 171
  St Wenceslas 150
Cihelná Gate 181
Cinemas 218, 219
Civic Forum 37, 144
Clam-Gallas Palace 80
  Prague's Best 49, 51
  Street-by-Street map 79
Clementinum **81**, 175
  architectural features 33
  Prague's Best 47
  Street-by-Street map 78
Cleopatra (Zrzavý) 164
Closely Observed Trains (film) 37
Coach travel 236
Codex of Jena 28
Commerce (Gutfreund) 42
Committee for the Defence of the Unjustly Persecuted 37
Communications and media 232–3
Communism 19, 36
  Museum of Communism 146
Concerts see Music
Concierges 187
Congress Centre Prague
  Vyšehrad Walk 180
Constance, Council of (1415) 29, 72
Consulates 225
Convents
  of the Barefooted Carmelites 135
  St Agnes's 12, 13, 25, 41, 42, 46, 85, **94–5**
  St Anne's 78
  St George's 42, 99, **100–101**
Conversion chart 227
Cook, Thomas 57
Corot, Jean Baptiste Camille 115
Cosmas, St 136
Counter-Reformation 32, 47, 74
Courbet, Gustave 115
Court of the Bishop of Prague 134
Crafts shops 212, 213
Cranach, Lucas the Elder 114
  Adam and Eve 114
  St Christine 94

Credit cards 230
Croatian Benedictines 153
Crown jewels 26, 101
Crowns (currency) 231
Crucifixion (Stevens) 44
Cubism 42
Cubist Houses **93**, 160, 174
  Street-by-Street map 84
Currency 231
Currency exchange 230
Customs and immigration 224
Cycling 241
Cyril, St 22, 23, 53, 138
Czech Airlines (ČSA) 234, 235
Czech Association of Persons with Disabilities 185, 187, 227
Czech Astronomical Society 177
Czech Industrial Museum 77
Czech Master
  Christ on Clouds 85
Czech Republic Information Centre 225
Czech Technical University 148
Czechoslovak Orthodox Church 152
Czechoslovak Republic 20, 36
Czechoslovak Socialist Republic (ČSSR) 37

**D**

Dalibor of Kozojedy 110
Dalibor Tower **110**
  Street-by-Street map 99
Daliborka 110
Damajan, Deodatus 80
Damian, St 136
Dance 218, 219
The Dancing House 59
Day of Liberation from Fascism 52
Day of the Republic 54
Decorative Arts, Museum of **86**
  Art Nouveau 149
  Prague's Best 41, 43
  Street-by-Street map 84
Defenestrations of Prague 28, 31, 107, 155
Degas, Edgar 115
Delacroix, Eugène 115
Delicatessens 215
Della Stella, Paolo 31, 111
Dentists 229
D'Este collection 114
Destinn, Emmy 127
Devětsil movement 36
Devil's Column 160, 181
Devil's Stream 131, 133
Dientzenhofer, Christoph 47, 129
  Břevnov Monastery 163
  Loreto, The 47, 118
  St Nicholas (Little Quarter) 47, 128

Dientzenhofer, Kilian Ignaz 47, 129
  Břevnov Monastery 163
  Church of Mary Magdalene (Karlsbad) 171
  Church of St John on the Rock 148, 153
  Church of St Thomas 127
  Dvořák Museum 154
  Golz-Kinský Palace 49, 51, 72
  The Loreto 47, 118
  St Nicholas (Little Quarter) 47, 128–9
  St Nicholas (Old Town) 72
  Villa Amerika 49
Diplomatic Health Centre 229
Disabled travellers 226, 227
  hotels 185, 187
  restaurants 193
Discos 208, 209
Discounts, in hotels 185
Dominic, St 139
Dominicans 77, 139
Don Miguel de Lardizábal (Goya) 115
Dopravní podnik hlavního města Prahy 238
Drahomíra 101
Drinks 196–7
Dryák, Alois 148
Dubček, Alexander 37
Dům Pánů z Kunštátu 80–81
Dům u Dvou Zlatých Medvědů 73
Dům umělců 86
Dürer, Albrecht 42
  The Feast of the Rosary 40, 114
Duty-free allowances 224
Dvořák, Antonín 41, 43, 154, 168
Dvořák, Karel 138, 163
Dvořák Hall (Rudolfinum) 86
Dvořák Museum 154
  Prague's Best 41, 43

**E**

Ecotourism 227
Edward VII, King of England 171
Elbe, River 56
Eleanor of Toledo (Bronzino) 115
Electricity 227
Elizabeth, St 139
Elizabeth of Pomerania 44
Emauzy (Slavonic Monastery) 153
Embassies 225
Embassy of the Czech Republic 187
Emergency telephone numbers 229
English-language performances 218
Entertainment 216–21
Equestrienne (Chagall) 115

Ernst, Max 115
*Eros* (de Vries) 126
Estates Theatre 12, 13, **67**
  Street-by-Street map 65
Ethnographical Museum 176
Etiquette, in restaurants 193
Europa Hotel *see* Hotel Europa
Events (seasonal) 52–5
Exhibition Ground **162**, 178
  Prague's Best 42

**F**

Fabricius, Philipp 107
Fanta, Josef 148
Faust House 153
  Street-by-Street map 149
Faustův dům 153
Fauves 42
*Feast of the Rosary* (Dürer) 114
Felix de Valois, St 136
Fénix Palace 145
Ferdinand I, Emperor 21, 30, 81
  Archbishop's Palace 111
  Belvedere 110
  Loreto, The 118
  Mausoleum 105
  Prague Castle 97
  Royal Garden 111
Ferdinand II, Emperor 21, 32, 126
  Church of St Giles 77
  defenestration (of 1618) 107, 110
Ferdinand III, Emperor 21
Ferdinand V, Emperor 21, 174
Ferrer, St Vincent 137
Festivals 52–5
  music 217
Fiala, Zden k 58
*Fighting Giants* (Platzer) 98
Filippi, Giovanni Maria 130
Films 218, 219
Fire services 229
Fischer, Jíří 179
Fischer von Erlach, Johann Bernhard 67, 80
*Five Songs* (Tulka) 156
Flekovský, Jakub 155
Food and drink 194–7
  shopping 215
  *see also* Restaurants
Forman, Miloš 65
Fortuna Czech Open 53
Fountains
  Křižík 53, 178
  Singing 48, 50, 111
  Venus 48
Francis of Assisi, St 137
Francis Xavier, St 138
Franciscan Garden **146**
  Street-by-Street map 144

Franciscans 67, 146
Františkánská zahrada 146
Franz II, Emperor 21, 121
Franz Ferdinand, Archduke 169
Franz Josef, Emperor 21, 34, 35
Franz Kafka Gallery 71
Frederick of the Palatinate 32, 74, 105
Freud, Sigmund 165
Fringe theatres 218
Funicular railway 11, **141**
Fux, Jan 134

**G**

Galerie Rudolphinum 86
Gallas de Campo, Jan 80
Gallery Křižovníků 81
Galli, Agostino 116
Gall's Town 73
Gambrinus, King of Beer 196
Gans, David 88
Garden on the Ramparts 110
Gardens
  Prague's Best 48–51
  *see also* Parks and gardens
Gauguin, Paul 42, 115
Gay and lesbian venues **208–9**
George, St 98
George of Poděbrady 21, 28, 29, 174
  Church of Our Lady before Týn 72
  Palace of the Lords of Kunštát 79
Ghetto *see* Jewish Quarter
Glass
  Bohemian 43
  Museum of Decorative Arts 86
  shopping 212, 213
Godyn, Abraham 167
Goethe, Johann Wolfgang von 171
Gogol, Maxim 171
*Golden Age of Czech Art* (Ženíšek) 156
Golden Horseshoe 130
Golden Lane **101**
  Street-by-Street map 99
Golem 90
*The Good Soldier Švejk* (Hašek) 35, 154
Gossaert, Jan 114
Gothic architecture 46
Gottwald, Klement 21, 36, 160
  proclaims Communist state 71, 72
Goya, Francisco de
  *Don Miguel de Lardizábal* 115
*Grand Meal* (Medek) 164
Grand Priory of the Knights of Malta 131, 133

Grand Priory Mill 58
Grand Priory Square 12, **131**
  Street-by-Street map 132
Greco, El
  *Head of Christ* 112, 115
Green Lobster 130
Green travel 238
*The Guardian* 233
Guarini, Guarino 128
Gutfreund, Otto 42, 135, 164

**H**

Habermel, Erasmus 86
Habsburg dynasty 19, 20, 110
Hanavský Pavilion 58, 161
Hanuš (clockmaker) 76
Harovník, Fabian 101
Hartig Garden 110
Hašek, Jaroslav 154
Havel, Václav 21, 98
  Civic Forum 144
  Velvet Revolution 36, 37
Havelské Město 73
Havlíček, Milan 161
Haydn, Josef 43
*Head of Christ* (El Greco) 112, 115
Health care 229
Health Centre Prague 229
Heermann, Johann Georg 166
Heermann, Paul 166
Heger, Filip 69
Heger, František 69
Heinsch, Jan Jiří 92, 152, 155
Heinsch, Josef 67
Henlein, Konrad 36
*Hercules* (Braun) 49, 80
Heydrich, Reinhard 36, 53, 152
High Synagogue 87
  Prague's Best 47
  Street-by-Street map 84
History of Prague 19–37, 43
Hitler, Adolf 36
*Hladová Zed'* 140–41
Hlahol Choir Building 143, 148
Hlavní nádraží 148, 236
Holbein, Hans the Elder 114
Holešovice Station 236
Holidays, public 55
Holocaust 84, 86
*Holy Family* (Brandl) 132
Holy Ghost, Church of the 92
  Street-by-Street map 85
Holy Infant of Prague 131, 132
Holy Rood, Church of the 98
Holy Rood Chapel (Karlstein Castle) 27
Holy Rood Rotunda 46
Holy Saviour, Church of the (Clementinum) 81
  Street-by-Street map 78
Holy Saviour, Church of the (St Agnes's Convent) 95

Holy Trinity, Church of the 130
*Homage to Prague* (Špillar) 66
Horowitz, Aaron Meshulam 86
Horse-drawn carriages 241
Hospitals 229
Hostels 186, 187
Hotel Central 148
Hotel Europa 13, **147**
  Street-by-Street map 145
Hotels **184–91**
  Hradčany 188, 190, 191
  Jewish Quarter 189, 190, 191
  Little Quarter 188, 189, 190, 191
  New Town 188, 189, 190, 191
  Old Town 188, 189, 190, 191
  Prague Castle 188, 190, 191
House at the... *see* At the...
House of Artists 86
House of the Black Madonna
  12, 65, 67, 93, 174
Hradčany 96–119
  area map 97
  hotels 188, 190, 191
  restaurants 201
  Street Finder maps 1–2
Hunger Wall **140**, 176–7
Hunting Château 179
Hus, Jan 19, 28, 29, 46, 137
  anniversary 53
  Bethlehem Chapel 77, 79
  Monument 64, 71, **72**
Husák, Gustáv 21, 37
Hussite Church 227
Hussites 19, 28–9, 46, 160
  Church of Our Lady before Týn
  72
  Council of Basle 152
  Jan Hus Monument 72
  occupy St Vitus's Cathedral 102
  Utraquists 77
Hvězdárna 140
Hynais, Vojtěch 35, 147, 157

**I**

Ibsen, Hendrik 171
Ignatius Loyola, St 152
Imperial Sanatorium (Karlsbad) 171
Impressionism 42, 115
Industrial Palace 162, 178
Information centres 225
Institute of Gentlewomen 151
Insurance 228, 229, 237
Interdenominational church
  services 227
International Church 227
*International Herald Tribune* 233
International Student Identity
  Cards (ISIC) 226
Internet access 232–3
Internet cafés 232–3
*The Invention of Destruction* (film)
  36

Iron Man 80
Italian Court (Kutná Hora) 170
Italian Hospital 130
Italian Street **130**
Ivan, Blessed 136

**J**

Jäger, Joseph 131
Jan Hus Monument 71, **72**
  Street-by-Street map 64
Jan Vratislav of Mitrovice 45
Jansa, Václav
  *Melantrichova Passage* 71
  *Old Town Square* 64
Jaroš, Tomáš 100, 111
Jazz 52, 54, **208**, 209
Jelení skok 171
Jerusalem Synagogue 227
Jesuit College **152**
  Street-by-Street map 149
Jesuits 30
  Baroque architecture 32
  Bethlehem Chapel 77
  Carolinum 67
  Church of St Ignatius 149, 152
  Clementinum 33, 47, 59, 78, 81
  cult of St John Nepomuk 137
Jewish Burial Society 87
Jewish Museum 43
Jewish Quarter 12, 82–95
  area map 83
  history 34, 35
  hotels 189, 190, 191
  restaurants 200–201
  sightseeing tours 241
  Street-by-Street map 84–5
  Street Finder map 3
  synagogues 46
Jewish Town Hall 87
  Street-by-Street map 84
Jews *see* Jewish Quarter; Old
  Jewish Cemetery; Synagogues
Jezuitská kolej 152
Jizdáma 111
Jižní Zahrady 110
John the Baptist, St 138
John of Luxemburg 20, 26, 74
John de Matha, St 136
John Nepomuk, St 117, 137
  Charles Bridge 137, 138
  statues of 85, 92, 153, 155
  tomb of 105
Josef I, Emperor 21
Josef II, Emperor 21, 73, 120
  Jewish Quarter 83
Josefov 82–95
Joseph, St 138
Jubilee Exhibition (1891) 35, 58,
  148, 178
  Exhibition Ground 161, 162
  Petřín Park 140, 141
Jude Thaddaeus, St 137

Judith Bridge 24–6, 58, 136, 138
Judith Tower 134
Julius II, Pope 114
Jungmann, Josef 144, 160
Jungmannovo Square 144
Just, St 44

**K**

Kafka, Bohumil
  statue of Žižka 160
Kafka, Franz 10, 36, 70, 145
  Golden Lane 101
  Kafka Museum 135
  tomb of 160
Kafka Museum 135
Kafkovo Muzeum 135
Kaiserstein Palace 53, 127
Kampa Island 12, 13, **131**
  Prague's Best 49, 50, 51
  Street-by-Street map 133
*Kampa Island* (Pinkas) 133
Kampa Museum of Modern Art
  12, **135**
Kaňka, František Maximilián 130,
  169
Kapucínský klášter 116–17
Kara, Rabbi Avigdor 88
Karlova Street 175
Karlove ulice 80
Karlovo náměstí 148–9, 152
Karlovy Vary 170–71
Karlsbad 170–71
Karlstein Castle 12, 26, 27, **168–9**
Karlštejn 169
Karlův most 136–9
Kelley, Edward 100, 153
Kepler, Johannes 43, 117
Kinský, Štěpán 72
Kinský family 49, 141, 176
Kinský Garden 176
Kinský Palace 12, 68, **72**, 176
  Prague's Best 49, 51
  Street-by-Street map 64
Kipling, Rudyard 171
Kisch, Egon Erwin 73
Klášter na Slovanech 153
Klášter sv. Anežky České 94–5
Klausen Synagogue **87**, 88
  Prague's Best 47
  Street-by-Street map 84
Klausová synagóga 87
Klementinum 81
Klimt, Gustav 42, 115
  *The Virgin* 165
Knights of the Cross Square
  **81**, 175
  Street-by-Street map 78
Knights of Malta 131, 134
Knights of St John 134
Koch, Jindřich 176
Kohl, Hieronymus
  *St Augustine* 125

Kohl, John Frederick
  *St Paul* 128
Kolowrat-Černín Garden 135
Konopiště Castle 114, **169**
Koruna Palace 144
Kostel Matky Boží před Týnem
  72
Kostel Panny Marie pod řetězem
  134
Kostel Panny Marie Sněžné 146
Kostel sv. Cyrila a Metoděje 152
Kostel sv. Ducha 92
Kostel sv. František 81
Kostel sv. Halva 73
Kostel sv. Haštala 93
Kostel sv. Ignáce 152
Kostel sv. Jakuba 67
Kostel sv. Jana Na skalce 153
Kostel sv. Jiljí 77
Kostel sv. Kateřiny 154
Kostel sv. Martina ve zdi 77
Kostel sv. Mikuláše (Little Quarter)
  128–9
Kostel sv. Mikuláše (Old Town)
  72–3
Kostel sv. Šimona a Judy 93
Kostel sv. Štěpána 154
Kostel sv. Tomáše 127
Kostel sv. Vavřince 140
Kostel sv. Voršily 155
Kracker, Johann Lukas
  *St Joseph* 129
Královská zahrada 111
Královský letohrádek 110
Královský palác 106–7
Kramář, Vincenc 42
Krásnohorská, Eliška 149
Křivoklát Castle **169**
Křižík, František 178
Křižík Fountain 178
Křižovnické náměstí 81
Krkonoše (Giant) Mountains 140
Kroměříže, Jan Milíč z 77
Kubistické domy 93
Kunratice forest 54
Kunštát, Lords of 80–81
Kupecký, Jan 100
Kupka, Frantisek 135
Kutná Hora 13, **170**
Kvapilová, Hana
  statue of 176
Kysela, František 102

**L**

Ladislav Posthumus 20
*Lamentation of Christ* (Lorenzo
  Monaco) 112
Language 224
Langweil, Antonín 43, 161
Lapidarium, National Museum
  178
*Last Judgment* (mosaic) 103

Late-night transport 217
Laterna Magika 144
Le Brun, Charles 115
Ledebour Garden 135
Lennon, John 131, 132
Leopold I, Emperor 166, 167
Leopold II, Emperor 21
  coronation 104
  Royal Route 71, 174, 175
Leopold Gate 180
Letná Park 161
  Prague's Best 51
Library, National 81
Libuše, Princess 20, 23, 180
  statues of 78, 181
*Libuše* (Smetana) 34, 157
Libuše's Baths 181
Lichtenstein Palace 53, 127
Lipany, Battle of (1434) 19, 28,
  179
Liqueurs 197
Literature, Museum of National
  120
Little Quarter 12, 13, 19, **122–41**,
  175
  area map 123
  history 24, 25
  hotels 188, 189, 190, 191
  restaurants 201–202
  Street-by-Street map 132–3
  Street Finder maps 1–2
Little Quarter Bridge Towers 58,
  123, 136, 175
  Street-by-Street map 124–5
Little Quarter Riverside 13
Little Quarter Square 12, 13, **127**,
  175
Little Quarter Town Hall 127
Little Quarter Water Tower 58
Lobkovický palác 101
Lobkowicz, Kateřina of 118
Lobkowicz, Polyxena of 131
Lobkowicz family 168
Lobkowicz Palace **101**, 130
  Prague's Best 43, 50
  Street-by-Street map 99
Longinus, St 181
Lorenzetti, Pietro 114
Lorenzo Monaco
  *Lamentation of Christ* 113, 114
Loreto, The 13, **118–19**
  Prague's Best 40, 43, 44, 47
Lost and found 229
Louis XIV, King of France 67
Löw, Rabbi 30, 80, 87, 91
  and the Golem 90
  tomb of 89
Lucerna Palace 54, 144
Ludmilla, St 22, 99
  statue of 137
  tomb of 101
Ludvíc II, King 21

Luitgard, St 137
Lurago, Anselmo 120, 129
Lurago, Carlo
  Church of St Ignatius 152
  Jesuit College 152
  Lobkowicz Palace 101
  Our Lady beneath the Chain
    134
Luxemburg dynasty 20

**M**

Mácha, Karel Hynek 141
*Madonna Aracoeli* 42
Maillol, Aristide
  *Pomona* 164
Main Post Office 233
Maisel, Mordechai
  High Synagogue 87
  Maisel Synagogue 84, 92
  tomb of 89
Maisel Synagogue **92**
  Prague's Best 41, 43
  Street-by-Street map 84
Maiselova synagóga 92
Malá Strana 122–41
Malls 214, 215
Malostranské náměstí 127
Maltese Square 131
  Street-by-Street map 132
Maltézské náměstí 131
Mánes, Josef 34
  Old Town Hall Clock 76
  tomb of 160
Manet, Edouard 114, 115
Mannerism 47
Marchfeld, Battle of (1278) 20
Marcomans 22
Marcu, Jan Marek 63
Margaret, St 139
Maria Theresa, Empress 21, 33,
  174
Marian pillar 42
Mariánské Lázně 171
Mariánské náměstí 80
Mariánské Square **80**
  Street-by-Street map 79
Marienbad **171**
Markets **214–15**
Marold's Panorama 179
Martinic, Jaroslav 107
Martinic Palace 50, **116**
Martinický palác 116
*Martyrdom of St Thomas* (Rubens)
  113
Mary, Virgin 44, 118, 119, 146
Mary Magdalene, Church of
  (Karlsbad) 171
Masaryk, Jan 117
Masaryk, Tomáš Garrigue 21, 36
Masarykovo nádraží 236
Master of the Třeboň Altar
  *The Resurrection of Christ* 41

Master of the Vyšší Brod Altarpiece
*The Annunciation of Our Lady*
94
Mathey, Jean-Baptiste 51, 166–7
Matisse, Henri 114
Matthew of Arras 102, 169
Matthias, Emperor 21, 30, 110
Matthias Gate 31, 97
Maulbertsch, Franz
*Struggle of Mankind to Know
Real History* 121
Maximilian I, Emperor 114
Maximilian II, Emperor 21, 105
Medek, Mikuláš
*Grand Meal* 164
Medical centres 229
Medical tourism 229
Medici, Cosimo de' 115
Medieval architecture 24–5,
46, 50
Melantrichova Passage 71
Memorial to František Palacký 59
Menzel, Jiří 37
Merciful Brethren 85
Methodist-Evangelical church
services 227
Methodius, St 22, 23, 53, 138
Metro 238, 242–3
Metronome (Letná Park) 36, 161
Michna, Pavel 141
Michna Palace **141**
Michnův palác 141
Míčovna 111
Mikeš, František 59
Military History, Museum of 116
Prague's Best 40, 43
Mill Colonnade (Karlsbad) 171
Mime 218
Ministerstvo pro místní rozvoj
149
Minorite Order 67
Mint 174
Mirror Chapel 81
Mirror Maze **140**, 177
Mládek, Jan and Meda 135
Mladota, Count Ferdinand 151,
153
Mlýnská kolonáda 171
Mocker, Josef 47, 169
Church of St Stephen 154
St Ludmilla 161
St Vitus's Cathedral 102
Modern and Contemporary Art,
Centre for *see* Trade Fair Palace
Monasteries
Břevnov 23, **163**
Capuchin 46, 47, **116–17**
Na Slovanech 59
Slavonic 45, 46, 47, 148, **153**
Strahov 13, 24–5, 32, 46–7,
**120–21**, 177
Zbraslav 42, **163**

Monet, Claude 115
Money 230–31
customs regulations 224
Montanelli Museum (MuMo) **127**
Monuments
Jan Hus 64, 71, **72**
Letná Park metronome 36, 161
National Memorial 160
St John Nepomuk 117
St Wenceslas 145, 146
to Victims of Communism
(2002) 141, 145
*see also* Statues
Monuments of the Nation's Past
101
Morzin Palace 51, 130
Street-by-Street map 124
Mostecká ulice 134–5
Mozart, Wolfgang Amadeus 120
*La Clemenza di Tito* 104
*Don Giovanni* 33, 67
plays organ in St Nicholas's 128
Mucha, Alfons 35, 149
*Allegory of Vigilance* 39
Municipal House 66
Mucha Museum 13, **147**
*St Cyril and St Methodius* 104
Mucha Museum 13, **147**
Munch, Edvard 42, 43, 115
Munich Agreement (1938) 36
Municipal House 13, 35, 52, **66–7**,
174
Mayor's Room 39
Street-by-Street map 65
Museums and galleries
Choco Story Museum 227
Czech Industrial Museum 77
Dvořák Museum 41, 43, **154**
Ethnographical Museum 176
Kafka Museum 135
Kampa Museum of Modern Art
12, **135**
Loreto, The 40, 43, 118
Montanelli Museum (MuMo)
**127**
Mucha Museum 13, **147**
Municipal Mass Transport 241
Museum of Communism 146
Museum of Decorative Arts 41,
43, **86**, 149
Museum of Military History 40,
43, 116
Museum of Miniatures 226,
227
Museum of Music 43, 132, **141**
Museum of National Literature
120
Muzeum Antonína Dvořáka 154
Muzeum Bedřicha Smetany 81
Muzeum Hlavního Města Prahy
161
Náprstek Museum 43, **77**

Museums and galleries (cont.)
National Museum 13, 41, 43,
145, **147**, 160, 178, 225
National Technical Museum 43,
**162**
Nelahozeves Castle 168
Picture Gallery of Prague Castle
100
Prague Museum 43, **161**
Prague's Best 40–43
Riding School 111
Schwarzenberg Palace 40, 43
Smetana Museum 40, 43, 59,
78, **81**
Star Hunting Lodge 163
State Jewish Museum 41, 43, 225
Sternberg Palace 13, **112–15**
Toy Museum 101
Trade Fair Palace 164–5
Troja Palace 166–7
Music 43, **220–21**
festivals 217
jazz 208, 209
Museum of Music 43, 132, **141**
rock and pop clubs 208, 209
Myslbek, Josef 163, 181
*Přemysl and Libuše* 181
*St Agnes* 94
St Ludmilla portal 161
*St Wenceslas* 146
*Záboj and Slavoj* 149

## N

Na Františku Hospital 85, 93
Na Slovanech Monastery 59
Náměstí Míru 161
Napoleon I, Emperor 34
Náprstek, Vojta 77
Náprstek Museum 43, **77**
Náprstkovo Muzeum 77
Národní divadlo 156–7
Národni Muzeum 147
Národní technické muzeum 162
National anthem 67
National Gallery
Golz-Kinský Palace 49, 72
Prague's Best 42
St Agnes's Convent 94–5
Sternberg Palace 112–15
Trade Fair Palace 164–5
Wallenstein Palace 126
Zbraslav Monastery 163
National Library 81
National Memorial 160
National Museum 13, **147**, 160
history 19, 34, 35
Hunting Château 179
Lapidarium 178
Náprstek Museum 77
Prague's Best 41, 43
Street-by-Street map 145
National Revival 34–5

National Technical Museum 43, **162**
National Theatre 13, 59, **156–7**
  history 19, 34, 35
Nativity, Church of the 119
Nazis 36, 43, 74, 87, 92
Nebozízek station 141
Nelahozeves Castle 168
Neo-Gothic architecture 47
Nephele Mound 88
Nepraš, Karel
  *Big Dialog* 165
Neruda, Jan 130, 175
Nerudova Street 12, 13, 33, **130**
  Royal Route Walk 175
  Street-by-Street map 124
Nerudova ulice 33, 124, 130
Neunhertz, Jiří 120
New Deanery 180
New Land Rolls (Royal Palace) 107
New Town 13, **142–57**
  area map 143
  history 26, 27, 34
  hotels 188, 189, 190, 191
  restaurants 202–204
  sightseeing tours 241
  Street-by-Street maps 144–5, 150–51
  Street Finder maps 3–6
New Town Hall 13, 28, **155**
New World 13, **116**
New Zealand Consulate 225
Newspapers 233
Nicholas Tolentino, St 137
Night buses 240
Nightclubs **208**, 209
Nightlife **208–9**
Norbert, St 120, 138
Nostitz, Count 67
Nostitz Palace 131, 132
Novák, Emanuel 149
Nové Město 142–57
Novoměstská radnice 155
Novotný, Antonín 21, 37
Nový Svět 116

**O**

Obrazárna Pražkého Hradu 100
Observation Path (Kinský Garden) 176
Observation Tower **140**, 177
  Street-by-Street map 79
Očko, Jan, Archbishop 26, 94
Old Jewish Cemetery 12, 13, 83, **88–9**
  Prague's Best 43
  Street-by-Street map 84
Old-New Synagogue 12, 13, **90–91**, 227
  history 26
  Prague's Best 45, 46
  Street-by-Street map 84

Old Royal Palace 106–7
  Prague's Best 50
  Street-by-Street map 99
Old School 92
Old Town 13, 24, **62–81**
  area map 63
  hotels 188, 189, 190, 191
  restaurants 198–9
  Royal Enclosure Walk 178–9
  Royal Route Walk 174
  sightseeing tours 241
  Street-by-Street maps 64–5, 78–9
  Street Finder maps 3–4
Old Town Bridge Tower 27, 139, 175
  Street-by-Street map 78
Old Town Hall 12, 13, **74–6**
  Clock 12, 13, 28, 34, 75, **76**
  Street-by-Street map 64
  Tower 75
Old Town Square 12, 13, 52, 63, **68–71**, 174
  East and North sides 68–9
  South side 70–71
  Street-by-Street map 64
*Old Town Square* (Jans) 64
Olšanské hřbitovy 160
Olšany cemeteries 52, **160**
Ondříček, František 116
Opening hours 225
  shops 210
Opera 145, 147, 220
Oppenheim, Rabbi David 88
Order of the Golden Fleece 126
Oriel Chapel 75
Orloj 76
Orthodox Church 152
Our Lady before Týn, Church of 12, 13, 69, **72**, 174
  history 29, 71
  Prague's Best 45, 46
  Street-by-Street map 65
Our Lady beneath the Chain, Church of 134
  Street-by-Street map 132
Our Lady of the Snows, Church of 146
  Prague's Best 46
  Street-by-Street map 144
Our Lady of Unceasing Succour, Church of 130
Our Lady Victorious, Church of **130–31**, 163
  Prague's Best 47
  Street-by-Street map 132
Ovocný trh 65

**P**

Palác Kinských 72
Palace Gardens 49, 51, **135**

Palaces
  music in 220
  Prague's Best 48–51
Palach, Jan 37, 146
Palacký, František (Memorial to) 59
Palacký Bridge 149, 181
Pálffy Garden 135
Palko, František
  *The Celebration of the Holy Trinity* 129
Palliardi, Ignaz 135
Panorama, Marold's 179
Pantheon 181
Pantomime 218
*Paradise* (Savery) 113
Paradise Garden 110
Pařížž (hotel) 84
Parking 241
Parks and gardens
  Botanical Gardens 51, 151, **153**
  Charles Square 148, 152
  Franciscan Garden 144, **146**
  Garden on the Ramparts 110
  Hartig Garden 110
  Kampa Island 49, 50, 51, 131, 133
  Kinský Garden 176
  Kolowrat-Černín Garden 135
  Letná Park 36, 37, 51, **161**
  Palace Gardens 49, 51, **135**
  Pálffy Garden 135
  Paradise Garden 110
  Petřín Park 51, 140, 141, **176–7**
  Prague's Best 48–51
  Rose Garden (Petřín Park) 177
  Royal Garden 12, 48, 51, **111**
  South Gardens 12, 48, 51, 98, **110**
  Stromovka 51, **162**
  Troja Palace 167, 179
  Veltrusy Château **168**
  Vojan Park 51, 133, **135**
  Vrtba Garden 51, **130**
  Vyšehrad Park 53, 181
  Wallenstein Palace and Garden 12, 13, 48, 51, **126**
Parler, Peter 169
  All Saints' Chapel 106, 107
  Charles Bridge 138
  Karlstein Castle 169
  Old Town Bridge Tower 27, 66, 78, 139
  St Barbara (Kutná Hora) 170
  St Vitus's Cathedral 102, 103, 105
  *Wenceslas IV* 27
Passports 224
Pensions 187
People Against Violence 37
Performing arts 218–19

*Pesach Haggadah* (manuscript) 41
Petřín Hill 51, 121, 140
Petřín Park **141**
 Petřín Park walk **176–7**
Petřínská Rozhledna 140
Pharmacies 229
Phonecards 232
Physical Culture and Sport, Museum of 141
Picasso, Pablo 42
Picture Gallery of Prague Castle 40, **100**
 Prague's Best 40
 Street-by-Street map 98
Pilsner 196
Pinkas, Rabbi 86
Pinkas, Soběslav 133
Pinkas Synagogue 12, 13, **86–7**, 88
 Prague's Best 46, 47
 Street-by-Street map 84
Pinkasova synagóga 86–7
Pissarro, Camille 115
Planetarium 179
Plastic People (rock band) 37
Platzer, Ignaz
 *Fighting Giants* 98
 Golz-Kinský Palace statues 68, 72
 *St John Nepomuk* 155
 statues in St Nicholas's 129
 Strahov Monastery 121
Plečnik, Josip 48, 110
Plzeň 196
Pohořelec 117
Police 228, 237
Polívka, Osvald 66, 69
Pollution 55, 229
*Pomona* (Maillol) 164
Poor Clares 25, 94
Post-Impressionism 42, 115
Post offices 233
Poste restante 233
Powder Gate 12, 13, **66**, 174
 Street-by-Street map 65
Powder Tower 100
 Street-by-Street map 98
Prachner, Peter 128
Prachner, Richard 128
Prager, Karel 156
Prague Burial Society 89
Prague Castle 12, 13, 19, 50, **96–119**
 area map 97
 Dalibor Tower 110
 history 23, 24, 25, 26, 29, 30–31, 32
 Lobkowicz Palace 43, 50
 Matthias Gate 31, 97
 Picture Gallery 40, 42, 43, 98, **100**

Prague Castle (cont.)
 Powder Tower 100
 Royal Garden 48, 51
 Royal Palace 12, 13, 99, **106–7**
 Royal Route 80
 South Gardens 48, 51, 98, 110
 "Story of Prague Castle" exhibition 10
 Street-by-Street map 98–9
 Street Finder map 2
Prague City Insurance Company 69
Prague Gallery 42
Prague Information Service (PIS) 224, 225
Prague Insurance Company 148
Prague Integrated Transport 226
Prague Museum 43, **161**
Prague Organization for Wheelchair Users 226, 227
*The Prague Post* 224, 233
Prague Public Transport Company 238
Prague Public Transport Information Centres 238
"Prague Spring" (1968) 37
Prague Spring Music Festival 52
Prague Uprising (1945) 36, 52, 74
Praha House 148
Prašná brána 66
Prašná věž 100
Pražská paroplavební společnost 57
Pražský hrad 96–119
Prčice 52
*Pregnant Woman and Death* (Schiele) 165
Premonstratensians 120
Přemysl 23, 181
Přemysl Otakar I, King 20, 25
Přemysl Otakar II, King 20, 24, 25, 106
Přemyslid dynasty 19, 20, 22–3, 26, 169
Přichovský, Archbishop Antonín 111
Private rooms 186, 187
Procopius, St 137
Public holidays 55
Pubs 192, 197, **206–7**
Purkyně, Jan (statue) 151

**Q**
Quitainer, Johann Anton 117, 120
Quitainer, Ondřej 118

**R**
Radio 233
Rail travel 236
Rajská zahrada 110
Red Army 36

Red Eagle 130
Reiner, Václav Vavřinec
 Church of the Nativity frescoes 119
 Church of Our Lady Victorious 163
 Church of St Giles frescoes 77
 Church of St James frescoes 67
 Church of St Thomas frescoes 127
 Vrtba Garden 130
Rejsek, Matthias 75
Religious services 227
Rembrandt 42, 114, 115
 *Scholar in his Study* 112
Renaissance 19, 30–31
 architecture 46–7, 50
Reni, Guido 100
Responsible tourism 227
Restaurace u Kalicha 154
Restaurants 192–205
 Hradčany 201
 Jewish Quarter 200–201
 Little Quarter 201–202
 New Town 202–204
 Old Town 198–200
 Prague Castle 201
*Resurrection of Christ* (Master of the Třebo Altar) 41
Riding School 111
Ried, Benedikt
 Powder Tower 100
 St Barbara (Kutná Hora) 170
 Vladislav Hall 106
Rock and pop clubs **208**, 209
Rodin, Auguste 42, 115
Romanesque architecture 24–5, 46
Romanticism 42
Rose Garden (Petřín Park) 177
Rotunda of St Martin 25, 46, 160, 181
Rotunda of St Vitus 22, 23
Rotundas, Romanesque 46
Rousseau, Henri "le Douanier" 42
Royal Court 66
 Prague's Best 48, 51
Royal Enclosure Walk 178–9
Royal Garden 12, **111**
Royal Hall 179
Royal Palace 12, 13, 99, **106–7**
Royal Route Walk 174–5
Rubens, Peter Paul 42, 43, 100, 113, 114–15, 127
 *Martyrdom of St Thomas* 113
Rudolfinum 13, 34, 59, **86**
 concerts 52, 54
 Galerie 86
 history 19
Rudolph, Crown Prince 86
Rudolph I, Emperor 167

Rudolph II, Emperor 19, 21, 86, 92
   art collection 42, 100, 114
   history 30–31, 46
   miraculous statue of Madonna
      and Child 116–17
   Prague Castle 97, 98
Rudolph Water Tunnel 179
Ruzy Airport 234–5

**S**

Sadeler, Aegidius
   *Vladislav Hall* 106
Safety 228–9
St Agnes of Bohemia Convent 12,
   13, 25, **94–5**
   Prague's Best 41, 42, 46
   Street-by-Street map 85
St Anne's Convent 78
*St Augustine* (Kohl) 125
St Barbara, Church of (Kutná
   Hora) 159, 170
St Castullus, Church of 93
   Street-by-Street map 85
St Catherine, Church of 95, **154**
St Clement, Church of 33, 37
St Cosmas and St Damian,
   Church of 150
St Cyril and St Methodius, Church
   of 13, 148, **152**
*St Cyril and St Methodius* (Mucha)
   104
St Francis, Church of 78, **80–81**
*St Francis Borgia* (Brokof) 33
St Gall, Church of 12, **73**
St George's Basilica 12, 13, 23, 25,
   99, **100–101**
   Prague's Best 44, 46
St George's Convent 99
   Prague's Best 40, 42
St Giles, Church of 77
   Street-by-Street map 79
St Ignatius, Church of 152
   Street-by-Street map 149
St James, Church of 67
   Prague's Best 45
   Street-by-Street map 65
*St John the Baptist* (Brokof) 131
*St John the Baptist* (Rodin) 114
*St John Nepomuk* (Brokof) 85, 92
   Charles Bridge 153
St John on the Rock, Church of
   47, **153**
   Street-by-Street map 148
St Joseph, Church of
   Street-by-Street map 132
*St Joseph* (Kracker) 129
St Lawrence, Basilica of 180
St Lawrence, Church of 16, **140**
   Petřín Park Walk 177
St Longinus's Rotunda 46
St Ludmilla, Church of 47, 161
St Margaret, Church of 163

St Martin in the Wall, Church of 77
St Martin's Rotunda 25, 46, 160, 181
   Prague's Best 46
   Vyšehrad Walk 180, 181
*St Michael* (Solimena) 128
St Nicholas, Church of (Little
   Quarter) 12, 13, 32, 127, **128–9**
   Prague's Best 44, 46, 47
   Street-by-Street map 125
St Nicholas, Church of (Old Town)
   68, **72–3**, 175, 227
   history 71
   Prague's Best 47
   Street-by-Street map 64
*St Nicholas* (Platzer) 129
*St Paul* (Kohl) 128
St Peter and St Paul, Church of
   59, 160
   Prague's Best 45, 47
   Vyšehrad Walk 181
St Roch, Church of (Olšany
   Cemeteries) 160
St Roch, Church of (Strahov
   Monastery) 47
St Simon and St Jude, Church of
   93
   Street-by-Street map 85
St Stephen, Church of 154–5
St Thomas, Church of 115, **127**
   Prague's Best 44, 47
   Street-by-Street map 125
St Ursula, Church of 155
*St Vitus* (Master Theodoric) 27
St Vitus Treasure 42
St Vitus's Cathedral 12, 13, 54,
   **102–5**
   Chapel of St Wenceslas 44
   Prague's Best 44, 46, 47
   St Wenceslas Chapel 26, 103,
      104, 105
   stained glass 97
   Street-by-Street map 98
St Vladimír, Church of
   (Marienbad) 171
St Wenceslas, Church of 150
St Wenceslas (Feast of) 54
*St Wenceslas and St Vitus*
   (Spränger) 19
St Wenceslas Chapel (St Vitus's
   Cathedral) 26, 103, 104, 105
St Wenceslas Crown 26
Sales 211
Šaloun, Ladislav
   Jan Hus Monument 72
   Zbraslav Monastery 163
Samo 22
Santa Casa 118, 119
Santini-Aichel, Giovanni 73
Sausages 192
Savery, Roelant
   *Paradise* 113
Saxons 32

Schiele, Egon 42, 115
   *Pregnant Woman and Death* 165
Schnirch, Bohuslav 156
*Scholar in his Study* (Rembrandt)
   112
Schönborn Palace 125
Schor, Jan Ferdinand 154
Schulz, Josef 86, 147, 156
Schwarzenberg Palace **116**
   Prague's Best 40, 43, 50
Schwarzenberský palác 116
Science museums 43
Seifert, Jaroslav 37, 101
Self-catering apartments 186, 187
*Self-portrait* (Rousseau) 112, 115
Senior travellers 226
Seurat, Georges 115
*Sgraffito*
   Ball Game Hall 111
   Calvary Chapel 177
   House at the Minute 175
   Lobkowicz Palace 101
   Martinic Palace 116
   Royal Palace 106
   Schwarzenberg Palace 50, 116
   Smetana Museum 81
   Štorch House 64
   Wiehl House 144
Shopping 210–15
Sicilian Golden Bull 25
Sightseeing tours 241
Sigismund, Emperor 160
Sigismund, King 20
Sigismund, St 138
Singing Fountain 48, 50, 111
Sisley, Alfred 115
Šitka Tower 59
Škréta, Karel 42, 73
   Church of Our Lady beneath
      the Chain paintings 134
   Church of St Gall paintings 73
   *Crucifixion* 128
Slánský Trial 36
Slavata, Vilém 107
Slavic tribes 22
Slavín 181
Slavkov, Battle of (1805) 34
Slavonic House 147
Slavonic Monastery Emauzy 153
   Prague's Best 45, 46, 47
   Street-by-Street map 148
Slovanský dům 147
Smetana, Bedřich 52, 149, 175
   *Dalibor* 110
   *Libuše* 34, 157
   tomb of 181
Smetana Museum **81**
   Prague's Best 40, 43
   Street-by-Street map 78
Smíchov Station 236
Smiřický Palace 127
Sněžka (mountain) 140

Soběslav I, King 106
Soběslav II, King 20
Sokol 141, 149
Soldati, Tommaso
  St Ignatius sculptures 152
Solimena, Francesco
  St Michael 128
South Gardens 12, **110**
  Prague's Best 48, 51
  Street-by-Street map 98
Špála, Václav 42
Španělská synagóga 92–3
Spanish Synagogue 13, **92–3**
  Street-by-Street map 85
Spas 170, 171
Speciality shops 214–15
Spezza, Andrea 126
Špička Gate 140, 180
Špillar, Karel
  Homage to Prague 66
Spires 46–7
Spirits 197, 224
Sports 220–21
Spränger, Bartholomeus
  St Wenceslas and St Vitus 19
Spytihněv, Prince 102
Stag's Leap 171
Stalin, Joseph
  statue of 36, 37, 161
Stamps, postage 233
Star Hunting Lodge 163
Stará Škola 92
Staré Město 62–81
Staroměstská radnice 74–5
Staroměstské náměstí 68–71
Staronová synagoga 90–91
Starý židovský hřbitov 88–9
State Jewish Museum 225
  Prague's Best 41, 43
State Opera 147
  Street-by-Street map 145
Státní opera Praha 147
Statues
  Charles IV 81
  on Charles Bridge 136–9
  Hana Kvapilová 176
  Hercules 49
  Jan Hus 71, 72
  Jan Purkyn 151
  Jan Žižka 160
  Přemysl and Princess Libuše 181
  Princess Libuše 78
Statues (cont.)
  on Rudolfinum 59
  St John the Baptist 131
  St John Nepomuk 85, 92
  St Joseph and St John 118
  St Wenceslas 145, 146
  Vltava 58
Stavovské divadlo 67
Štefánik's Observatory 140, 177
Sternberg, Count 166

Sternberg, Franz Josef 112
Sternberg Palace 13, **112–15**, 127
  Prague's Best 40, 42–3, 51
  Visitors' Checklist 113
Šternberský palác 112–15
Stevens, Antonín
  Crucifixion 44
Štorch House 70
  Street-by-Street map 64
Štork, Lorenc 73
"Story of Prague Castle" exhibition 10
Strahov Gospel (book) 121
Strahov Monastery 13, **120–21**, 177
  history 24, 25
  Philosophical Hall 32, 120
  Prague's Best 46, 47
Strahov stadium 36
Strahovský klášter 120–21
Street signs 241
Street stalls 214
Střelecký Island 53
Stromovka 51
Stromovka Park 162
Struggle of Mankind to Know Real History (Maulbertsch) 121
Students 226, 227
Štvanice Island 56
Sucharda, Stanislav
  New Town Hall sculpture 79
Sucharda, Vojtěch
  Apostles 76
Sudeten German Party 36
Svoboda, Ludvík 21
Synagogues
  High 47, 84, **87**
  Jerusalem 227
  Klausen 47, 84, **87**, 88
  Maisel 41, 43, 84, **92**
  Old-New 12, 13, 46, 45, 46, 84, **90–91**, 227
  Pinkas 12, 13, 46, 47, 84, **86–7**, 88
  Prague's Best 44–7
  Spanish 13, 85, **92–3**

## T

Tábor Gate 180
Taborites 19, 28
Táborský, Jan 76
Tauc, Gustav Makarius 37
Taxes
  in hotels 185
  in restaurants 193
  in shops 210
Taxis 240
Technology museums 43
Telephones 232
  in hotels 185
Television 233
Temperature chart 55
Terezín 43, 87

Theatines 130
Theatres 218, 219
Theodoric, Master 100
  St Vitus 27
Theresian Way (Royal Palace) 107
Thirty Years' War (1618–48) 19, 30, 32, 107, 138
Thomas, St 139
Thomas, Edward 34
Thun-Hohenstein Palace 130
  Street-by-Street map 124
Thurn, Count 107
Tickets
  entertainment 216–17
  travel 234
Tina B 54
Tintoretto 43, 100, 115
Tipping
  in hotels 185
  in restaurants 193
Titian 43
  Toilet of a Young Lady 100
Tobacconists 233
Toilet of a Young Lady (Titian) 100
Torah 87, 92
Toulouse-Lautrec, Henri de 115
Tour operators 225
Tourist information offices 71, 224, 225
Town Halls
  Jewish 84, **87**
  Little Quarter 127
  New Town 13, **155**
  Old Town 12, 13, 28, 34, 64, **74–5**, 76, 175
Toy Museum 101
Trade Fair Palace 42, **164–5**
Trains 236
Trams 239
Transport 234–43
  air 234–5
  arriving in Prague 236–7
  buses 240
  cars 236–7, 241
  coaches 236
  late-night 217
  metro 238, 242–3
  trains 236
  trams 239
Traveller's cheques 230
Trinitarian Order 136
Troja Palace **166–7**, 179
  Prague's Best 42, 50, **51**
Trojský zámek 166–7
Tulka, Josef
  Five Songs 156
Turba Palace 131
Tuscany Palace 50
Twain, Mark 171
The Two Suns 175
Týn School 69
Tyrš House 141

## U

U Fleků 155
U Halánků 77
U Kalicha 154
U Lazara 70
U Pinkasů
  Street-by-Street map 144
U Rotta 64
U Tří pštrosů 134
  Street-by-Street map 133
U Zlatého hroznu 171
Uměleckoprůmyslové muzeum 86
Union Café 36
United Kingdom Embassy 225
United States Embassy 225
Universities
  Carolinum 12, 13, 19, 26, 27, 65, 67
  Clementinum 33, 47, 59, 78, 81, 175
  Czech Technical University 148
Urban V, Pope 26
Ursuline Order 155
Utraquists 28, 72, 77

## V

Václav, Prince of Opava 153
Václava A Vojtěcha 102
Václavské náměstí 146
Valdštejnský palác 126
Van Cleve
  Cardinal Cesi's Garden 112
Van Gogh, Vincent 115
  Variant of the Krumlov Madonna 95
Vegetarians 193
Veletržní Palác 164
Velká Kunratická 54
Velkopřevorské náměstí 131
Veltrusy Château 168
Velvet Revolution (1989) 19, 36, 37
  celebration of 54
  Civic Forum 144
  Letná Park 161
  Monument to the Victims of Communism 145
  Wenceslas Square rally 146
Veronese, Paolo 100
Villa Amerika 154
  Dvořák Museum 41, 154
  Prague's Best 49, 51
Villa Müller 163
Vinohrady Theatre 161
The Virgin (Klimt) 165
Visas 224
Vítkov Hill 160
Vitus, St 27, 136, 139
Vladislav I, King 20

Vladislav II Jagiello, King 21, 24
  Church of Our Lady beneath the Chain 134
  Dalibor Tower 110
  Powder Gate 66
  Prague Castle 97
  Royal Palace 29, 106
  Strahov Monastery 46
Vladislav Hall (Royal Palace) 107
  history 29, 30, 106
  Prague's Best 50
Vladislav Hall (Sadeler) 106
Vlašská ulice 130
Vltava River 40, 53, 54, 56–9
Vltava Statue 58
Vojan Park 135
  Prague's Best 51
  Street-by-Street map 133
Vojanovy sady 135
Volflin of Kamen 75
Votive panel of Archbishop Jan Očko of Vlašim 94
Vouet, Simon 115
Vratislav, Count of Mitrovice 67
Vratislav I, Prince 24, 46, 100, 101
Vratislav II, Prince 20, 25, 180, 181
Vries, Adriaen de 100, 111
  statue of Eros 126
  tomb of 127
Vrtba Garden 51, 130
Vrtbovská zahrada 130
Vyletěl, Josef 171
Vyšehrad 12, 160
  history 22, 32
  Špička Gate 140
  Walk 180–81
Vyšehrad Cemetery 160, 181
Vyšehrad Codex 24, 25
Vyšehrad Park 53, 160, 181
Vysoká synagóga 87
Výstaviště 162
Výtoň 43
Výtoň Excise House 59

## W

Wagner, Antonín 59, 157
Wagner, Richard 171
Walks 172–81, 240
  Petřín Park 176–7
  Royal Enclosure 178–9
  Royal Route 174–5
  Vyšehrad 180–81
Wallenstein, Count Albrecht von 32, 48, 125, 126, 141
Wallenstein Palace and Garden 12, 13, 48, 51, 125, 126
  Prague's Best 48, 51
Warsaw Pact 37
Weather in Prague 52–5
Weber, Carl Maria von 171
Weiss, František 79

Wenceslas I, King 20, 67, 169
Wenceslas II, King 20, 127, 163
Wenceslas III, King 20
Wenceslas IV, King 20, 27, 29, 137
  statue of 139
  Zbraslav Monastery 163
Wenceslas, St 19, 20
  Monument 145, 146
  murder 22–3, 103, 104
  paintings of 70
  St Vitus's Cathedral 102
  shrine 26
  statues of 136, 138
  Štorch House decorations 64
  tomb of 13, 103
Wenceslas Square 13, 146
  Street-by-Street map 144–5
  Street Finder maps 3–6
Westphalia, Treaty of (1648) 32
Wheelchair access see Disabled travellers
White Mountain, Battle of the (1620) 67, 74, 77, 93, 105
  history 31, 32–3
  site of 163
White Swan 130
Wiehl, Antonín 144
Wiehl House
  Street-by-Street map 144
Wine 197
  duty-free allowances 224
Wirch, Johann Georg 152
Wirch, Johann Joseph 111
Wohlmut, Bonifaz 73, 106, 111
Women, safety 228–9
World music 220
World War I 35
World War II 19, 36
Wycliffe, John 77

## Z

Záboj and Slavoj (Myslbek) 149
Zahrada Na valech 110
Zápotocký, Antonín 21
Zbraslavský klášter 163
Želivský, Jan 146, 155
Zemach, Bezalel 88
Zemach, Mordechai 88
Zeman, Karel 36
Ženíšek, František 147
  Golden Age of Czech Art 156
Židovská radnice 87
Zítek, Josef 86, 156, 171
Žižka, Jan 28, 29, 160
  statue of 160
Žižkov 54, 160–61
Zlatá ulička 101
Zoo 162
Zoologická zahrada 162
Zrcadlová kaple 81
Zrcadlové bludiště 140
Zrzavý, Jan 42
  Cleopatra 164

# Acknowledgments

Dorling Kindersley wishes to thank the following people who contributed to the preparation of this book.

## Main Contributor
Vladimír Soukup was born in Prague in 1949. He worked for the daily newpaper, *Evening Prague*, for 20 years, eventually becoming Deputy Chief Editor. He has written a wide range of popular guides to Prague.

## Additional Contributors
Ben Sullivan, Lynn Reich, Wendy Wrangham.

## Design and Editorial
*Managing Editor* Carolyn Ryder
*Managing Art Editor* Steve Knowlden
*Senior Editor* Georgina Matthews
*Senior Art Editor* Vanessa Courtier
*Editorial Director* David Lamb
*Art Director* Anne-Marie Bulat
*Production Controller* Hilary Stephens
*Picture Research* Susie Peachey, Ellen Root
*Designer* Nicola Erdpresser, Sangita Patel
*Consultant* Helena Svojsikova
*Maps* Caroline Bowie, Simon Farbrother, James Mills-Hicks, David Pugh (DKCartography)
*Revisions Team*
Tora Agarwala, Emma Anacootee, Jasneet Arora, Shruti Bahl, Mark Baker, Claire Baranowski, Kate Berens, Marta Bescos, Hilary Bird, Louise Cleghorn, Michelle Crane, Russell Davies, Stephanie Driver, Emer FitzGerald, Fay Franklin, Anna Freiberger, Camilla Gersh, Alistair Gunn, Lydia Halliday, Elaine Harries, Charlie Hawkings, Kaberi Hazarika, Christine Heilman, Claire Jones, Jan Kaplan, Juliet Kenny, Dr Tomáš Kleisner, Rakesh Kumar Pal, Maite Lantaron, Jude Ledger, Susannah Marriott, Wilf Matos, Alison McGill, Jacy Meyer, Sonal Modha, Casper Morris, Vikki Nousiainen, Catherine Palmi, Helen Partington, Marianne Petrou, Filip Polonský, Arun Pottirayil, Private-Prague-Guide.com, Khushboo Priya, Robert Purnell, Rada Radojicic, Azeem Siddiqui, Sands Publishing Solutions, Beverly Smart, Tracy Smith, Scott Stickland, Marian Sucha, Will Tizzard, Daphne Trotter, Conrad Van Dyk, Vinita Venugopal, Ajay Verma, Deepika Verma, Christopher Vinz, Debra Wolter.

## Additional Photography
Mark Baker; DK Studio/Steve Gorton; Nigel Hudson; Ian O'Leary; Otto Palan; Filip Polonský; Rough Guides/Jon Cunningham, /Eddie Gerald, /Natascha Sturny, M Soskova, Clive Streeter, Alan Williams, Peter Wilson, Wendy Wrangham.

## Picture Credits
a = above; b = below/bottom; c = centre; f = far; l = left; r = right; t = top.

Works of art on the pages detailed have been reproduced with the permission of the following copyright holders: Aristide Maillol *Pomona* 1910 © ADAG, Paris, and DACS, London, 2011: 166bc; Gustav Makarius Tauc (An der Aulenkaut 31, Wiesbaden, Germany) under commission of the Minorite Order in Rome: 37br.

The Publishers are grateful to the following individuals, companies and picture libraries for permission to reproduce their photographs:

**Alamy Images**: Petr Bonek 40tr; Frank Chmura 234bl; © CTK/ Rene Fluger 27crb; CZ Prague/ Dennis Chang 232cla, 238bl; Chris Fredriksson 81br, 195c; isifa Image Service s.r.o 119cra; B. O'Kane 13c; Profimedia International S.R.O/ Michaela Dusíková 84tr, 179bl, 226tl; Robert Harding Picture Library 10bl; Josef Sedmak 108–9; **Archiv für Kunst und Geschichte, Berlin**: 19b, 20tr, 20bc(d), 20br(d), 21tl(d), 21tc(d), 21tr(d), 21bc(d), 22bl, 25crb(d), 31ca(d), 34bl, 36cla(d), 37clb, 37bl(d), 45tl, 52br(d), 107crb, 116tr, Erich Lessing 30cl(d), 33bl(d), 90tr, 91br;
**Archív Hlavniho Mesta. Prahy (Clam-GallasůvPalác)**: 25clb, 26bl, 29br, 30br, 32bc, 35cb, 35bc, 74br, 136br, 137br(d), 138crb.

**Barock Restaurant, Prague**: 200bl; **Bildarchiv Preussischer Kulturbesitz**: 4tr(d), 21bl(d), 31br,

36br, 70tr(d), 106bl(d); **Bridgeman Art Library, London**: Prado, Madrid 31tl; Rosegarten Museum, Constance 28cla.
**Budweiser Budvar**: 196cr, 197tr.

**Cafe Imperial, Prague**: 204br;
**Cedaz, Ltd**: 235tr;
**Česká Tisková Kancelár**: 21br, 37cra;
**Comstock**: George Gerster 12cla; Jean-Loup **Charmet**: 20bl(d), 23cra, 33br, 35tl, 35bl, 36cra(d), 36bl, 64cl, 71tc;
**Zdenek Chrappek**: 52cl; **Corbis**: Christophe Boisvieux 82, 158; Gail Mooney 195tl; Scheufler Collection 8-9; **Joe Cornish**: 148br; **Czech National Bank**: 231.

**La Degustation**: 200tr; **Dreamstime.com**: Artur Bogacki 172; Courtyardpix 122; Frbird 62; Louis Henault 2-3; Liberty 12bc; Lukyslukys 146br; Mihaiciolan 145ca; Quixoticsnd 222-223; Vitaly Titov & Maria Sidelnikova 12tr; Zkk600 60-1.

**EU Ecolabel Help Desk**: 227cra;
**Courtesy of Eurolines UK**: 236br;
**Mary Evans Picture Library**: 138br, 223.

**Fotolia**: © Tanya 64br.

**Golden Well Hotel, Prague**: 190tr, 202tl;
**Grafoprint Neubert**: 33cb, 40clb, 118cl.

**Robert Harding Picture Library**: Michael Jenner 128cl; Christopher Rennie105tr; Peter Scholey 32cl, 129cla;
**Hidden Places Residences & Boutique Hotels**: 186bl; **Hutchison Library**: Libuše Taylor 53br, 54c, 176bc.

**The Image Bank**: Andrea Pistolesi 16b;
**iStockphoto.com**: Narvikk 235bl.

**Kancelář Prezidenta Republiky**: 22–3, 23tc, 23bl, 23br, 24cla;
**Oldrich Karasek**: 11tr, 58cb, 64cla, 103bl; 103br, 134tr, 135bl; 176tr, 197crb, 217tr, 233tl;
**Karlštejn**: 27tl; Vladimír Hyhlík: 26–7; Kempinski Hotel Hybernska: 191br;
**Karel Kestner**: 37bc; **Klementinum**: 25tl;
**Dalibor Kusák**: 168–9 all, 170–1 all.

**Ivan Malý**: 216cr.

**Lehka hlava, Prague**: 198bl;
**The Lobkowicz Collections**: 99br;
**Luka Lu Restaurant, Prague**: 201br.

**Mosaic House, Prague**: 189tc;
**Muzeum Hlavního Města Prahy**: 34–5;
**Muzeum hl. M. Prahy/Müllerova vila**: 163bl;
**Muzeum Montanelli**: The secret of Pavla Aubrechtova, The Kabinet of Vladimir Gebauer photo by Oto Palan 124cla; **Muzeum Poštovní Známky**: 149cl.

**Národní Galerie v Praze**: 26br; Grafická sbírka 29bl, 33tl, 69bl, 71cb, 102tr, 104br, 121tl, 125cb, 129br, 138bc, 157br, 175bl, 180bl; Klášter sv. Anežky 41tr, 85tl, 94–5 all, 133bl; Klášter sv. Jiří 18, 39cl,, Šternberský palác 40cl, 112–3 all, 114–5 all, Veletržní Palac 164–5 all; Zbraslav Monastry 42bl;
**Národní Muzeum v Praze**: 147br; Vlasta Dvořáková 22crb, 28–9, 28bl, 28bc, 28br, 29t, 29cl, 29cr, 29crb, 31bl, 75bl, 77br, Jarmila Kutová 22cl, 22clb, 24bl, Dagmar Landová 30bl, Muzeum Antonína Dvořáka 41b, Muzeum Bedřicha Smetany 34cl, Prokop Paul 77b, Tyršovo Muzeum; 149bl; **Národní Technické Muzeum**: Gabriel Urbánek 43tr.

**Obrazárna Pražského Hradu**: 100bl;
**Österreichische Nationalbibliothek, Wien**: 27cb, 28cb.

**Le Patio**: 203tr; **Photographers Direct**: Chris Barton 10cra; Eddie Gerald 11bc; **Photolibrary**: Robert Harding Travel/Yadid Levy 194c.
**Pivovarské Muzeum**: 196tr; **Pivovary Staropramen**: 197ftl; Plzenska Restaurant: 199tl;
**Prague Information Service**: www.prague-info. cz 133cra; **Bohumír Prokůpek**: 27bl, 32clb, 120cl, 121cr, 121bl.
**Reciprocity Images**: www.photographersdirect. com/Jason Langley 240br; **Rex Features Ltd**: Alfred 37tr; **Riverside Praha**: 184br;
**ROPID**: 238cra, 239cl, 239cr, 240tl, 243cr.

**SABMiller**: 196cl, 196crb, 196br, 197tl, 197tc, 197ftr; **SaSaZu, Prague**: 205tc;
**Sotheby's/ Thames and Hudson**: 106cl; **STA Travel Group**: 226c; **Státní Ústredni Archiv**: 25br; **Státní Ústav Památkové Péče**: 25c; **Státní Židovské Muzeum**: 41cr, 87tc, 87clb, 92tl;
**Lubomír Stiburek, www.czfoto.cz**: 57bc, 163tr,

243tc, 249bca, 250cr;
**Marian Sucha**: 57tl, 127tr, 174tr, 197bl;
**SuperStock**: age fotostock 142; age fotostock/
Christian Beier 38; Hemis.fr 13br, 182-3;
imagebroker.net 96;
**Svatovítský Poklad, Pražský Hrad**: 23tr, 26clb,
42tr.

**La Truffe, Prague**: 192bl, 199br.

**U Emy Destinnove**: 204t;
**Uměleckoprůmyslové Muzeum v Praze**: 41tl,
149c, 149clb, 149cb, Gabriel Urbánek 30clb,
43bl;
**Universal Restaurant, Prague**: 203bl;
**Univerzita Karlova**: 27ca;
**U Pinkasu Restaurant**: 194cla.
**Peter Wilson**: 4b, 193tl.

**ZEFA**: 35cr; **ZZS HMP**: 229bl.
**Front endpaper:**
**Corbis**: Christophe Boisvieux Rtr ;
**Dreamstime.com**: Courtyardpix Lbc;  Frbird Rcr;
**SuperStock**: age fotostock Rbr; imagebroker.
net Lcl.

**Map cover:**
**4Corners**: Pietro Canali.

**Jacket Picture Credits**

Front main and spine top:
**4Corners**: Pietro Canali.

All other images © Dorling Kindersley.
For further information,
see: www.dkimages.com

**Special Editions of DK Travel Guides**
DK Travel Guides can be purchased in bulk
quantities at discounted prices for use in
promotions or as premiums. We are also able
to offer special editions and personalized
jackets, corporate imprints, and excerpts from
all of our books, tailored specifically to meet
your own needs.

To find out more, please contact:
*in the United States* **SpecialSales@dk.com**
*in the UK* **travelspecialsales@uk.dk.com**
*in Canada DK Special Sales at* **general@
tourmaline.ca**
*in Australia* **business.development@pearson.
com.au**

# Phrase Book

## In Emergency

| | | |
|---|---|---|
| Help! | Pomoc! | po-mots |
| Stop! | Zastavte! | za-stav-te |
| Call a doctor! | Zavolejte doktora! | za-vo-ley-te dok-to-ra! |
| Call an ambulance! | Zavolejte sanitku! | za-vo-ley-te sa-nit-ku! |
| Call the police! | Zavolejte policii! | za-vo-ley-te poli-tsi-yi! |
| Call the fire brigade! | Zavolejte hasiče | za-vol-ey-te ha-si-che |
| Where is the telephone? | Kde je telefón? | gde ye tele-fohn? |
| the nearest hospital? | nejbližší nemocnice? | ney-blish-ee ne-mots-nyitse? |

## Communication Essentials

| | | |
|---|---|---|
| Yes/No | Ano/Ne | ano/ne |
| Please | Prosím | pro-seem |
| Thank you | Děkuji vám | dye-ku-ji vahm |
| Excuse me | Prosím vás | pro-seem vahs |
| Hello | Dobrý den | do-bree den |
| Goodbye | Na shledanou | na s-hle-da-no |
| Good evening | Dobrý večer | dob-ree vech-er |
| morning | ráno | rah-no |
| afternoon | odpoledne | od-po-led-ne |
| evening | večer | ve-cher |
| yesterday | včera | vche-ra |
| today | dnes | dnes |
| tomorrow | zítra | zeet-ra |
| here | tady | ta-di |
| there | tam | tam |
| What? | Co? | tso? |
| When? | Kdy? | gdi? |
| Why? | Proč? | proch? |
| Where? | Kde? | gde? |

## Useful Phrases

| | | |
|---|---|---|
| How are you? | Jak se máte? | yak-se mah-te? |
| Very well, thank you. | Velmi dobře děkuji. | vel-mi dob-rzhe dye kuji. |
| Pleased to meet you. | Těší mě. | tyesh-ee mye |
| See you soon. | Uvidíme se brzy. | u-vi-dyee-me-se-br-zi |
| That's fine. | To je v pořádku. | to ye vpo-rzhahdku |
| Where is/are…? | Kde je/jsou …? | gde ye/yso …? |
| How long does it take to get to? | Jak dlouho to trvá se dostat do..? | yak dlo ho to tr-va se do-stat do…? |
| How do I get to…? | Jak se dostanu k..? | yak se do-sta-nu k …? |
| Do you speak English? | Mluvíte anglicky? | mlu-vee-te an-glits-ki? |
| I don't understand. | Nerozumím. | ne-ro-zu-meem |
| Could you speak more slowly? | Mohl(a)* byste mluvit trochu pomaleji? | mohl- (a) bis-te mlu-vit tro-khu po-maley? |
| Pardon? | Prosím? | pro-seem? |
| I'm lost. | Ztratil(a)* jsem se. | stra-tyil (a) ysem se. |

## Useful Words

| | | |
|---|---|---|
| big | velký | vel-kee |
| small | malý | mal-ee |
| hot | horký | hor-kee |
| cold | studený | stu-den-ee |
| good | dobrý | dob-ree |
| bad | špatný | shpat-nee |
| well | dobře | dob-rzhe |
| open | otevřeno | ot-ev-rzhe-no |
| closed | zavřeno | zav-rzhe-no |
| left | do leva | do le-va |
| right | do prava | do pra-va |
| straight on | rovně | rov-nye |
| near | blízko | blee-sko |
| far | daleko | da-le-ko |
| up | nahoru | na-ho-ru |
| down | dolů | do-loo |
| early | brzy | br-zi |
| late | pozdě | poz-dye |
| entrance | vchod | vkhod |
| exit | východ | vee-khod |
| toilets | toalety | toa-leti |
| free, unoccupied | volný | vol-nee |
| free, no charge | zdarma | zdar-ma |

## Making a Telephone Call

| | | |
|---|---|---|
| I'd like to place a call. | Chtěl(a)* bych volat | khtyel(a) bikh vo-lat |
| I'd like to make a reverse-charge call. | Chtěl(a)* bych volat na účet volaného. | khtyel(a) bikh volat na oo-chet volan-eh-ho |
| I'll try again later. | Zkusím to později. | skus-eem to poz-dyey |
| Can I leave a message? | Mohu nechat zprávu? | mo-hu ne-khat sprah-vu? |
| Hold on. | Počkejte. | poch-key-te |
| Could you speak up a little, please? | Mohl(a)* byste mluvit hlasitěji? | mo-hl (a) bis-te mluvit hla-si-tyey? |
| local call | místní hovor | meest-nyee hov-or |

## Sightseeing

| | | |
|---|---|---|
| art gallery | galerie | ga-ler-riye |
| bus stop | autobusová zastávka | au-to-bus-o-vah za-stah-vka |
| church | kostel | kos-tel |
| garden | zahrada | za hra-da |
| library | knihovna | knyi-hov-na |
| museum | muzeum | muz-e-um |
| railway station | nádraží | nah-dra-zhee |
| tourist information | turistické informace | toorist-tske in-for-ma-tse |
| closed for the public holiday | státní svátek | staht-nyee svah-tek |

## Shopping

| | | |
|---|---|---|
| How much does this cost? | Co to stojí? | tso to sto-yee? |
| I would like … | Chtěl(a)* bych …. | khtyel(a) bikh… |
| Do you have …? | Máte …? | maa-te …? |
| I'm just looking. | Jenom se dívám. | ye-nom se dyee-vahm |
| Do you take credit cards? | Berete kreditní karty? | be-re-te kred-it nyee karti? |
| What time do you open/ close? | V kolik otevíráte/ zavíráte? | v ko-lik o-te-vee-rah-te/ za vee rah-te? |
| this one | tento | ten-to |
| that one | tamten | tam-ten |
| expensive | drahý | dra-hee |
| cheap | levný | lev-nee |
| size | velikost | vel-ik-ost |
| white | bílý | bee-lee |
| black | černý | cher-nee |
| red | červený | cher-ven-ee |
| yellow | žlutý | zhlu-tee |
| green | zelený | zel-en-ee |
| blue | modrý | mod-ree |
| brown | hnědý | hnyed-ee |

## Types of Shop

| | | |
|---|---|---|
| antique shop | starožitnictví | sta-ro zhit--nyits-tvee |
| bank | banka | bank a |
| bakery | pekárna | pe-kahr-na |
| bookstore | knihkupectví | knih-kupets-tvee |
| butcher | řeznictví | rzhez-nyits-tvee |
| camera shop | obchod s fotoaparáty | op-khot sfoto-aparahti |
| chemist (prescriptions etc) | lékárna | leh-kah-rna |
| chemist (cosmetics, toiletries etc) | drogerie | drog-erye |
| delicatessen | lahůdky | la-hoo-dki |
| department store | obchodní dům | op-khod-nyee doom |
| grocery | potraviny | pot-ra-vini |
| glass | sklo | sklo |
| hairdresser (ladies) | kadeřnictví | ka-derzh-nyits-tvee |
| (mens) | holič | ho-lich |
| market | trh | trkh |
| newsstand | novinový stánek | no-vi-novee stah-nek |
| post office | pošta | posh-ta |
| supermarket | samoobsluha | sa-mo-ob-slu-ha |
| tobacconist | tabák | ta-bahk |
| travel agency | cestovní kancelář | tses-tov-nyi kantse-laarzh |

*alternatives for a female speaker are shown in brackets*

## Staying in a Hotel

| | | |
|---|---|---|
| Do you have a vacant room? | **Máte volný pokoj?** | mah-te vol-nee po-koy? |
| double room | **dvoulůžkový pokoj** | dvo-loozh-kovee po-koy |
| with double bed | **s dvojitou postelí** | sdvoy-to **pos**-telee |
| twin room | **pokoj s dvěma postelemi** | po-koy sdvye-ma pos-tel-emi |
| room with a bath | **pokoj s koupelnou** | po-koy s ko-pel-no |
| porter | **vrátný** | vraht-nee |
| hall porter | **nosič** | nos-ich |
| key | **klíč** | kleech |
| I have a reservation. | **Mám reservaci.** | mahm rez-ervatsi |

## Eating Out

| | | |
|---|---|---|
| Have you got a table for …? | **Máte stůl pro …?** | mah-te stool pro …? |
| I'd like to reserve a table. | **Chtěl(a)\* bych rezervovat stůl.** | khtyel(a) bikh rez-er-vov-at stool |
| breakfast | **snídaně** | snyee-danye |
| lunch | **oběd** | ob-yed |
| dinner | **večeře** | vech e-rzhe |
| The bill, please. | **Prosím, účet.** | pro-seem oo-chet |
| I am a vegetarian. | **Jsem vegetarián(ka)\*.** | ysem veghe-tariahn(ka) |
| waitress! | **slečno** | slech-no |
| waiter! | **pane vrchní!** | pane vrkh-nyee! |
| fixed price menu | **standardní menu** | stan-dard-nyee men-u |
| dish of the day | **nabídka dne** | nab-eed-ka dne |
| starter | **předkrm** | przhed-krm |
| main course | **hlavní jídlo** | hlav-nyee yeed-lo |
| vegetables | **zelenina** | zel-en-yin-a |
| dessert | **zákusek** | zah-kusek |
| cover charge | **poplatek** | pop-la-tek |
| wine list | **nápojový lístek** | nah-po-yo-vee lee-stek |
| rare (steak) | **krvavý** | kr-va-vee |
| medium | **středně udělaný** | strzhed-nye ud-yel-an-ee |
| well done | **dobře udělaný** | dobrzhe-ud-yel-an-ee |
| glass | **sklenice** | sklen-yitse |
| bottle | **láhev** | lah-hev |
| knife | **nůž** | noozh |
| fork | **vidlička** | vid-lich-ka |
| spoon | **lžíce** | lzhee-tse |

## Menu Decoder

| | | |
|---|---|---|
| **biftek** | bif-tek | steak |
| **bílé víno** | bee-leh vee-no | white wine |
| **bramborové knedlíky** | bram-bo-ro-veh kne-dleeki | potato dumplings |
| **brambory** | bram-bo-ri | potatoes |
| **chléb** | khlehb | bread |
| **cibule** | tsi-bu-le | onion |
| **citrónový džus** | tsi-tron-o-vee dzhuus | lemon juice |
| **cukr** | tsukr | sugar |
| **čaj** | chay | tea |
| **čerstvé ovoce** | cher-stveh-o-vo-ce | fresh fruit |
| **červené víno** | cher-ven-eh vee-no | red wine |
| **česnek** | ches-nek | garlic |
| **dort** | dort | cake |
| **fazole** | fa-zo-le | beans |
| **grilované** | gril-ov-a-neh | grilled |
| **houby** | ho-bi | mushrooms |
| **houska** | hous-ka | roll |
| **houskové knedlíky** | ho-sko-veh kne-dleeki | bread dumplings |
| **hovězí** | hov-ye-zee | beef |
| **hranolky** | hran-ol-ki | chips |
| **husa** | hu-sa | goose |
| **jablko** | ya-bl-ko | apple |
| **jahody** | ya-ho-di | strawberries |
| **jehněčí** | ye-hnye-chee | lamb |
| **kachna** | kakh-na | duck |
| **kapr** | ka-pr | carp |
| **káva** | kah-va | coffee |
| **krevety** | krev-et-i | prawns |
| **kuře** | ku-rzhe | chicken |
| **kyselé zelí** | kis-el-eh zel-ee | sauerkraut |
| **maso** | ma-so | meat |
| **máslo** | mah-slo | butter |
| **minerálka** | min-er-ahl-ka | mineral water |
| **perliva/ neperliva** | purl-i-vah/ ne-purl-i-vah | fizzy/ still |
| **mléko** | mleh-ko | milk |

| | | |
|---|---|---|
| **mořská jídla** | morzh-skah-yeed-la | seafood |
| **ocet** | ots-et | vinegar |
| **okurka** | o-ku-rka | cucumber |
| **olej** | oley | oil |
| **párek** | paa-rek | sausage/frankfurter |
| **pečené** | petsh-en-eh | baked |
| **pečené** | pech-en-eh | roast |
| **pepř** | peprzh | pepper |
| **polévka** | pol-eh-vka | soup |
| **pomeranč** | po-me-ranch | orange |
| **pomerančový džus** | po-me-ran-ch--o-vee dzhuus | orange juice |
| **pivo** | pi-vo | beer |
| **rajské** | rayskeh | tomato |
| **ryba** | rib-a | fish |
| **rýže** | ree-zhe | rice |
| **salát** | sal-at | salad |
| **sůl** | sool | salt |
| **sýr** | seer | cheese |
| **šunka** | shun-ka | ham |
| **vařená /uzená** | varzh-enah u-zenah | cooked smoked |
| **telecí** | te-le-tsee | veal |
| **tuna** | tu-na | tuna |
| **vajíčko** | va-yee-chko | egg |
| **vařené** | varzh-en-eh | boiled |
| **vepřové** | vep-rzho-veh | pork |
| **voda** | vo-da | water |
| **vývar** | vee- var | broth |
| **zelí** | zel-ee | cabbage |
| **zelenina** | zel-enyina | vegetables |
| **zmrzlina** | zmrz-lin-a | ice cream |

## Numbers

| | | |
|---|---|---|
| 1 | **jedna** | yed-na |
| 2 | **dvě** | dvye |
| 3 | **tři** | trzhi |
| 4 | **čtyři** | chti-rzhi |
| 5 | **pět** | pyet |
| 6 | **šest** | shest |
| 7 | **sedm** | sedm |
| 8 | **osm** | osm |
| 9 | **devět** | dev-yet |
| 10 | **deset** | des-et |
| 11 | **jedenáct** | ye-de-nahtst |
| 12 | **dvanáct** | dva-nahtst |
| 13 | **třináct** | trzhi-nahtst |
| 14 | **čtrnáct** | chtr-nahtst |
| 15 | **patnáct** | pat-nahtst |
| 16 | **šestnáct** | shest-nahtst |
| 17 | **sedmnáct** | sedm-nahtst |
| 18 | **osmnáct** | osm-nahtst |
| 19 | **devatenáct** | de-va-te-nahtst |
| 20 | **dvacet** | dva-tset |
| 21 | **dvacet jedna** | dva-tset yed-na |
| 22 | **dvacet dva** | dva-tset dva |
| 23 | **dvacet tři** | dva-tset-trzhi |
| 24 | **dvacet čtyři** | dva-tset chti-rzhi |
| 25 | **dvacet pět** | dva-tset pyet |
| 30 | **třicet** | trzhi-tset |
| 40 | **čtyřicet** | chti-rzhi-tset |
| 50 | **padesát** | pa-de-saht |
| 60 | **šedesát** | she-de-saht |
| 70 | **sedmdesát** | sedm-de-saht |
| 80 | **osmdesát** | osm-de-saht |
| 90 | **devadesát** | de-va-de-saht |
| 100 | **sto** | sto |
| 1,000 | **tisíc** | tyi-seets |
| 2,000 | **dva tisíce** | dva tyi-see-tse |
| 5,000 | **pět tisíc** | pyet tyi-seets |
| 1,000,000 | **milión** | mi-li-ohn |

## Time

| | | |
|---|---|---|
| one minute | **jedna minuta** | yed-na min-uta |
| one hour | **jedna hodina** | yed-na hod-yin-a |
| half an hour | **půl hodiny** | pool hod-yin-i |
| day | **den** | den |
| week | **týden** | tee-den |
| Monday | **pondělí** | pon-dye-lee |
| Tuesday | **úterý** | oo-ter-ee |
| Wednesday | **středa** | strzhe-da |
| Thursday | **čtvrtek** | chtvr-tek |
| Friday | **pátek** | pah-tek |
| Saturday | **sobota** | so-bo-ta |
| Sunday | **neděle** | ned-yel-e |

*alternatives for a female speaker are shown in brackets*